WORLD
SCENOGRAPHY
1975-1990

EDITED BY PETER McKINNON & ERIC FIELDING

INTERNATIONAL ORGANISATION OF
SCENOGRAPHERS, THEATRE
ARCHITECTS AND TECHNICIANS

EDITORS: Peter McKinnon & Eric Fielding
DESIGNER: Randal Boutilier at 12thirteen

Published by OISTAT
International Organisation of Scenographers, Theatre Architects and Technicians
Suite A, 2F, No.7, Sec.2, Renai Rd.
Taipei 10055
Taiwan

ISBN 978-92-990063-0-6 Hardcover
ISBN 978-92-990063-1-3 Softcover

Printed and bound in China
by Artron Color Printing Co., Ltd.

{ TABLE OF CONTENTS }

{ DEDICATION }

This book is
respectfully dedicated to
Professor René Hainaux,
whose four-volume series
Stage Design Throughout the World, 1935-1975
was the genesis of this work,
the immensity of which
in a pre-computer age
is monumental.

{ EDITORIAL BOARD }

{ CONTRIBUTING RESEARCHERS }

Ossei Agyeman
GHANA

Zain Ahmed
PAKISTAN

Marcelo Allasino
ARGENTINA

Philippe Amand
MEXICO

Ana Paula Merenholz De Aquino
BRAZIL

Otavio Arbelaiz
COLOMBIA

Beatriz Arteaga
URUGUAY

Ivana Bakal
CROATIA

Jorge Ballina
MEXICO

Donatella Barbieri
UNITED KINGDOM

Andy Bargilly
CYPRUS

Ekaterina Barysheva
RUSSIA

Lian Bell
IRELAND

Susan Benson
CANADA

Jade Bettin
UNITED STATES

Lovisa Björkman
SWEDEN

Camilla Bjørnvad
DENMARK

Jody L. Blake
UNITED STATES

Sándor Böröcz
HUNGARY

Adam Bresnick
SPAIN

Lada Čale Feldman
CROATIA

Louisa Carroll
IRELAND

Paulo Eduardo Carvalho
PORTUGAL

Jorge Castrillón
GUATEMALA

Jean Cazaban
ROMANIA

Livia Cazaban
ROMANIA

Jan Chambers
UNITED STATES

Keren Chiaroni
NEW ZEALAND

Sorin Chitsu
ROMANIA

Jean Chollet
FRANCE

Barbara Cohen Stratyner
UNITED STATES

Emily Collett
UNITED KINGDOM

Ruphin Coudyzer
SOUTH AFRICA

Tâmara Cubas
URUGUAY

Jane Daly
IRELAND

Peter de Kimpe
NETHERLANDS

Edith Del Campo
CHILE

Mairéad Delaney
IRELAND

José Dias
BRAZIL

Arturo Díaz
MEXICO

Radivoje Dinulovic
SERBIA

Reynaldo Disla
DOMINICAN REPUBLIC

Kate Dorney
UNITED KINGDOM

Ann Mari Engel
SWEDEN

Thomas Engel
GERMANY

Edwin Ermini
VENEZUELA

Eric Fielding
UNITED STATES

Sara Franqueira
PORTUGAL

Marcel Freydefont
FRANCE

Sandra Gredig
SWITZERLAND

Moisés Guevara
VENEZUELA

Carmelinda Guimarães
BRAZIL

Ian Hammond
NEW ZEALAND

Frank Hänig
GERMANY

Dorita Hannah
NEW ZEALAND

Kazue Hatano
JAPAN

Hanna Helavuori
FINLAND

Roberto Henrique King
PANAMA

Ian Herbert
UNITED KINGDOM

Justin Hill
SINGAPORE

Tal Itzhaki
ISRAEL

Primož Jesenko
SLOVENIA

Dio Kangelari
GREECE

Sam Kasule
UGANDA

Mary Kerr
CANADA

Ketevan Kintsurashvili
GEORGIA

Ammy Kjellsdotter
SWEDEN

Agnieszka Kubaś
POLAND

Pälvi Laine
FINLAND

Rosie Lam Tung Pui-man
HONG KONG

Monika Larini
ESTONIA

1975

The British Conservative Party chooses its first female leader, Margaret Thatcher • Oil goes over $13.00 per barrel • The Vietnam War ends • New York City avoids bankruptcy when President Ford signs a $2.3 billion loan • The IRA bombs London Hilton Hotel • The Suez Canal reopens for the first time since the Six-Day War • King Faisal of Saudi Arabia assassinated • Baader-Meinhof guerrillas take 11 hostages at West German embassy in Stockholm • Britain's inflation rate jumps to 25% • Beginning of 15 years of civil war in Lebanon • The UK votes to stay in the European Community • Angola gains independence from Portugal • Suriname gains independence from Netherlands • Bill Gates and Paul Allen create Microsoft • US Apollo and Soviet Soyuz 9 spacecraft link up in space • Spanish dictator Franco dies • The British Conservative Party chooses its first female leader, Margaret Thatcher • Oil goes over $13.00 per barrel • The Vietnam War ends • New York City avoids bankruptcy when President Ford signs a $2.3 billion loan • The IRA bombs London Hilton Hotel • The Suez Canal reopens for the first time since the Six-Day War • King Faisal of Saudi Arabia assassinated • Baader-Meinhof guerrillas take 11 hostages at West German embassy in Stockholm • Britain's inflation rate jumps to 25% • Beginning of 15 years of civil war in Lebanon • The UK votes to stay in the European Community • Angola gains independence from Portugal • Suriname gains independence from

The Rocky Horror Show

Brian Thomson (Australia)
& Sue Blane (UK)
Set & Costume Design

The Rocky Horror Show began its life at the Upstairs Theatre at the Royal Court Theatre in London in 1973. Brian Thomson and Jim Sharman had already worked together on a number of productions in Australia and London, and neither of them could have anticipated the worldwide phenomenon that *Rocky* would become. Their work together precipitated an entirely new approach to design in the Australian theatre.

This was one of Sue Blane's first professional productions as a solo designer, and undoubtedly her big break. Designing for this production led her to design the US version, and later the costumes for the movie as well as the sequel. So intrinsic is her connection to the design of the show that her name is now part of the audience participation script for the production. She has since gone on to design for opera, musical, theatre and dance, returning regularly to design any new productions of *Rocky Horror* in the UK.

The work, and its outrageous costumes, has inspired many interpretations, recreations, and homages, not only in theatre, but also in fashion, make-up, and music. The success of the show and its popular design confirmed the success of the Royal Court's black box studio, the Theatre Upstairs, which had opened three years earlier.

The production has become part of popular culture, and the costume designs have played a big part in that, often recreated down to tiny details for audience participation nights and fancy dress or *Rocky Horror*-themed parties. Blane has received both an MBE and the Royal Designer for Industry award for services to theatre design.

Equus
John Napier (UK)
Set & Costume Design

Equus was John Napier's first production as a designer at the National Theatre, winning him an Olivier award and establishing him as one of the world's leading production designers. The play requires actors to impersonate the horses that obsess the disturbed youth at its centre. The author specifies that "any literalism which could suggest the cosy familiarity of a domestic animal — or worse, a pantomime horse — should be avoided." Napier realised Peter Shaffer's directions by creating stylised horses' heads, which were acceptable as both real animals and the horse gods of the boy's imagination. The head is a skeletal structure attached to a padded leather band that runs around the chin and sits above, rather than over, the wearer's head to increase his height. The shape is created from bands of leather and what appears to be silver wire, but is actually a type of cane covered in silver metal foil. This gives it rigidity and stability while being light for the wearer. Further height is added by the hooves, which are constructed from metal rods. The actor is clearly visible. The overall effect was, in the words of the theatre critic of *Punch* magazine, "gravely spectacular and unearthly."

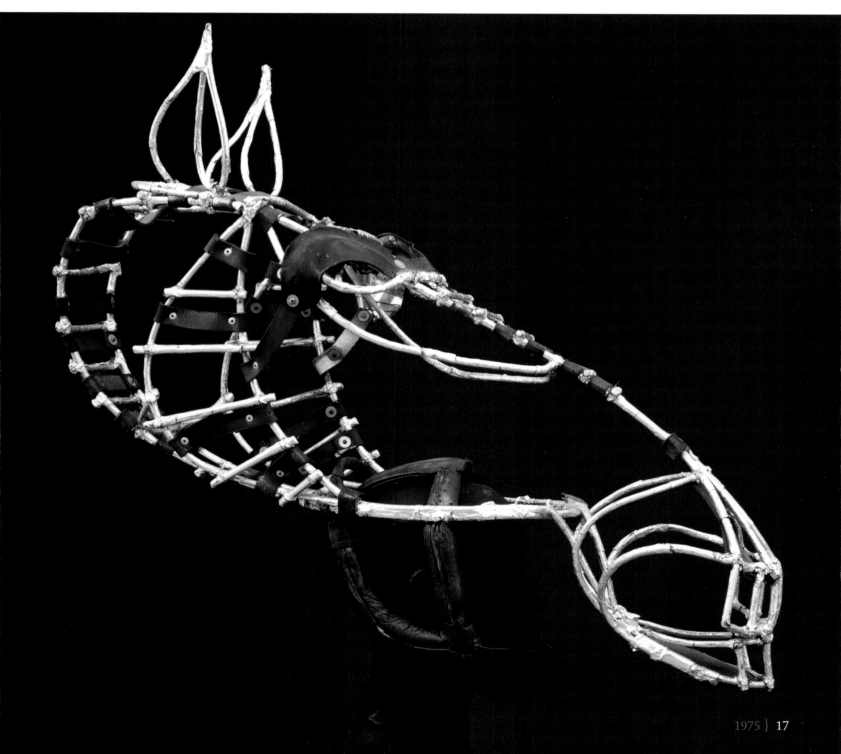

The Money Tree

Julian Beck & William Shari (USA)
Set Design

The Money Tower was created in Pittsburgh in 1975 and toured several European countries through 1976. A complete Italian version was performed in 1976. The structure was five stories high. On the bottom were the poor; next the workers' level, with a plexiglass steel furnace; then the bourgeoisie; then the police/technocrats; and finally the elite, with a plexiglass bank full of dollars, topped by a neon dollar sign. A small elevator rose through the centre of the tower, operated by the workers by pulling a rope. In the Italian version, the tower was completely dismantled by the end of the play, all accompanied by music and poetry. The plot of the play, which was almost always performed outdoors, concerned the nonviolent social struggle to overcome the power of money.

Samoan Fire Knife Dance *(Siva Aailao)*

Aggie Grey's Resort (Western Samoa)
Performance Design

Aggie Grey's Resort has long been associated with the development of the Samoan Fire Knife Dance (Siva Aailao). Through continuous performances of fire-dancing since the 1950s, this resort offers visitors an encounter with Samoa's culture, at the same time enriching that culture and helping ensure its sustainability. Poolside performances are part of the traditional fiafia, or Samoan meal, set in an ornately carved fale opening onto the pool. Resort architecture is thus adapted to the needs of scenography. A similar adaptation can be seen in the use of the restored 100-year-old church on the resort grounds as a venue for various cultural functions.

Design developments in the dance itself may be seen in modifications to the gestural implements of the dance — the Siva Aailao (the knife); the nifo oti (or baton) — and to the basic choreography, first developed in its current form in the late 1950s and 1960s. The years 1975 to 1990 saw the emergence of increasingly youthful artists extending the vocabulary of the dance and stylizing the knife and baton.

Originally part of a sequence of war-dances used to intimidate as well as indicate victory, the contemporary fire-dance is now linked to alternative competitive rituals, much like the incorporation of the ritual Maori haka into the New Zealand rugby field. The Polynesian Cultural Center of Samoa now recognizes this formalized rivalry in the annual World Fire Knife Dance Competition. A number of fire-dancing champions began their careers at Aggie Grey's.

A Little Night Music

**Boris Aronson (Russia/USA),
Florence Klotz & Tharon Musser (USA)**
Set, Costume & Lighting Design

Stephen Sondheim's musical *A Little Night Music* was inspired by
the Ingmar Bergman film *Smiles of a Summer Night*. To deal with
the cinematic nature of the source material, scenic designer Boris
Aronson utilized a set of moving screens with painted silver birches
to assist in shifting the scene from one locale to another. *The New
York Times* review described the production — winner of 1973 Tony
Awards for best musical and best costume design and nominated for
best scenic and lighting design — as "...heady, civilized, sophisticated,
and enchanting...[Aronson's] villa is a delight; he has devised a front-
cloth that is pure Swedish Drottningholm baroque. The costumes
by Florence Klotz are sumptuous and knowingly aware, while the
lighting by Tharon Musser puts all the soft and cold smiles into this
particular summer night." [Review by Clive Barnes, *New York Times*,
26 Feb 1973]

Split Enz

Noel Crombie (New Zealand)
Costume Design

These designs defined a look for the band and their live performances, which were a significant aspect of their success as one of New Zealand's first and most famous musical exports. The aesthetic defined by Noel Crombie's colourful costumes and their wild haircuts went on to be reproduced in their music videos and television appearances.

The designs were intrinsically involved in the cultural event that Split Enz became for New Zealand, and New Zealand music. Looking back on this band, their music, their costumes, their hair, and their performances, it is possible to see this as a defining moment in New Zealand culture.

As one the earliest of these examples, Split Enz heralded a new approach to musical performance, one that employed theatrical methods and devices. Aside from the makeup, costumes, and hairstyles, Raewyn Turner's lights also had a significant impact.

Where previously rock lighting was very simple, Turner introduced a complex lighting palette to this performance medium. Gobos, film loops, glass slides, and other lighting textures were used. The monochromatic costumes were lit with complimentary colours flashing back and forth to create after images and cinaesthetic effects on the retina.

Ivanov

Mart Kitaev (Latvia)
Set Design

The design of the space for *Ivanov* created an impression of decay and deathly emptiness. Facing the audience was a black-box closed space, shaped by three surfaces of coarse sacking and painted in silvery tones. Soaring over the stage was a smoky gauze curtain, also silvery in tone, calling up the image of a funeral shroud. All the furniture was coated with grey covers, making them reminiscent of gravestones. The stage was lit through silvery filters. The overall image created by the designer fully conformed to the director's general interpretation of Chekhov's play, its central motif being the loneliness of the protagonist in his cold home in the company of strangers.

Romeo and Juliet

Sergei Barkhin (USSR/Russia)
Set Design

The playfulness of Sergei Barkhin's art was especially
evident in this 1975 student production, a real hit of
the season. The design suggested that the students
themselves had drawn and painted the huge capital
letters (Ionic for the Capulets, Corinthian for Montagues)
in vivid colours. In the fight scene, paintbrushes were
the weapons. Throughout the play, the performers were
strewing the stage with sawdust ("the cultural layer of
history") and various fruits. A pile of eggs was thrown
at an alabaster wall, then crushed and trampled. The
eggshells were used to drink potions or poison. For all
the outward absurdity of the set design, its components
contained serious meanings. The result was the sharp
juxtaposition of the remnants of Renaissance architecture
and the boggy mass of sawdust, epitomizing the
impersonal powers that are capable of annihilating love.

In 1977 Barkhin's sketches of the sets for *Romeo
and Juliet* received first prize at the 2nd Triennial
of Set Designers from the Baltic region, Leningrad,
and Moscow.

Strider: The Story of a Horse
(Kholstomer)

Eduard Kochergin (USSR/Russia)
Set Design

"In *Kholstomer*, based on Tolstoy's *The Story of a Horse*, I wanted to see a stable on stage and at the same time the universe," said director Georgi Tovstonogov. Designer Eduard Kochergin created multiple dimensions by using a highly precise arrangement of the acting space in the form of a bowl and employing the simplest of all materials —canvas. One of the critics referred to the visual image as "the world stable" where a centaur, wearing a canvas shirt, tells the Biblical story of the life of a horse.

Kochergin's designs helped tell the story of a suffering-laced life of the horse, nicknamed Kholstomer, from birth to death. The storyteller on stage was the brilliant Soviet actor Eugeni Lebedev. But what was created on stage could hardly be called a set. More precisely, it was a theatrical sculpture, shaped out of canvas like a cup or saddle. It lacked any right angles. The canvas slowly flowed over the stage floor to the walls, inflating unevenly like sores on the body of a horse, like imprints of its horrible life in old age that has come.

The Red Eagle *(Al Nesr Al Ahmar)*

Sakina Mohamed Ali (Egypt)
Set & Costume Design

The Red Eagle concerns the crisis when a ruling class faces the stark contradiction between reality and dreams, between principles and necessity. The hero Saladin does not like war, but is determined to cleanse his land of the enemies who have divided the world into two groups: the masters who rule from palaces, and the slaves whose only place on the earth is their graves.

The designer used an abstract expressionist style. Using a non-realistic style was more appropriate for the very dramatic text. At the technical level, the designer used a large rotating disk with another smaller rotating disk in it. Many artistic motifs were used to express the dramatic story.

The Little Square
(Il campiello)

Luciano Damiani (Italy)
Set & Costume Design

The design is one of the most significant in Luciano Damiani's career at the Teatro Piccolo di Milano and in his collaboration with Giorgio Strehler. It represents an important mix of realistic and figurative stage setting.

A Chorus Line
Robin Wagner & Tharon Musser (USA)
Set & Lighting Design

This was probably the most important production in the collaboration of "The Dream Team" of Broadway production in the 1970s and '80s: designers Robin Wagner, Theoni V. Aldredge, and Tharon Musser, and director/choreographer Michael Bennett. It was also one of the first shows with a credited sound designer, Abe Jacob.

Its startling use of an empty stage with performers dressed only in rehearsal dance clothes—until more traditional sets and costumes appeared in the finale—was a first in a large commercial musical production. It was an inspiration to other designers. For lighting designers it was a seminal production because it introduced computerized lighting control into the Broadway Theatre.

A Chorus Line played 6,137 performances on Broadway and toured all over the world, making the producers and artists wealthy. The original Broadway production won a number of Tony Awards in 1976, including Best Musical and Best Lighting Design. The London production won the 1976 Laurence Olivier Award as Best Musical of the Year.

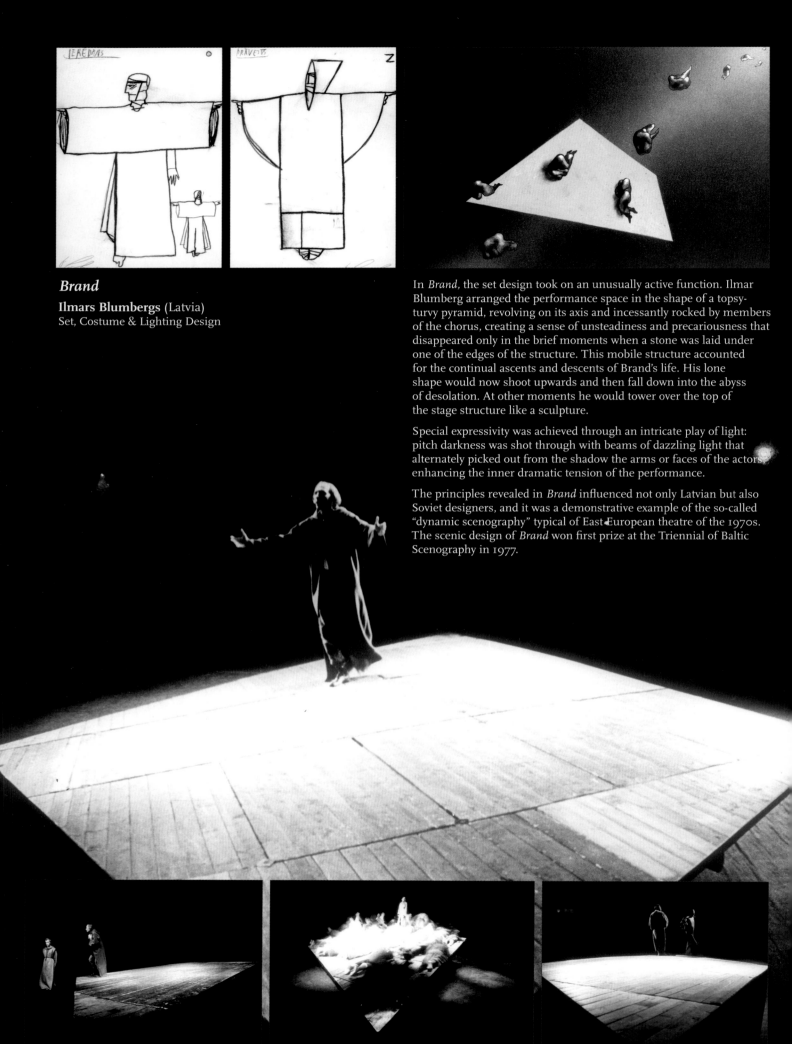

Brand

Ilmars Blumbergs (Latvia)
Set, Costume & Lighting Design

In *Brand*, the set design took on an unusually active function. Ilmar Blumberg arranged the performance space in the shape of a topsy-turvy pyramid, revolving on its axis and incessantly rocked by members of the chorus, creating a sense of unsteadiness and precariousness that disappeared only in the brief moments when a stone was laid under one of the edges of the structure. This mobile structure accounted for the continual ascents and descents of Brand's life. His lone shape would now shoot upwards and then fall down into the abyss of desolation. At other moments he would tower over the top of the stage structure like a sculpture.

Special expressivity was achieved through an intricate play of light: pitch darkness was shot through with beams of dazzling light that alternately picked out from the shadow the arms or faces of the actors, enhancing the inner dramatic tension of the performance.

The principles revealed in *Brand* influenced not only Latvian but also Soviet designers, and it was a demonstrative example of the so-called "dynamic scenography" typical of East European theatre of the 1970s. The scenic design of *Brand* won first prize at the Triennial of Baltic Scenography in 1977.

The Lady Bagdat (Bağdat Khatun)
Refik Eren (Turkey)
Set Design

Bağdat Khatun (The Lady Bagdat) was written by Güngör Dilmen, a Turkish playwright with an international reputation for his mythological and historical plays. Taken from 14th-century Anatolian history, it tells the story of the Chobanid princess Bağdat Khatun and her tragic end, caused by her greed for power and the throne. This first production of the play featured sets and costumes by Refik and Hale Eren, who put their imprint on Turkish theatre design with their collaboration on more than 300 plays over 50 years. Their concept was based on stylized 14th-century Anatolian decoration and architecture. The scenery was simplified to a high degree to provide a free acting space and to highlight the performers' actions. Nevertheless it evoked the atmosphere of the period and successfully conveyed the spirit of the play with its carefully applied authentic motifs, rough materials, and muted colors.

Ayten Gökçer, one of the brightest stars in the history of Turkish theatre, appeared in her elaborately worked authentic costumes as a Turkish "Lady Macbeth," enchanting the Turkish audiences. The production won many awards and has been staged in many cities in Turkey and also in Germany.

Ivan the Terrible
Simon Vrisaladze (USSR/Russia)
Set Design

Yuri Grigorovitch's ballet Ivan the Terrible, choreographed to the film score and other pieces by Sergei Prokofiev, entered the repertoire of the Bolshoi Theatre in 1975. Designer Simon Versaladze made the stage as bare as possible for the dancers, yet managed to depict the specific locales and convey the spirit of tragedy that permeated the period. The design was largely based on motifs borrowed from ancient Russian icons and frescoes. In the background were three half-cylinders, resembling monastery towers or the apses of old Russian churches, used in varying combinations of their convex and concave sides. Worthy of special mention are the belfry, with real bells, and the curtain made of thin metallic rings, resembling both chain armor and shackles. The design was further enhanced by the imaginative use of lighting that varied from semi-darkness to a blood-red glow. Versaladze's costumes were both easy to dance in and authentic from an ethnic and historical point of view.

Fragments from an Unfinished Novel
(Útržky z nedokončeného románu)

Jan Konečný
(Czechoslovakia/Czech Republic)
Set Design

This student of Josef Svoboda, also an active interior designer, worked here on a set for a studio-type theatre space, where the audience members didn't simply sit in a frontal, proscenium position, but surrounded the playing area on several sides. The interplay of this simple geometric shape and the "realistic" second-hand furniture achieved an existential tension, which supported the feeling of being restricted in an imaginary cage, which was especially timely under the totalitarian communist regime in the Czechoslovakia of the day.

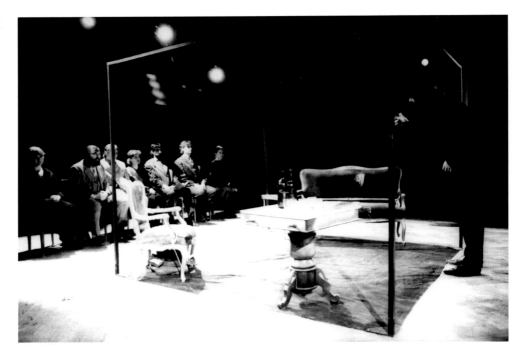

Optimistic Tragedy (Optimistinen tragedia)

Måns Hedström (Finland)
Set & Costume Design

Måns Hedström, together with his artistic production team, created new process-based working practices between dramatist, director, and scenographer. The entire set for *Optimistic Tragedy* was made of tarpaulin or canvas, a realistic, concrete material which was used on boats. The acting ensemble was able to produce the sails, the tent, or the storm with their own movements using this very simple scenographic element. The actors' movement, rhythm, and choreography made the simple scenography alive and transformative.

His experiments with environmental scenography and minimalism became the hallmarks of Finnish stage design. He was a conceptual thinker, and his innovative use of space, his choice of significant materials, and his simple visual solutions challenged the aesthetics of scenography and its approaches.

American Anti-Bicentennial Pageant

Peter Schumann (Germany/USA)
Puppet Design

The Bread and Puppet Theatre, founded in New York in 1961, is a loose association of performers under the direction of founder Peter Schumann. His maxim for the company is "...theatre is like bread, more like a necessity..."

"Deeply involved in the contemporary reaction against what is perceived as the over-intellectualization of Western culture, as epitomized in its powerful tradition of literary theatre, Schumann and his associates work with larger-than-life puppets to create a non-narrative theatre that addresses contemporary issues, such as... the 1975 *Anti-Bicentennial* at the University of California — an angry and moving elegy to the last Indian survivor of white genocide in the state—... through disturbing visual images rather than words..." [*Cambridge Guide to American Theatre* by Don B. Wilmeth & Tice Mller]

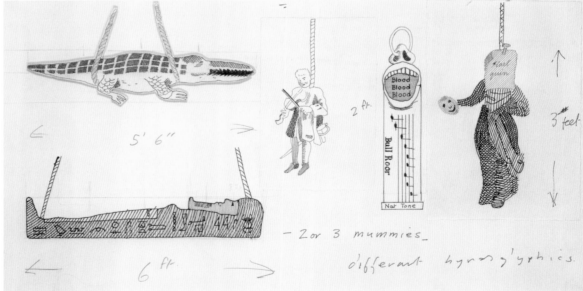

Rake's Progress

David Hockney (UK)
Set & Costume Design

While not his first work for the stage, this hugely successful design led to further collaborations for David Hockney with Glyndebourne and other major opera companies in the US and the UK. He had completed his own series of etchings based on Hogarth's while still a student at the Royal College of Art, which was what led to this commission. However it was to Hogarth, rather than his own work, that Hockney went for his inspiration.

Throughout the 20th century, great painters have been employed to design sets and costumes, with varying degrees of success. Hockney is among the most successful, as his bold sense of form and colour is admirably suited to the stage. Embracing the challenge of a new medium, Hockney capitalized on his ability to absorb a subject and then embody it visually, using only the essential elements, thereby giving a great simplicity to his stage pictures and creating the essence of a character, theme, or period. For many critics his work has become the definitive design for this opera, perfectly matching Stravinsky's idiom. "The paramount task is to... find an equivalent form and colour for the music," Hockney later wrote. The artist's involvement not only drew a wider audience to Glyndebourne, but, in John Cox's words, made a difficult opera "audible through the eye."

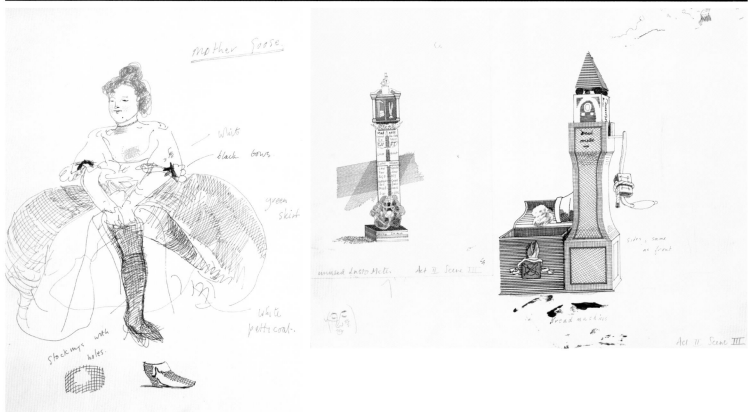

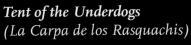

Tent of the Underdogs
(La Carpa de los Rasquachis)

Luis Valdez (USA)
Set Design

La Carpa de los Rasquachis, written and directed by Valdez, is from the early El Teatro Campesino theatre canon. The set was made with what was at hand: burlap potato sacks used by the Central Valley farm workers who were the theatre's original audience. Designed to travel, the set toured the United States, Mexico, and Europe extensively starting in 1972. It continues to be a part of the El Teatro Campesino repertoire and is considered the exemplary play of the early Chicano Theatre Movement.

By Feet and Hands
(De Pies y Manos)

Guillhermo de la Torre (Argentina)
Set Design

Guillermo de La Torre is a major character in the modern scenography scene in Argentina. He studied at NYU under a Fulbright grant, and has also taken courses in Paris, London, and Madrid.

His work can be described as poetic realism, which suggests overcoming illusion using spacial elements. His synthesis of elements — making knowledge and procedures concrete in space, thereby intensifying the theatre action in a subtle way — distinguishes his creativity.

His professional work covers nearly all Argentine theatre history in the last half of the 20th century. Latin American countries live in a state of constant politic and economic oscillations, where the first victims are culture and theatre. This requires theatre artists to persevere in the profession and try to solve the countless challenges of a production with creativity and inventiveness rather than money. De La Torre is a great example of how a talented creator stands out even more when he succeeds with fewer resources.

One of his most outstanding designs, *De pies y manos* played out in a unique space that transformed itself through the lighting of more than a dozen metallic structures. On the floor, a mound of stories represented by hundreds of objects piled up helped make this work one of the landmarks in Argentinian design.

Baal

Raul Belem (Brazil)
Set & Costume Design

This design represents the breakout moment of national recognition for designer Raul Belém Machado. He is the greatest name of the Brazilian scenography outside Rio or Sao Paulo, working in Belo Horizonte, the capital of Minas Gerais. Raul started his work at the beginning of the 1970s, and *Baal* was the most significant production of that decade in Minas Gerais.

Baal was designed like a piece of furniture, put together with fittings without the use of nails or screws, which allowed for dozens of different configurations. It became a playful puzzle with great spacial force.

Raul Belém, in addition to being a scenographer, is a theatre architect, costume designer, and one of the greatest stage managers in Brazil. He has been the director for the technical centre of the arts palace in Belo Horizonte for many years, and is a great art educator. For more than three decades, he has influenced many new scenic and costume designers.

He is, undoubtedly, one of the greatest figures in Brazilian scenography.

The Cherry Orchard

Valery Levental (USSR/Russia)
Set Design

In a design that was strikingly different from the previous, predominantly open-space stagings at the Taganka Theatre, Valeri Levental reshaped the acting space into a picturesque environment. White gauze curtains, creating a distinctive sense of frailty, fluttered not in the sitting-room but over the graveyard that became "home" for Ranevskaya and the locale for Efros's production.

The few remaining pieces of furniture, painted in white with slipcovers of white Holland, were placed among crosses, gravestones, and marble benches. Only the old redwood bookcase appeared to be a real solid object in this illusory environment. In the spirit of Japanese art where it is a funeral color, white was predominant in sets and costumes. These Oriental motifs continued in the design of the orchard: in the foreground, just one branch was left blooming while a mass of artificial white blossom covered the stage floor. People were evicted not from their ancestral estate, but from their family vault. The exquisite beauty of the environment didn't conceal the conflicts inherent in the play but enhanced and accentuated them.

The Revenger's Tragedy

Kristian Fredrikson
(New Zealand/Australia)
Set & Costume Design

Kristian Fredrikson was one of the most influential designers in the Australian theatre. Early in his career, he worked as a resident designer for the Melbourne Theatre Company, and this production is a superb example of the work he did while at the company.

The production marked a "golden era" of design for the still-emerging Melbourne Theatre Company when, led by Kristian Fredrikson, a permanent group of artisans and realizers (cutters, milliners, scenic artists, prop makers, etc.) was able to hone and develop their skills.

Till Eulenspiegel (Thyl Ulenspegel)
Evgeni Lysik (Ukraine)
Design

The staging of the ballet *Till Eulenspiegel*, choreographed by Valentin Yelizaryev and designed by Eugeni Lysik, marked the emergence of a new theatre of "pictorial choreography." Dismissing many details of the original story, the authors of the ballet focused not so much on the characters portrayed by Charles de Coster as on the notions personified by them.

The central conflict was the struggle between Freedom and Oppression. Its visual image was the highly expressive and monumental stage design as well as the original costumes created by Lysik. After that staging, Lysik gained a reputation as the most tragically expressive of artists in Soviet musical theatre. His imaginative set design appeared to be, if not the main character, then at least the major driving force of the performance, helping to profoundly and epically express its central theme.

Gee Girls—The Liberation is Near (Jösses flickor—befrielsen är nära)
Måns Hedström (Sweden)
Set & Costume Design

Måns Hedström's philosophy was to erase the boundary between the actor and the audience, which can, for example, be seen in *Gee Girls—the Liberation is Near*. It's possible to define his professional role with the title "visual designer" which describes his career in a good way. A significant phrase for Hedström's work is "less is more" and he made the visual impressions from his scenographies, costumes and posters an indispensable part in the theatre process. *Gee Girls* is a landmark in Swedish theatre history because of its political and feminist history. It was played 140 times at the Stockholm City Theatre and well reviewed in the press. It was remade in 2008 with a new second part. He received his training at the School of Art and Design in Helsinki.

The Resistible Rise of Arturo Ui
(Der aufhaltsame Aufstieg des Arturo Ui)
Daniil Lider (Ukraine)
Set Design

This single set was used as the basis for two productions — Brecht's *The Resistible Rise of Arturo Ui* and Shakespeare's *Macbeth*. What both stagings had in common was the theme of the triumph of base instincts and the release of the darkest forces from the lower depths of human soul. The set design was emphatically neutral in relation to the tradition of theatre as the venue for spectacles. It ignored such elements as footlights, wings, revolve, and curtains. From somewhere deep down, the sewer pipes appeared as a multifunctional component of the design. The model of the sets for *The Resistible Rise of Arturo Ui* was exhibited at PQ'75.

For his sets for *The Resistible Rise of Arturo Ui* and *Macbeth* Daniil Lider was awarded the Gold Medal at the Second Quadrennial in Vilnius.

Clowns of Avignon
(Klauni z Avugnonu)

Helena Anýžová
(Czechoslovakia/Czech Republic)
Costume Design

Compared to other designers of her generation, Helena Anýžová's concept for the costume design seems subtle and unobtrusive (like the handwriting on the design), while revealing a hint of eroticism and ironic detachment. Even though the actors in this production are swathed in drapery, the natural proportions of the human figure are respected, but subtly touched up by the arrangement of the fabrics, the textile samples, and the accessories. These economic, stylized interventions express a simple charm, gentle humour, and comic playfulness.

The Miracle in Sargan
(Čudo u Šarganu)

Petar Pašić (Serbia/Yugoslavia)
Set Design

Right from its start, Atelje 212 became well known for its avant-garde repertoire. The first directors of the theatre were Radoš Novaković and Bojan Stupica, but Mira Trailović soon became director. *The Miracle in Sargan* was a tragi-comedy with two plot lines: one set "today" and the other dealing with a soldier in WWI. The two threads are linked in the person of a beggar who takes on peoples' troubles. It was an extraordinary production that showed very realistically the life of the socially rejected, poorly educated and unstable people who find themselves caught between the country and city life.

Peter Grimes

Timothy O'Brien & Tazeena Firth (UK)
Set Design

Timothy O'Brien: "The romantic evocation of actual places in the original production thirty years before gave way to a more epic approach. We felt that *Peter Grimes* should be set in an evocative, abstracted space. At the same time, the people on stage, their clothes and the things they handle should have a gritty reality.

"We began with the floor. Tilted towards the audience, textured in sand, we inlaid an area of worn planking downstage, reminiscent of a boardwalk. On the sand, we laid pebbles, graded in size by the tides, and amongst them we threw down sequins so that the beach glittered in the sun.

"The side walls were sail-shaped and softly sprayed in horizontal sepia bands. Downstage the walls were barely as high as a man and upstage as high as the sky. The sky was a screen, made up of a pale translucent sheet of plastic fronted with a gauze, on to which we sprayed softer bands of sepia.

"Within the space were things that came and went: two fishing boats, a capstan, steel posts with wires and curtains between them, benches, tables and nets, and Grimes's hut, made from part of an upturned boat.

"Most of the changes of scene took place in front of the audience, but the change from the Borough on Sunday morning to Grimes's hut was made behind a front curtain, softly banded in sepia and dressed with a projection of clouds."

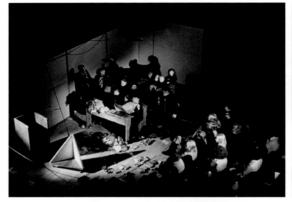

The Dead Class
(Umarła klasa)

Tadeusz Kantor (Poland)
Set & Costume Design

In the early 60s Tadeusz Kantor began to create his own theatre, Cricot 2. Instead of traditional scenery he designed "objects", to constitute the essence of the show. Kantor's aesthetics can be described as "antiscenography". He opposed all decoration, preferring a subdued color range of black, gray and white.

The quintessence of these assumptions was his award-winning 1975 staging of *The Dead Class*, which toured the world and was played more than two thousand times over seventeen years. In this "shocking" and "cruel" play the game space was clearly separated with ropes. A narrow, long rectangle was surrounded by spectators in front and on its right side. The left side of the wall was closed; an entrance for the actors located at the back. The hall/room was dark, but the acting area was exactly lit—white, uniform light, without any changes and shades. Stacks of dried books and notebooks. In school benches, twelve old men in funeral suits and black dresses, with white faces and empty eyes, were waiting for the teacher. The class, which began here soon, was stretched between the two poles—childhood and death. *The Dead Class* was in fact a celebration of the poetic fight against the spectres of doom and destruction, of man's inevitably lethal journey into oblivion.

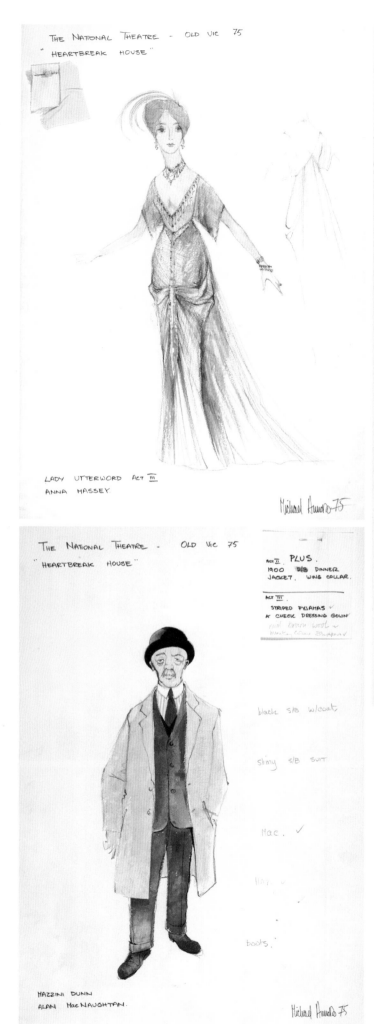

THE NATIONAL THEATRE - OLD VIC 75
"HEARTBREAK HOUSE"

LADY UTTERWORD ACT III
ANNA MASSEY.

Michael Annals 75

THE NATIONAL THEATRE - OLD VIC 75
"HEARTBREAK HOUSE"

ACT II PLUS.
1900 D/B DINNER
JACKET. WING COLLAR.

ACT III.
STRIPED PYJAMAS
& CHECK DRESSING GOWN

black s/b w/coat

shiny s/b suit

Mac. ✓

boots.

MAZZINI DUNN
ALAN MacNAUGHTAN.

Michael Annals 75

Heartbreak House

Michael Annals (UK)
Set & Costume Design

Michael Annals' 15-year association with Britain's National Theatre began early, with a *Saint Joan* seen in Chichester in 1963 and later in the fledgling company's opening season at the Old Vic, where he had already designed for the Old Vic Company. He had a huge success the following year with *The Royal Hunt of the Sun*. About John Schlesinger's production of *Heartbreak House* in 1975, "It was something which had to be approached with a completely fresh mind," he told the critic Irving Wardle. "As a movie director, John has a much more visually constructive eye than many other directors I've worked with."

Other memorable designs for Laurence Olivier's National Theatre Company included the 1971 *Long Day's Journey Into Night*. Commercial success came with his definitive sets and costumes for Michael Frayn's worldwide hit, *Noises Off*, in 1982.

Macbeth *(Makbet)*

Vladimir Marenić (Croatia/Serbia)
Set Design

Vladimir Mareni's set for *Macbeth*, directed
by Arsenije Jovanović at the National Theatre
in Belgrade, made a strong impression
on the spectator with its monumentality
but also with the solid red colour that
covered its whole space. Critics described it
variously as the inside of a ship, a cauldron,
a landscape of our subconscious, a bizarre,
phantasmagorical Bosch-like scene, and a
bloody bathroom. From the walls of this
egglike space stare many dark holes, from
which only hints of horrors presented
themselves. The spectator's imagination
was invited to complete the picture. The
colouring of Milena Nitčeva's costumes
was complementary to the stage set: red
and black rustic materials, stylised and
simply cut for the realistic characters,
more imaginative for the witches and the
characters from the underworld. Vladimir
Marenić has been characterised by critics
as an artist who demonstrates remarkable
creativity: some of his set designs are so
dominant that they determine the meaning
of the play.

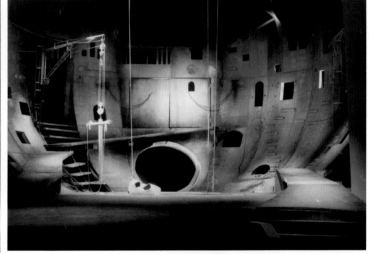

The Corsair *(Der Korsar)*

Toni Businger (Switzerland)
Set & Costume Design

Toni Businger was engaged at the Bregenzer Festspiele from 1972 until 1979. His stage designs became one of the principal reasons for people to visit the Bregenz festival.

He received the Innerschweizer Kulturpreis (cultural award of central Switzerland) in 1980 and the Johann-Melchior-Wyrsch-Preis (Johann-Melchior-Wyrsch award) in 1990, both honouring his complete works.

A Night in Venice *(Eine Nacht in Venedig)*

Toni Businger (Switzerland)
Set & Costume Design

In 1975 he created sets for the two festival productions, *Eine Nacht in Venedig* and *Der Korsar*. 1975 was a very successful season, attracting over 50,000 spectators. The last performance of *Eine Nacht in Venedig* was on August 1st and the premiere of *Der Korsar* was on August 2nd. To facilitate an easy and swift transformation of the set, Businger based the two designs on the same elements. The set of *Eine Nacht in Venedig* gained additional rooftops, crescents, and palm trees to create an oriental atmosphere. The festival management wanted ships on the lake during the show, so Businger designed a pirate ship. Traditionally the festival ends with fireworks, which were started from this ship and created a glamorous finale for the season.

Oedipus at Colonus

Dionysis Fotopoulos (Greece)
Set & Costume Design

The throne that dominates this set by Dionysis Fotopoulos, and the tattered robe he designed for the great Greek actor Alexis Minotis, are tightly linked to the mental state of the tragic hero and offer an ontological slant on Oedipus as the "Marble Emperor" (or sleeping hero) at Colonus.

The set is a particularly important milestone for the artist himself, for the National Theatre of Greece, and for the history of the Epidaurus Festival. Until that time, sets had been dominated, almost without exception, by palatial architectural volumes; this design signalled the new-found freedom enjoyed by artists following the fall of the military dictatorship.

White Marriage *(Białe małżeństwo)*

Zofia de Ines (Poland)

Costume Design

The highly original costumes designed by Zofia de Ines for *White Marriage* aided in the creation of a dark phantasmagoria. The soft sculptures—made of canvas stuffed with sponge—both stylish, surreal and erotic, revealed the monstrous sexuality of the characters. Mother with maternity obsession had many budding pregnancy bellies. Aunt wore front bum. A lot of phalluses-mushrooms grew from the father costume. Yet, young girls were wearing short petticoats, exposing their breasts and legs.

The Devils of Loudun
(Diabły z Loudun)

Andrzej Majewski (Poland)
Set & Costume Design

The Polish première of Penderecki's *The Devils of Loudun*, directed by Kazimierz Dejmek with scenery by Andrzej Majewski, was on 8 June 1975. It went on to play 75 times over five years, touring extensively.

Majewski divided his permanent playing area into two spaces: the proscenium and the main stage. In the foreground (the proscenium) intimate chamber scenes were played out, sometimes in two or three places simultaneously, often in parallel with the action on the main stage, which depicted a huge space, extending to the horizon, its contents marking the dominance of religion and the church.

Above, on a tangle of ropes and chains, hung a meteorite, which changed its position and appearance from scene to scene. Illuminated mosaic lamps—producing patterns like sunlight sifted through stained glass—were revealed in the interior of the cathedral setting for the trial of Urbain Grandier. Finally, it would develop into a dry hillock—Golgotha, where Grandier would be martyred in a scene reminiscent of medieval Italian paintings. The opera, in its theatrical texture, hovered like a Passion Play somewhere between mystery and rhetoric.

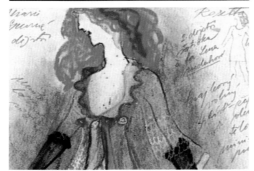

655,000 • Tidal Wave in Philippines kills 5,000 • First commercial Concorde flights take off • 32 African nations boycott Montreal Olympics • First Legionnaires Disease affects 4,000 delegates in Pennsylvania • Soweto riots in South Africa mark beginning of the end of apartheid • Palestinian extremists hijack Air France plane to Entebbe, Uganda • United States Bicentennial is celebrated • Mao Tse-tung dies • Eccentric American billionaire Howard Hughes dies • Fidel Castro becomes president of Cuba • Apple computer company is formed by Steve Jobs and Steve Wozniak • NASA unveils first space shuttle • American panel warns of CFC damage to ozone layer • VHS home VCR introduced to compete with Sony Betamax system • Landing vehicles from the US Viking spacecraft set down on Mars • Earthquake in China kills 655,000 • Tidal Wave in Philippines kills 5,000 • First commercial Concorde flights take off • 32 African nations boycott Montreal Olympics • First Legionnaires Disease affects 4,000 delegates in Pennsylvania • Soweto riots in South Africa mark beginning of the end of apartheid • Palestinian extremists hijack Air France plane to Entebbe, Uganda • United States Bicentennial is celebrated • Mao Tse-tung dies • Eccentric American billionaire Howard Hughes dies • Fidel Castro becomes president of Cuba • Apple computer company is formed by Steve Jobs and Steve Wozniak • NASA unveils first space shuttle • American

1976

Firebird

Tetsuhiko Maeda (Japan)
Set Design

He designs mainly for classic and contemporary dance, and his designs always try to create a sculptural style with the dancers on the stage. The production was unique for its time in its use of very modern materials for the set.

The Misadventures of The New Satan (or The New Devil of Hellsbottom)
(Põrgupõhja Uus Vanapagan)

Georg Sander (Estonia)
Set Design

This production heralded the arrival in the 1970s of a new generation of stage directors exploring total metaphorical-physical theatre. Probably the most significant production of its era, this staging is also considered to be one of the most "theatrical" productions in Estonian theatre history. The scenography played a great role in its success, and was considered the most important metaphor for the whole production, with its apocalyptic vision of the future shown through national classics.

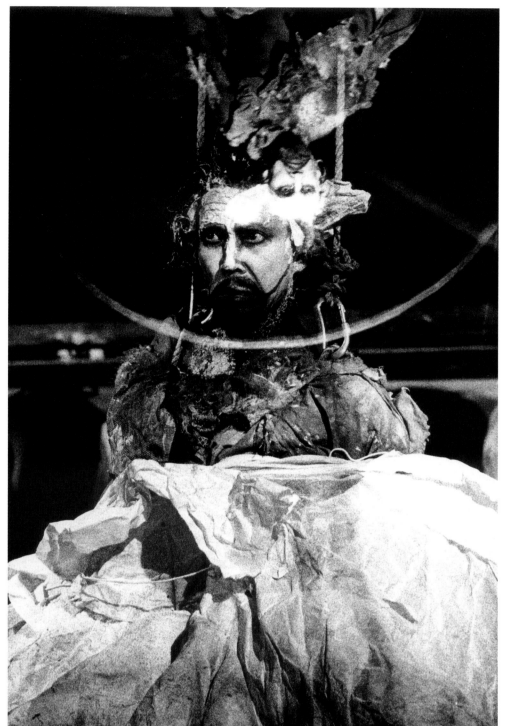

Storm *(Arashi)*

Akaji Maro (Japan)
Set Design

The stage creates a space for the Buto dancers, who might leave the audience filled with awe or revulsion, unable to relate to any of it, or be deeply affected by it. It might be seen as being full and alive, and at the same time empty.

While the designs are drawn up and constructed using a global approach, the choreography and storytelling are also progressing. But the production as a whole shouldn't be limited to one country or realm or point of view, even if it is required by the work.

The theme and the contents of a work not only need to counterbalance each other, but must work together to make a work vivid and rich. A production should not simply explain the theme and the contents, but should reveal a work's universality.

The dancers are never principal, nor even secondary. The designs are never principal nor secondary either. This dynamic, like a master-servant relationship, should be highly and complexly explored.

When a work is totally evaluated, it's also evaluated from part to part. Each part must be well harmonized. If the glory is granted only for design, the production is a failure.

Book of Splendors
(le Livre des Splendeurs)
Richard Foreman (USA)
Set, Costume & Lighting Design

The Book of Splendors was first created by *avant garde* director/designer/playwright Richard Foreman for the 1976 Festival d'Automne in Paris and then presented in 1977 at his New York home, the Ontological-Hysteric Theater. The production featured stop-and-go action, recorded comments by the author, his signature dotted-line strings, and a parade of imagery (furniture and props were accorded as much focus and expressiveness as the actors). "Foreman seeks to disrupt the audience's logical and teleological thought processes and 'force people to another level of consciousness.'" [*Cambridge Guide to American Theatre* by Don B. Wilmeth & Tice Mller]

Midsummer Night's Dream

Susan Benson (Canada)
Set & Costume Design

Robin Phillips' first year as artistic director of the Stratford Shakespearean Festival was in 1975, and this production was one of the first collaborations between him, Susan Benson, and light designer Michael J Whitfield. Their creative teamwork was a high mark in the development of a strong Canadian stage design aesthetic. Her work continued at Stratford for another 30 years.

The Good Woman of Setzuan
(Der gute mench von Sezuan)

Nina Schiøttz (Denmark)
Set & Costume Design

This is a fine example of cooperation between director and scenographer and of the high-level production values that can be achieved by a provincial theatre. The evolving scenery showed great simplicity and symbolism, using an almost cubist language. The stylized costumes combined European tradition with Chinese stylistics and symbols.

The Little Square *(Il Campiello)*

Deirdre Clancy (UK)
Costume Design

This was the inaugural production at the National Theatre's Olivier stage, attended by HM Queen Elizabeth II, and takes a proud place on Deirdre Clancy's own website, where she mentions it as one of the 18 productions she has designed for The Royal National Theatre. Her talent in both visual and verbal communication has ensured that her historically correct and highly researched design process has made her way of working very influential with her contemporaries and with younger designers. She was one of the group of UK designers who won the Golden Triga at PQ'79. She is also a published author, writing on costume design and costume history. She has won both Olivier and BAFTA awards for her costume designs.

The Shadows

Tatiana Selvinskaya (USSR/Russia)
Set & Costume Design

The Shadows was one of the most astonishing productions of Soviet theatre in the 1970s. Director Felix Berman came up with a coarse but very neat interpretation of the amoral world depicted by the writer. Tatiana Selvinskays's scenery encompassed both Petersburg in its ceremonial glory and the ugly outskirts of the capital.

In the middle of the stage, gigantic circus lions lie tail-to-tail, as though guarding access to an enormous table covered with green broadcloth, conceived both as a sign of the omnipotence of officialdom and as a platform for the show-booth interludes. The uniforms of the Petersburg bureaucrats were transformed into the liveries of circus hands. Female attire fluttered like the riding habits of horsewomen. The dandies wore tight trousers with tassels and fringes like performing poodles. Above the stage was a chandelier resembling either a candlelit circus arena or the swing bridges of Petersburg. In the course of the action, the space would break up, revealing its seamy side. *The Shadows* was shown at many theatre festivals and became a breakthrough for national theatre.

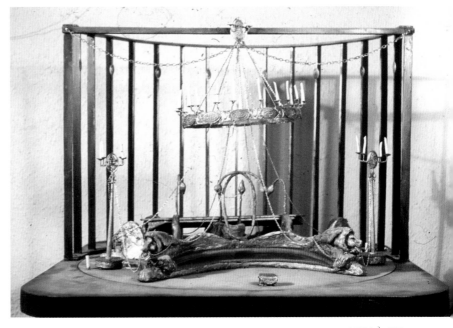

Romeo & Juliet

Phillip Silver (Canada)
Set & Lighting Design

The Citadel Theatre was established in 1963 and by the early 1970s plans were underway to build a larger home for the company to open in 1976. Artistic director John Neville chose *Romeo and Juliet* to be the first production in the new theatre. The set and lighting designer was Phillip Silver, who served as the theatre's resident designer 1967 to 1978.

Neville challenged Silver to not only serve Shakespeare's play, but to define the standards of production audiences might expect in the new facility. In Silver's design, the play began on a bare stage, dressed only with the remnants of building construction materials, but, as the Chorus (in modern dress) concluded the opening speech, the white marble floor of Verona, four two-level towers, and white side walls appeared, along with the characters of the play in period costume. Throughout the performance, Silver's unit set provided a simple but powerful background for the play, achieving changes of location through variations of the positions of four motorized towers.

Jakov Bogomolov

Vladimir Serebrovsky
(USSR/Russia)
Set Design

In staging *Yakov Bogomolov*, Serebrovsky faced the problem of how to depict nature, which had been largely ignored by designers in the 1960s and 1970s. In this case, the designer was inspired by the experiences of the post-Itinerant artist Stanislav Zhukovsky, so he created a spacious, sun-lit veranda overlooking the summer garden stretching out deep into the stage. The artist's intention was to let the audience "breathe in the coolness of the garden on stage and admire its beauty as though they were positioned inside."

At the Nice View *(Kod lepog izgleda)*

Dušan Ristić (Serbia)
Set Design

With his unconventional approach, the Italian director Paolo Magelli, who worked a lot in former Yugoslavia and in Belgrade extensively in this period, distinguished himself from the other theatre directors in Belgrade. His assertiveness in the realm of contemporary theatre and graphic on-stage action drove absurdity to the edge of the possible. This was all displayed in the production *At the Nice View*, which premiered on 19 March 1976. The designers were the top Serbian theatre designers at the time: Dusan Ristic (sets) and Bozana Jovanovic (costume). Those designers collaborated with Magelli on more than one occasion. The scene painting was done by the young Miljen Kreka Kljakovic, who later established himself as an important production director in the Yugoslav and international film industry. With his brilliant cast (Milena Dravic, Dragan Nikolic, Petar Kralj, Vlastimir-Djuza Stojiljkovic and Bora Todorovic) the production exposed dormant aggression in human beings, placing them in the realm of absurdity.

Tales of Ensign Stål
(Fänrik Ståls sägner)

Ralf Forsström (Finland)
Set Design

In 1976 Forsström created the scenography for *The Tales of Ensign Stål* at the Swedish Theatre. The design could be considered the first postmodern scenography in Finland with its illusionistic fairy-tale world of anachronisms. During this same period, and at the beginning of 1980s, he experimented with fabric décor that enabled him to create abstract forms, colors, and movements with the help of light.

Long Day's Journey into Night
(Lungul drum al zilei catre noapte)

Dan Jitianu (Romania)
Set Design

The stage set is dominated—at the wish of director Liviu Ciulei—by "Venetian" window shutters, specific to New Orleans and appropriate to the idea of "a house, not a home," to a drifting life, to hopeless relationships. The numerous windows (the playwright demanded them, too) do not change; on the contrary they underline the increasingly tense atmosphere inside the house.

The Wedding (Casatoria)

Paul Bortnovschi (Romania)
Set Design

A realistic yet stylized stage set, considered one of the best of its time: an arrangement of more or less useful objects on a platform, a large space that can be changed by sliding the walls, so that the stage opens out into the background, offering playing space for the actors

The Left-hander (*Levsha*)

Boris Messerer (USSR/Russia)
Set & Costume Design

For the ballet *Levsha* (*The Lefthander*) Messerer wanted to design sets and costumes that would mark a new stage in his artistic career, integrating current trends in world set design and breaking off from the conventional approach to versions of Russian fairy tales laid down by Boris Kustodyev. He succeeded with flying colours.

The stage was dressed in black velvet. To the right of the audience there was a moving vertical picture with a gigantic flower, calling up images from popular folk prints and embroidery. But although the stage was "wearing" one and the same "garment," the sets changed from one point on Levsha's itinerary to another (Tula, St. Petersburg, London), showing their emblematic architectural monuments. They conveyed perfectly the impetuosity of the performance rhythm, set by the composer and the choreographer, and its non-stop action captured the rapid race of Platonov's carriage.

Cervantes

Józef Szajna (Poland)
Set Design

"Józef Szajna—painter, designer, director— was the creator of a very personal formula of a visual narrative theatre. He used to say: "I change my life into the picture" – and this idea assimilated most of his non-theatrical experiences and fully realized in his original morality plays.

In *Cervantes*, which was a clear extension of the existing exploration, Szajna read the prose of Don Quixote and Sancho Panza with his painter's eyes. He took only the mood of Cervantes' work, creating his own set of symbols, characters and spoken dialogue, connected with his personal reflections on the text, visionary organization of stage space and the intense, expressive acting of his actors.

Using pictures-metaphors (ex. huge-ladder Trojan horse, invasion of barrels, self-immolation of the Knight), Szajna created an archi serious performance with ironic counterpoints such as a white dove, a live cock and a pig in a magnificent palace foyer.

Szajna received a special award for this artistic vision at the 13th Kalisz Theatre Meetings."
— Agnieszka Kubaś

To Clothe the Naked (Vestire gli ignudi)

Maurizio Balò (Italy)
Set Design

For designer Maurizio Balò, creation grows out of dialogue with the director. This is one of the more important set designs from the beginning of his career, when the image of a room with doors and windows was an essential theme and element of his poetics. This design also marks the beginning of his creative collaboration with the director Massimo Castri.

The Crucible (Dokimasia)

Giorgos Patsas (Greece)
Set Design

The design was notable Thessaloniki's theatre during this period. The metal crown of thorns traps the people of history, with a backdrop of the nail-pierced hands of Jesus Christ (a detail from Bellini's "Pieta").

1977

President • French is adopted as the official language of Quebec • Nobel Peace Prize is awarded to Amnesty International • Menachem Begin becomes Israel's 6th prime minister • World Trade Center in New York City is completed • Steve Biko "dies in custody" in South Africa • The last execution by guillotine in France • Palestinians hijack Lufthansa airliner demanding release of Baader-Meinhof terrorist group • Egypt president Anwar al-Sadat recognizes state of Israel • First Apple II computer goes on sale • GPS inaugurated by US Department of Defense • First MRI Scanner is tested • NASA space shuttle makes first test flight off back of jetliner • Unmanned Voyager spacecraft launched to explore outer solar system • Jimmy Carter elected US President

• French is adopted as the official language of Quebec • Nobel Peace Prize is awarded to Amnesty International • Menachem Begin becomes Israel's 6th prime minister • World Trade Center in New York City is completed • Steve Biko "dies in custody" in South Africa • The last execution by guillotine in France • Palestinians hijack Lufthansa airliner demanding release of Baader-Meinhof terrorist group • Egypt president Anwar al-Sadat recognizes state of Israel • First Apple II computer goes on sale • GPS inaugurated by US Department of Defense • First MRI Scanner is tested • NASA space shuttle makes first test flight off back of jetliner • Unmanned Voyager spacecraft launched to explore outer solar system •

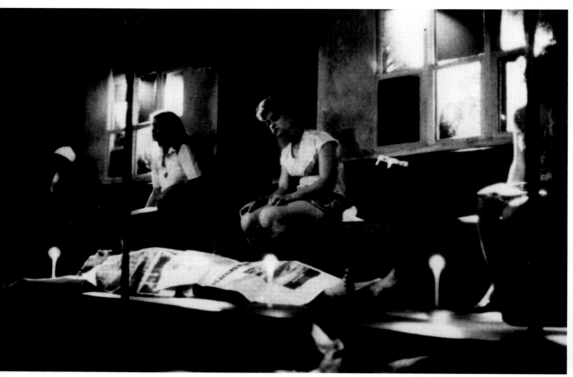

The Last Car
(O Ultimo Carro)
Germano Blum (Brazil)
Set Design

The Last Car was unique for its time because of its scenographic approach where the audience was surrounded by the set. The play—that presents a train trip around the Carioca slums—dealt with political and social issues that are still relevant today. Exhibited at PQ'79, it was and still is remembered as a landmark of Brazilian scenography.

The Journey to Golgotha
(Olugendo lwe Gologoosa)
Leonard Ondur (Uganda)
Set & Lighting Design

It was extremely dangerous to be an artist under Idi Amin's regime and some artists lost their lives for using their work to comment on the state of the country; however, this production and its surreptitious allegorical use of the cross against the backdrop of an empty stage was able to speak eloquently about Uganda while escaping the eyes of the censor. It paved the way for other artists and companies to search for ways of representing the devastation of the regime without getting into trouble.

The scenic environment symbolises the wasteland that Uganda has become and brings together the performers and the audience in a world of suffering and death. On stage, there are symbols of religion, sacrifice, blood, and death. While this is at the heart of the story of the passion, Kiyingi used it as a reference for a country bleeding under Amin's rule.

Hamlet
Ezio Toffolutti (Italy)
Set & Costume Design

This production of *Hamlet* arrived at the Avignon Festival from another theatre stage, a classic theatrical closed space where the court of Denmark was seen as a labyrinth. In Avignon, the space changed and with it the set design, which became an interesting adaptation of a non-theatrical open space. The labyrinth became a trench because Toffolutti, inspired by the space, wanted to create a closer connection with the viewer using an image nearer to the audience's sensibility, and so chose a war setting.

Dead Souls

Valery Levental (USSR/Russia)
Set Design

The set design solution for this opera was suggested by its two coexisting tonal layers: the folk song of the peasants and the musical characteristics of the world of landlords. The composer alternated two operas performed side by side, the characters of each living the lives of their own, with the conflict between them of a philosophic rather than a dramatic nature. Valery Levental turned the two levels of the stage into two gigantic steps. The former accommodated the landlords, fussing around and trading in dead souls. Above them were Russian peasants, dragging themselves along a road. The simplicity of their level was in sharp contrast with the intricate *mise-en-scene* below. In this way the designer separated the authentic from the sham, the eternal from the transient.

Dead Souls became one of Boris Pokrovsky's best works for the Bolshoi Theatre. In 2002 it was awarded the Gold Medal by the Irina Arkhipova Foundation for outstanding contribution to the development of operatic art.

"CESARET ANA"
ILK ETÜDLER.

Mother Courage

Metin Deniz (Turkey)
Set Design

Brecht's *Mother Courage and Her Children* was staged by the Tepebaşı Experimental Stage in one of the scenery workshops of the Istanbul Municipal Theatre. The company was an offshoot of the lively progressive intellectual climate of 1960s Turkey, which was severely interrupted by the military coup in 1971. Under the shadow of the military regime, these young professionals continued to put on plays of social protest and criticism.

This production was revolutionary in its environmental layout. Metin Deniz was the most innovative and rule-breaking stage designer in the history of modern Turkish theatre. "I always considered the stage as a huge statue, a statue which people can move around," he said. A Brecht production in an experimental theatre was ideal for realizing his vision.

He built a big circular platform to serve as the stage and placed the audience inside the circle. Mother Courage's wagon was replaced by a rotten Jeep found in a junkyard, which she dragged around the audience throughout the performance. The contradiction of a motor vehicle moved by hand illustrated Brecht's alienation effect, and the "vicious circle" of the acting was a reference to the hopeless struggle of ordinary people under a capitalist regime.

The waltz became popular in the late 1700s. It was banned at first by some authorities who thought it immoral for couples to dance so closely, but by the mid-1800s, it was accepted everywhere. The faster Viennese form, characterized by swift, gliding turns, expressed the vivacity and brilliance of the Hapsburg court. The waltz was a dance form Balanchine revisited and explored often over his career, but never on as grand a scale as the 1977 *Vienna Waltzes. Vienna Waltzes* — Balanchine's homage to the pleasures and delights of an age that epitomized imperial grandeur — transforms from sylvan forest glen to sassy dance hall to glittering society cafe to, at last, a majestic mirrored ballroom through Rouben Ter-Arutunian's evolving scenery. The music selected for each section of the ballet is associated with the transformation of the waltz across society and over the years.

Vienna Waltzes

Rouben Ter-Arutunian
(Georgia/USA)
Set Design

Untitled

Pilobolus Collective (USA)
Choreographic Design

Original founders Robby Barnett, Jonathan Wolken, Michael Tracy, and Moses Pendleton met in 1971 in a modern dance class at Dartmouth University taught by Alison Chase. The four men, all non-dancers, collaboratively developed an improvised athletic choreography that made use of acrobatics and gymnastics and sometimes bordered on contortion. Success with this approach prompted them to form Pilobolus, which they named after a spirited barnyard fungus. The four brought Chase and Martha Clarke on board as equal partners in artistic direction, and within the first year the company had established itself as something entirely new in the world of dance. Their work was known for its elements of humor and visual illusion, as well as a sculptural physicality in which multiple bodies combined to make unique and ever-changing forms. Scenographically, Pilobolus created a genre in which the performers became the scenic element. Their aesthetic not only changed the way we look at dance, but also blurred the lines between performance and scenography, paving the way for other dance/movement artists and companies.

The company's awards include the Berlin Critic's Prize, Scotsman Award at the Edinburgh Festival, and a Primetime Emmy Award. In June 2000, Pilobolus received the Samuel H. Scripps American Dance Festival Award for lifetime achievement in choreography, and in 2010 it won the Dance Magazine Award for lasting contribution to the field — the only time a collective has won the award.

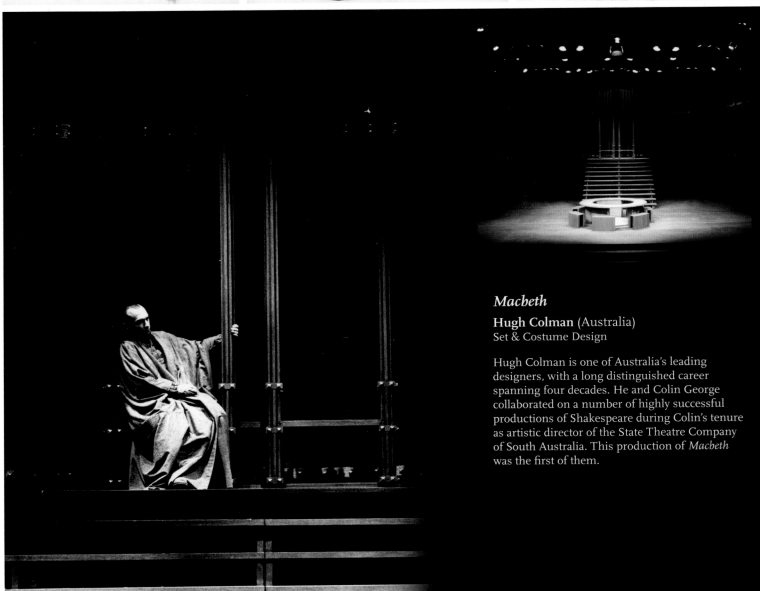

Macbeth

Hugh Colman (Australia)
Set & Costume Design

Hugh Colman is one of Australia's leading designers, with a long distinguished career spanning four decades. He and Colin George collaborated on a number of highly successful productions of Shakespeare during Colin's tenure as artistic director of the State Theatre Company of South Australia. This production of *Macbeth* was the first of them.

Danton's Death
(Dantonin kuolema)

Juha Lukala (Finland)
Set Design

Juha Lukala was the stage designer of the Turku City Theatre. In his early works during the 1960s, he was influenced by the kinetic theatre made famous in Josef Svoboda's Laterna Magica. Lukala started creating his own Finnish versions of kinetic theatre in 1960s, eventually focusing more on architectural theatre. During the Turku City Theatre period from 1971 to 1977 under directors Ralf Långbacka and Kalle Holmberg, the stage was developed into a living dynamic organism which could easily be transformed to change its function. The space offered an ideal situation and starting point for action

Långbacka's adaptation of *Danton's Death* required a flexible scenography so that all the scenes could be realized with film-like fade-out cutting technique. This meant that the previous scene could still be present when the new scene was already taking shape, with the help of the lighting design. The scenographer created a landscape where the presence of a guillotine could be perceived and sensed throughout the performance. The faded gray color scale of the set allowed the costume designer to use rich colors and materials, making it easier for the audience to identify the characters.

The Tempest

Luciano Damiani (Italy)
Set Design

Probably the most important product of the collaboration between Luciano Damiani and Giorgio Strehler, this set design presented an empty space for the poetry of staging, and was very much in tune with Shakespeare's text as translated by Agostino Lombardo.

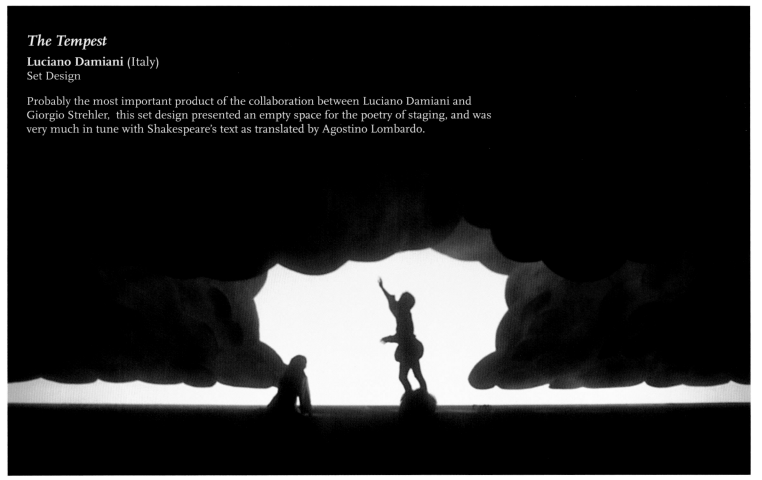

Danton's Death
(A Morte de Danton, Dantons Tod)
Luis Carlos Mendes Ripper (Brazil)
Set Design

The Tower of Babel
(Torre de Babel, La tour de Babel)
Luis Carlos Mendes Ripper (Brazil)
Set Design

Luis Carlos Ripper, a very active stage designer in Brazil and especially in the city of Rio de Janeiro, was a director, teacher, and designer (set, lighting, and costumes). Ripper was also an architect, focusing on theatre spaces and developing projects all over the country. As a theatre director he worked in more than a dozen productions, but his strengths also included his scenographic instruction. He demonstrated a highly loaded dramatic language in his work, and a focused on a synthesis of elements in his artistic search. He experimented with this language on the traditional Italian stage—in productions like *The Tower of Babel*—as well as in alternative public spaces—in productions like *Danton's Death*, produced in the galleries of the subway installation/construction in Rio during the mid-1980s.

The Cherry Orchard
Santo Loquasto (USA)
Set & Costume Design

Santo Loquasto has been nominated for 14 Tony Awards, is a three-time Tony winner, and the winner of the Irene Sharaff/Robert L.B. Tobin Award for Lifetime Achievement in Theatrical Design. He was nominated for the Tony four times in 1977 for his set and costume design work on *American Buffalo* and *The Cherry Orchard* that ran simultaneously on Broadway, winning the best costume design award for *Cherry Orchard*.

"To stage a classic is an easy thing but to restore that classic to the hands, mind, and blood of its creator is in itself an act of creativity. And that is precisely what Andrei Serban and his team of collaborators and clowns have done with their production of Anton Chekhov's *The Cherry Orchard*...

"Apart from the ballroom scene, the designer, Santo Loquasto (here surpassing even himself), has arranged for no setting as such. There is a vast white carpet, the suggestion of white walls at the side and a huge curtain across the back of the stage, flown right up to the flies. There are sometimes light projections behind this curtain—marvelous lighting, by the way, from Jennifer Tipton—but for the most part it is a spectral backdrop to various props and bits of furniture." [Review by Frank Rich, *New York Times*, 18 February 1977]

Rumstick Road

Jim Clayburgh & Elizabeth LeCompte (USA)
Production Design

"It is true that *Sakonnet Point* is the first show that Elizabeth LeCompte and Spalding Gray (to become known as The Wooster Group) made together—but, generally, most people, including people here, think of *Rumstick Road* as the more archetypal early Wooster Group show. *Sakonnet Point* was performed on a revision of the set for The Performance Group's *Mother Courage*—originally the shows were done in rep, one on Thursday and Friday and the other on Saturday and Sunday—so they shared the 'environmental' seating and atmosphere that was a foundation of the work of TPG and it's director, Richard Schechner. (LeCompte and Gray were both in *Mother Courage* by the way.) With *Rumstick Road*, LeCompte was able to realize a vision that was distinctly her own. If you're going to choose only one I would encourage you towards *Rumstick Road* as the more important early piece." [Clay Hapaz, Wooster Group]

Michelangelo Buonarroti

Miodrag Tabački (Yugoslavia/Serbia)
Set & Costume Design

Michelangelo Buonarrotti belongs to a group of
early avant-garde plays by the most renowned
and venerated of Croatian modernist writers and
playwrights, Miroslav Krleza. It was long considered
to be unperformable, not least because of its imagined
setting. It demanded that the designer recreate the
scaffolding in the Sistine Chapel, which would then
withdraw in the scenes depicting Michelangelo's
nightmares. Miodrag Tabacki not only realised the
huge scaffolding, but extended it beyond the usual
limits of the proscenium, connecting the
performance space with the audience.

The Merchant of Venice

Ichiro Takada (Japan)
Set Design

Ichiro Takada is one of Japan's most renowned theatre designers.
For the past half century, his work has been seen throughout
Japan and at such international venues as La Scala. His designs
have been exhibited many times at the Prague Quadrennial.
The symbolism in this set design for *The Merchant of Venice* is
expressed through various organic objects.

He Who Gets Slapped
(Ten, který dostává políčky)

Fára Libor (Czechoslovakia/
Czech Republic)
Set Design

Two strong creative personalities, scenic artist
Fára Libor and director Miroslav Macháček,
come together in this performance, which
takes place in the circus. The model, which
makes use of collage and elements of pop art,
is a scenic expression of this versatile artist's
work in free and graphic creation (including
theatre posters and programmes). Fára's
activities were extremely important in the
context of the progressive art trends of the
1960s and 1970s, which continued beyond
the official Czech artistic scene during the
"normalization" era.

The Trojan Women (*Troades*)

Yannis Tsarouchis (Greece)
Set & Costume Design

In designing and directing *The Trojan Women* Tsarouchis broke the relationship with antiquity and the ancient theatre of Epidaurus by utilizing more contemporary costumes and covering the historic ruins with fabric. This was a very important production in Tsarouchis' career.

Variations (Warjacje)

Jerzy Grzegorzewski (Poland)
Set Design

Jerzy Grzegorzewski's *Variations* is a theatre of dreams, a collage of various texts assembled into a unified whole. The show begins gradually, almost imperceptibly. The half-light reveals silhouettes. A distant horizon gives an impression of extraordinary depth and intriguing light. Combining cubism and pop art, Grzegorzewski has constructed a completely imaginary space, even though the objects collected on stage are literal quotations from reality: bizarre plexiglass shapes, the guts of countless pianos, the wings of aeroplanes and gliders. The actors were more static than the scenery, intimidated by those strange, looming windows on the proscenium and the drowsily swinging wings. Not a cluttered apartment but a cluttered mind.

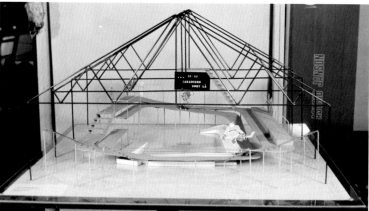

Les Canadiens

Astrid Janson (Canada)
Set & Costume Design

This was originally produced at the Centaur Theater in Montreal, which at that time had a very large national influence in English theatre. It captured the imagination of the Canadian public, who enjoyed seeing their national game played onstage.

Les Canadiens was an allegory for French Canada: hockey supremacy, with its star players representing the spirit of independence, a rallying point for political and cultural dissatisfaction within the existing Canadian political system. The production played in the round, in a spiral, designed to maximize the possibilities of speed for the actors, who were on roller skates and skateboards. Close proximity to the audience added to the "arena" feeling, and hundreds of life-sized puppets were part of the interaction with the spectators. The use of a special plastic floor surface for "ice" and electronic machines for "score keeping" were elements new to theatre in 1977.

The production was also significant in drawing in new non-traditional theatregoers for Toronto Workshop Productions, a primarily political theatre company.

The Tent Project
(Tältprojektet: vi äro tusenden...)
Sören Brunes (Sweden)
Set Design

Sören Brunes is one of the most active scenographers in Sweden, working with theatres and independent groups as well as exploring new spaces for performance. Cube-like or spherical rooms, whose contents are cut out of reality, are sometimes a starting point for Brunes. In *The Tent Project* the aim of his scenography was to erase the borders between stage and auditorium in order to get everyone included. This project was a unique event, uniting many Swedish independent theatre and music groups to tell a common story about the rise of Swedish society, from a very political standpoint. It toured all over Sweden, visiting 31 locations and being performed 82 times.

Volpone or the Fox

Drago Turina (Yugoslavia/Croatia)
Set Design

Drago Turina: "The seemingly simple idea for the realisation the play *Volpone* (produced in front of the Lord Mayor's palace in the Dalmatian seaside City of Trogir in the hot summer of 1977) was to suggest medieval pageantry by using three wagons/cages and a circular belt that that encompassed the audience. The belt was used to bring in actors as well as various scenic elements, such as miniature Venetian architecture vistas, boats, numerous furniture, props of different kinds and sizes, etc. It also served as a reminder that Volpone, The Fox, is a character of such pure greediness, that his boundless appetite to collect a fortune by grinding people down at any cost, is the essence of evil in an eternal, hellish vicious circle."

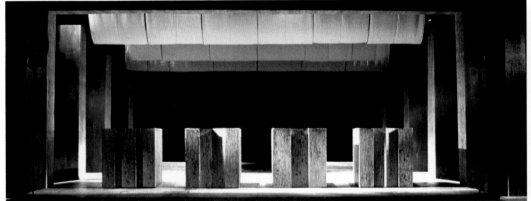

Julius Caesar

Ichiro Takada (Japan)
Set Design

His designs looked very symbolic but they were based in realism and he has always intended to maintain the texture of realism on the stage. His wonderful skill in cut-outs worked to reinforce the sense of realism through his fine knife work.

Shadows *(Сенки)*

Georgi Ivanov (Bulgaria)
Set & Lighting Design

The design epitomizes Georgi Ivanov's metaphorical approach to scenography.

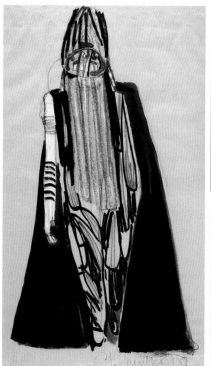

Oresteia

Niels Hamel (Netherlands)
Design

As an abstract-expressionistic visual artist, Niels Hamel always reached for a form of total theatre in which the actors were a vital part of the visual concept. He found a soul mate in unconventional theatre director Erik Vos, with whom he collaborated for 20 years. In 1975 their company Toneelgroep De Appel relocated to a former train depot in Scheveningen, The Hague. They used movable seating for the audience to help realize a changeable theatrical environment.

For the *Oresteia*, the audience sat around a circular area. Wooden poles, sails, ropes, and a rough wooden staircase constructed in the middle of this theatrical space functioned as temple stairs and alternatively as a ship from which the rowers let down their oars.

In addition to the text, Hamel found inspiration in a relief by the American artist Lee Bontecou. For his costumes he used raw materials like jute, feathers, rope, and metal in contrast to the more traditional designs modeled after Greek peploi.

signed as Egypt makes peace with Israel • After nearly 30 years the Volkswagen Beetle stops production • Worldwide unemployment rises after several decades of near full employment • Gold reaches an all time high of $200 per ounce • Rhodesia's leaders agree on transfer to black majority rule • Indira Ghandi faces fraud charges in India • Jim Jones instructs his church members to commit suicide in Guyana • Eric Fielding marries Cecelia Ann Harris • World's population estimated at 4.4 billion • Argentina wins World Cup in Argentina

1978

• US introduces first ever cellular mobile phone system • First computer bulletin board system is created • First test tube baby born in England • Camp David Peace Treaty signed as Egypt makes peace with Israel • After nearly 30 years the Volkswagen Beetle stops production • Worldwide unemployment rises after several decades of near full employment • Gold reaches an all time high of $200 per ounce • Rhodesia's leaders agree on transfer to black majority rule • Indira Ghandi faces fraud charges in India • Jim Jones instructs his church members to commit suicide in Guyana • Eric Fielding marries Cecelia Ann Harris • World's population estimated at 4.4 billion • Argentina wins World Cup in Argentina • US introduces first ever cellular mobile phone system • First computer bulletin board system is created • First test tube baby born in England • Camp David Peace Treaty signed as Egypt makes peace

Angel

Ming Cho Lee (China/USA)
Set Design

While it was a critical and financial failure, *Angel*—the 1978 musical adaptation of the novel and play, *Look Homeward Angel*—featured a handsome scenic design by Ming Cho Lee, a Chinese-born American theatrical set designer. During his award-winning career, Lee has designed for opera, ballet, Broadway, regional theatres (such as Arena Stage, the Mark Taper Forum, and the Guthrie Theater), as well as more than 30 productions for Joseph Papp at The Public Theater, including the original Off-Broadway production of *Hair*. Since 1969 he has been a professor of scenic design at the Yale School of Drama influencing generations of America's emerging designers.

The image here shows Lee's beautifully crafted maquette for the principal setting of the musical *Angel*: the Dixieland Boarding House in Altamount, North Carolina, during the autumn of 1916.

Faust - a fantasy (Faust en fantasi)

Claus Rostrup (Denmark)
Set & Costume Design

This performance marked a high point in the collaboration between Kaspar Rostrup and Claus Rostrup, who created several productions in the form of open space theatre in Gladsaxe Theatre. The action took place on wagons pushed around the stage space, surrounded by the audience. It was the first time this kind of staging was performed in Danish theatre. The production was inspired by the theatre of the middle ages and by Luca Ronconi's 1969 *Orlando Furioso*.

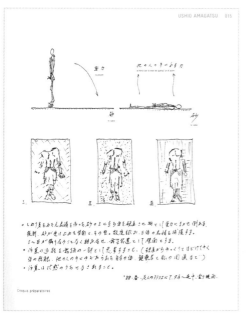

Croquis préparatoires

Shijima: The Darkness
Calms Down in Space

Ushio Amagatsu (Japan)
Production Design

Ushio Amagatsu: "For me stage art is equally important elements along with the dancer's movement, the lighting and music. Because they are means that are used to help create that invisible 'something' we give expression to on the stage. This may be a rather abstract way of describing it, but I think in terms of a sort of 'bridge' that is strung between us dancers, and the audience. And the among the elements used to create that 'something' in the time-space of that bridge are the stage art, music and the movements of the dancers. It is not the case that the movement of the dancers is the 'main' element and the music and stage art a 'sub' elements, rather they are all three 'sub' elements supporting the invisible bridge between us and the audience. And the important thing is that this 'something' is created and appears in each performance.

"As an object of a stiffened body, stands on the various patterned moistened sands and falling on his back with gravitation naturally. There are taken the three expressions of his back on the sands, after repeating several times of above procedure. The combinations and the variations of the expression of their back which never positioned next to each other create the wall as the set.

"I consider this procedure as a part of movement as the Butoh. The consideration of this which means to interpret the catching the sense of the relief from the stiff, and the feeling with the body has been left by others, and the thinking of the relation between the watchers and themselves and so on.

"This working process has to be done in a complete silence."

On The Twentieth Century

Robin Wagner (USA)
Set Design

Veteran Broadway designer Robin Wagner—whose early use of large-scale automated scenery in musicals like *Chess* and *Dreamgirls* has now become standard in American theatre—won his first Tony Award for his handsome, art deco "train set" for *On the Twentieth Century*. Wagner's set design credits include the original productions of *Hair*, *Promises, Promises, Jesus Christ Superstar, A Chorus Line*, and *Angels in America*. He has been nominated for ten Tony Awards for best set design during his 50-year career, and has won three, for *Twentieth Century* (1978), *City of Angels* (1990), and *The Producers* (2001).

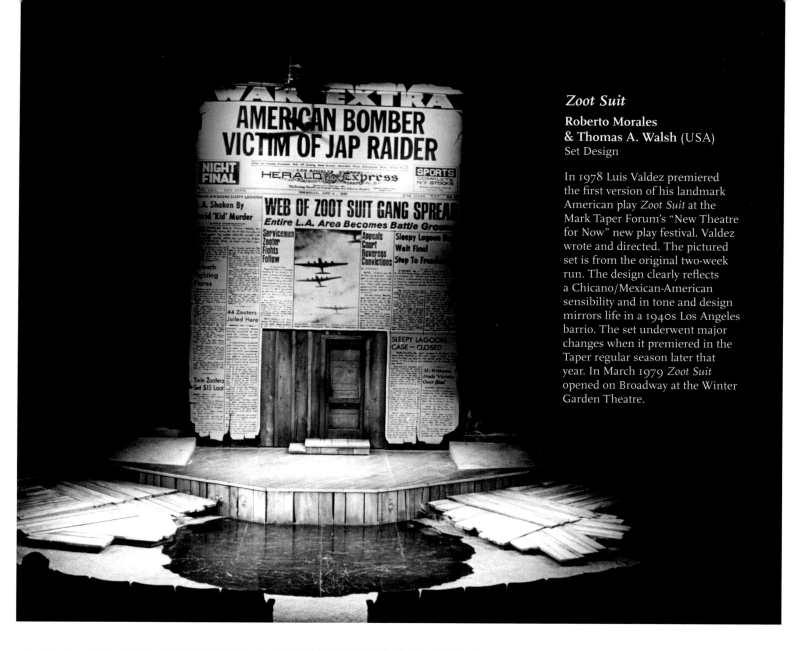

Zoot Suit

Roberto Morales
& Thomas A. Walsh (USA)
Set Design

In 1978 Luis Valdez premiered the first version of his landmark American play *Zoot Suit* at the Mark Taper Forum's "New Theatre for Now" new play festival. Valdez wrote and directed. The pictured set is from the original two-week run. The design clearly reflects a Chicano/Mexican-American sensibility and in tone and design mirrors life in a 1940s Los Angeles barrio. The set underwent major changes when it premiered in the Taper regular season later that year. In March 1979 *Zoot Suit* opened on Broadway at the Winter Garden Theatre.

Project Round Tower
(*Projekt Rundetårn*)

Kirsten Dehlholm
& Per Flink Basse (Denmark)
Set & Costume Design

From 1977 to 1986, Theatre of Images experimented with space, visual tableaux, sound, and light. The company performed outside the traditional theatre, in streets and squares as well as in museums and spectacular buildings. It united different art forms and developed into the internationally acclaimed group Hotel Pro Forma, inspiring a more open use of the concept of theatre.

Antichrist *(Антихрист)*

Neyko Neykov (Bulgaria)
Set, Costume & Lighting Design

The stage design of *Antichrist* won the 1979 Pentcho Guerguiev award from the Union of Bulgarian Artists for scenography, and the scenography award of the Union of Bulgarian Actors at the 1979 National Festival of Bulgarian Drama and Theatre.

Betrayal

John Bury (UK)
Set Design

John Bury shared the Gold Medal for stage design at PQ'75 and was a member of the British team that won the Golden Triga at PQ'79. A lighting designer as well as a scenographer, he has had a gigantic influence on stage design in both the UK and abroad. He began his career with Joan Littlewood's Theatre Workshop, later enjoying a long and fruitful partnership with Peter Hall, both at the National Theatre and at Glyndebourne. Shown here are designs for one of Hall's many works with Harold Pinter, the 1978 *Betrayal*. Bury described them as "small and intimate moments remembered— moving backwards through time. But never a clue as to a world outside these moments. The designer followed suit."

Bury helped establish a way of designing for theatre in Britain that left behind the notion of "the painterly" to embrace the three dimensionality of the stage space, stressing the elemental quality of that space. He promoted interaction, with lighting as key. (He also designed the lighting for this production.) At the same time, he pursued an unashamed historical realism through costume, which "had to be designed with great conviction and in the strictest period, with not a hint that these things might never have happened."

The Insect Play *(Ze života hmyzu)*

Jan Vančura (Czechoslovakia/
Czech Republic)
Set & Costume Design

The use of plastic and industrial design in this
production, emphasized by the penetrating
colors in the costumes which personified
the insects, anticipated the arrival of Czech
postmodernism. The striking shape of the
costumes stood out on the minimalist stage
design. Jan Vančura received a silver medal at
PQ'79 for this design.

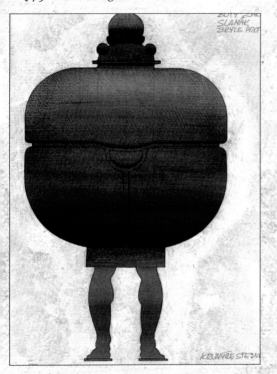

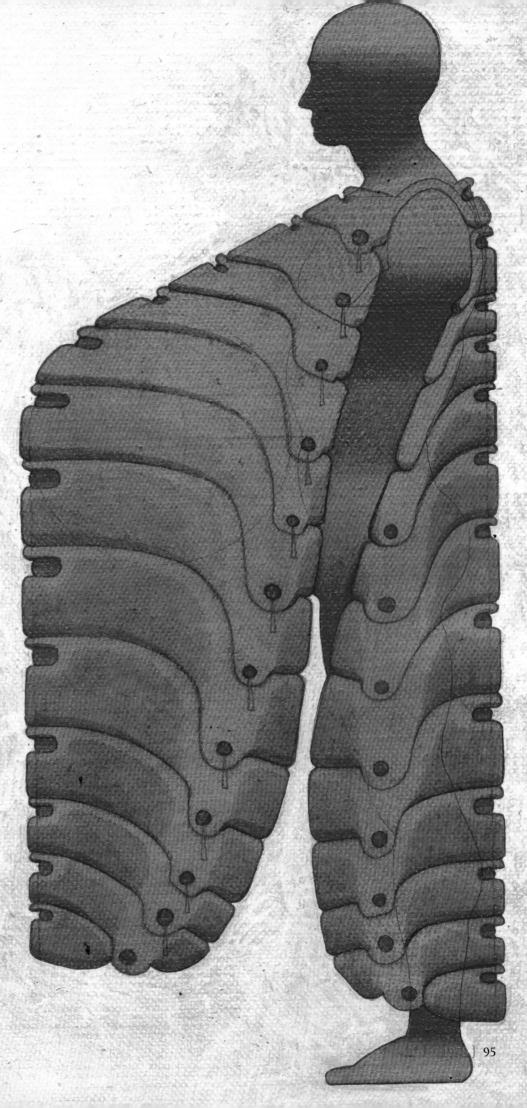

95

MACDUFF マクダフ 1 II-3 バンクォーの ヨロイ使用 星のみ 替える

バンクォ 3 II-3

マクベス夫人 3 II-2 本替 計 2枚 片ソデのみ 引抜 SILVER 2 WHITE PURPLE ++

魔女 3

Kabuki Macbeth

Shozo Sato (Japan/USA)
Set & Costume Design

Shozo Sato, professor emeritus of the Art
and Design Faculty of the University of
Illinois at Urbana-Champaign, came to
Illinois from Japan as an artist-in-residence
in 1969 and made his life's work the
establishment of the study of Japanese
culture at the University of Illinois. In the
theatre world, Shozo Sato is known for
his Kabuki interpretations of European
classics, which came to be known as
"Kabuki fusion." The first of these
productions, *Kabuki Macbeth*, premiered
in 1979 as a student production at the
University of Illinois. *Kabuki Macbeth*
is noted as having an interpretation
that connects with a kind of original
theatricality intended by Shakespeare, but
often lost in contemporary productions.
What followed *Kabuki Macbeth* is a body
of work in a new genre that played all over
the world, including productions of *Kabuki
Medea*, *Kabuki Faust*, *Kabuki Othello*,
Achilles: A Kabuki Play, *Iago's Plot*, *Kabuki
Lady Macbeth*, and, most recently, *Othello's
Passion*. Sato's fusion of Kabuki and
European classics reframes each dramatic
form, with the cultural attributes of one
strengthening and reinforcing the other,
and merges them into something wholly
new. The approach has been emulated by
other Kabuki troupes, but Sato's production
of *Kabuki Macbeth* is recognized as being
the first. *Kabuki Macbeth* was subsequently
produced professionally at the Wisdom
Bridge Theatre in Chicago.

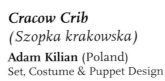

Cracow Crib
(Szopka krakowska)

Adam Kilian (Poland)
Set, Costume & Puppet Design

One of the main representatives of the folk trend in the Polish theatre was Adam Kilian, who created his own recognizable style, drawing inspiration from the colourful world of costumes, paper cutouts or painting on glass, and above all, from the architecture and colour of the crib in Krakow, where he saw the roots of Polish puppet theatre. Its three part, two-level architecture was a hierarchical space precisely defined for a dramatic situation.

Cracow Crib, made in the Puppet Theatre "Pleciuga" in Szczecin in 1978, raised the traditional scheme of nativity scenes to another level, placing it in the living world plan of Krakow. Kilian described the aesthetics of the crib as "absurd," because the poor, dilapidated stable must be presented as artfully and generously as possible. The natural co-existence of simplicity and richness in Kilian's theatrical language are capable of conveying both joy and tragedy in their purest form. Such a creative attitude, taken from a popular vision of the world, was to be consistently implemented by the designer in subsequent productions in both the puppet theatre and his dramatic and musical works.

Woyzeck

Cristina Reis (Portugal)
Set Design

This design points to the fragmentary and erratic sequence of scenes as a possible image of Woyzeck's perplexed mind. Viewed as a struggle between an interiorized oppression and Woyzeck's restless imagination, this perplexity imposes a contrast between the fragmentary disposal of scenes and the permanent movement of people, thus offering a kind of journey through ruins. Cristina Reis puts six different rostra on the stage (as an open fan) that converge on a centre near to the audience. Some of them evoke outdoor places (inhabited mainly by Woyzeck and the commoners) but no mimetic grass ever enters that section, rather barren "earth"; furthermore, the slopes are so steep that they evoke imminent danger. The opposite world is made up of stairs, doors (but no walls), façades and glass, where people in rich—or formal—costumes signal a sophisticated world. It was celebrated as another visionary creation by this designer, finely consolidating her post-structuralist approach to scenographic design.

Spartacus

Boris Messerer (USSR/Russia)
Set Design

The set design for this production of *Spartacus* was radically different from previous interpretations. Boris Messerer used the Roman amphitheatre as its central element. A few additional elements helped advance the narrative, but the action was set entirely within the space of the arena. The backdrop for the scenes, showing the school of gladiators, was iron bars arranged in the semi-circle of the arcade, a very precise rendering of the atmosphere of violence. Quite contrasting was the design for the scene "The Triumph of Rome," for which the structure was transformed to create the porticos and temples of the Roman Forum. The white of the steps and of the characters' costumes was perfectly in tune with the sense of solemn spectacle. The final scene had an especially powerful emotional effect, when Spartacus and his comrades, chained to the grid and lit by powerful floodlights, are raised into the air.

The End of the World (El Fin del Mundo)

El Teatro Campesino (USA)
Scenic Design

The set of *El Fin del Mundo*, written and directed by Luis Valdez, went through multiple design evolutions until it reached a level of symbology and functionality that supported the Dia de los Muertos (Day of the Dead) referencing, the bold presence of the eight to twelve Calavera (skeleton)-robed actors, and Valdez's quick-paced direction and broad physicality. Like all of El Teatro Campesino's work, the set was made to travel to their target audiences. In 1978 and 1980, it toured extensively in the United States and Europe. The frame of the looming skeleton was made of PCP pipe and the limbs were made of Styrofoam-filled burlap casings. The tennis shoes were made with plywood, newspaper, chicken wire, and burlap gleaned from trash bins.

Oedipus

Maurizio Balò (Italy)
Set & Costume Design

This set design continues Maurizio Balò's creative collaboration with Massimo Castri. Here, in an open-air theatre, Balò uses his usual poetics of "doors," which is disturbing because this is a closed set in an open space.

Oedipus Rex

Cameron Porteous (Canada)
Set & Costume Design

Cameron Porteous: "With its startling bare stage, this very stylish production of *Oedipus Rex* was a spectacle of simplicity set in 2000 pounds of sand. Those who saw it still talk about the sculptural beauty. The Emily Carr School of Art voted it the best example of living sculpture for the year. (I don't think the City of Vancouver was as thrilled as theatre-goers, for I hear they are still getting sand out of the office equipment.)"

Margaret Thatcher elected UK prime minister • SALT II arms limitation talks signed by US and USSR • Three Mile Island nuclear accident • Ayatollah Khomeini returns to Iran and takes over government • 63 Americans taken hostage in American Embassy in Tehran • Dictator Idi Amin is deposed in Uganda • Saddam Hussein becomes president of Iraq • Lord Mountbatten assassinated by the IRA • Iranian radicals invade US embassy in Tehran • China institutes one child per family rule • Price of oil reaches new record of $24 per barrel • Sony introduces the Walkman • Voyager I photo reveals Jupiter's rings • Snowboard invented • USSR invades Afghanistan •

1979

Margaret Thatcher elected UK prime minister • SALT II arms limitation talks signed by US and USSR • Three Mile Island nuclear accident • Ayatollah Khomeini returns to Iran and takes over government • 63 Americans taken hostage in American Embassy in Tehran • Dictator Idi Amin is deposed in Uganda • Saddam Hussein becomes president of Iraq • Lord Mountbatten assassinated by the IRA • Iranian radicals invade US embassy in Tehran • China institutes one child per family rule • Price of oil reaches new record of $24 per barrel • Sony introduces the Walkman • Voyager I photo reveals Jupiter's rings • Snowboard invented • USSR invades Afghanistan • Margaret Thatcher elected UK prime minister • SALT II arms limitation talks signed by US and USSR • Three Mile Island nuclear accident • Ayatollah

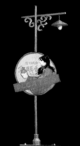

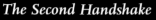

The Second Handshake

Zhang Lian (China)
Set & Costume Design

The period between 1975 and 1990 witnessed a dramatic change in stage design in China. Advances in the education of theatre and fine art technique enabled designers to constantly present new looks.

In *The Second Handshake*, bright "life fragments" were outlined within a black velvet curtain. Concise scene changes combined with stage properties that featured a strong sense of time and place not only represented Chinese history, but also gripped the audience's imagination.

The Bourgeois Gentleman
(Úrhatnám polgár)

Nelly Vágó (Hungary)
Costume Design

Nelly Vágó's designs highlighted the director's concept, yet were in harmony with the actors' character, offering very wearable costumes of quality materials. During her career spanning more than four decades, she created designs of lasting value for the opera, ballet and theatre. Her costumes avoid the routine, and her renderings can be regarded as independent works of art, achieving a life well beyond their function. Her drawings have been exhibited in several scenography contests and received gold medals at PQ, Novi Sad, Graz, and Milan.

Chikamatsu Lovers' Suicide Story

Setsu Asakura (Japan)
Set Design

Before she became a theatre designer, Setsu Asakura was a popular painter in Japan. Her designs are strikingly painting-like, implementing the beautiful art of graphics. When she begins to design a set, she always likens the stage to the blank canvas on which she is drawing with her free imagination.

Richard III

Mirian Shveldidze (USSR/Georgia)
Set Design

Robert Sturua's production had little in common with traditional Shakespeare stagings. It was styled as a grotesque political tragicomedy. The sets were intentionally sparse. Parts of the sets and props were directly engaged in the action. Thus, the main symbol of the performance, the crown, was lovingly played with, snatched from the contenders' hands, put on. The stairway to the orchestra pit called up the road to and from hell. Long poles with instruments of torture and ravens nesting on their tops awaited their next victim. The final battle scene was especially spectacular. The torsos of the fighters and their hands holding huge swords broke through the gigantic backcloth with the map of England on it, making it heave like sea waves. Richard died in its ragged mass, as Richmond stepped over his body and rushed toward the throne and the crown.

This production became a major event of not only of Soviet but also world theatre, touring with great success to many countries. In 1981 it was awarded the State Shota Rustaveli Prize in Theatre.

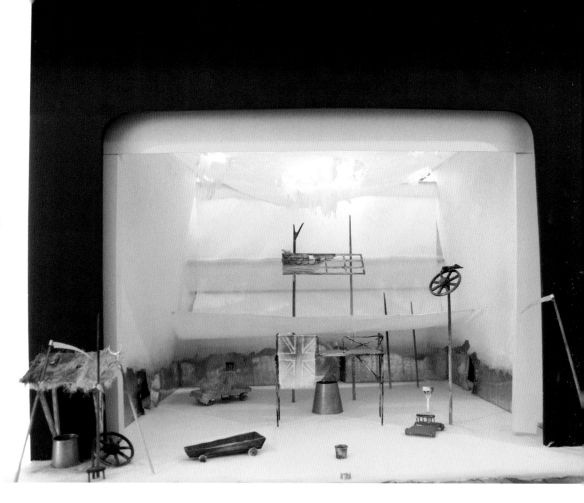

The Tempest *(Furtuna)*

Liviu Ciulei (Romania)
Set Design

Set on a large space that allowed for moments of high acting intensity, Liviu Ciulei's set was symbolically surrounded by a bloody ditch full of half-submerged objects: books, a Mona Lisa, a fragment of an equestrian statue, a knight's armour, a clock, a guitar, and other items—the emotional images of a shipwrecked world.

The Seagull

Sergei Barkhin (Russia)
Set Design

In designing the sets for *The Seagull* at the Vilnius Youth Theatre, Sergei Barkhin turned to the "condemned" and half-forgotten traditions of 19th century theatre, specifically the method of "scene-by-scene" design in various period styles. Thus, predominant in the first part was the idyllic landscape set between expressly theatrical flat wings. Centre stage, the wings spread apart, revealing the magical lake and the silhouette of the manor, the moonlit sky and, in the foreground, the alley strewn with leaves. In the second part, the visual image changed dramatically into a vast and ostensibly deserted space of the "black box," within which white rectangular cornices outlined details of the interior, designed in the cold style Scandinavian art nouveau. All the furniture rested on very thin legs, creating a sense of instability. In Barkhin's concept, the juxtaposition of the two theatrical environments, enhanced by the entire structure of the play, allowed the conflict inherent in *The Seagull* to be fully realized.

Macunaíma

Naum Alves de Souza (Brazil)
Costume Design

Macunaíma was staged by Antunes Filho, considered Brazil's great theatrical director of the second half of the 20th century. For the period from 1975 to 1990, *Macunaíma* was the most significant theatre production in Brazil. The work traveled to more than 50 countries and at least 90 different cities, including almost all major cities of Brazil, influencing and transforming local theatre. Created in a neutral space (black box), the scenery was created by the movement of the actors with their colourful costumes, the movement of their bodies, hand props (mostly made from newspaper), and lighting effects.

Gerald Rabkin, critic for New York's *The Soho Weekly News*, summarized the June 1979 performance of *Macunaíma* as a work "that conveys a pure theatrical excitement. Good theatre doesn't need translation. With sensual mischievousness, *Macunaíma* lives out an adventurous journey of joy and despair that—like *Peer Gynt*—touches the deepest parts of the modern soul."

Bouquet *(Kytice)*

Jana Zbořilová (Czechoslovakia/
Czech Republic)
Set & Costume Design

Designer Jana Zbořilová has been influenced by
the openness, simplicity, and variability of action
scenography as well as by the imaginative poetics of
Brno's Goose on a String Theatre, with whom she has
worked since the 1970s. She was a co-creator of the
poetic tradition of this studio-type theatre, known for
its productions full of tenderness mixed with cruelty,
but also full of imaginative humour, as seen in this
production of *Bouquet*. The stylized costumes contain
oddly transformed elements of folklore, imbued with
a wry detachment bordering on caricature, and also
elements from gloomy poetic ballads.

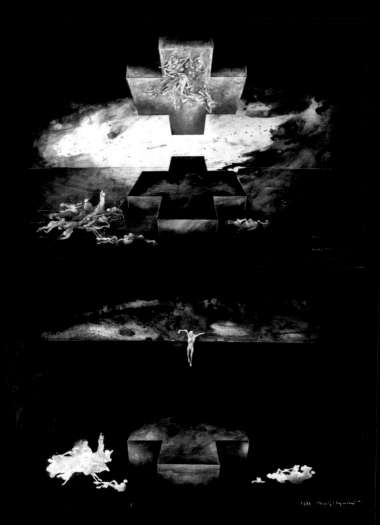

The Passion and Death of Our Lord Jesus Christ
(Passio et mors Domini Nostri Iesu Christi secundum / Pasja)

Andrzej Majewski (Poland)
Set Design

Andrzej Majewski had always insisted that his stage designs were born out of the spirit of painting. His directing debut confirmed this. In this architecturally constructed setting, Majewski saw the gospel of Luke most of all through the words of the composer: "*Passion* is the suffering and death of Christ, but also the suffering and death of Auschwitz, the tragic experience of mid-20th-century humanity."

In the first scene, a platform in the shape of a Greek cross rose from the trapdoor—the symbol of martyrdom and death. A 170-member choir stood on it. Human plaster casts slowly emerged from the darkness, emphasized by a painterly use of lighting to show dynamic movement against a static setting. In the second part, the sky gradually revealed a symmetrical, filled with the remains of the tomb cross— symbol of contemporary suffering. In its upper part Majewski placed a mass of human bodies, symbolizing martyrdom in the gas chambers, while beneath it a choir sang "Pulver mortis Et in deduxisti me" ("The dust of death has enveloped me.") In the finale, darkness swallowed everything but a tormented body—the figure of Christ.

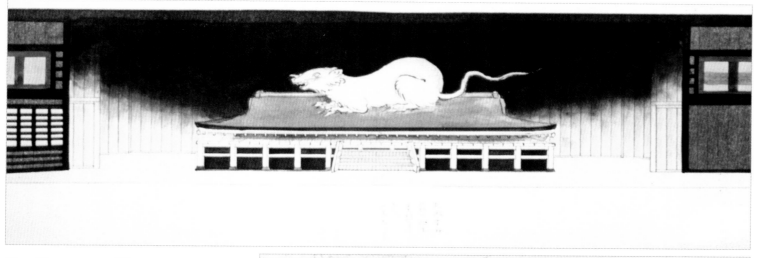

Ten Characters of Date

Kumaji Kugimachi (Japan)
Set Design

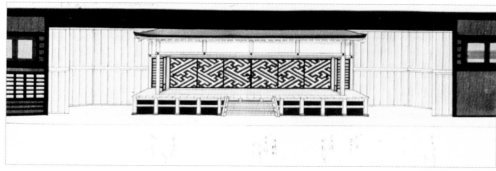

Kumaji Kugimachi is considered by some to be the original Kabuki set designer. Before him there were no set designers who were identified as such. His sets are like beautiful watercolour paintings, with sophisticated coloring and shadows. His well-honed drawing skills are inimitable. There were no theatre designers by the end of the 20th century who came close to matching him in technique.

Chalk (Giz)

Alvaro Apocalypse (Brazil)
Puppet Design

The Group Giramundo is undeniably the most important puppet theater group in Brazil and in all South America. Alvaro Apocalypse, the group's head for more than 40 years, was a great researcher in the area of puppet animation. Having trained hundreds of followers around Brazil, he left published educational material that still informs many followers of this art. His group has its headquarters in Belo Horizonte, Minas Gerais, and keeps its amazing heritage of more than 1,000 puppets in a museum open to the public. The group has taken part of dozens of international festivals, and has been honored with many awards and prizes. Alvaro died in 2003; his work was featured at the Prague Quadrennial of that year.

Sweeney Todd, The Demon Barber of Fleet Street

Eugene Lee & Franne Lee (USA)
Set & Costume Design

Eugene Lee won the Tony Award for set design and Franne Lee won
the Tony and Drama Desk Awards for costume design for their work
on the 1979 Broadway production of Steven Sondheim's black operetta,
Sweeney Todd, The Demon Barber of Fleet Street, directed by Hal Prince.

"The set *[for Sweeney Todd]*, a great contraption like a foundry with
iron beams, moving bridges, and clanking wheels and belts, is grim
and exuberant at the same time. When a back panel, a festering mass
of rusty corrugated iron, lifts, a doleful scene of industrial London is
exposed. In stylized attitudes, and gutter costumes, a whole London
underworld appears, serving, in the manner of *The Threepenny Opera*,
as populace and as sardonic chorus." [Review by Richard Eder, *New York
Times*, 2 March 1979]

Three Sisters

Vladimir Serebrovsky (Russia)
Set Design

In *Three Sisters*, designer Vladimir Serebrovsky was faced with the problem of "inscribing" a real period interior within the framework of a modern performance. He elected to show the interior of the Prozorovs' house in full keeping with the stage direction: "A sitting-room with columns and a big hall behind it." His idea was that the entire play should be performed in this interior. The layout was rational and unpretentious, just like the openness of the interior to nature and the light coming through its tall windows. There was special spirituality in the restrained and refined coloration, in the light stripes of the Empire-style wallpapers and upholstery. One had the impression that nothing could be added to or taken away from this interior, that the emergence of any new person or object would destroy its harmony.

The Duelist (Rváč)

Otakar Schindler (Czechoslovakia/Czech Republic)
Set & Costume Design

Poetic stylization and minimalist expression, which included the audience in its scenic picture (birch stumps were placed in the audience as well) and a natural connection of the interior and exterior elements, give evidence of this artist's hand. Otakar Schindler, in his long collaboration with the director Kačer, was one of the leading Czech interpreters of Russian classics.

Beautiful Vida
(Lepa Vida)

Meta Hočevar (Slovenia)
Set & Costume Design

Meta Hočevar's design for *Beautiful Vida* received the award for the best stage design by Ulupus at the Festival Sterijevo Pozorje, Novi Sad, Yugoslavia.

Hamlet
Hugh Colman (Australia)
Set & Costume Design

Hugh Colman and Colin George collaborated on a number of productions of Shakespeare during Colin's tenure as artistic director of the State Theatre Company of South Australia. This production of *Hamlet* is a particularly strong example of their work together.

Vassa Zheleznova
Igor Popov (USSR/Russia)
Set Design

In his sets for this production, Popov was seeking to convey a sense of cold emptiness and at the same time invasive constraint. Almost half the stage was cut off by a curved wall, extending from the left side of the proscenium arch toward centre stage. This dingy green wall, with its molded Art Nouveau ornament and two doorways, resembled the one in the old Moscow Art Theatre that separated the foyer and the auditorium.

The Third Pole (A treia teapa)
Vittorio Holtier (Romania)
Set & Costume Design

This was a stage design for an historical play about the famous Prince Vlad Tepes ("Vlad the Impaler"). The set design limited itself to the essentials: on the horizon were projected the vertical lines of three poles, alternatingly illuminated, which underlined the thoughtful dramatic nature of the dialogue and pointed out the differences or similarities between the characters.

Richard III
Tatiana Selvinskaya (USSR/Russia)
Set & Costume Design

For this production, Tatiana Selvinskaya decided to turn to "live set design." She invented a game for the actors to play, using soft mobile drapes and "dummies" on sticks with cross-pieces. A cloth could turn into a winged monster, and when sacks were thrown on to the "dummies," they became victims of Richard's crimes since they resembled the silhouettes of draped human figures. The "dummies" could represent the crowd of people who bunched up or fell out across the stage. The tallest "puppet" first looked like a riding horseman, then like some fantastic plant. This method of making "live set design" by way of playing with a cloth turned into a puppet, a costume, or another plastic form is typical of Tatiana Selvinskaya's work in theatre and was used in many of her productions.

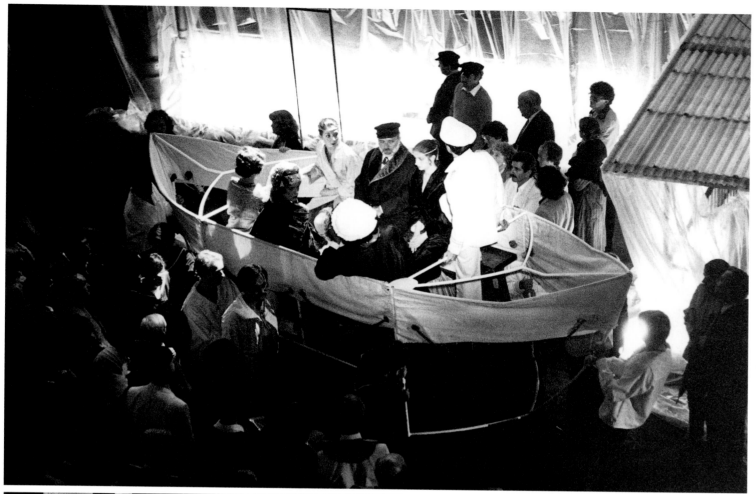

Sinking of the Titanic (Der Untergang der Titanic)

Martin Rupprecht (Germany FGR)
Set & Costume Design

The opera, a work commissioned for the Berlin Festival of Art, the so called Festwochen, deals with the catastrophe of 1912. The creative team developed a unique solution to bring the drama close to the public: the Deutsche Oper becomes the Titanic. People of all classes, first-class, emigrants, seamen—and the 300 members of the opera audience—go on board outside the opera house. The construction of a deck on stage, the installation of "cages" for the third-class passengers in the substage and the use of other areas of the Deutsche Oper allowed the public to follow the actors everywhere through phases of flight, phases of fear. They experience these feelings through music but also through the atmosphere of narrow passages or wide dance halls.

Idomeneo

John Truscott (Australia)
Set & Costume Design

In 1978, John Truscott returned to live in Australia after having spent the previous 15 years working in London and then Hollywood. In 1968 he won two Academy Awards for his work on *Camelot* (one for design and one for art direction). *Idomeneo* was the first production he designed upon his return.

Amadeus

John Bury (UK)
Set, Costume & Lighting Design

This was one of the high points of a lifetime collaboration with the director Peter Hall, at the National Theatre, Glyndebourne and beyond. Bury's lighting in particular was suggestive of real space and atmosphere, through its reference to shutters.

Bury contributed to the establishment of a way of designing for theatre in Britain that left firmly behind the notion of 'the pictorial' whilst embracing the three dimensionality of the stage space and its elemental quality, promoting interaction with lighting as key. All this whilst pursuing a unashamed historical 'realism' through costume, which as quoted in Goodwin 'had to be designed with great conviction and in the strictest period, with not a hint that these things might never have happened.'

Through the success of this piece and his repeated success at the Prague Quadrennials (gold medal for stage design at PQ'75; exhibited at PQ'79; British Golden Triga at PQ'83), Bury's approach to design—an embedding of three-dimensional integrity into the process—gained international relevance and influence. His set and lighting design for *Amadeus* won him a Tony Award in 1981.

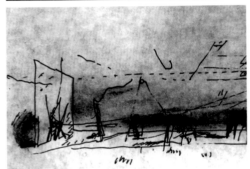

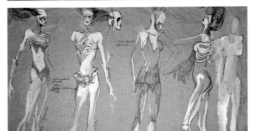

is 13.58% • Solidarity Trade Union formed in Poland and shipyard workers go on strike • Yassar Arafat elected president of Palestinian National Council • Japan becomes world's largest auto producing country • US leads boycott of Moscow Olympics in protest of Soviet invasion of Afghanistan • Iran and Iraq begin a war that lasts 8 years • Former Beatle John Lennon is shot to death • 6.0 magnitude earthquake in southern Italy kills more than 3,000 people • First domestic camcorders available in Japan • First fax machines in Japan • CNN becomes first 24-hour news station • Invention of Post-It Notes • Yearly inflation rate in USA is 13.58% •

1980

First fax machines in Japan • CNN becomes first 24-hour news station • Invention of Post-It Notes • Yearly inflation rate in USA is 13.58% • Solidarity Trade Union formed in Poland and shipyard workers go on strike • Yassar Arafat elected president of Palestinian National Council • Japan becomes world's largest auto producing country • US leads boycott of Moscow Olympics in protest of Soviet invasion of Afghanistan • Iran and Iraq begin a war that lasts 8 years • Former Beatle John Lennon is shot to death • 6.0 magnitude earthquake in southern Italy kills more than 3,000 people • First domestic camcorders available in Japan • First fax machines in Japan • CNN becomes first 24-hour news station • Invention of Post-It Notes • Yearly inflation rate in USA is 13.58% • Solidarity Trade Union formed in Poland and shipyard workers go on strike • Yassar Arafat elected president of Palestinian National Council • Japan becomes world's largest auto producing country •

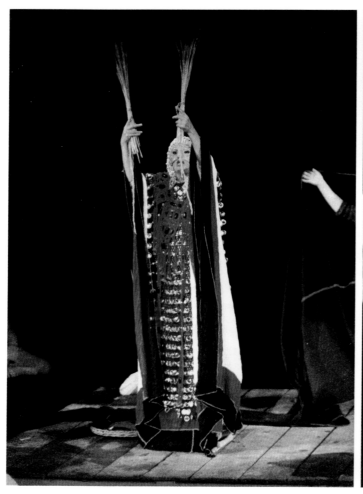

The Suppliants (Ικέτιδες)

Giorgos Ziakas (Greece)
Set & Costume Design

This can be viewed as a costume design milestone for ancient drama productions at the Epidaurus Festival. It was the next milestone after Dionysis Fotopoulos' costume design (1975). It was absolute simplicity. It created a very personal, modern style through the relationship with traditional costume. The wig was abolished.

Montserrat

Mao Jingang (China)
Set & Costume Design

Mao Jingang designed a round wall and stairs to encircle the performing area, creating a sense of pressure. A war mural was painted on the entire wall, inlaid with colorful stones. It depicted scenes of a brutal massacre by the colonial army, documented the colonial crimes, and depicted the fierce struggles of the people, creating the specific environment and atmosphere needed for the play.

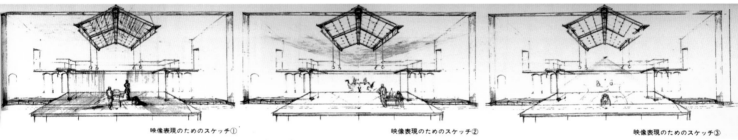

映像表現のためのスケッチ①　　　　　　　　映像表現のためのスケッチ②　　　　　　　　映像表現のためのスケッチ③

The Elephant Man
Kaoru Kanamori (Japan)
Set Design

"The stage set of *The Elephant Man* was constructed with the big simple patterned floor as a raked stage and there was a glass ceiling which showed different angles. Sometimes on the floor and in the space of both side stages there were two [big framed panels] with stretched black cords vertically. There were arranged props on the stage, like a bed or table and chairs. The director and scenographer intended to create a certain strong design of the style for the space.

"The big difference between scenographer and a painter or sculptor is he must think about the effect of the dimensional process of time and space in a two- and three-dimensional manner, and [then] compose the design on the stage in the fourth dimension." — Kaoru Kanamori

This design was featured in the Japanese exhibition at PQ'83.

Parintins Street Festival
(Festa Popular de Parintins)

Group Caprichoso (Brazil)
Performance Design

This Amazon festival presents three days of parades during which decorated floats, big props, special effects, fireworks, and dazzling costumes create one of the major scenographic parties held every year in Brazil. Everything is made in collaboration by a group of designers, technicians, and prop designers, and the entire community participates.

Genroku Minato Uta

Setsu Asakura (Japan)
Set Design

Her designs sometimes required new materials which helped the development of knowledge and technology in the theatre.

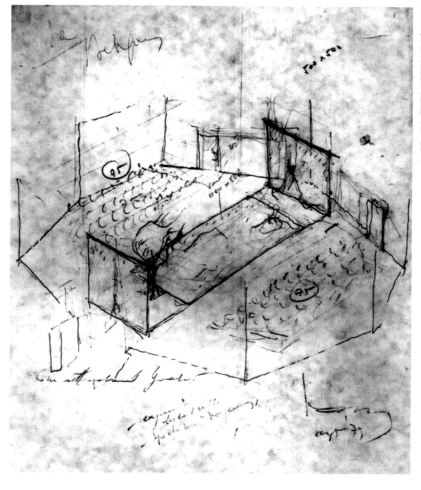

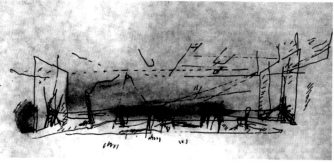

Waiting for Godot (Asteptand pe Godot)

Paul Bortnovski (Romania)
Set Design

The stage designer chose a set of great simplicity, stripped to its essentials, moonlit under the spotlights—all of which were appropriate to the way indicated by Becket and enclosed in the theatre space that was set between the seats of the spectators. The tree that miraculously turns green in this space became the tangible sign of unquenchable hope.

Cruel Games

Oleg Sheintsis (USSR/Russia)
Set Design

Stage left featured a red metallic wheel, stretching out behind the set, which was a cold and comfortless room. From the first moments of the action, the sharp graphic quality of the wheel and the harsh electronic music that played each time it began to roll introduced an element of anxiety. In the culminating moment, the wheel rim carried one of the characters away from the performance and out of this life. It then became the tragic wheel of death. It contained other meanings: the urban fantasy, the pulse of the big city, the mechanisms that set things going. Director Mark Zakharov observed that it was "a kind of materialization of fast-running time, fate, the steamroller that runs us over with its soulless metal." Later the wheel called up the image of the merry-go-round of life. But it turned out to be just an amusement facility in a park, almost a domestic kind of entertainment, a present from Santa Claus.

The Hundredth Bride

Wang Linyou (China)
Set Design

The Hundredth Bride was created and staged by the National Opera House of China in 1980 based on the story of Avanty. The stage designer once went to Urumqi, Kashgar and other places of Xinjiang to experience life and collect materials. And in the creation, special attention was paid to the ancient Islamic characteristics and the decorative style of plastic arts. In 1981, it was awarded the first prize for stage design by Ministry of Culture of the People's Republic of China. This is also the first award issued by the Ministry of Culture after China's reform and opening-up.

The Sunny South

Ian Robinson (Australia)
Set Design

This was a highly successful example of the creative partnership of Ian Robinson and Richard Wherrett, who had worked together at Sydney's Nimrod Theatre. This was the first production by the newly created Sydney Theatre Company at its home in the Drama Theatre at the Sydney Opera House, and was directed by the first artistic director, Richard Wherrett.

The Haggadah: A Passover Cantata

Julie Taymor (USA)
Set & Costume Design

Best known as the director of the long-running Broadway musical version of Disney's *The Lion King* (for which she became the first woman to win the Tony Award for directing a musical in addition to a Tony for costume design), Julie Taymor began her career in theatre as designer as well as a director. One of the first productions she worked on after returning to the USA (following her study and work in France, Japan, Java, and Bali) was *The Haggadah*, produced at the New York Shakespeare Festival in 1980. This musical retelling of the Passover seder was conceived, composed, and directed by Elizabeth Swados, with set, costumes, masks, and puppets designed by Taymor.

This production of *Danton's Death* showed clearly the new approach to theatre that the creative team Dieter Dorn (director), Jürgen Rose (scenic and costume design) and Max Keller (lighting design) undertook at that time and developed further over the following decades. What has become "normal" in today's theatre was then completely new: a modern setting for a historical play, complete with contemporary costumes and a new way of lighting.

This revolution drama of German author Georg Buechner has been interpreted in many different ways, mostly trying to demonstrate the "good and evil" of the revolution. With his set, Jürgen Rose opened a completely new vision on that play. He placed the revolution in the bourgeois middle class ambiance of modern times, creating a closed, abstract world. It was a space with many doors—original doors taken from demolished houses. This space is neutral at the beginning; later on it is painted with traces of actual life, including the graffitti of "hunger" or other inscriptions. The revolution is taking place behind these doors.

The leaders Danton and Robespierre and their officers negotiate in an off-space, and represent a leading class afraid of the people they are leading. The then-active RAF terrorists or the much-discussed activities of the East German Secret Police seemed to have influenced Rose in his creation of the space and the corresponding costumes. At the end of the revolution, the politicians act like civil servants, killing and then counting the dead. Robespierre and Danton can be seen as wax figures in the off-space under the guillotine photographed by journalists and passers-by, although they are still alive. This political statement by director Dieter Dorn was translated and interpreted by Juergen Rose in the last scene, where murder becomes a bureaucratic measure, and individuals do not count.

"Jürgen Rose always builds a world, but he does it with a variety of spaces. The confrontation with the stage, the stage house, includes the artistic space that is being built into the stage house and that creates its own stage" says H.J. dramaturg Ruckhäberle in a documentation about Rose's work. "... What is real? What looks real? What has to be precise so that another play with illusion is possible?" The scene for *Danton* is contemporary and it is real, because he uses real materials, but at the same time it is not a concrete place that is quoted. H.J. Ruckhäberle: "In the 70s and 80s, Jürgen Rose has radically explored the material of his sets. Away from the decoration, from the "illusion" of the real, towards the theatrical design."

Danton's Death *(Dantons Tod)*

Jürgen Rose (Germany FRG)
Set Design

Satyagraha

Robert Israel (USA)
Set & Costume Design

Satyagraha (which translates as "truth force")
is based on the story of Mohandas Ghandi
and is the second in Philip Glass' *Portrait
Trilogy* about men who changed the world
(*Einstein on the Beach* 1976, *Satyagraha* 1980,
Akhnaten 1984). Unlike *Einstein on the Beach*,
which embraced a minimalist post-modern
approach, *Satyagraha* employed a structure
more similar to traditional epic opera, with
one significant exception. The text, taken
from the Hindu scripture the Bhagavad Gita,
was sung in Sanscrit without translation,
assuring that few if any in the audience
would comprehend it. The words became a
repetitive abstract musical element, rather
than a means of conveying storyline, while the
design elements supported the continuity of
the episodic structure, but further abstracted
the presentation of the story. Grounded by
Israel's static pyramid structure, a white-clad
chorus created slowly moving sculptural
tableaus. These scenes were brightly
illuminated by Richard Riddell's powerful
industrial instruments, but also muted and
flattened behind a white scrim for the entire
performance. This fusion of visual and aural
elements worked beyond the scope of the text
to create a visceral, emotional, and profound
journey for audiences.

Satyagraha premiered in the Netherlands
(Rotterdam, Utrecht, and The Hague) and
was subsequently performed in North
America, the UK, and West Germany. Israel's
costume designs for *Satyagraha* are part of
the permanent collection of the Museum of
Modern Art in New York City.

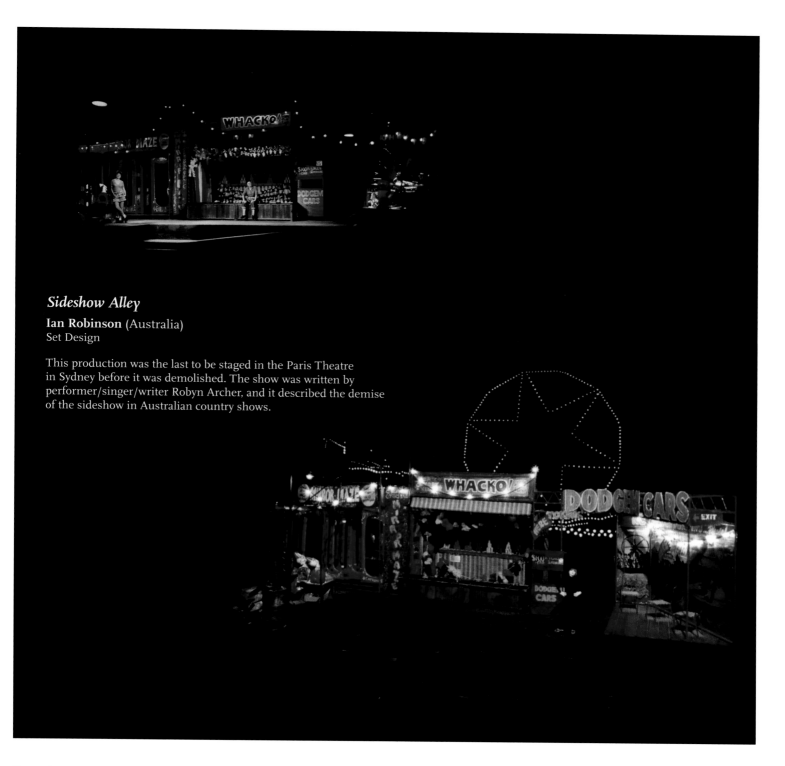

Sideshow Alley

Ian Robinson (Australia)
Set Design

This production was the last to be staged in the Paris Theatre in Sydney before it was demolished. The show was written by performer/singer/writer Robyn Archer, and it described the demise of the sideshow in Australian country shows.

Tear Heart (*Rasga Coração*)

Marcos Flaksman (Brazil)
Set & Costume Design

Scenographer Marcos Flaxman is still one of the greatest names in Brazilian theatre, and he also worked in television and theatre architecture.

The production of *Tear Heart* was set at the height of the dictatorship that the country had lived under since 1964. The play, written by Oduvaldo Viana, represented an enormous resistance to the political regime of the time.

The design broke with the theatrical simplicity that was very popular in designs of that time, creating instead a space filled with different floor plans and movement. The production also included an exquisite performance by one of the greatest Brazilian actors of all time, Raul Cortez.

Lola

Hysen Devolli (Albania)
Set Design

Hysen Devolli completed his studies in 1952 at the Academy of Fine Arts in Bucharest. He has been one of the leading scenographers for the Albanian National Theatre, which was established in 1945. During 30 years on the stage of this theatre he created more than 300 designs for opera, ballet, and theatre. His stage designs were distinguished by their functional and conventional character. He was given the title of "Meritorious Artist" for his outstanding artistic service by the state.

The Cunning Little Vixen
(Příhody Lišky Bystroušky)

Maria Björnson (UK/France)
Costume Design

Maria Björnson came to international attention with a series of Janacek opera designs for Scottish Opera and Welsh National Opera with director David Pountney. They gave her the opportunity to reveal her creativity by experimenting with interesting anthropomorphic forms. The costumes deployed a visual language that made everyday objects, such as an apron, a transformative element of performance. Her drawing of the Hens has influenced designers and directors all over the world through its expressiveness. It made Janacek's work real and something that audiences could relate to. This project—part of the Janacek cycle—cemented her working relationship with Pountney, one that eventually brought the latter to lead the English National Opera, ushering in its "powerhouse" years.

Her obituary in the *Independent* newspaper mentioned this as one of the most notable of her designs, which totaled 136 productions over 32 years. They remain an important and influential set of costume drawings, used particularly in teaching and in publications because of the way they show embodiment and movement as key in the design process. They won her the silver medal for costume at PQ'83, where the theme was Janacek.

The set design for *Cunning Little Vixen* was no less innovative, with a stage floor that at one point split down its center. "The singers took one look at it and said they could never work on a surface like that," she said. "Meanwhile the children who were to take part rushed on to the floor and started having a whale of a time running about and rolling on the set. They thought it was the best thing since Christmas, and pretty soon the adults were won over, too."

Wielopole, Wielopole

Tadeusz Kantor (Poland)
Set & Costume Design

"Tadeusz Kantor was an untiring animator of artistic life in Poland after World War II, one of its main driving forces.

Completed in Florence in 1980, *Wielopole, Wielopole* consisted of five parts: Weddings, Insults, The Crucifixion, Adam Leaves for the Front, The Last Supper. The action took place on a low, rectangular platform. The audience sat frontally to the scene. The rear platform was formed with a large sliding walls of old straight boards. In the background, from left, a wardrobe, chairs, on the right, a rostrum moved on wheels with a window wall. In the foreground, right, a freshly dug mound with a cross and a shovel stuck into it. Beyond, receding into the depths, a dozen of the same small crosses. On the left, set sideways, a bed—the so-called deathbed, the archetype of the machinery of death. All dull with age. And finally, Kantor, a conductor, a master of ceremony, constantly present on stage. He created a spectacle that seemed to work like a symphony." — Agnieszka Kubaś

Don Juan is Coming Back from War
(Don Žuan se vraća iz rata)

Dušan Ristić (Croatia/Serbia)
Set Design

For Horvath's piece *Don Juan Comes Back from the War* directed by Paolo Magelli at the Yugoslav Drama Theatre, Dušan Ristić's set evoked an attic space, which was later transformed into a street, a café, a hospital, a village cemetery. It was partly lit from beneath by two apertures in the floor that let in a diffuse, autumnal light, elongating the characters' shadows. Magelli decided on an expressionistic style to correspond with Horvath's play, to which Ristić's set and Božana Jovanović's costumes made a great contribution. Painter, scenographer, and costume designer, Ristić created more than 200 stage sets and was widely known for his inventiveness, research, and erudition. His work was often inspired by surrealism.

Caligula

Paul Bortnovski (Romania)
Set Design

A world announcing its end, suggested by a set of ruins, dilapidated marble buildings, while the few remaining lights glitter and flicker strangely.

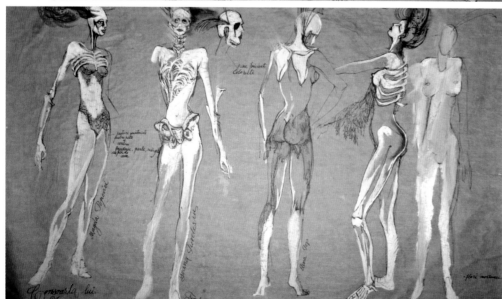

Maestro and Margaret
(Maestrul si Margareta)

Lia Mantoc (Romania)
Costume Design

Lia Mantoc's designs for this production by the great Romanian director Catalina Buzoianu has been described as "an arrangement of costumes that gives us a historical image of the transitional period of the 20th century that Mihail Bulgakov wrote about, as well as his fascinating vision, full of sarcasm, colored by mystery."

hostages • First high speed train service in Europe begins between Paris and Lyon • Thatcher government in England begins privatisation of nationalised industries • IRA member Bobby Sands dies while on hunger strike • Wreck of Titanic located in the North Atlantic • Muhammad Ali finally retires • Pope John Paul II shot in the Vatican • Lady Diana Spencer marries Prince Charles • Egyptian president Anwar Sadat assassinated • Antigua and Barbuda gain independence from Great Britain • Scientists identify the AIDS virus • First flight of US space shuttle Columbia • European Rocket "Ariane" is launched • IBM launches its first PC • The term "internet" is first mentioned • China clones the first fish • Iran releases 52 American hostages • First high speed train service in Europe begins between Paris and Lyon • Thatcher government in England begins privatisation of nationalised industries • IRA member Bobby Sands dies while on hunger strike • Wreck of Titanic located in the North Atlantic • Muhammad Ali finally retires • Pope John Paul II shot in the Vatican • Lady Diana Spencer marries Prince Charles • Egyptian president Anwar Sadat assassinated • Antigua and Barbuda gain independence from Great Britain • Scientists identify the AIDS virus • First flight of US space shuttle Columbia • European Rocket "Ariane" is launched • IBM launches its first PC • The term "internet" is first mentioned • China clones the first fish • Iran releases 52 American hostages • First high

1981

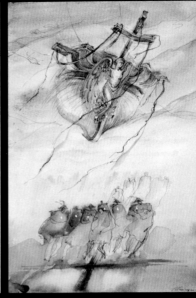

Juno and Avos (*Yunona i Avos*)

Oleg Sheintsis
& Valentina Komolova (USSR/Russia)
Set & Costume Design

Aware of the need to make this rock opera large-scale and spectacular, Oleg Sheintsnis came up with the original idea of dividing the stage into five slanting platforms, like a kind of stage-sized Rubik Cube that, according to director Mark Zakharov, "contained a multitude of various amusing combinations".

Part of a sail, soaring above the stage, was perceived as a full-size ship that was ceremonially launched on the glass flooring of the platforms lit from underneath. Some soulless force, engaged in insoluble conflict with the dominant lyrical theme, seemed to be hiding in the cold glitter of the metallic surfaces, the menacingly frozen folds of the drapes, the gesture of the bronze figure crowning the bow of the ship

Director Zakharov has repeatedly stressed that it took flawless taste and superb professional standards to make costumes for *Juno and Avos*. Indeed, the artist was faced with a complex task of designing a very wide spectrum of costumes: from historical and ethnic (uniforms of the 19th century Russian naval officers, Spanish garments) to the costume of a universal personality like Woman with Child. Besides, costumes for a rock-opera had to be eye-catching in movement, since many of the scenes were choreographed. Costume designer Valentina Komolova created a wonderful colour palette, using contrasting combinations of colours (green and white for the Russian officers, black and red for the Spaniards) and an intricate blend of smoky-white and pale-yellow tinges in the apparel of Conchita. The attire of Woman with Child was a mixture of pastel lilac and grey and pink.

Juno and Avos became a cult show in the former USSR and later in Russia. It has played to packed houses for over quarter of a century.

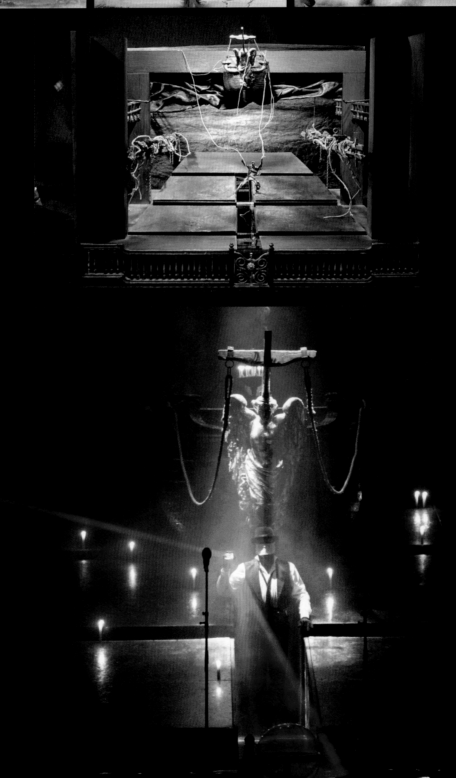

The True Story of Ah Q

Xue Dianjie (China)
Set & Costume Design

Xun used Brecht's narrative approach in the design of this play. White lighting was released from exposed lamps, and the scenes were painted on ragged linens in traditional ink and brush style. Set changes were facilitated by the movement of two traverse tables.

 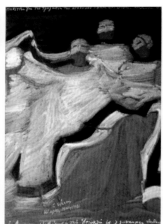   

The Seven against Thebes (Επτά επί Θήβας)

Giorgos Ziakas (Greece)
Set & Costume Design

The production featured an internationally significant design that opened up new avenues for communication. A photo of the costume decorates the cover of a major book on ancient drama productions: Hellmut Flashar, *Inszenierung der Antike* (Verlag S.H.Beck, Munich, 1991).

ѪНГЄЛ

УДОЖНІК

ЧЄРТОЖНІК

The Alphabet Story (*Хождение по буквам*)

Silva Bachvarova (Bulgaria)
Set, Costume & Puppet Design

In its combination of text, chants, and puppet manipulation, the production offered brilliant theatrical imagery based on the spirit of Christian rituals and iconic art, attracting both young and adult audiences. The performance was played abroad, evoking great interest in its original form and vision.

ТРЄТ

One String of Koto

Yasuhiro Ishii (Japan)
Set Design

Yasuhiro Ishii studied architecture at Waseda University. In the world of Japanese theatre design, his works beautifully express both structural and pictorial beauty.

Woza Albert

Mbongeni Ngema, Percy Mtwa & Barney Simon
(South Africa)
Set Design

Temple Hauptfleisch writes, "If any single play may be said to represent all the exuberance and power of South African theatre in the 1980s to the world, it would undoubtedly be *Woza Albert*. It was not the only, or necessarily the best, workshopped play to come out of the struggle, but was certainly the most travelled and the best known. Based on an idea by Mbongeni Ngema and Percy Mtwa and shaped under the direction of Barney Simon, the Earth Players' exhilarating performance piece opened to rave reviews at the Market Theatre in 1981."

The "black-box" bare-stage style of presentation can be traced from *Woza Albert!* through *Asinamali* and on to *You Strike the Woman, You Strike the Rock*. Material austerity did not, however, signal a lack of recognition of the visual component of the medium of theatre. Instead, it homed in on the body of the performer and its expressive capacity, and it demanded innovative and resourceful, if minimal, solutions to design challenges. An example of this approach was the use of the red clown noses on the faces of Mbongeni and Percy in *Woza Albert!* The noses produced lightning-fast transformations of identity in addition to acting as racial and political signifiers.

Songs for Faidra
(Lauluja Faidralle)
Juha Lukala (Finland)
Set Design

In this scenography for *Songs for Faidra*, the reflecting mirror—which multiplied the movements of the protagonist and at the same time blinded the audience—signified the postmodern idea of a divided self.

Orphan of Zhao Family
Zhao Yingmian (China)
Set Design

This version of a play in the traditional repertoire offered something new in its performance. The first curtain and the second curtain were removed, and actors moved the striped screen to achieve a rhythmic conversion of space. An image of *Taotie* (a mythical ferocious animal) and black velvet were used to create a dark psychological atmosphere.

Cats

John Napier (UK)
Set & Costume Design

Cats represents one of the most extraordinary stage designs in recent times, notable for its opening moments in which the front rows of the audience were swung round in their seats with the stage, so that they lost their bearings to become immersed in the scaled-up world of John Napier's rubbish dump set. *Cats* enjoyed productions around the world and played continuously for several decades, winning awards and accolades worldwide. It was seminal in defining the mega-musical, and its all-encompassing design freed even the largest shows from the confines of the proscenium stage.

Kappa Senoh (Japan)
Set Design

The distinctive composition of Kappa Senoh's theatre designs is based on good research and a study of painting, a style that he has worked to develop.

Translations

Eileen Diss (UK)
Set Design

Eileen Diss (born in 1931) is a highly regarded set designer, whose huge talent as a production designer for film and television earned her three BAFTA wins, four BAFTA nominations, and a Royal Television Society Lifetime Achievement Award. Through television she became connected with Harold Pinter, who introduced her to theatre. This design, imbued with the realism that characterized her film work, contributed to the fact that this important play, arguably Brian Friel's best, was taken seriously in London during a period of conflict, known as "the troubles," in Northern Ireland.

Diss describes the *Translations* set as follows: "Donegal in 1833, when the Royal Engineers were doing a map survey of Ireland, changing Irish names for English ones. The characters, Irish and English, gather in a disused barn, now a 'hedge school,' the only source of education for the rural Irish." The highly realistic set in the intimate space of the old Hampstead theatre would have ensured that the audience was very much inside the action. The naturalistic costumes, designed by Lindy Hemming, would have complemented the space well. (Lindy Hemming is also highly decorated as a cinema and theatre designer specializing in costume, nominated for several awards and winner of an Oscar.)

Yerma

Giorgos Patsas (Greece)
Set & Costume Design

The scene was a threshing floor, round and earthy, with dry barren soil. The curtain was a very large black circle, which acted as a symbolic threat to the action. A wild fertility overflowed from all directions. Poles took on the role of huge phallic symbols, which brought to mind the game of love and death.

Scaffolding *(Echafaudages)*

Pat Van Hemelrijck (Belgium)
Set Design

This production was the signature piece by the collective Radeis, which was founded in 1977. They had a breakthrough at the Festival of Fools in Amsterdam, and performed their wordless productions at every possible festival in Europe, also touring Canada, Hong Kong, and Venezuela. With *Echafaudages (Scaffolding)*, they travelled around the world, ending at the Olympic Arts Festival in Los Angeles in 1984 where they decided to dissolve the group at its peak.

This production has been recognized as one of the most influential performances in podium art. The collective Radeis (Josse De Pauw, Pat Van Hemelrijck, and Dirk Pauwels) has been very important to establishing the reputation of Flemish theatre abroad.

Pirosmani, Pirosmani...

Adomas Yatsovskis (Lithuania)
Set Design

The ballet *Romeo and Juliet* at the Bolshoi Theatre was ground breaking in every respect. For the first time in the history of stagings of this ballet, choreographer Grigorovitch made a dance version not of Shakespeare's tragedy but of Prokofiev's romantic musical concept. The stage space was completely available for the dancers. The signs of real life appear only at a distance and behind the gauze curtain: the gothic cityscape of Verona, the mysterious moon-lit garden, Friar Laurence's monastic cell pierced by sunlight, the opulent palazzo of the Capulet family decorated with sculptures and bright lustrous columns. The picturesque backdrops looked like illustrations from an ancient book emerging in the clouds of reminiscence. The designer's sensitivity to music was amazing. One had the impression that it was the costumes that orchestrated the dance, which in turn grew out of the music.

Dreamgirls
Robin Wagner & Tharon Musser (USA)
Set & Lighting Design

"*Dreamgirls* is a musical with almost 40 numbers, and virtually everything, from record-contract negotiations to lovers' quarrels, is sung. More crucially, [composer Henry] Krieger has created an individual musical voice for every major player and interweaves them all at will... What's more, the score's method is reinforced visually by Robin Wagner's set. Mr. Wagner has designed a few mobile, abstract scenic elements—aluminum towers and bridges—and keeps them moving to form an almost infinite number of configurations. Like the show's voices, the set pieces—gloriously abetted by Tharon Musser's lighting and Theoni V. Aldredge's costumes—keep coming together and falling apart to create explosive variations on a theme." [Review by Frank Rich, *New York Times*, 21 December 1891]

Dreamgirls was the final collaboration of director Michael Bennett and designers Robin Wagner, Theoni Aldredge, and Tharon Musser. Wagner received the 1982 Drama Desk Award for his set design and Musser received the Tony and Drama Desk Awards for her lighting design.

Bluebeard *(Kékszakáll)*

Judit Schäffer (Hungary)
Costume Design

Judit Schäffer's costume designs offer a dazzling element ito each production. Her precision and her choice of materials are outstanding, and the dramatic value of the costumes is extraordinary. Her drawings and costumes are preserved in national libraries and museum collections in Hungary. The designs can often be caricatures, but she is also successful in merging the techniques and properties of classical styles with contemporary fashion.

The Man From Mukinupin
Anna French (Australia)
Set & Costume Design

Mounted at the Melbourne Theatre
Company, this was the second
Australian production of the
highly successful play by Dorothy
Hewett. The play had premiered in
Perth, Western Australia, having
been commissioned by the West
Australian Theatre Company. The
costume designs are a very good
example of the level of detail that is a
hallmark of Anna French's work as a
costume designer.

Goldilocks (Zlatovláska)
Petr Matásek (Czechoslovakia/Czech Republic)
Set & Puppet Design

The puppet scenography of this fairytale
performance connects the traditions of Czech
puppetry and wood carving with modern artistic and
scenic styling, which reached its peak in the 1970s
and 1980s. This performance is a good example
of the significant achievements of Drak Theatre,
which enjoyed much success beyond the borders of
Czechoslovakia and where the artist Petr Matásek
and director Josef Krofta worked together.

Antigone

Isabel Echarri & Diego Echeverry (Spain)
Set & Costume Design

Echarri and Echeverry are a design team whose work is seen throughout France and internationally. Their design for Antigone was featured in the French exhibition at PQ'83.

On foot (Pieszo)

Jerzy Juk Kowarski (Poland)
Set Design

In Krakow and then Warsaw in 1981, performances of *On Foot* by Slawomir Mrozek were sold out every night. Director Jerzy Jarocki, with the artistic vision of Jerzy Juk Kowarski, created a spectacle that is an important part of Polish contemporary history.

Its characters wander around the no man's land between the fronts, during the brief period of democracy in Poland when the German occupiers withdrew, and the Soviet 'liberator' had not yet entered. The action went beyond the architectural division of audience and performing area, as muddy, sodden earth was poured from the stage on to a rectangular platform in the auditorium. Tracks, dividing the stage into east and west, were the tracks for a train that can never arrive, because its rails hit blank walls. In this spring field, people waited in the mud and rain between two realities: the endless nightmare of occupation and war, and the anticipation of the unknown. Finally, toy planes bearing the red Soviet star were released over the heads of the audience, a metaphor for imminent totalitarianism.

On the Razzle

Carl Toms (UK)
Set & Costume Design

Carl Toms was a steady and highly respected purveyor of elegant sets for theatre, ballet, and opera from the 1970s onward, working regularly with Tom Stoppard. This production and *Rough Crossing*, also documented in this volume are European plays adapted by Stoppard for the National Theatre, which show his careful style. Of *On the Razzle*, from Nestroy, staged in 1981, he wrote: "A complicated fast-moving farce involving five sets which had to change in view; two large carrying platforms tracked diagonally up and down stage, one masking the other when it was in place. Flying pieces complete the set." He won the 1974 Tony and Drama Desk awards for stage design, and the 1981 Olivier.

Nahod Simeon

Vladislav Lalicki (Yugoslavia/Serbia)
Set & Costume Design

Dejan Mijač decided to give new life to this minor piece by the leading 19th Century Serbian playwright Jovan Sterija Popović by opting for some radical changes, such as moving the tragedy into a comic frame and simplifying the characters to their basic traits. This approach makes costumes, masks and scenery even more important, as the means by which the impression of "distinctness" is created. To achieve it, set and costume designer Vladislav Lalicki, with the help of jewellery designer Vladislav Petrović, produced some of the most beautiful costumes of his career. Against a shiny background of metal foil move luxurious images of the Orient. Most of the actors, with faces half hidden, are driven to complement their costume with their body, instead of the other way around. Lalicki, set designer, costume designer and illustrator, created over 500 set and costume designs for the theatre and more than 200 television and film sets.

Danton's Death *(Dantons Tod)*

Volker Pfüller (Germany FRG)
Set & Costume Design

This production was especially important for the collaborative team, because it became a "cult" hit that everybody in the GDR and the theatre community from West Berlin that could enter the GDR wanted to see. Revolution was presented as a punch theatre; the leading characters were shown as persons driven by their own interests. Although Danton and Robespierre are very different characters, the result of their acting is the same. They are both driven by egoistic motives, the two extremes being two sides of one medal. Director Alexander Lang and designer Volker Pfüller did not present the play as a historical drama but rather as a contemporary situation, in spite of the partially historic costumes. Dealing with this serious play in a manner of a punch theatre was provocative and very new to the GDR population. Nevertheless *Danton's Death* was performed for many years and was one of the most successful plays in the German Democratic Republic.

France by Carlos the Jackal • Argentina invades Falkland Islands • Israel returns Sinai to Egypt • Disney futuristic park EPCOT opens • International Whaling Commission ends commercial whaling • Doctors perform first implant of permanent artificial heart • Solidarity leader Lech Walesa released from jail • Italy wins World Cup in Spain • Communist party leader Leonid Brezhnev dies of heart attack • Vietnam Veterans Memorial in Washington DC dedicated • First CD player sold in Japan • Grace Kelly dies in car crash • Wave of terrorist attacks in France by Carlos the Jackal • Argentina invades Falkland Islands • Israel returns Sinai to Egypt • Disney futuristic park EPCOT opens • International Whaling Commission ends commercial whaling • Doctors perform first implant of permanent artificial heart • Solidarity leader Lech Walesa released from jail • Italy wins World Cup in Spain • Communist party leader Leonid Brezhnev dies of heart attack • Vietnam Veterans Memorial in Washington DC dedicated • First CD player sold in Japan • Grace Kelly dies in car crash • Wave of terrorist attacks in France by Carlos the Jackal • Argentina invades Falkland Islands • Israel returns Sinai to Egypt • Disney futuristic park EPCOT opens • International Whaling Commission ends commercial whaling • Doctors perform first implant of permanent artificial heart • Solidarity leader Lech Walesa released from jail • Italy wins World Cup in Spain • Communist

1982

Antigone

Sally Jacobs (UK)
Set & Costume Design

Sally Jacobs was the set and costume designer for Peter Brook's landmark productions of *Marat/Sade* and *A Midsummer Night's Dream*, along with a number of other productions for the Royal Shakespeare Festival in the 1960s and 1970s. Following the Broadway transfer of *Marat/Sade* in 1965 (and after designing the film version of the play in 1966), Jacobs began designing in both in Europe and the United States. One of her designs for the New York Shakespeare Festival was Joseph Chaikin's 1982 production of *Antigone* that featured actor F. Murray Abraham as Creon.

White Weapons
(Armas blancas)

Alejandro Luna
(México)
Set, Costume
& Lighting Design

White Weapons is representative of the experimental theatre at the University of Mexico, a professional theatre with great freedom of speech and innovative esthetics. The wide range of designer Alejandro Luna was particularly shown in this experimental production of three early short plays by Rascón Banda staged in a nonconventional space: a theatre underground. Luna's use of that difficult space and in particular his lighting design created an ideal framework for director Julio Castillo, who was known for the singularity of his stage images.

The parallel development of set, costume, and lighting design added to the dramatic text and the actor's creation of characters, creating a violent and tense atmosphere shared by audiences placed in front of this unusual stage. The critically acclaimed play took part in several international festivals in Mexico and toured also to places like Venezuela, where it was a great success.

Rigoletto

Patrick Robertson (UK)
Set Design

Jonathan Miller's "mafioso" *Rigoletto*, set in New York's "Little Italy" in the 1950s, was an immediate success and remains in the English National Opera's repertoire to this day. It owed a great deal to Patrick Robertson's sets and Rosemary Vercoe's costumes. Edward Hopper's paintings provided the inspiration for the sets, particularly in Act 3, as illustrated.

Nine

William Ivey Long (USA)
Costume Design

"*Nine* tells the same story as [Federico Fellini's film] *8 ½*—that of a creatively and emotionally blocked film director in midlife crisis—[but] it does not make the mistake of slavishly replicating the film's imagery... [T]he setting is once again an Italian spa, where fantasy, reality and flashback intermingle as the hero, Guido, sorts out the many formative women in his life.

"With the exception of [Guido] and his playmates, the entire cast of *Nine* is women—22 of all shapes and sizes, each with her own pedestal on Lawrence Miller's expansive white-tiled spa set. Mr. Tune uses the women as a Greek chorus and, with the aid of William Ivey Long's spectacular costumes, as the show's real scenery. Placed against a void, they give *Nine* its colors, its characters, its voices, even its Venetian gondolas—and remind us that the musical, in fact, unfolds inside Guido's troubled head." [Review by Frank Rich, *New York Times*, 10 May 1982]

William Ivey Long received the 1982 Drama Desk Award and the Tony Award for his costume design for *Nine*, the first of five Tony awards he has received in his rich and varied career.

New Genji Story

Hachiro Nakajima (Japan)
Set Design

Hachiro Nakjima's designs for the Kabuki
stage have a distinctive sense of color. His
calculations of the lighting design for Kabuki
theatre work extremely well.

The Mikado

Susan Benson (UK/Canada)
Set & Costume Design

This was the first production of a Gilbert and Sullivan operetta done after the design copyright of the D'Oyly Carte Opera Company expired. It later moved to Broadway, where it received a Tony nomination for best direction. The creative team followed up on this success with a series of Gilbert and Sullivan smash hits. Their vision opened the door to new designs of Gilbert and Sullivan worldwide.

Hecuba (Hekuba)

Marin Držić (Croatia)
Set Design

Marin Držić's design for Zlatko Kauzlaric-Atac's *Hecuba* has a special place in the 60-year history of the Dubrovnik festival. By choosing the space under Fort Minceta for the production of the first Croatian renaissance tragedy, director Ivica Boban and his designer established a new, symbolic relationship between the action of the play—the fall of Troy—and the city of Dubrovnic. This relationship was further emphasized by the division of the acting space into two areas: the lower one a sandy beach in front of the camp of the Trojan women, the higher one the camp of the Greek arm. The areas were connected by a wooden bridge bordered by huge animal ribs, suggesting the remnants of the fatal Trojan horse. One rib occupied the forestage as well, evoking both a wrecked ship and a leftover carcass. The correlation between animal and human is a recurrent motif in the tragedy, making the open entrails of the horse to which the bridge leads function as the setting for both Achilles's grave and Polyxena's sacrifice.

The Thirteenth Chairman
(Тринадесетият председател)

Vassil Rokomanov (Bulgaria)
Set & Costume Design

"Through this early work I found my own perspective on the metaphorical possibilities of an independent physical object when it is changed to a specific decision covering all components of the show. It is a personal artistic approach to the so-called 'Aesop language' in which the highly ideological text of the early perestroika period was made theatrically viable.

"The actors involved in the show found that even from a static position (similar to the earlier 'fixed theatre' of V. E. Meyerhold), they could communicate with the audience on a theatrical rather than an agitational level, through a visual metaphor emanating from the skin of a sacrificed bull. The provincial theatre troupe of Kardjali town gained the confidence to solve more complex problems creatively using the resources of contemporary theatre, one of which is the actor communicating actively with the stage designer's suggestions.

"The performance was greeted with acclaim from the local audience and from the specialist critics."

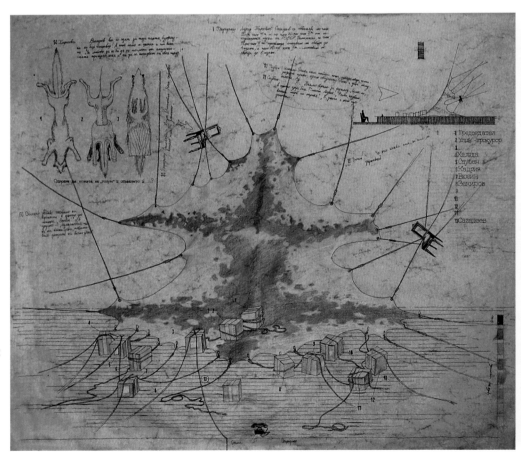

Rush Hour *(Час Пик)*

Georgi Ivanov (Bulgaria)
Set & Lighting Design

Critic D. Grozdanov noted that, in Ivanov's work, the author's "boundless stage" is always part of the dramatic picture. Ivanov develops it by means of symbols and analogy, features of his designs that have been critically acclaimed. "He develops the imagery, emphasizes the conflicts, oppositions, and problems of the dramatic text and its context. That is why, from *Music from Shatrovets* through *The Forest* to *Rush Hour*, [Ivanov's] design always metaphorically conveys the dramaturgy," said Grozdanov.

Kings and Queens
(Könige und Königinnen)

Johannes Schütz (Germany FRG)
Set Design

The theatre in Concordia Bremen was small, and the audience and dancers were on one level and were very close together. Johannes Schuetz chose to bring them even closer by conceiving the auditorium and stage as one space. He became famous for his abstract and empty stages (as seen in the German exhibition at PQ'07). For *Kings and Queens,* he built a space that had three scarlet walls with high window openings. These windows continued behind the public. When the "court" appears in the windows, these look like theatre boxes. The only prop was a sofa. A golden thread linked two columns, one on stage and one in the auditorium.

The space created around the dance company and the audience constituted a strong link between the two. The small theatre looked very wide, with its circular set design, and the audience actually became part of the court, viewing what was happening on the stage from the king's or queen's perspective.

In the 1980s, dance was only beginning to liberate itself from the corset of classical ballet. This production of *Kings and Queens*, in combination with the design of the space, had a great deal of influence on other productions, and toured internationally.

Amadeus

Kazue Hatano (Japan)
Set & Costume Design

Kazue Hatano's design of this period drama was especially well-shaped, and the scene changes had to be exactingly calculated in order to work in the irregularly limited theatre space. The structure of her design was very true to the idea of the playwright.

Sink the Ruined Capital

Kappa Senoh (Japan)
Set Design

Kappa Senoh's challenging set designs are a strong stimulus for actors. He used to work as a designer for television and has exceptionally good eye for detail.

Giselle

Marie-Louise Ekman (Sweden)
Set & Costume Design

Marie-Louise Ekman—scenographer, costume designer, filmmaker and visual artist—was educated at the University College of Arts Crafts and Design in Stockholm and is a professor emeritus at The Royal University College of Fine Arts. She is a member of the Swedish Academy and theatre director of the Royal Dramatic Theatre in Stockholm, where she previously worked as a scenographer and costume designer.

Ekman is a multifaceted artist with a provocative style, and she has become a prominent person in Swedish cultural life. She has worked with a lot of different artistic techniques, media, and genres. Recurring themes are relationships, identity, dreams, and everyday life. She often works in close collaboration with other artists, including choreographer Mats Ek and his Cullberg Ballet.

The Cullberg Ballet is today probably the best-known Swedish contemporary dance company. Their masterpiece *Giselle* was performed more than 300 times in 28 different countries, and Ekman's scenography for it has been much praised.

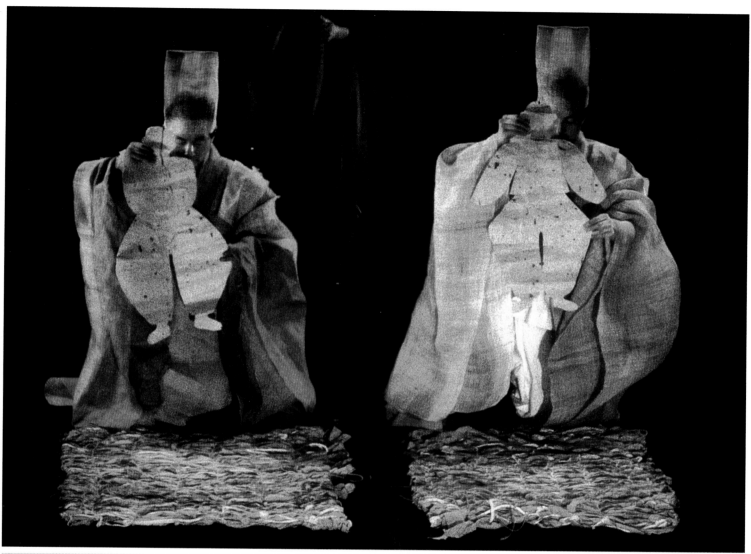

Blood Wedding (*Bodas de sangre*)

Byong-boc Lee (Korea)
Set & Costume Design

Lee Byong-Boc trained at Ewha Women's University and at the Académie de Coupe de Paris. She started her work as a costume and set designer in 1966, designing more than 100 productions over many years, including her early *Blood Wedding* in 1982, which she also designed in 1985, 1988 and in 1998. Jong-Ok Kim's adaptation became a regular part of the Chayu Theatre Company's repertoire, and was very well received both in Korea and Europe. The review in France's *Le Publicain Lorrain* described it: "The play unfolds on a dimly lit stage. Masks and pantomime double the significance o f the faces and movement, singing and tone of voice enhance the refined beauty of the play. Lorca's funeral, the dark face of life, is in the production symbolized by light, a powerful light concentrated upon the costumes and masks, which are further emphasised by the contrast of black and white."

A Man is a Man *(Mann ist Mann)*

Shigeo Okajima (Japan)
Set Design

Shigeo Okajima is known as the Japanese authority on Bertolt Brecht. His designs are modified with the Japanese flavor and in a contemporary light. Most of his works are shown at the "Brechit no Shibaigoya" (Brecht Theatre). This design won a silver medal in stage design at PQ'83.

Afonso Henriques

João Brites (Portugal)
Set Design

This was a first and powerful example of what would soon become the specific aesthetics of O Bando: Building stage machines with multiple functions and a close relationship with the actors, who would use them as utilitarian props. In this case the main prop served as a curious symbol for cradle, throne and coffin, thus allowing for a compact representation of a historical figure not devoid of a comical undertone. The practicality of the set suited the needs of a touring company that wanted to reach new audiences especially outside the big cities.

The Mission *(Der Auftrag)*

Erich Wonder (Austria/Germany)
Set Design

Heiner Mueller lived in the German Democratic Republic but had the exceptional opportunity to cross the Iron Curtain and work periodically in West Germany. For an East German author to direct his own play in a typical West German industrial town of the Ruhr area was most unusual. The scenographer Erich Wonder, born in Austria, had visited East Germany many times and developed strong impressions of both the life of the people and the atmosphere in the cities, which were much different from the West. He was able to incorporate this understanding into this staging. Mueller and Wonder collaborated in many productions. This one was invited in 1982 to the "Theatertreffen," where the best 10 German language productions chosen by a jury were shown.

Too True to Be Good

Jim Plaxton (Canada)
Set & Costume Design

This was a startlingly innovative and metaphoric design during the years when the Shaw Festival was renowned for the visual aspects of its productions. It was set on a tiny thrust stage in a former second-floor courthouse. This design was exhibited at PQ'85 and was awarded a special mention.

Twelfth Night

Agim Zajmi (Albania)
Set Design

Agim Zajmi is one of the creators of contemporary Albanian scenography and one of the outstanding arts personalities in the country. He studied scenography with Professors Bobishov and Akimov at the "Repin" Academy of Arts in St. Petersburg, Russia. He was appointed the scenographer of the Opera and Ballet Theatre in 1961 and of the National Theatre in Tirana in 1963. Over a 50-year career he designed sets and costumes for theatre, opera, and ballet in theatre throughout Albania, Kosovo and Macedonia. For his outstanding artistic merit he was given the title "Artist of the People." His scenographic works are based on artistic invention but also have a functional character.

The Dove and the Poppy
(Kyyhky ja unikko)

Tiina Makkonen (Finland)
Set, Costume & Poster Design

Tiina Makkonen (1952-2011) was the first Finnish scenography to introduce the idea of mental space in scenography. Her early works from 1981 to 1986 at the Vaasa Municipal Theatre emphasized the experience of space. In a similar way that Gaston Bachelard dealt with the experience of private space in his book *La poetique de l'espace*. Makkonen created holistic/comprehensive installations and expanded the concept of scenography. She was one of the first ones to make site-specific set designs, abandoning the traditional theatre stages.

The Dove and the Poppy was based on a novel by Timo K. Mukka, a Finnish writer and poet whose works depict the sexual fervor and ecstatic religiousness of the Lapp people in Finland. The play is a sad ballad of Pieti, who has lost the will to live, and Darja, who brings love into Pieti's empty life before Pieti kills her.

Le Grand Macabre

Timothy O'Brien (UK)
Set & Costume Design

Originally a designer for television, where he was head of design for ABC until 1966, Timothy O'Brien realized a prolific amount of stage work during this period, much of it in collaboration with Tazeena Firth. Art critic Brian Robertson described his style as "sumptuous simplicity." Of his sets for *Le Grand Macabre*, one of many commissions for English National Opera, he says: "Ligeti's 'beautiful Breughel Land' is the world on the brink of destruction. The motorway is all that remains above the rubbish-silted city. It is a stage for the last act of mankind. Hearses are used for bridal cars. The Chief of Police has the head of a bird." On design in general, he suggests, "There is no such thing as a good set for a bad production. A sweating brick wall in *Hamlet* that works is good design. An exquisite Palladian playing space is useless if it frames a failure."

Love and Pigeons

**Olga Tvardovskaya
& Vladimir Makushenko** (USSR/Russia)
Set Design

The original set design by Olga Tvardovskaya and Vladimir Makushenko transfromed Viktor Gurkin's touching and amusing story into a kind of parable. Its backdrop, a huge TV screen with dark and rounded angles, showed a landscape that looked like the work of some naïve artist: little houses with tiled roofs, leafy trees, a small bridge over a canal with swans. Attached to the angles of the screen were bouquets of paper flowers, and above it was a blue clapboard pigeon loft, flanked by a loo and a shed. In the foreground, was a nickel-plated bed; at some distance, a simple grey table. The designers didn't merely show the characters' lives, they also expressed their feelings and vision of the world, while mildly criticizing various aspects of the 1970s: the simple-hearted and slightly weird protagonist, the corny narrative patterns, the "pretty shots" from soap-opera (like a swing twined with flowers in a "resort" scene). The production was very popular, and audiences appreciated its combination of lyricism and light parody.

The Magic Flute (*Die Zauberflöte*)

Achim Freyer (Germany)
Set & Costume Design

Achim Freyer, painter, set-and-costume designer and director, designed several productions of *The Magic Flute* in different periods of his career. This one is an excellent example of what was defined as "theatre of images." In this period, at the beginning of the 1980s, this type of staging, with its colourful, joyful, and symbolic images and costumes, marks a strong contrast to the tendency toward abstract and dark spaces in stage design. It opened a new path in the interpretation of this famous opera. The production was shown nine years after its Hamburg premiere at the Mozart Festival in Vienna, and even then it was the highlight of the festival. One critic wrote: "Everything that was shown to celebrate Mozart was blown away by this nine-year-old production after the first moments. What remains is the comforting certainty that theatre can still be beautiful nowadays, that it can be wise, vital, sometimes even naive, in spite of all the education."

Achim Freyer won the Gold Medal for his lifetime achievement at PQ'99.

Way Upstream

Alan Tagg (UK)
Set & Costume Design

This is one of many designs Alan Tagg made for the prolific British playwright Alan Ayckbourn, often working with Ayckbourn's preferred "in the round" staging. For *Way Upstream*, a very dark, apocalyptic comedy set in and around a motor cruiser, he flooded the stage of the National Theatre's Lyttelton auditorium, a proscenium stage. Of the production he wrote: "The water-filled tank in which this boat moved—on rails beneath the surface—was 30-feet by 40-feet and deep as a man. But the boat seen here, the one we used, is not the model we wanted. That one and the factory adapting it were burned in a fire just before rehearsals. Also, the tank leaked (until it was put right), causing much merriment in the media.'

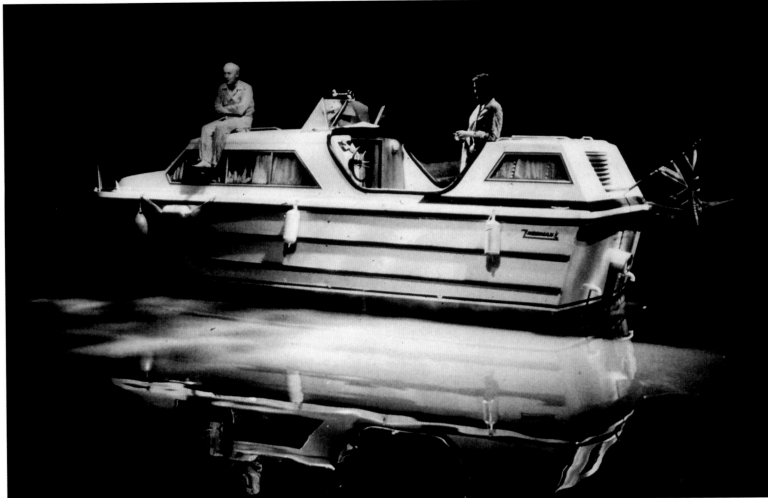

The Hobbit *(Hobit)*

Geroslav Zarić
(Yugoslavia/Serbia)
Set Design

The Buha Theatre was loudly praised by critics for its production of *The Hobbit*, calling it "A play that widely opens the door for spectators' imagination, a play that appeals more to spectator's spirit than to his physical eye." Designer Geroslav Zarić successfully resisted the trap that anyone who designs a space for a magical story can easily fall into: going over the top with the details and leaving nothing to the viewer's imagination. Zarić "lays out this magic world along the edges of the auditorium and in this way he imprints the conception of freer and more dynamic space in the experience of youngest audience instead of well known communicational and spatial pattern that traditional theatre burdened us with. In a glance, the performances, with its simple, but also striking, set design by Geroslav Zarić, was a small feast for the eyes of the spectators."

The Tempest

Nadine Baylis (UK)
Set & Costume Design

Nadine Baylis is one of the most successful designers of dance costumes today, particularly for contemporary dance. Particularly skilled at designing body tights, she can convey, through this most minimalist of costumes, the mood and character of each particular work. Her long-term relationship with Glen Tetley was especially noteworthy in *The Tempest*, staged by Ballet Rambert and later revived by the Norwegian Ballet. The design revealed a fantastic world of billowing fabric, the setting offering cloth sails transformed by projections, with an immense nylon sheet to suggest the sea. "The sea of silk, 16 yards square, became an integral part of the ballet," she said.

Hamlet

Gilles Aillaud (Germany)
Set Design

Built from a former cinema, the Schaubuehne was
conceived as a flexible space that can be used as one
auditorium or be divided into three. The floor consists
of scissor platforms, the ceiling of a technical grid. The
concrete walls have no covering. This ambience was used
for the performance of a *Hamlet* that lasted almost six hours.

The set design for this production was new, because it
used the auditorium as "set." The richness of the language
combined with the pure design of the space gave the
audience the chance to imagine all the different places
where the tragedy plays. The space created a distance to the
play, but at the time it was a wonderful body of resonance
for the tragedy.

The Golubnjaca (Golubnjača)

Radovan Marušić (Bosnia & Herzegovina)
Set Design

The Golubnjača, written by Jovan Radulović, was played on a big boarded stage resembling a drainage pit. Vladimir Stamenković wrote: "Simple as it is unique, the idea of set designer Radovan Marušić is to make the stage slightly concave, tilted down toward the yawning, dark black abyss... That black hole, of course, is one of those fabled mass graves into which the Ustašas, during the last war, threw their unfortunate victims." This unadorned stage design grounds the performance of the actors and supports the tension as it builds up. It also makes the chilling, horrible hole the focal point of the stage. This play, directed by Dejan Mijač for the Serbian National Theatre in Novi Sad, raised much controversy because it spoke openly about war crimes and the tension between two ethnic groups in the former Yugoslavia.

Guys and Dolls

John Gunter (UK) **& Sue Blane** (UK)
Set & Costume Design

Laurence Olivier had always wanted
to stage *Guys and Dolls* at the National
Theatre, but it was left to the NT's third
director, Richard Eyre, to finally stage it in
1982. The production was a huge success,
supported by John Gunter's vibrant neon-
lit sets, and Gunter's design received
particular acclaim. Playing on the contrast
between a grimy version of New York in
the daytime and the neon-lit city at night,
the design is said to have "cracked," or
mastered, the National Theatre's Olivier
space. The design reflects the fruitful
long-term collaboration between Gunter
and director Richard Eyre at the National
Theatre. It was a successful production
for the National Theatre, critically and
financially, transferring to the West End
for an extended run and winning the
1982 Olivier Award for best set design.

The Screens *(Les Paravents, Parawany)*

Jerzy Grzegorzewski (Poland)
Set & Costume Design

In his staging of Jean Genet's *The Screens*—the work which he chose to launch his artistic
directorship of the Studio Theatre in Warsaw—Jerzy Grzegorzewski created magnificent
theatre of the imagination, using airplane wings, stands, fragments of different decora-
tions, chairs of the era and screens. Into this strange poetic world of two cultures—Islamic
and western—entered prostitutes, mourners, soldiers, thugs, both living and dead. Genet
illustrated a world devoid of values. Following him, Grzegorzewski used his very specific art
to illustrate Genet's thesis with semantic costumes, aggressive characterization of the actors
(reflected in their facial expressions) and the rhythmic motions of ballet. Music extracted
episodes from the various shades of grey, replacing the light that was far from the intensity
of the midday sun or the deep black of night. The screens hid the emptiness—or perhaps
the incomprehensible and ineffable mystery—of existence.

It is theatre as was to be expected and foreseeable.
(Het is theater zoals te verwachten en te voorzien was.)

Jan Fabre (Belgium)
Set Design

In 1982, Jan Fabre put a fragmentation bomb under the padded seats of the theatre for *It Is Theatre As Was to Be Expected and Foreseen*, an eight-hour performance. The bombardment continued two years later with *The Power of Theatrical Madness* at the invitation of the Venice Biennale. These two pieces are mentioned in all the literature on contemporary theatre and have travelled around the world. In the meantime, Jan Fabre has grown into one of the most versatile artists on the international scene. He breaks with the codes of the existing theatre by introducing "real time performance"— sometimes called "living installations"—and exploring radical choreographic possibilities to renew classical dance.

in the US to 12 million, the highest figure since 1941 • IRA bomb exploded outside Harrods during the pre-Christmas shopping season • The Worlds population is estimated at 4.72 billion • The Philippines' opposition leader, Benigno Aquino, assassinated • China's population reaches 1 billion • Civil war breaks out in Zimbabwe • Brinks robbery at Heathrow Airport, three tons of gold bars valued at $37.5 million stolen • Maze prisoners break out from Maze High Security Prison near Lisburn, Northern Ireland • Terrorist suicide bomber destroys the United States Embassy in Beirut, killing 63 • The first mobile phones are introduced in the US. • The US deploys nuclear missiles in England and West Germany • Margaret Thatcher wins landslide victory in the UK • ARPANET officially changes to use the Internet Protocol creating the Internet • IBM releases the IBM PC XT • US Space Shuttle Challenger is launched on its maiden flight • Microsoft Word is first released • The first person to receive an artificial heart, Barney Clark, dies after 112 days • Unemployment rises in the US to 12 million, the highest figure since 1941 • IRA bomb exploded outside Harrods during the pre-Christmas shopping season • The Worlds population is estimated at 4.72 billion • The Philippines' opposition leader, Benigno Aquino, assassinated • China's population reaches 1 billion • Civil war breaks out in Zimbabwe • Brinks robbery at Heathrow Airport, three tons of gold bars valued at $37.5

1983

The Sun Festival

Joe Bleakley (New Zealand)
Event Design

Joe Bleakley's work with the experimental theatre troupe Red Mole established him as a significant designer in the 1970s and early 1980s. However, with *The Sun Festival* he began to move into larger-scale performances, engaging with more ritualistic elements, the spectacle, and the local community. This summer festival gathered schoolchildren from around Wellington into a symbolic "rite of passage" ceremony. Together with their families, children led the ceremony in processions from various points in the city to converge at the water's edge in Oriental Bay. With live music, seven-story floating scaffolds, and an elaborate fireworks display, the event also became a significant moment in bringing together a diverse collection of New Zealand's artists and inventors. Bleakley went on to design for events such as the 1990 Auckland Commonwealth Games and was the art director for cinematic spectacles such as the *Lord of the Rings* trilogy and Peter Jackson's *King Kong*.

Not only did the Sun Festival succeed in bringing together various artistic disciplines and scientific ideas, it also managed to collaborate with a large public. New Zealand was beginning to seek a distinct national identity beyond colonial associations with the British Empire and the Commonwealth. The intention was to establish an event not linked to European or Maori culture, but rather use something that unites all cultures, that was the celebration of sun and light. The Sun Festival still stands as an expression of a multicultural nationality, with a broad range of cultural backgrounds and outlooks being expressed, as well as a diverse range of artistic practises being employed in the event.

Cats (*Macskák*)

Béla Götz (Hungary)
Set Design

This was the first ever production of *Cats* that was
allowed to be produced without the original John Napier
sets and costumes. In his set at the Madách Theatre
(which nowadays is exclusively dedicated to musicals),
Béla Götz created a space configuration and visual design
unique for 1983. The show ran from 1983 to 1999 for
more than 1,000 nights. The unbelievably successful
range of set elements, with its large conveyor belts and
stage lifts, is still functional today and was used again in
2010, always playing to full houses.

A Bicycle

Sun-Hi Shin (Korea)
Set & Costume Design

"[The design] is an image drama where living people appear and disappear like ghosts according to the flow of the unconscious mind. The three generations riding on bicycle are a metaphor of the repetitive tragedy of Korean fratricide, families killing one another. The director emphasized the image of an endless road and the writer emphasized the abrupt entrance and exit of the characters. I received a strong impression from a reservoir named 'Yeosoo Snake' and a pine tree forest.

"I expressed continuance through the winding yellow dirt road that the bicycle had been ridden along. I intended the sorrow and frustration to look like a solemn ornamental wall painting when I covered the [bicycle] wheels with gold and put them up on the pine trees."

— Sun-Hi Shin

Caesar and Cleopatra
Cameron Porteous (Canada)
Set & Costume Design

Cameron Porteous designed all but one of the shows at the Vancouver Playhouse during Christopher Newton's tenure as artistic director from 1973 to 1979. (The exception was Liviu Ciulei's stupendous production of *Leonce and Lena*.) This remarkable collaboration (often with light designer Jeffery Dallas) continued when Newton took over the directorship of the Shaw Festival in 1980 and lasted more than 30 years.

This production of *Caesar and Cleopatra* was exemplary in showing the scale and singular artistic vision that Porteous forged at the Shaw Festival. It, and indeed many productions like it at Shaw at the time, showed a real scenographic "coming of age," both of the Festival and in English Canada generally. Many younger designers at the time were greatly influenced by Porteous' work through assisting more senior designers at the Festival.

K2
Ming Cho Lee (China/USA)
Set Design

Master designer and design educator Ming Cho Lee received the Tony Award for Outstanding Set Design for his work on *K2*. The New York Times review of the Washington Arena Stage production described his work this way:

"One must extol the production artistry behind *K2*, beginning with the director and including the set designer, Ming Cho Lee.... The set is a threatening glacial wall entirely filling the stage of the Kreeger Theater. The audience faces the action at a perpendicular, as if it were watching movie. Through artful change of lighting by Al Lee Hughes, we feel the shortening of the day and the encroachment of the sub-zero weather. With the addition of simulated storms and avalanche the audience is inundated with authenticity."
(Mel Gussow, *New York Times*, 5 May 1982)

Don Giovanni/Donna Giovanni

Carmen Parra (Mexico)
& Tolita Figueroa (Mexico)
Set Design

Don Giovanni was a major success of Mexican theatre that was performed and acclaimed internationally. The show later changed its title to *Donna Giovanni*. It is the only Mexican production ever to have been given a cover photograph on major world theatre magazines like *Theater Heute*. It toured through the whole world during its run of several years.

The provocative staging of the opera of a male archetype with a cast of all women was made more vivid by the fact that none of the performers was an opera singer. The very intense images on the subject of women's eroticism and the accent on the "drama giocoso" made the production so original and so theatrical that it overcame the audiences' doubts and fulfilled their musical expectations. The set and costume designs contributed largely to its success.

The Spring and Autumn of the Taiping Heavenly Kingdom

Xing Dalun (China)
Set Design

The set's white walls, black pillars, and repeated lines created a grand and solemn architectural display. The details of the screen and the court demonstrated the luxury of the Taiping Heavenly Kingdom. A large mural painting with a landscape and battle map became a unique way for the army of the Taiping Heavenly Kingdom to show off its success. A large-scale flag placed on the proscenium indicated the "spring" and "autumn" of the Taiping Heavenly Kingdom with changing colors and lights. Scene modeling featured a multi-screen projection.

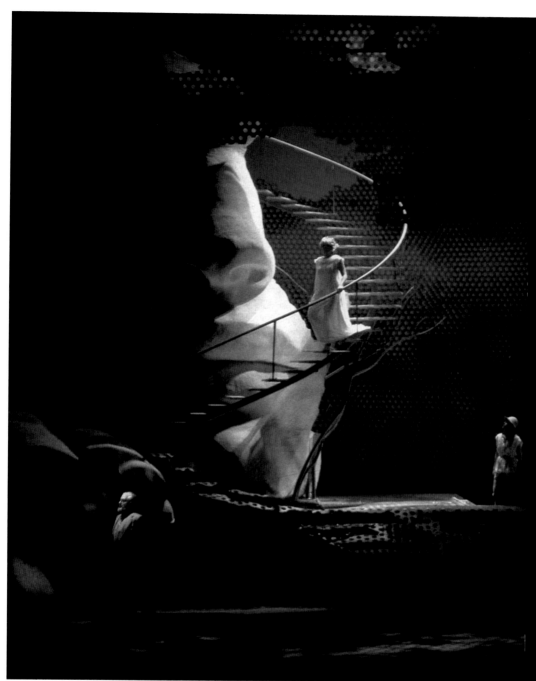

The Midsummer Marriage
Robin Don (UK)
Set & Costume Design

This memorable design is on the cover of the publication *British Theatre Design 83-87*. Its designer is quoted as saying, "There are shadows, dangers, and death in the opera, but its main song is of fruitfulness and joy. The design attempted to echo a phrase from Michael Tippett's definition of a modern composer's task: 'to create... in an age of mediocrity and shattered dreams, images of abounding, generous, exuberant beauty.'"

Robin Don's background in engineering, combined with a fine art education, has enabled him to created extraordinarily beautiful and lithe work, using often elemental materials (plaster, metal, wood) to great effect. He was part of the British team that successfully won the Golden Triga at PQ'79, and also exhibited works in 1983, 1987, and 1999. He has also worked extensively with directors such as John Copley.

Mary Stuart
Shigeki Kawamori (Japan)
Costume Design

Shigeki Kawamori was the recipient of the gold medal for costume design at PQ'75. He mainly worked for the Haiyu-za (Actors' Theatre) Company for more than five decades after he graduated in aeronautics from the University of Tokyo. His superb costume designs are underscored by his accurate understanding of the characters.

Wozzeck

Annelies Corrodi (Switzerland)
Set, Costume & Projection Design

Annelies Corrodi's unique work has always inspired other artists. She helped develop advanced lighting techniques, working with companies like Pani and Niethammer. Known for her projections with painted slides, she predominantly used slides with collages of photographs and paintings to create an oppressive atmosphere in *Wozzeck*.

Drawing one of the main slides, which she does herself, takes about 30 to 35 hours. One production can demand from 80 to 120 slides, each measuring 18 x 18 cm. Several projectors show a number of slides simultaneously to create an impressive atmosphere. Most of the time Corrodi uses a cyclorama as a projection screen, which adds to the acoustics. The projections can be adjusted in moments, so no pauses need to be made for scene changes.

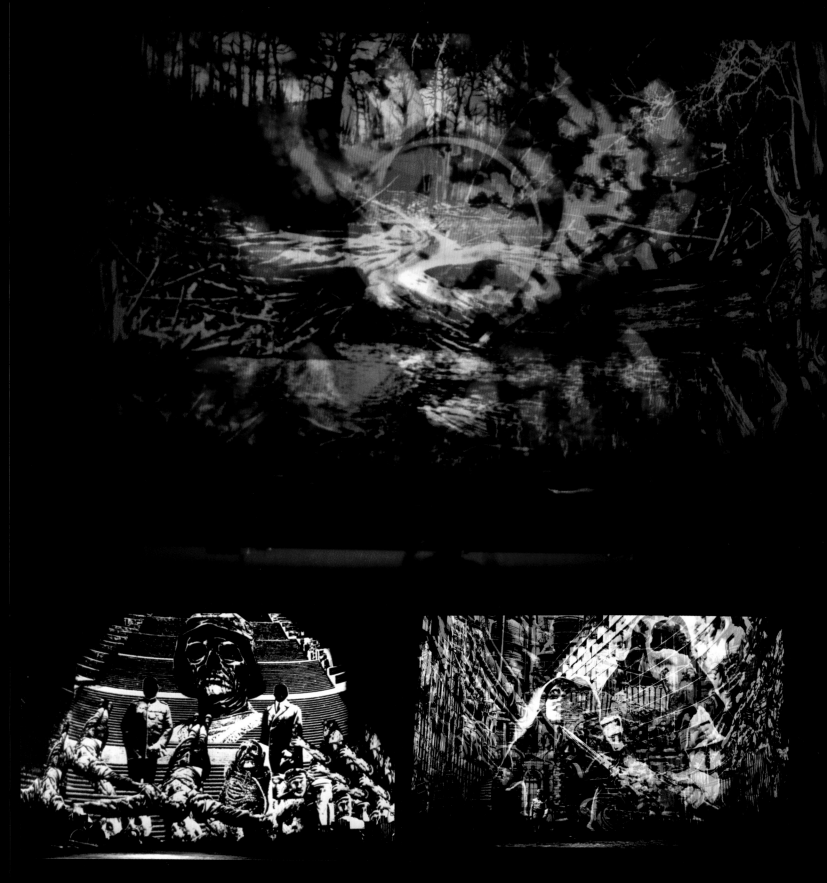

In *Wozzeck*, photographic projections of mixed media collages in black and white insinuated "a vast exploding city" as director Pierre Médecin described it in an interview. Corrodis' nightmarish scenery evokes the turning point in World War I, a time in which civilization was at such a loss that it encouraged the rise of totalitarian regimes, notably in Germany. The only color visible was the Red Moon (blood).

The stage floor consisted of paving stones and gullies filled with piles of scrap metal, debris, and rusty materials. Scene changes had to be quick as the opera played without intermission and no curtain interrupted the action.

OD on Paradise

Jim Plaxton (Canada)
Set & Lighting Design

This production proved that was possible
to have large-stage production values in an
alternative theatre. It introduced Theatre
Passe Muraille in its current configuration,
and it was given the Dora Award for
outstanding new play and set design.

Peer Gynt

Liu Yuansheng (China)
Set Design

The stage was covered with white branches as a constant mark throughout the play. They were
trees, but also symbols of trees, and became either a corner of the woods or the woods at a corner.
They grew around an empty space in the middle of forest and in the village of the Heige town.
They were mysteriously a scene out of real life, but also an illusion. As the basic installation, they
not only represented the pastoral and lyrical style shown in most of the scenes, but also formed
the scenes of grotesquery and mystery. At the end, the revolving stage began to rotate and the
defeated Peer Gynt stumbled toward the last crossroad in his life.

Rusalka

Stefanos Lazaridis (Greece/UK)
Set & Costume Design

Born in Ethiopia of Greek parents, Stephanos Lazaridis trained in Geneva and in London, where he made his home. Russian director Yuri Lyubimov was a major influence on his work. In theatre he worked with the Royal Shakespeare Company, among others. The costume drawings and set model for Act 3 of *Rusalka* illustrated here are representative of his long association with English National Opera. During a period when conceptual opera design was at its peak, he was considered the master of the genre. He was also a regular designer for the huge lake stage at the Bregenz Opera Festival, one of his many international clients.

Body
Tetsuhiko Maeda (Japan)
Set Design

Tetsuhiko Maeda's set design created a delicate space for dancers. It gave the impression of spaciousness, and the movement of the dancers looked beautiful in the space.

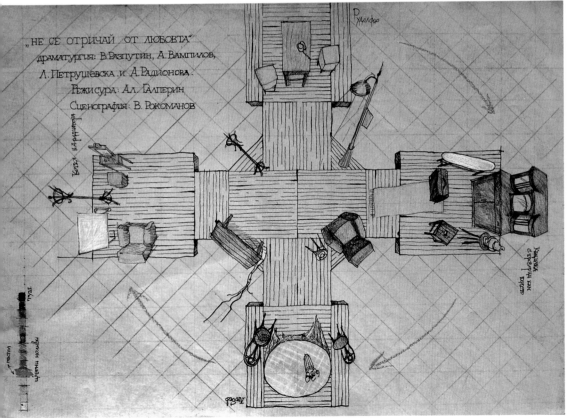

Do Not Deny The Love
(*Не се отричай от любовта*)

Vassil Rokomanov (Bulgaria)
Set & Costume Design

This is one of the first plays, very rare for Bulgaria at the time, to have been produced successfully in an alternative space. The project explored a new relationship between the actors and the stage. The audience was seated between the arms of a cross, in which the playing space was set.

The actors and the director were able to experiment with four different texts in this new playing environment. The experimental nature of the show, demonstrated in the absurdity in the script by Ludmila Petrushevska, created a sometimes-insurmountable barrier between actors and audience. Part of the show was initially cut, then after another rehearsal, was returned to the performances.

Due to the mobile nature of the scenography and lack of distance between actors and spectators, the play was staged in many different places, from theatre lobbies to administrative and cultural institutions to cafes and discotheques.

On the Life of the Marionettes
(De la vida de las marionetas)

Alejandro Luna (Mexico)
Set, Costume & Lighting Design

On the Life of the Marionettes was probably Mexico's most complete theatrical production ever. The oppressive atmosphere of Ingmar Bergman's film inspired some of the richest acting ever achieved by Mexican players. Placed on a very small stage, Luna's design helped create a sensation—shared by actors and audience—of being trapped. The disjointed game playing with space and time was masterly realized by Luna and director Ludwik Margules through an always-surprising change of sets.

This was the culmination of the creative relationship between Luna and Margules, two of Mexico's greatest artists. Margules declared at that time, "Alejandro is my co-director and I am his co-scenographer."

This production enjoyed a major audience and critic success, was honored by all of the critics associations, and is mentioned in all historical reviews as one of the highest achievements in Mexican theatre.

The Ring of the Nibelung
(Der Ring des Nibelungen)

Lars Juhl (Denmark)
Set & Costume Design

This scenography for Wagner's Ring Cycle became a convincing example of how an elegant and pure stylistic language can be developed. The performance was a milestone for Den Jyske Opera and was repeated in the period 1993 to 1996, where it was shown on screen in Copenhagen's Tivoli gardens and was released on video. Asian theatre inspired the steady, unchangeable stage construction and changing locations. The characters appear as beautifully modelled and expressive figures in the scenery.

The Descent of the Middle Class
(Amurgul burghez)

Emilia Jivanov (Romania)
Set Design

Here is an exemplarily elaborate set designed
as a receptacle, adaptable and open to the
play's many characters and dramatic moments.
It differed significantly from a matrix set, or
series of scenic devices, which would have
structured and determined the layout of
the events in the play. The production was
honored by the Theatrical Association of
Romania.

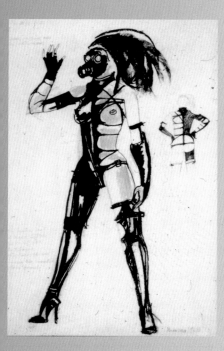

The Soldiers *(Les Soldats, Die Soldaten)*

Ralph Koltai (Germany/UK)
Set Design

A teacher for most of his career, Ralph Koltai became head of theatre design at Central St Martins College of Art and Design in 1966, creating an environment in which students were encouraged to experiment with concepts and develop as individual practitioners, with less emphasis placed on the teaching of craft skills. Practitioners such as Alison Chitty and John Napier refer to Koltai's influence as a teacher.

He said of this production, "Ken Russell requested four acting areas. The model photograph shows a surreal composition—a metaphor for a story about the degradation of women by men. The four acting areas are top left, top right, linking gantry centre, and stage floor. The production photograph show the ability to 'transform' these areas with very powerful projectors positioned at the rear of the stalls."

In the introduction to the monograph on his work, *Ralph Koltai: Designer for the Stage,* Koltai states that: "...for the designer to succeed requires pronounced critical faculty, for he must also remain true to himself as a creative artist." This design represents Koltai's approach to design, often on a grand scale, which emerges from concept to make a strong visual statement. It also reflects an overall trend within Britain toward design based on concept, as opposed to more representational work, although the two approaches exist concurrently. It was honoured at PQ'83.

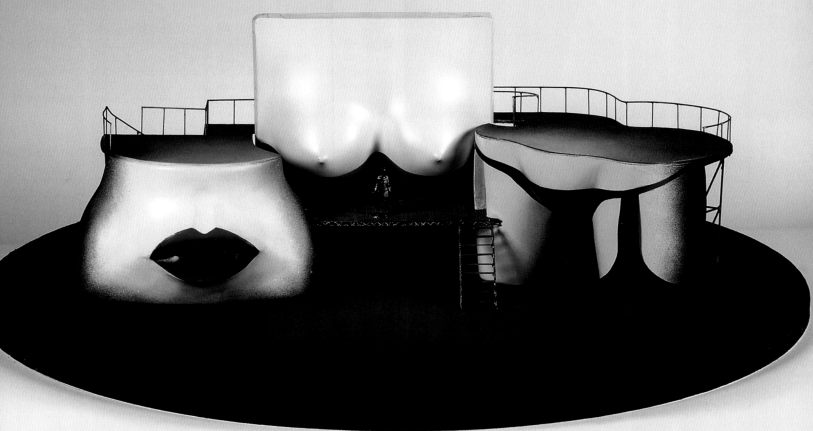

Oedipus

Tony Geddes, Pamela Maling & Joe Hayes (New Zealand)
Set, Costume, & Lighting Design

Oedipus was an innovative and original production that demonstrated the effectiveness of this particular grouping of artists. A simple stage set with a number of gauze screens defined the performance space. Texts projected onto these screens made veils and transparent layers out of the very words the performers were speaking. This is characteristic of other works such as *Pravda* (1986) where this team continued their investigation of stage typography. Also of note is how the design interacted with the layers of vocalization in the performance, where the recorded song is overlaid live by the performers speaking the same lyrics. Once again this created "veils" of meaning, where the audience absorbed the storyline through layers of representation. This occurred before subtitling was used first by Houston Grand Opera, and represents one of the very early innovations with this feature of operatic performance.

This production is an example of the collaboration between four theatre artists, whose work defined the productions of Christchurch's Court Theatre during this era. Director Elric Hooper, set designer Tony Geddes, costume designer Pamela Maling, and lighting designer Joe Hayes developed a strong synthesis between all the performing elements. This might not have been possible in larger cities where practitioners tend to move around more between companies and collaborators.

Raymonda

Nicholas Georgiadis (Greece/UK)
Set & Costume Design

Nicholas Georgiadis was hugely influential throughout his extensive career as a designer, painter, and teacher. He ran the Slade course for 30 years. If he had a style it was a refusal to opt for what Royal Ballet Kenneth MacMillan's widow Deborah calls "virtual reality" or design that is merely flat reproduction. Instead he worked allusively and metaphorically, playing with space, scale, and emphasis to isolate and dramatize certain elements. He collaborated with Rudolf Nureyev on both Nureyev's original choreography (*The Tempest* and *Washington Square*) and his productions of the classics, among them Nureyev's first version of *Raymonda* for the Royal Ballet touring group.

One of the most important international designers of his generation, he taught for many years and co-founded the Society of British Theatre Designers in 1971. He was the first designer to receive the Evening Standard Award for outstanding achievement in ballet in 1982. He was made CBE in 1984 and admitted to the Greek Academy of Arts in 1999.

Lulu

David Borovsky (Russia)
Costume Design

Grey tones prevailed in the design of sets and costumes for this production. The musicians in the pit were covered by iron bars, with the conductor's head sticking out above them. This solution was on the one hand preconditioned by the theme of circus, and on the other by the time to which the director and designer transferred the action—the 1930s, the epoch of totalitarian rule and fascism. After the animal trainer introduced the characters in the Prologue, the bars were lifted to an upright position, so that the entire stage was "behind bars." The stage space was blocked off by the fire curtain and when the action began one of the sectors of its iron surface opened to reveal the locale that was designated with architectural details, textures, and objects typifying the period. In the next episode, another sector was revealed, and each time the wall would be moved farther upstage. In the final scene, all that was left of the massive iron wall was the bare framework. The heroine died from the knife of the assassin and White Pierrot tenderly laid her body on to the bars of the orchestra pit, from which the last chords of the opera were sounding.

1984

Indira Ghandi assassinated • Widespread famine in Ethiopia leads to 10 million people facing starvation • UK and China agree Hong Kong will revert to China in 1997 • Truck bomb destroys US embassy in Beirut, Lebanon • USSR boycotts Los Angeles Olympics in retaliation for western boycott in 1980 • Twelve month strike by coal miners begins in British coal industry • Ethiopian famine begins • Winter Olympic Games held in Sarajevo, Yugoslavia • First Apple Macintosh computer goes on sale • First commercial CD players introduced • Genetic fingerprinting or DNA profiling developed • Michael Jackson sells over 37 million copies of Thriller album • Indian Prime minister Indira Ghandi assassinated • Widespread famine in Ethiopia leads to 10 million people facing starvation • UK and China agree Hong Kong will revert to China in 1997 • Truck bomb destroys US embassy in Beirut, Lebanon • USSR boycotts Los Angeles Olympics in retaliation for western boycott in 1980 • Twelve month strike by coal miners begins in British coal industry • Ethiopian famine begins • Winter Olympic Games held in Sarajevo, Yugoslavia • First Apple Macintosh computer goes on sale • First commercial CD players introduced • Genetic fingerprinting or DNA profiling developed • Michael Jackson sells over 37 million copies of Thriller album • Indian Prime minister Indira Ghandi assassinated • Widespread famine in Ethiopia leads to 10 million people

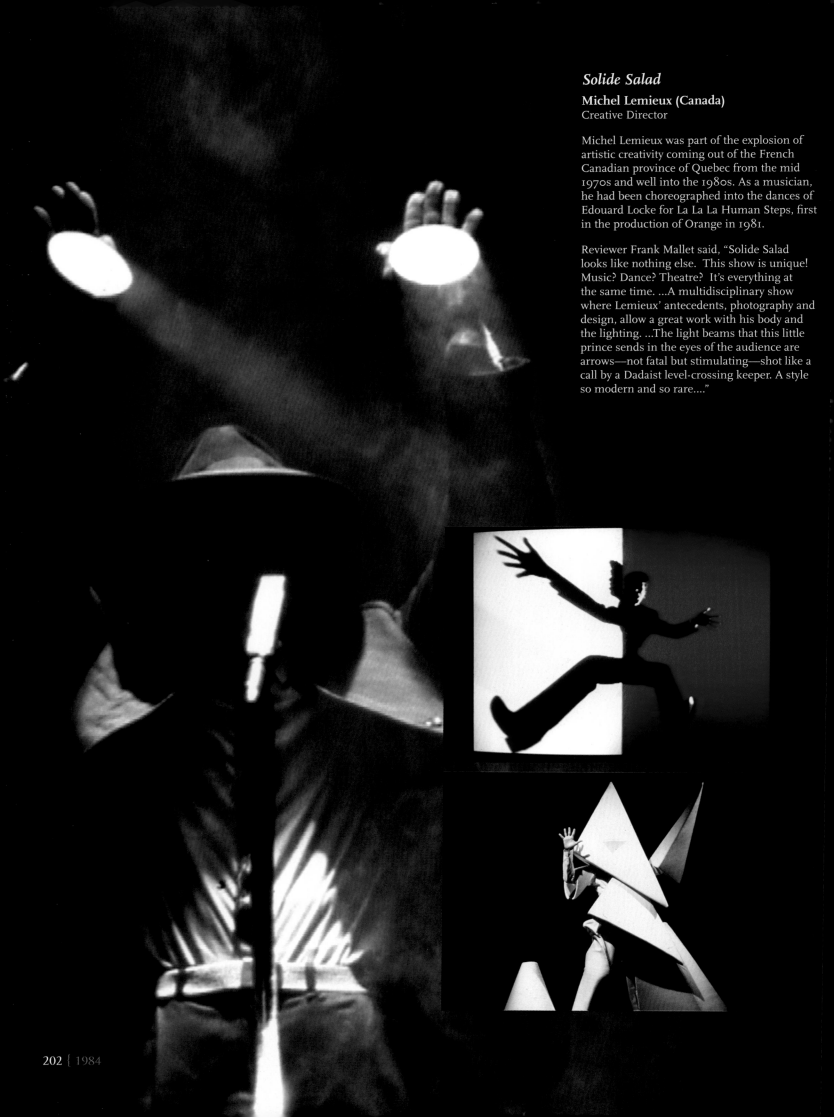

Solide Salad

Michel Lemieux (Canada)
Creative Director

Michel Lemieux was part of the explosion of artistic creativity coming out of the French Canadian province of Quebec from the mid 1970s and well into the 1980s. As a musician, he had been choreographed into the dances of Edouard Locke for La La La Human Steps, first in the production of Orange in 1981.

Reviewer Frank Mallet said, "Solide Salad looks like nothing else. This show is unique! Music? Dance? Theatre? It's everything at the same time. ...A multidisciplinary show where Lemieux' antecedents, photography and design, allow a great work with his body and the lighting. ...The light beams that this little prince sends in the eyes of the audience are arrows—not fatal but stimulating—shot like a call by a Dadaist level-crossing keeper. A style so modern and so rare...."

Venice Preserv'd

Alison Chitty (UK)
Set & Costume Design

As resident designer at the National Theatre, this is one of the productions that enabled Alison Chitty to establish and maintain a high standard of development and presentation of ideas. These drawing are representative of a body of work which made Chitty a force in the industry at this point in time.

The fabric samples show how Chitty achieves her effect: using a black fabric with a lurex pattern to suggest the watered silk of the overskirt, which she has drawn with such subtle precision. Another fabric incorporating lurex gives enough life and subtle sparkle to the costume, so that the third fabric can be a heavy black, just the kind of fabric designers were taught not to use.

Sunday in the Park with George

Tony Straiges, Patricia Zipprodt & Ann Hould-Ward (USA)
Set & Costume Design

Sunday in the Park With George was a musical and visual exploration of the creation of artist George Seurat's most famous canvas, ''A Sunday Afternoon on the Island of la Grande Jatte.''

"In a fantastic set by Tony Straiges—an animated toy box complete with pop-ups—[Seurat] gradually assembles bits and pieces of the painting, amending and banishing life-size portions of it before our eyes... [W]hen Seurat finishes 'La Grande Jatte' at the end of Act I, we're moved not because a plot has been resolved but because a harmonic work of art has been born. As achieved on stage—replete with pointillist lighting by Richard Nelson and costumes by Patricia Zipprodt and Ann Hould-Ward—the 'fixing' of the picture is an electrifying *coup de theatre*." [Review by Frank Rich, New York Times, 3 May 1984]

Tony Straiges won the 1985 Tony and Drama Desk Awards for his scenic design while Zipprodt and Hould-Ward were honored with nominations for their costume design for *Sunday in the Park*.

The Mission *(A missão: Recordações de uma revolução)*
Cristina Reis (Portugal)
Set Design

This performance responded mainly to a kind of disenchantment with Portugal's 'Carnation Revolution' of 1974. But it also matched a certain moral crisis among the artists themselves. Rehearsals were long and painful, and the whole enterprise seemed to prompt melancholia. The set-design took on the theatricality involved in that fictional universe, with its underlying emptiness, silence, discontinuities, through the use of left-overs from other set designs as well as the image of an industrial container, a large orange box variously used as an infernal mechanism, strict lens or radioscopic tool to examine treason and the oblivion of history. The performance, the first professional production of Müller in Portugal, had a great impact as a display of strong inventiveness within post-structuralist aesthetics. Director Luís Miguel Cintra asserted that the set design was the main clue to the staging itself and named Cristina Reis as co-director of the performance.

It was shown in Venice, at the Biennale theatre section, and was seen by the author Heiner Müller himself, who praised the performance.

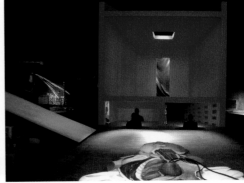

Bumboat!
Kalyani Kausikan (Singapore)
Lighting Design

This was a very significant production that brought together an emerging team of designers, performers, writers, and theatre practitioners. The stripped-bare set was designed for dance and small theatre pieces. The production was the first in Singapore to use lighting importantly and seriously on a bare stage.

The Snow Queen
(Снежната Кралица)

Asen Stoychev (Bulgaria)
Set, Costume & Lighting Design

In this design, Asen Stoychev emphasized the richness of visual texture and surface. The sets and costumes were made of " fabrics" created from hand-processed and unsustainable materials, one of the first successful examples of such bold use of these materials in theatre design in Bulgaria. The extensive use of collage in the costume and set design renderings was also a new development in the scenography practice of this period. The sketches and the production itself influenced the work of many young designers and students.

Puck (Пук)

Silva Bachvarova (Bulgaria)
Set, Costume & Puppet Design

These puppets opened up new creative opportunities for the acting team and made a strong emotional connection with the audience. The production relied on the transformation of objects and costume elements into puppet characters and the creation of a metaphorical underwater world using prosaic objects. The show, recognized as one of Bulgaria's best and most innovative puppet theatre pieces, played in many national and international festivals, and it received many awards.

Rapunzel In Suburbia

Kim Carpenter (Australia)
Set & Costume Design

Kim Carpenter is one of Australia's leading exponents of visual theatre and as artistic director of the company he founded in 1988, Theatre of Image, a rare example of the director/designer in Australia. This production of an adaptation of the poems of acclaimed Australian writer Dorothy Hewett is an eloquent example of the work that described the aspirations of and ultimately led to the formation of this company. Carpenter's work was described as " fascinating and highly charged visual feasts" in the *World Encyclopedia of Contemporary Theatre*, Don Rubin, ed.

The Vampires
Adrianne Lobel (USA)
Set Design

[*The Vampires* is an] excursion into the dark heart of a crazy all-American family. ...The topsy-turvy set has been smartly designed by Adrianne Lobel... the staging is neo-sitcom; the production looks like a hopped-up, surreal version of 'The Donna Reed Show'..." [Review by Frank Rich, *New York Times*, 12 April 1984]

Designer Adrianne Lobel received the 1984 Obie Award for outstanding scenic design for her work on *The Vampires*. She has designed extensively for theatre, opera, and dance throughout the US and around the world, working frequently with director Peter Sellars.

The Archaeology of Sleep
Julian Beck (USA)
Set Design

The Archaeology of Sleep was Julian Beck's last play for the Living Theatre before his death in 1985. Through an examination of the science of sleep, five sleepers and their doubles/shadows voyage through the alpha/beta/gamma/delta cycles of sleep toward a collective dream of liberation. The play premiered at Maison de la Culture in Nantes, France, in June 1983 and was subsequently staged in New York. The set consisted of five beds, a railroad of sleep on a raised platform/runway at the rear of the stage where a small platform could move back and forth across the runway, as well as many small props. The lighting, one of Julian Beck's specialties, was elaborate. In the photo one sees Julian Beck as the evil sleep doctor, experimenting on two actor/cats.

Birds (Ὄρνιθες)

Apostolos Vettas (Greece)
Set & Costume Design

As with *Cyclops*, *The Birds* was produced for another small experimental group, requiring that the stage could be set up easily and quickly during tours of open-air theatres.

The Flight (Menekülés)

László Székely (Hungary)
Set Design

The 1984 premiere of Bulgakov's *Flight* for the Katona József Theatre received the theatre critics' prize in several categories. The abstract power and visual logic of his tripartite black box was considered outstanding by theatre professionals.

Masquerade *(Maskarada)*

Drago Turina (Yugoslavia/Croatia)
Set Design

"Lermontov's drama *Masquerade* is by a poetic masterpiece where I found passion as well as chilliness, utmost love and hate, love of an angel and the demon, I decided on an obscure white/black for sumptuously decadent rooms of the XIX century in Russia, with card playing as well as rich masked balls.

My starting point was a basic wide arc, consisting of columns and coronet with black/gold details, the remaining space filled in with doors and windows drapery, off white colour. The audience noticed the the drapery crating a bizzare cold atmosphere; rigid forever, "frozen", icelike.

The design's austerity had an ethereal quality in concordance with the music, dancing, acting." Drago Turina

The Big Magic (La grande magia)

Ezio Frigerio (Italy)
Set Design

The design is a wonderful example of Ezio Frigerio's work at the Teatro Piccolo di Milano with Giorgio Strehler and his company. It demonstrates the designer's essential values of image and simplicity. In this production, he created an atmosphere that recalls the world of Federico Fellini.

Folichon

Acar Başkut (Turkey)
Set Design

"What is a stage designer? He is one of the distinguished instruments in a big orchestra. Sometimes he plays solo, sometimes he mingles in the whole sound, sometimes he remains completely silent."

So writes Acar Başkut, a prominent figure in the generation that established modern stage design in Turkey. Beginning in 1965, he designed hundreds of productions, most of them in the Ankara and Istanbul State Operas. Besides his career in theatre, he was a renowned painter, and his designs were distinguished for their high artistic quality. He also had a solid knowledge of theatre technique, gained during his education and practice in Germany.

Folichon is a popular Turkish operetta. The scenery for this 1984 production displays the main features of Başkut's artistry: his skill in conveying the spirit of the music and making the spectator feel the elegance, charm, and glamour glittering inside the proscenium arch.

Blue Snake

Jerrard Smith (Canada)
Set & Costume Design

Blue Snake was a significant departure for the National Ballet of Canada under the guidance of Erik Bruhn. The work was far removed from their usual repertoire and was a popular success. It also provided an opportunity for the performers to be more involved in the process of the design, visiting the shop at various stages of the build to try elements of the set with which they were to interact. *Blue Snake* became a popular piece in the company's touring repertoire, and it prompted Rhombus Media to make a documentary film which was widely viewed.

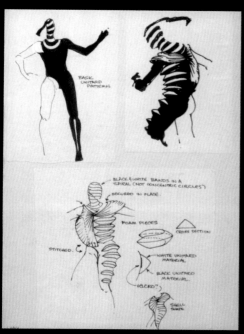

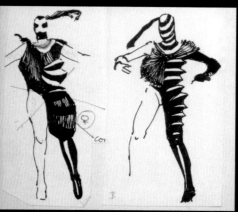

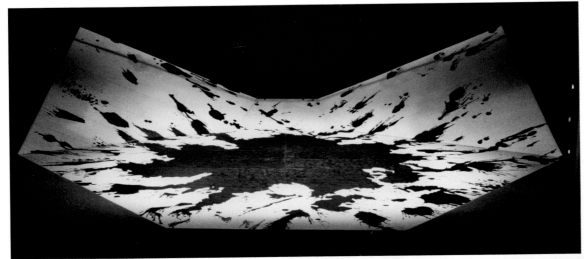

Revelation and Fall

Michael Pearce (Australia)
Set & Costume Design

This work was commissioned for the 1984 Adelaide Arts Festival, and formed part of a triple bill presented at the festival.

The Mask

Kuan-Yen Nieh (Taiwan)
Set & Lighting Design

Kuan-Yen (Alan) Nieh is one of Taiwan's
most influential and senior designers. He
was among the first to embrace a western
influence in his work methodology, especially
in his use of computer assisted drawing. His
production of *The Mask* is an early indication
of his work in a non-traditional form while
still being rooted in a Taiwanese aesthetic.

Sacra Conversazione

Peter McKinnon (Canada)
Lighting Design

This piece was commissioned by the Banff Centre for the Arts and
was later transferred to The Toronto Dance Theatre and became a
mainstay of their repertoire for the next ten years, touring nationally
and internationally. It was unusual for a contemporary dance piece,
for its large scale and range of scenic looks.

The American section of *The Civil Wars* was a series of twelve brief interludes intended to connect the larger scenes and provide time for set changes. David Byrne was the composer of these mostly wordless pieces, and choreography was by Suzushi Hanayagi.

With no singers, *The Knee Plays* told its story through nine dancers wearing white doctor's smocks. The style of presentation was influenced by Japanese Bunraku puppetry and Noh and Kabuki theater. The designs, by Jun Matsuno with Wilson and Byrne, were modular white squares resembling Japanese shoji screens that moved fluidly to redefine the space for each scene.

Byrne's music, however, took its inspiration not from Japan but from the Dirty Dozen Brass Band of New Orleans. The instrumentation was for a brass ensemble, and incorporated a number of traditional tunes, including "In the Upper Room," "The Gift of Sound," "Theadora is Dozing," "I Bid You Good Night," and "I Tried."

New York Times critic John Rockwell wrote "The 'plot' traces the transformation of a tree into a boat into a book into a tree again, almost as a cycle of nature [...] All of which means little in words, but much in stage pictures." [*New York Times*, 29 April 1984]

Wilson coined the term "knee play," meaning an interlude between scenes, for the opera *Einstein on the Beach*. The term emerges from Wilson's conception of these pieces as connective tissue linking the "meat" of a performance.

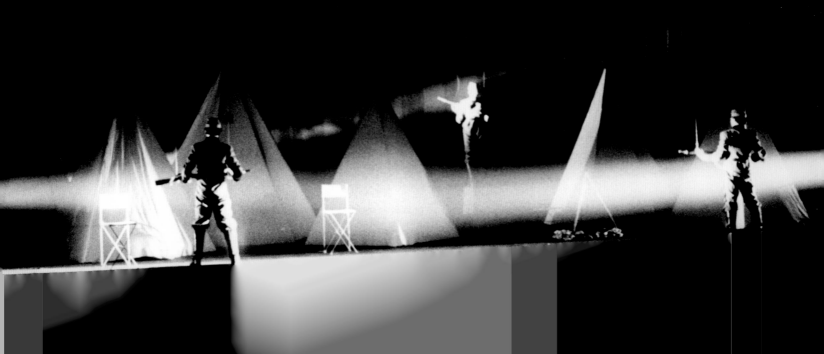

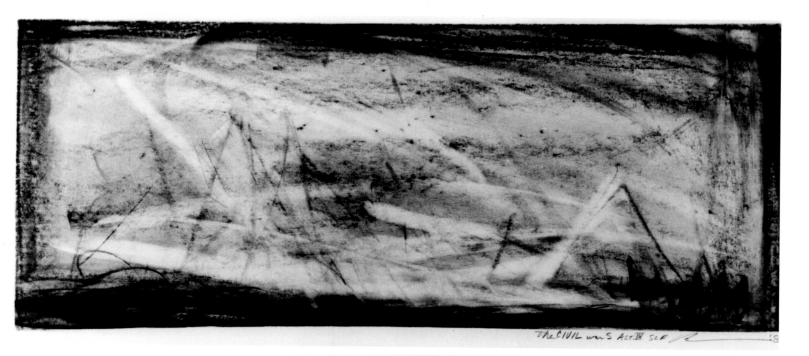

The CIVIL warS Act IV ScE

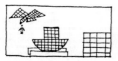

Knee Play 4
A large bird flies from the sky.
The boat appears with people on board.
The bird takes a man from the boat and flies
away.

Knee Play 5
The boat is beached on rocks.
Three people write graffiti on it.

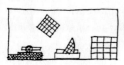

Knee Play 6
The boat sails along a coast.
On shore, two people load a cannon and fire
at the boat.
The boat is hit and breaks up.
The hull sinks and the cabin floats on.

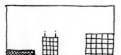

Knee Play 7
The cabin lands on the shores of Japan and
Admiral Perry gets out to greet a fisherman.
The Admiral entertains the fisherman with
a puppet show.

Knee Play 8
The boat hull sinks below the sea.

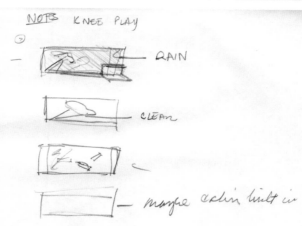

NOTES KNEE PLAY

RAIN

CLEAN

maybe cabin built in

*the CIVIL warS: a tree is
best measured when it is
down (The Knee Plays)*

Robert Wilson (USA)
Set, Costume & Lighting Design

Good

Kazue Hatano (Japan)
Set & Costume Design

Kazue Hatano debuted as a young female theatre designer, rare at the time in Japan, and received the Minister of Culture and Education Award in 1972. She approaches design intellectually and has always worked to maintain an aesthetic form and concept of the production. Her set and costumes designs are based on research that she conducted around the world. Her designs are refined and elegant, both the classics as well as the modern repertory. She has developed a good sense of coloring.

Waiting for Godot

Axel Manthey (Germany)
Set & Costume Design

The collaboration of Juergen Gosch and Axel Manthey had already reached its peak. Manthey greatly admired the work of Juergen Gosch, who came as a guest from the GDR. In this phase of their collaboration Manthey created his language of stage imagery, which he subsequently developed further and completed in his own productions. Gosch appreciated Manthey mainly as a partner to talk and think with. According to Gosch. Manthey was also a capable dramaturg and a very precise observer of the actors.

The King Goes Forth to France
(Kuningas lähtee Ranskaan)

Ralf Forsström (Finland)
Set & Costume Design

Ralf Forsström, born in 1943, is a freelance scenographer of set and costume design. He has worked in free theater groups in Finland and in Scandinavia, as a house designer in Swedish Theatre (Svenska Teatern in Finland), Stockholm City Theater Sweden and Helsinki City Theatre. As a free lance designer he has made several opera and theater productions for different companies, also outside Finland (Sweden and Norway); a very profound figure in the Finnish scenography and visual thinking.

His design for a Finnish opera Aulis Sallinen's Kuningas lähtee Ranskaan (*The King Goes Forth to France*) made of the castle of Olavinlinna 1984 was a science fiction environment where the costumes were a combination of middle ages, the Renaissance and 1980's. The set was made of rag rugs woven from green house plastic. A stretch fabric above symbolized the Ice Age. The movement and dynamism was brought with costumes, their visual affluence, their 80's camp attitude and music-TV aesthetics and japonism, kabuki-resemplance. The costume dramaturgy had the idea that the clothes will become more and more enormous and imposing (the characters could barely move in the costumes) while they themselves become more and more hollow from inside. Forsström thus created a metaphor for the inner emptiness of power and was able to grasp the time scale of Haavikko's multilayered libretto.

This scenography started this very strong period of visuality in the Finnish theatre. Suddenly visual spectacle was highly discussed, also simulaniously fiercely admired and critized.

The Niebelung *(Nibelungen)*

Jochen Finke (Germany GDR)
Set Design

This production was an important one for the producing company, the National Theatre (Schauspielhaus) Dresden. The abstract design played a major role in raising the importance of Dresden as a theatre capital. Until then, the leading productions were shown in the capital, East Berlin, and productions in other cities were considered less important. This meant at the time that local censorship was not as severe as that in the capital, and theatre could be more experimental. The design, an abstract space, served as model for many other productions. The inner life of the characters and the conflict between private and public life was reflected in the design.

A Midsummer Night's Dream *(San Ivanjske Noći)*

Drago Turina (Yugoslavia/Croatia)
Set Design

Born in 1934, Drago Turina is one of Croatia's leading designers. He is known as a daring and constructive artist, who often receives awards at international festivals. Scenography by Turina has frequently represented Croatia the Prague Quadrennial.

A Loud Solitude *(Hlučná samota)*

Jan Dušek (Czechoslovakia/Czech Republic)
Set & Costume Design

The artist was able, through his various modifications and groupings of "waste" material
(such as bundles of old paper) to turn them into an aesthetic and meaningful element which
corresponded to the poetic and philosophical literary intent of Bohumil Hrabal's play, set in
a junk shop. The production was one of Evald Schorm's most balanced during his time at the
Theatre on the Balustrade, a positive outcome achieved largely due to the creative collaboration
of its director and scenographer.

The Ring of the Nibelung
(Ring des Nibelungen)

Peter Sykora (Poland/Germany)
Set & Costume Design

This Ring Cycle was not only an international breakthrough for designer Peter Sykora, but also for Goetz Friedrich and the creative team. The production was exported to Tokyo and New York City and became a mainstay of the Deutsche Oper, where it was performed for the last time in April 2010. The tunnel that dominated the whole cycle was a very strong artistic element of, one idea becoming different variations for each opera.

The stage became a "tunnel of time," where every figure, every situation existed now and in the past. Sykora transformed the stage into a monstrous, science-fiction structure, something between a channel tunnel and an underground tube that narrowed in its perspective, thus created the illusion of endlessness. Changing elements within this tunnel were staged for the four operas, giving it a certain attractive dynamic.

Sykora enjoyed creating large spaces that were often built as complex structures. Sometimes they were like gigantic toys, breaking up the rigidity of the space using stage technology. In the *Ring* this combination of the dominant tunnel with transparent curtains for the Rhine scene, an opening stage floor with blinking stage technology for the Nibelungs, and bunker architecture from the Third Reich for Hunding's hat, to name just a few of the elements, revealed the genius of Goetz Friedrich's interpretation.

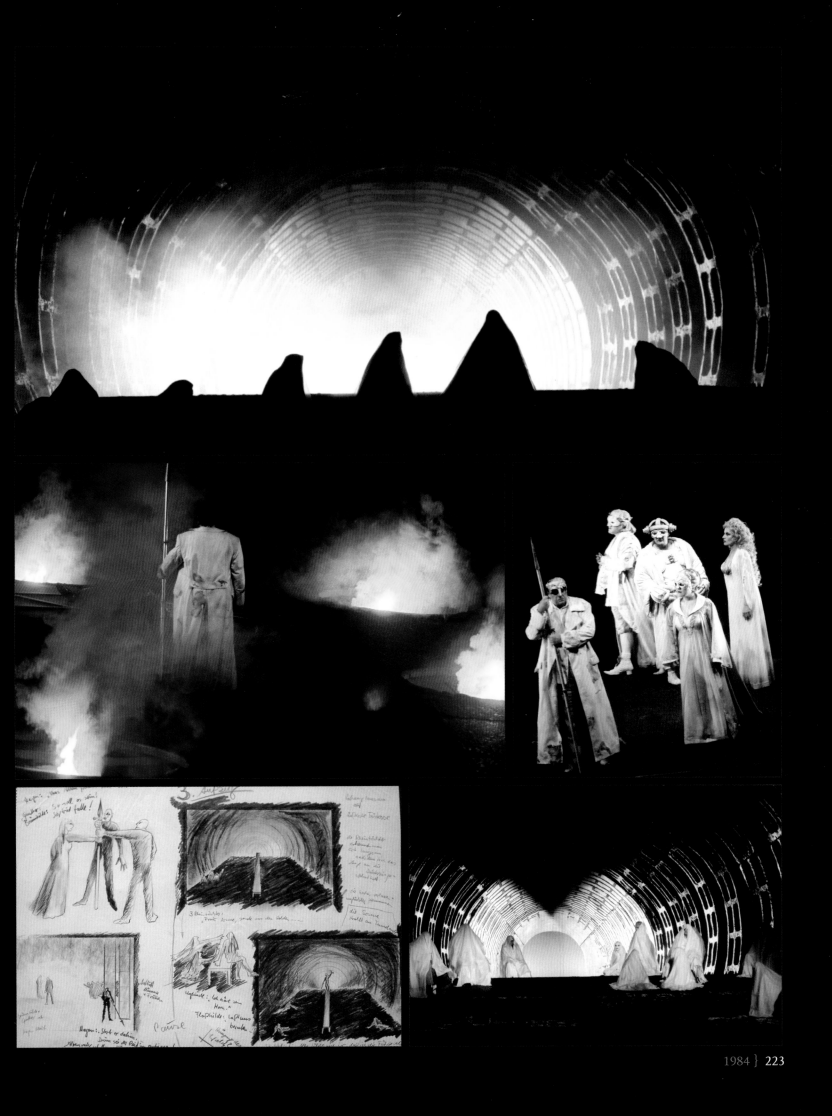

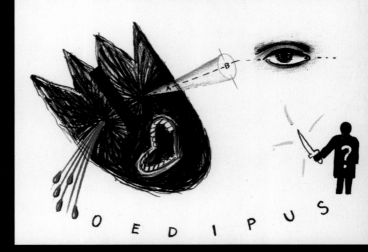

Oedipus

Axel Manthey (Germany)
Set & Costume Design

Juergen Gosch and Axel Manthey worked on nine productions between 1980 and 1985, always attracting much attention, though there was often strong protest against their work. *Oedipus* was their sixth collaboration. Gosch "forces the audience into a distant view of a tragedy that is unfathomable. It was an extraordinary production, defying all routine", wrote the critic Heinz Klunker in the magazine *Theatre Heute*. Manthey, who appreciated Gosch a lot and who developed may of his own discoveries of spaces and images thanks to him, proved himself again as a practitioner and minimalist, as Gosch has said, with "just five blocks of styrofoam and a house made of linen."

It was invited to the 1984 "Theatretreffen" in Berlin where the 10 most important productions of German speaking theatre are selected by a jury every year.

Nippon no Yoake

Akaji Maro (Japan)
Set Design

Dairakudakan, founded and directed by Akaji Maro, was the first company to introduce Japan's Butoh dance-theater on a large scale to the United States. Their work is a fusion of German dance expressionism and Japanese experimentation that became Butoh in the 1960s.

Henry V

Bob Crowley (Ireland/UK)
Set & Costume Design

This is part of the body of work Crowley created for the Royal Shakespeare Company. According to him, he has divided his life between the RSC and the National, but slightly more for RSC, so its selection is fitting. He was just a few seasons into his professional career when he designed this production, and it illustrates the direction of his work as well as his important creative partnership with Adrian Noble. His work for the company consistently imagined empty but visually arresting and interesting spaces for the actors to work with, and included costumes that played with historical accuracy.

His work is illustrative of a strong visual style that came to be associated with one of the leading theatre companies in the UK. The designer has been honoured with many awards both in the UK and the USA, including Tonys, Drama Desk Awards, Oliviers and the Royal Design for Industry.

In The Summer House (In het Tuinhuis)

Paul Gallis (Netherlands)
Set & Costume Design

With the mounting of black panels in the stage frame, which created various horizontal and vertical spatial cut-outs, scenographer Paul Gallis gives the staging of *In het Tuinhuis* an exciting twist, while avoiding the naturalism prescribed by author Jane Bowles. As the scene proceeds, the frame enlarges, and is supported with light and colour: the spectator perceives the scenes in 'close up' as if they were movie stills. A renowned designer since the seventies, Paul Gallis is a self-taught man with a fabulous photographic memory. His typical style seems to consist of constant renewal, varying between hyperrealism, stylization and abstraction. For this staging he seemed to revert to the realism of artists such as Ralston Crawford or Edward Hopper, investing it with contemporary technical ingenuity.

Turandot

Andrzej Majewski (Poland)
Set & Costume Design

Andrzej Majewski worked continuously since the 1960s, spending the years 1966-2005 as chief stage designer of the Wielki Theatre in Warsaw. He has designed over 350 performances around the world (including Covent Garden, the Paris Opera and the Teatro Colon in Buenos Aires).

His scenography for *Turandot*, directed by Marek Weiss-Grzesinski, was the quintessence of his style. The monumental, dynamic scenery characterized by an expressionistic treatment of shapes and colors, and the desire to allegorise. Majewski symbolically used the vertical layout of the scene. Above, in the distance, was visible the outline of the palace of the emperor of China against a starry sky. A little lower stood colorfully adorned Guardsmen and courtiers. At the bottom of the scene—just as at the bottom of the social ladder—a modestly dressed, grey crowd. Towering over all, the three-metre Princess Turandot in a silver-blue dress with a mask on her face—cold, inaccessible and mysterious. The critique of totalitarian systems combined with the exotic in the set designs of Andrzej Majewski. Next to signs of power: bars, chains, gong shield with beveled heads, appeared favored by Majewski—returning like Chinese fetishes—motives of bird claws and dragon wings.

Three Sisters (*Drei Schwestern, Tri sestry*)

Karl-Ernst Hermann (Germany)
Set Design

For this production, all three spaces of the theatre were used; three spaces became one by opening the roller shutters. The total length of the space was about 50 metres, the width about 16 metres. The result was a cinesmascope effect. Herrmann's design was the historical reconstruction of a Russian country house and of an alley that seemed real to many spectators. The production was highly praised, but in the context of 1980s, many also found the realism very conservative. In any case, it was a spectacular and unique set that really brought the ambience and the smell of the countryside into theatre.

Animal Farm

Jennifer Carey (UK)
Set, Mask & Costume Design

Jennifer Carey trained as a fine artist, beginning her theatre work in 1972 when she assisted John Bury at the then-new National Theatre. Of her 1984 design for Peter Hall's adaptation of Orwell's *Animal Farm,* she writes: "We searched for an innocent style. A young schoolboy narrated. The animals and humans were masked; four legs were achieved with crutches; the scale of chickens was solved by wearing the whole animal on the head. The toy farm scenery moved, turned, and opened, revealing new parts of the farm."

Rough Crossing

Carl Toms (UK)
Set & Costume Design

Carl Toms was a steady and highly respected purveyor of elegant sets for theatre, ballet, and opera from the 1970s onward. His description of the 1984 *Rough Crossing*, adapted from Molnar: "The play is set on a luxury liner in the 1930s. The design showed, I hope, an ironical, witty view of the nautical style then, not merely a pastiche. Both acts called for fast, open, choreographic scene changes."

The Cherry Orchard

Joe Hayes (New Zealand)
Lighting Design

This design — as well as that for *Away* included later in this volume—represents a body of work that defined an extensive partnership between Hayes and his collaborators. The transformative power of Hayes' lighting enabled the featured set designs and productions to exceed the physical boundaries of the architecture, making it possible to construct dense visual worlds of performance. Hayes' lighting designs played a major role in the featured productions, extending the familiar boundaries of the architecture.

From the textured patterns of *The Cherry Orchard*, to abstract shapes in *Pravda*, and the bright horizons of *Away*, Hayes' designs demonstrate the power of light to transform space and performance, provoking endless worlds and atmospheres.

Crime and Punishment
(*Priestuplenije i nakazanie, Zbrodnia i kara*)

Krystyna Zachwatowicz (Poland)
Set & Costume Design

Crime and Punishment was Andrzej Wajda's third staging of Dostoevsky in collaboration with the designer Krystyna Zachwatowicz. It was a surgical dissection of the crime drama, played on a limited stage space. A kind of labyrinth was constructed with wood and glass walls, a maze of nooks and crannies—stuffy, cramped cubicles at the same time both intimate and devoid of privacy. In it an interior journey into the depths of the characters took place, penetrating the depths of man, revealing what is unclear, illogical, irrational. Spectators watched the fragmentary events from behind a wooden railing, through walls and dusty windows, often fragmentarily, only in reflection. As a result, they became the ones who spy, who must piece together all the scraps of physical evidence—and judge.

Hezbollah • Achille Lauro hijacked by Palestinian terrorists • British coal miner strike ends • Mikhail Gorbachev becomes Soviet leader • Reagan and Gorbachev meet • Greenpeace vessel bombed and sunk in Auckland harbour by French agents • 9,000 people killed in Mexico City earthquake • South Africa invades Angola • Riots and protests in South Africa townships against apartheid policies • US Food and Drug Administration approves blood test for AIDS • The first "dot com" domain name is registered • Microsoft releases first version of Windows • Peter McKinnon marries Patricia Fraser • UK starts screening blood donations for AIDS • British scientists discover hole in the earth's ozone layer • Various artists record "We Are The World" to raise money for famine relief • TWA Flight 847 hijacked by Hezbollah • Achille Lauro hijacked by Palestinian terrorists • British coal miner strike ends • Mikhail Gorbachev becomes Soviet leader • Reagan and Gorbachev meet • Greenpeace vessel bombed and sunk in Auckland harbour by French agents • 9,000 people killed in Mexico City earthquake • South Africa invades Angola • Riots and protests in South Africa townships against apartheid policies • US Food and Drug Administration approves blood test for AIDS • The first "dot com" domain name is registered • Microsoft releases first version of Windows • Peter McKinnon marries Patricia Fraser • UK starts screening blood donations

1985

The Mahabharata

Jean-Guy Lecat (France)
Set Design

Peter Brook tells us that "theatre is life in a more concentrated form.'

"The phrase perfectly illustrates our research work at the Théâtre des Bouffes du Nord since 1974. When we create a show, there is a human being at centre stage. ...Everything surrounding this actor must be in harmony, in proportion, and on a human scale, and contract between each being requires a real intimacy. In his creative process, Peter Brook chooses not to have a set, or rather only suggested sets. He thus leaves freedom to the actors to find the elements which will be their starting point and the foundation for the images that the audience members will have to build themselves with their imaginations. Emptiness in theatre stimulates the imagination.

"In 1983, in *The Mahabharata*, an actor lost in the vastness of the Himalayas instantly finds himself at the bottom of a lake. Lakeside, his enemies observe him, looking over a simple piece of plastic laid out by two other actors, representing the water's surface; no complex prop could compete with this freedom and lightness.

"At the Bouffes du Nord the walls are realistic and abstract at the same time. On tour my work was not only to adapt different spaces in the way that the word suggests, but to modify them from the inside through working and creative processes. What matters with a space is that it serves the needs of the story being told. Furthermore, it has to become a vital and glowing space in performance.

"But when we did *The Mahabharata*, what was important was the intimate relationship that had been built up over ten years with the real purpose of all the work we were doing with Peter Brook, leading to his internal understanding of what *The Mahabharata* needed."

(Jean-Guy Lecat, *One Show, One Audience, One Single Space*, 2007, OISTAT)

The Mahabharata On Tour:

BAM Majestic/Harvey Theatre, Brooklyn, New York

Boulbon Quarry, Avignon, France

Granite Quarry, Perth, Australia

Barcelona, Spain

Three Venetian Twins
(Trei gemeni venetieni)
Stefania Cenean (Romania)
Set & Costume Design

The play's multiple gags and comical situations naturally corresponded to its wealth of scenographic elements, which supported them in a suitably chromatic environment.

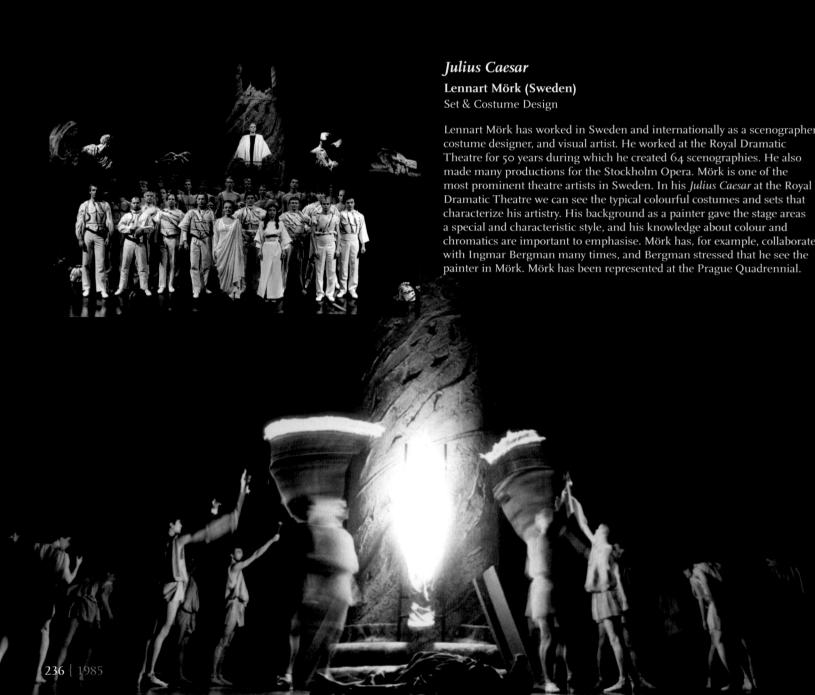

Julius Caesar
Lennart Mörk (Sweden)
Set & Costume Design

Lennart Mörk has worked in Sweden and internationally as a scenographer, costume designer, and visual artist. He worked at the Royal Dramatic Theatre for 50 years during which he created 64 scenographies. He also made many productions for the Stockholm Opera. Mörk is one of the most prominent theatre artists in Sweden. In his *Julius Caesar* at the Royal Dramatic Theatre we can see the typical colourful costumes and sets that characterize his artistry. His background as a painter gave the stage areas a special and characteristic style, and his knowledge about colour and chromatics are important to emphasise. Mörk has, for example, collaborated with Ingmar Bergman many times, and Bergman stressed that he see the painter in Mörk. Mörk has been represented at the Prague Quadrennial.

The Rake's Progress

Alejandro Luna & Lucile Donay (México)
Set, Costume & Lighting Design

Another production in the long and rich collaboration between Alejandro Luna and Ludwik Margules, the production was a major scandal for conventional opera audiences because of its contemporary design. A new breed of Mexican directors and designers arrived on the opera scene with this production.

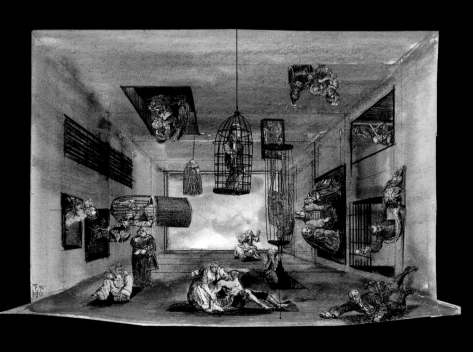

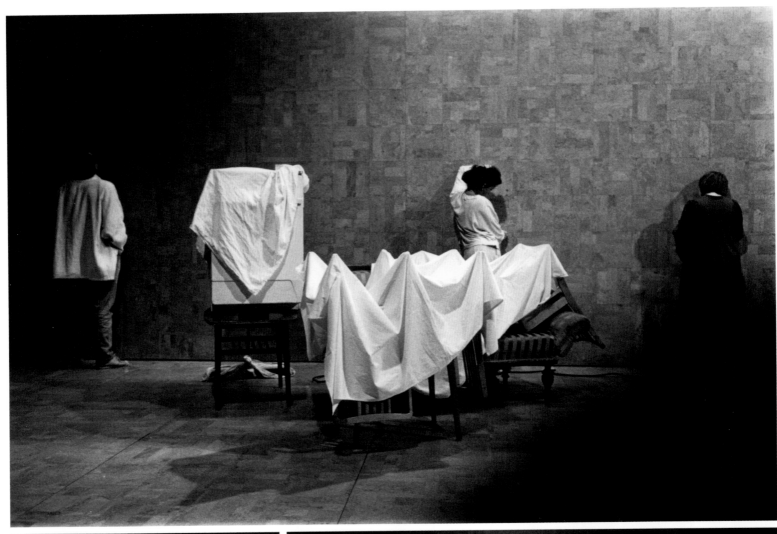

Tartuffe

**Måns Hedström, Riitta Riihonen &
Kimmo Viskari** (Finland)
Set and Costume Design

Måns Hedström (1943-2005) graduated as an
interior architect from the School of Industrial
Arts in 1968. He started designing for the
Helsinki Student Theatre, the experimental
theatre of its time, and became freelance
house designer of the KOM Theatre, founded
in 1969. He had a great influence on Finnish
modern scenographic thinking during
the 1960s and 1970s and taught future
generations of scenographers at the University
of Applied Arts. Hedström had a great interest
in minimalistic, inexpensive set design, which
is easy to construct, break down, and move
from one place to another.

Cerceau

Igor Popov (USSR/Russia)
Set Design

One of the central motifs of this production of *Cerceau* was the magic of a changing space. The house is the central locale and one of the key personages, which by the vision of the designer was erected right on the stage. The house was real, two-storied, made of wood, with a veranda, a banister, windows, and doors. As the performance unfolded, wooden planks were nailed on and torn off. The characters ran up the inside stairs, danced on the banister, performed a solemn ceremony on the veranda—all this within a few steps of the audience. Something was continually changing in the house and in the lives of the characters. Planked together tightly in the beginning, The House "set itself free" toward the end, and it turned out that behind its quite indecorous appearance was a late 19th-century manor, decorated in traditional period style. *Cerceau* played to packed audiences in Russia and was successfully presented at international theatre festivals in Rotterdam, London, and Stuttgart.

The Ring Cycle
(Der Ring des Nibelungen)

Robert Israel (USA)
Set & Costume Design

This production of The Ring Cycle was the first in the United States to fully embrace the experimental aesthetic that had become associated with European Wagnerian productions. In 1985 Seattle Opera produced *Die Walküre* as a trial approach to The Ring Cycle. Israel's contemporary visual aesthetic, in conjunction with Francois Rochaix's experimental staging, defied the traditional early 20th-century Wagnerian style that Americans had come to expect. The production stirred up great controversy among opera-goers and critics, who reacted in the extreme, both positively and negatively. The excitement generated by *Die Walküre* spurred the company on to stage the entire Ring Cycle in 1986, which was then revised and produced again in 1987. Scenographically, Israel chose to focus on the contradictions between artifice and illusion with an approach that evoked a juxtaposition of Brecht and surrealistic realism. Stylized Victorian Valkyries rode through the air on wooden carousel horses. Seigfried and the dragon battled among forests painted on canvas flats, which fell crashing to the ground. Rivers and then fire were created with stages full of undulating and swirling fabric. Eventually the fire evolved to become a full three minutes of stage-wide flame that burned 20 feet high, and was so hot that the heat could be felt in every seat in the theatre. This production brought international attention to Seattle Opera and laid the groundwork for its becoming a world-renowned opera company.

Lima Barreto

José Dias (Brazil)
Set Design

The production design for *Lima Barreto* received many awards in Rio de Janeiro because it translated, in a very simple way, the complex text by Lima Barreto. One of the first designs in Rio to effectively use minimalism, the set employed four elements that moved in different ways, opening up the space for many interpretations.

José Dias, a major Brazilian designers with 300 designs for theatre in his portfolio, is undoubtedly one of the greatest theatre figures in Rio. He has also been a television designer and a theatre architect. One of the few scenic artists in Brazil to hold a doctorate, he has headed/coordinated the department of scenography at UFRJ, Rio de Janeiro's federal university, for many years. He has received almost most of the artistic awards offered in Brazil, and he was part of PQ'79.

The Kalevala

Reija Hirvikoski (Finland)
Set & Costume Design

Reija Hirvikoski, a freelance set and costume designer who holds a doctor of arts from the University of Applied Arts 1984, wrote her dissertation on the role and position of the set designer. Hirvikoski is also the president of the Finnish OISTAT Centre and was the chair of the OISTAT Scenography Commission from 2009 to 2011. She was awarded the Jussi prize (the Finnish Academy Award) for her design of *Snow Queen* in 1987.

Since 1979 she designed more than 100 productions for leading Finnish theatres. Many of her designs have been world premieres. Her visual design for the dance theatre performance *The Kalevala* deconstructed the traditional imagery of this national masculine epic, creating instead a rich mixture of feminine and masculine metaphors using metal and aluminium together with bright colors. The scenographic objects told the story. It was an example of a new richness of empty space created with lighting design Claude Naville, resulting in a dreamlike rich inner mental landscape, poetic and at the same time active.

Lohengrin

Kenneth Rowell (Australia)
Set & Costume Design

Kenneth Rowell was one of Australia's most celebrated designers. He spent a large part of his career working in London, returning to live in Australia in 1982. He regularly designed for The Australian Opera and The Australian Ballet as well as Australia's regional opera and ballet companies. This production of *Lohengrin* is a superb example of his work as both set and costume designer, and was produced by the Victorian State Opera.

Grotesque *(Groteska)*

Petr Lébl (Czechoslovakia/
Czech Republic)
Set & Costume Design

It is difficult to express through
photography or costume design
alone the artistic importance of this
adaptation of an American novel in
then-communist Czechoslovakia.
The amateur theatre group Doprapo,
which became legendary because of
this performance, successfully created
the original vision of this director
and fine artist. It was a theatre of
surprising freedom of imagination
and original visual language, whose
great variety irritated some critics
and audience members. It was an
excellent beginning for the creative
career of Petr Lébl, one of the most
prominent Czech directors and
scenographers of the 1990s, an artist
who, although categorized as "post-
modern," goes well beyond this trend
in his individuality.

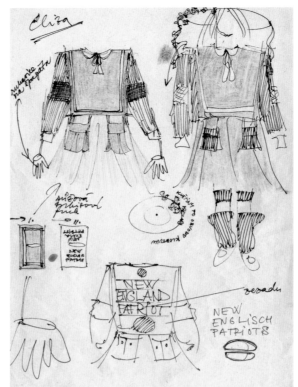
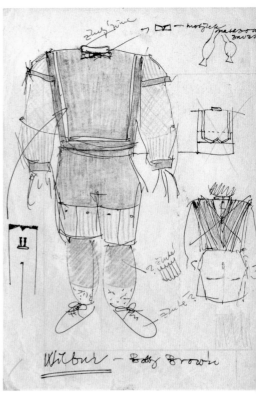

Les Miserables

John Napier (UK)
Set Design

Still playing in London and exported to almost
every country in the world, *Les Miserables*
owes some of its standing as the world's most
successful musical to John Napier's sets and
Andreane Neofitou's costumes. The show's
many scenes make full use of the stage revolve
as they flow into one another, but it is the
moment when the two jaws of the students'
barricade rise from either side of the stage
to join together that stays in the mind. Says
Napier: "My starting point was the play's
biggest moment, the barricade. Once that
was solved everything else fell into place. The
barricade could split, lift, and revolve, and was
a mass of *objets trouvés* which the actors picked
up from time to time and used."

Asinamali

Mannie Manim (South Africa)
Lighting Design

The photograph of this production vividly demonstrates how its presentation relied solely on the primary resources of the actors. Lighting design by Mannie Manim was unfussy and stark, emphasizing the presence and power of male bodies confined within an empty and enclosed space. The impact of the play (for South African audiences) depended on unleashing the energy of those bodies within the confines of a small intimate open stage, rather than adhering to the safe aesthetic distance provided by a proscenium arch theatre. Shaved heads and khaki prison uniforms were potent signifiers of prison identity, which became a metaphor for the status of the black South African male: emasculated and deprived of singularity as a subject and citizen.

Asinamali!—it takes its title from a Zulu slogan meaning "We have no money!"—toured internationally, including performances at the Lincoln Center South Africa Festival in 1986.

This production of *The Cherry Orchard* represents a particularly successful example of Boyce's lifelong passion for Chekhov's work and Russian culture. Swathes of crumpled brown paper covered the walls of Boyce's set. Here the design becomes integral to the storytelling with the brown paper being used in the final scene to wrap the family heirlooms as they prepare to move out of their family home. The work marks a significant approach in Boyce's work where the use of materials and design elements can produce powerfully charged moments of storytelling and poetry.

Designers that followed like Tony Rabbit and Dorita Hannah continued to push the material quality of their scenographic performances further, in ways inspired by Boyce's own treatment of materials and space in works like this.

The Cherry Orchard

Raymond Boyce (Great Britain/New Zealand)
Set Design

Everybody Wants to Live (*Kulam Rutzim Lich'yot*)

Ruth Dar (Israel)
Set & Costume Design

In this design, Ruth Dar managed to transform Hanoch Levin's grotesque creatures into potent relevant theatrical metaphors. This design welded the enormously fruitful collaboration of Dar and Levin, which became the hallmark of the Cameri Theatre through the 1980s. It was in the mid-1980s that many of the theatres in Israel shared a common vision of "encouraging theatrical involvement in current events and strengthening theatre's links with the community". (*World Encyclopedia of Contemporary Theatre*, Don Rubin ed.)

Matthew Honest (*Matěj Poctivý*)

Miroslav Melena (Czechoslovakia/Czech Republic)
Set & Costume Design

This empty setting left room for the extreme physical (almost acrobatic) action of the actors, and was connected through its function and aesthetic effect both to the poetics of the interwar avant-garde and to contemporary action scenography. Miroslav Melena's contribution to the humour and free playfulness of the performance was the fruit of a long collaboration with Studio Y and its artistic director, Jan Schmid. He also embraced the group's leanings toward improvisation.

Electra (Électre)

Yannis Kokkos (Greece/France)
Set & Costume Design

Yannis Kokkos, a French scenographer born in Athens, won the "Moliere du décorateur scénographe" award in 1987 for his design for *L'Échange* by Paul Claudel produced at Théâtre national de Chaillot. That same year his design for *Electra*, also produced at the Théâtre national de Chaillot, was featured in the French exhibition at PQ'87, where he was awarded the gold medal for scenography.

Les Liaisons Dangereuses

Bob Crowley (UK)
Set & Costume Design

"For the Royal Shakespeare Company production of *Les Liaisons Dangereuses*, the stage at the Music Box Theater has been remodeled into a sex-drenched boudoir of late 18th-century France. Signs of reckless carnal abandon are everywhere. Huge linen sheets, rumpled from hectic use, drape the proscenium and boxes. Lacy silk underthings tumble in messy profusion from the hastily slammed drawers of a towering chiffonnier. Tall slatted screens, the better for servants to peep through, cast distorted shadows. All that's missing is a proper regal bed. Instead, there's a constellation of settees and chaise lounges: this is an arena for men and women who copulate on the run. The setting, at once in period and nightmarishly abstracted in Bob Crowley's inspired design, does not belie the action." [Review by Frank Rich, *New York Times*, 1 May 1987]

Les Liaisons Dangereuses premiered at The Other Place in Stratford-upon-Avon on 24 September 1985. That production subsequently transferred to London where it was first presented in The Pit at the Barbican in January 1986 and then at the Ambassadors Theatre in the West End in October 1986. The Broadway production opened at the Music Box Theatre in April 1987.

The Mysteries
William Dudley (UK)
Set & Costume Design

This was one of the high points of a long collaboration between Bill Bryden and Bill Dudley, in which Tony Harrison's vernacular was matched by a visual language created from the everyday but transformed into the extraordinary in the National Theatre's Cottesloe space. Dudley, who designed both set and costumes, says, "I had to find an unpatronizing modern equivalent to the spiritual certainties of the medieval guild workers who acted and made the plays. Where, for instance, they used stonemason's techniques to raise God up for the creation, we used a fork lift truck; hurricane lamps and dustbin braziers became the firmament." Of the completion of the trilogy in 1985, he adds: "*Doomsday* today says nuclear destruction, and I wanted to give some of that feeling. Not corny mushroom clouds, but not old-fashioned hell-fire either—that would have been too warm and cheerful. I remembered an image from the National's early days: two blokes down in the drum of what was going to be the Olivier's revolve... They were welding amid a labyrinth of steelwork, and the light of their torches was eerie, satanic. We got this effect in the Final Judgment scene by using the cold white glow of carbon arcs. " Dudley's designs for *The Mysteries* won him one of his four Olivier awards.

The Princess of the Stars

Jerrard Smith (Canada)
Set & Costume Design

The Princess of the Stars by R. Murray Schafer marked my introduction to theatre design, and the success of the Qirst production in 1981 led to a continued collaboration with Schafer, including the 1983 production of *RA* at the Ontario Science Center and the 1985 remount of *The Princess of the Stars* at the Banff Centre. This collaboration has continued to the present day and has allowed me to develop a portfolio of designs for site-specific theatre.

As a result of working on *RA*, I met Robert Desrosiers and designed for Desrosiers Dance Theatre for two years leading up to the commission of *Blue Snake* by the National Ballet. I was asked to design sets and costumes for this work which went on to have a touring life and in addition, introduced me to the larger dance community where I had the pleasure of designing a number of works with various companies and choreographers.
— Jerrard Smith

RED GEL IN EYES

A RANDOM PATTERN OF HOLES TO
MINIMIZE WIND RESISTANCE

CANOEISTS WEAR BLACK HOODED
PONCHOS AND BLACK GLOVES

A.S.M. WITH
WALKIE-TALKIE

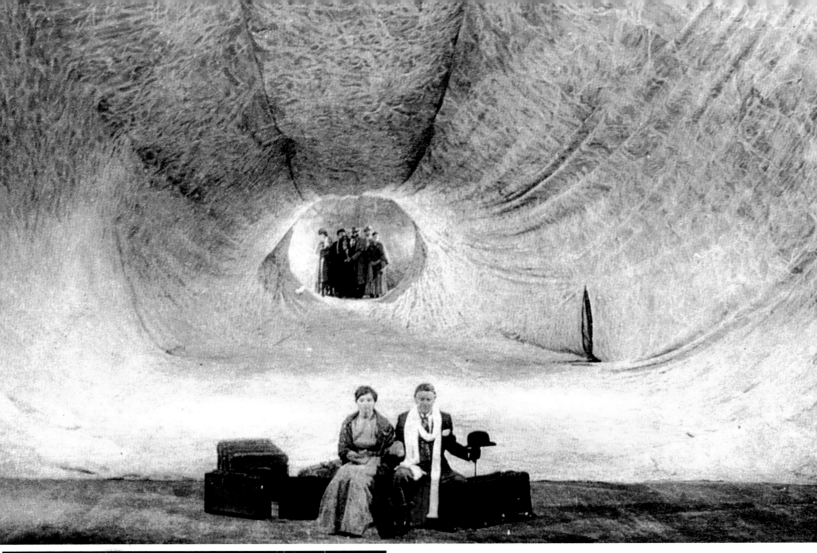

The Cherry Orchard
(Livada de visini)

Romulus Fenes (Romania)
Set & Costume Design

On the stage was an imagined "time-tunnel," through which the characters appeared and disappeared, the whole play having been given a new existential perspective throughout.

Confiteor *(Konfiteor)*

Miodrag Tabački (Yugoslavia/Serbia)
Set Design

For Slobodan Šnajder's production of Janez Pipan's play about the destiny of a Communist intellectual whose ideals are constantly clashing with reality, designer Miodrag Tabački created a set resembling the inside of a whale, a dinosaur, or maybe even a man. The play takes place within a great thoracic skeleton that is pierced with harpoons as the leading character's disappointments pile up. Distinguished theatre critic Jovan Hristić associates Tabački's work with Orwell's essay "Inside the Whale," while Jasen Boko, another well-known critic, sees in it a connection with Jonah from the Old Testament, or a man caught up in his own insides. The true value of this set, which Tabački realised for the National Theatre in Belgrade, lies in the multitude of associations that it gives to the spectator.

Xerxes

David Fielding (UK)
Set & Costume Design

This very successful and elegant production created a space that sliced the action into ordered sections, layering the Vauxhall Pleasure Garden of 18th-century England with ancient Persia in an architectural frame reminiscent of a museum, in which this juxtaposition finds a balance. Demonstrating a conceptual way of working that was also elegant and narrative, it made use of post-modern referencing without overwhelming the space. It has been critically acclaimed since its premiere at English National Opera, in 1985 and in subsequent revivals including ENO, Lyric Opera of Chicago, New York City Opera, and San Francisco Opera.

Tsar Maximilian *(Car Maksymilian)*

Rajmund Strzelecki (Poland)
Puppet Design

Son and disciple of the set designer Zenobiusz Strzelecki (with whom he collaborated on staging *Tsar Maximilian*), textile designer, graphic artist, painter, and illustrator Rajmund Strzelecki was considered the leading stage designer in Polish puppet theatre after World War II.

This set design, for the Puppet Theatre "Arlekin" in Lodz, was built of rough beams and hay. The tsar's simple throne was surrounded by cloth banners and candles, recalling the battlefield or a rural house rather than the palace of a ruler. The tsar figure was carelessly cut from a piece of cracked board, with a sliding hidden head between his arms, separated from the hunched figure with a fur beard. His ill-fitting red plush coat, shiny golden crown and a scepter drew attention by a collision of textures, different from the rough wood. Strzelecki's inspiration was both Polish folk art and the aesthetics of the Orient. He was the first who used in Poland previously unknown Indonesian *wayang* style; for other stage projects he constructed a puppet inspired by Mongolian-style lettering.

CAR MAKSYMILIAN

The Mother (Matka)

Jan Banucha (Poland)
Set & Costume Design

Jan Banucha's trademark was an ascetic simplicity, an aversion to showiness, but in his projects there was no shortage of surprising ideas and crazy experiments. He was at home with different styles and conventions, and his work on both classic and contemporary texts produced interesting results. A prime example is his set design for Stanislaw Ignacy Witkiewicz's *Mother*, for which he won many honors/awards.

The scene was an empty playing area with a black velvet floor and walls painted in a dirty blue color. A tin lampshade on a long string hung from the ceiling. Only a single chair on stage. Costumes, as recommended by the author, were black and white. Only the shawl that the mother was knitting shimmered with color. Rarely in the theatre is a prop as indispensable an element as this. The mother used her needlework as an umbilical cord that linked her to her son. Witkiewicz offers a dual incarnation of the essence of motherhood and blindness, aptly summarized in Banucha's cage-like space.

Libyan sponsorship of terrorist organizations • Breakthrough in US-USSR arms talks between Reagan and Gorbachev leads to commitment to disarm • Spain and Portugal join the EEC • Soviet Nuclear reactor at Chernobyl Explodes releasing radioactive material across much of Europe • Gorbachev steps up reform program in Russia introducing Perestroika and Glasnost • Comet Halley reaches the closest point to the earth during its second visit to the solar system in the 20th century • Bovine spongiform encephalopathy (BSE) commonly known as mad cow disease, first identified • The experimental airplane Voyager completed the first non-stop, around-the-world flight • A British newspaper reveals that Israel has secret nuclear weapons • Argentina Wins 1986 World Cup in Mexico • The United Kingdom and France announce plans to construct the Channel Tunnel • Space Shuttle Challenger explodes shortly after launch, killing all on board • The Soviet Union launches the Mir space station • IBM unveils the first laptop computer • Internet Mail Access Protocol defined for e-mail transfer • US bombs Libya in protest at Libyan sponsorship of terrorist organizations • Breakthrough in US-USSR arms talks between Reagan and Gorbachev leads to commitment to disarm • Spain and Portugal join the EEC • Soviet Nuclear reactor at Chernobyl Explodes releasing radioactive material across much of Europe • Gorbachev steps up reform program in Russia introducing Perestroika

1986

Titus Andronicus

Hu Miaosheng (China)
Set Design

The set featured a fixed platform with steps zigzagging down to the stage. Six square pillars 1.2 meters wide were combined with the platform and steps in different configurations to indicate different locations. The square cylinders were movable and were synchronized with the entrance and exits of the characters.

MATTI TRÄGT EINEN TISCH

Mr Puntila and His Man Matti
(Herr Puntila und sein Knecht Matti)

Nicos Kouroushis (Cyprus)
Set Design

Nicos Kouroushis is a visual artist who has had a very important influence on stage and costume design in Cyprus. Many of his designs have been innovative and memorable. This design used cheap materials—such as corrugated cardboard—in an aesthetically brilliant way.

Čaruga (Galócza)

László Székely (Hungary)
Set Design

Both designs by László Székely were made for the Katona József Theatre. The set designs for Kušan's *Čaruga*, which premiered in 1986, transgressed the usual boundaries of the applied arts, and could be seen as free-standing artworks. His colored tint-drawings, supplemented with tempera, are also notable as exhibits at the Prague Quadriennal.

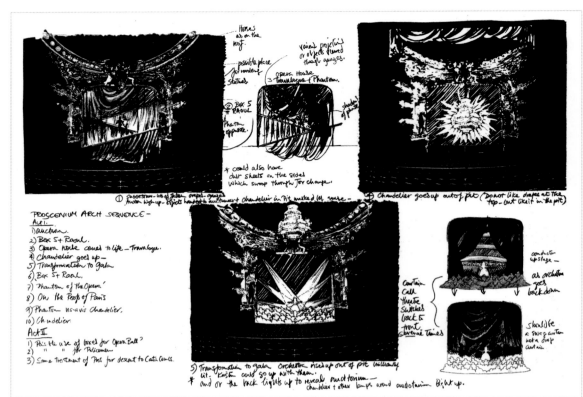

Phantom of the Opera

Maria Bjonson (France/UK)
Set & Costume Design

The huge and ongoing international success of *Phantom of the Opera* has made the name of the late Maria Björnson a household word in stage design. For it she designed about 180 lavish costumes as well as the breathtaking scenery. "I like to create a physical platform from which a show can be launched. In *Phantom*, the journey down and across the lake was the key scene and I worked more on this than on any other part of the show. At first I had the idea of using a hi-tech approach again, with a tilting floor and lots of chasing fibroptics … Then came the idea of candles, and the old machinery of Her Majesty's theatre was just right to present them rising up out of the stage."

The designs have won massive recognition, including the 1988 Tony and Drama Desk Awards for best costume design and best set design.

Shakespeare the Sadist
(Film und Frau)

Tihomir Milovac
(Yugoslavia/Croatia)
Set Design

Branko Brezovac is one of the most daring directors of Croatian alternative theatre, known for his emphasis on Russian and German avant-garde visionaries. This connection manifests itself in the creation of multiple, mobile, and changing acting platforms, which demand constant shifts of attention from the spectators and strenuous physical engagement from the actors. His *Shakespeare the Sadist* was one of the first to experiment with the use of film projections, by which the spectator would be confused and forced to establish dramaturgical connections by himself, while the actors would be compelled to fight for their stage presence against the overpowering imposition of canonical film images. Films by Godard, Dreyer, and others covered the entire front of the constructivist set in seemingly arbitrary juxtaposition to the trivial textual material, but in fact they were deliberately inserted to create an atmosphere of a broken humanist utopia. Tihomir Milovac is an art historian who started to work in the 1980s as a stage designer while a member of Brezovac's independent group, Coccolemocco. He went on to create designs for state-sponsored theatre institutions in Croatia in the 1990s, but also for Brezovec's later productions, with which he gained an international recognition.

Event in the City of Goga
(Dogodek v mestu gogi)

Meta Hočevar (Slovenia)
Set & Costume Design

Meta Hočevar's design for *Event in the City of Goga* won the award at the Festival Sterijevo Pozorje, Novi Sad, by the Association of Artists of Vojvodina for the best stage design in Yugoslavia.

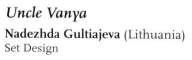

Uncle Vanya

Nadezhda Gultiajeva (Lithuania)
Set Design

This production of *Uncle Vanya* is illustrative of Eimuntas Nekrosius' distinctive treatment of space. In Gultiayeva's set, which incorporated pieces of furniture precisely as indicated in Chekhov's stage directions, the architecture of the big house, with its vertical pillars and horizontal cross-beams, and the distinctly Chekhovian motif of nature (represented by an easel with a forest landscape upstage) provided an eloquent pictorial milieu. Directional lights enabled the audience to see both the entire acting area and separate "shots" accentuating this or that aspect of an episode. Small props, like Yelena Andreyevna's bottles of scent, the samovar, and the bear skin, were used effectively. The designer's consideration for the textures of the materials used in the production and their explicit authenticity accounted for the acute sense of warmth of the space. The production became a major event and one of the most "evocative" stagings of *Uncle Vanya* in Soviet theatre.

Robert Lewis Stephenson's
The Strange Case of Dr. Jekyll & Mr. Hyde

Ladislav Vychodil (Czechoslovakia) & **Don Childs** (USA)
Set & Lighting Design

The design for *Robert Lewis Stephenson's The Strange Case of Dr. Jekyll & Mr. Hyde* at San Diego Rep called for no less than 14 locations and some 120 set changes. "Faced with such multiscene challenges, Vychodil tended to create a simultaneous set, in effect a version of montage in which a sense of interwoven destinies is graphically evident. ...In *Dr. Jekyll and Mr. Hyde*, primarily because of the relatively low height of the stage and the sheer number of locales, scenic units were shunted on and off the thrust stage: often they were also rotated onstage to create a shift of scene. Typical in this design is Vychodil's near signature of patterned lines or cords to integrate the elements of a set as well as to function as indications of walls or ceilings: here the lines are jagged and angular (and luminescent) to reflect the sustained anxieties embodied in the play." [from "Svoboda and Vychodil," Jarka M. Burian, *Theatre Crafts*, October 1987]

The Tempest

Vadim Fomitšev (Estonia)
Set Design

Director Evald Hearmaküla himself played Prospero in this Shakespearean revival. The production was seen as a rebirth of subtle theatre aesthetics and was praised for its dreamy atmosphere, in which the design played an important role. It approached the play and theatre with an open structure.

You Strike the Woman, You Strike the Rock
(WaThint'Abafazi, wathint'umbokotho)

Sarah Roberts (South Africa)
Set Design

The rallying cry of the 1956 march of 20,000 women to the Union Buildings in Pretoria in protest against the extension of the pass system to black women is taken up and repeated as the title of this work. Although clearly positioned within the tradition of minimalism, the play and production differed from both *Woza Albert!* and *Asinamali!* in that its the action was rooted in a more particular setting or location. The other two plays required the flexibility of a bare stage, which allowed a cinematic fluidity in terms of spatio-temporal shifts. The world of *Strike the Rock* is specific—it is the world of the migrant to the city, forced to inhabit a vacant street lot where recycling the remnants discarded by more affluent members of society ensured survival and triumph over brutal adversity. A large scrap of distressed and fraying black builders' plastic and a few props, the tools of the vendors' trades, comprised the setting.

The Merchant of Venice

Judit Schäffer (Hungary)
Costume Design

Judit Schäffer's costume designs offer a dazzling element into each production. Her precision and her choice of materials are outstanding, and the dramatic value of the costumes is extraordinary. Her drawings and costumes are preserved in national libraries and museum collections in Hungary. The designs can often be caricatures, but she is also successful in merging the techniques and properties of classical styles with contemporary fashion.

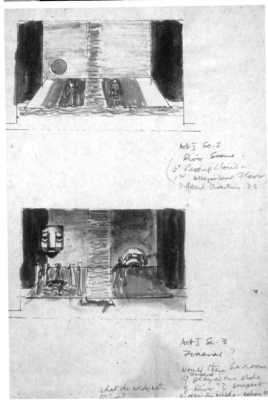

Act I Sc. 2
River Scene
2° Passing Cloud
1st Allegorical Flower
D'Agat Direction D.S

Act I Sc. 3
Funeral?
Would there be room
of super
of players one side
of River? suspect
pattern in middle echoes too

what do we do with
River?

The Mask of Orpheus

Jocelyn Herbert (UK)
Set & Costume Design

This design reflects Jocelyn Herbert's interest in the creation and use of masks—a key strand in her long career. Alan Strachan's obituary in *The Guardian* newspaper describes *The Mask of Orpheus,* her last work in opera, as her most innovative approach to this aspect of staging.

Working in collaboration with Harrison Birtwistle from the earliest stages of his musical composition, Herbert created a response that was by all accounts visually stunning—Strachan's obituary refers to the river of blue silk as one of its most effective moments. Herbert herself speaks of "a very complicated libretto involving singers, mimes, and puppets—and where the sun was almost a character, as the voice of Apollo."

Throughout Herbert's career, the simplicity of her designs focused attention on the actors and the writing. Where scenery and set pieces do appear, they are in themselves significant to the action. There was often no set, merely bare walls and floors. Sparse structures, visible rigging, gauzes, and shadows were used to create ambience rather than realistic effects. Peter Hall calls her one of the two designers that changed the course of British theatre design; the other was John Bury.

Isis

Sakina Mohamed Ali (Egypt)
Set & Costume Design

Isis is a play written by Tawfiq el-Hakim in 1955 about the goddess of Ancient Egyptian religious beliefs, whose worship spread throughout the Greco-Roman world. She was worshipped as the ideal mother and wife as well as the matron of nature and magic. Isis is the goddess of motherhood, magic, and fertility. In later myths, she had a brother, Osiris, who became her husband and with whom she conceived Horus. Isis was instrumental in the resurrection of Osiris when he was murdered by Seth. Her magical skills restored his body to life after she gathered the body parts that had been strewn about the earth by Seth. This myth became very important in later Egyptian religious beliefs.

Presented at the Egyptian National Theatre in 1986, *Isis* was directed by Karam Metawea, with set and costume design by Sakina Mohamed Ali. Sakina used a rich color palette, and alternated her designs between realistic and expressive styles. She had particular success in the costume for the character of the Pharaoh, with its simple elements and innovative expressive touches. The set featured a beautifully composed nest made of reeds and grass, which disappeared for a moment at the news of Osiris' death. Well-designed interiors were successfully used for the large number of scenes that showed different time and place, revealing both internal scenes (the courts of the warring kingdoms) and external ones (the rural markets).

A Doll's House

Kazue Hatano (Japan)
Set & Costume Design

This production of Ibsen's *A Doll's House* was excellent and beautifully done. The director effectively used the set to chart each character's psychological transition from the beginning to the catastrophic ending. The play opened with noise and sound in the dark and gradually revealed a stream of light touching on a long row of thin pillars that stood in a crescent curve.

Designer Kazue Hatano's well-designed set created a modern atmosphere, but helped a great deal in imagining and understanding the feudal society of 19th century Norway. This effectively simple oval-shaped set had a large raked rostrum featuring the row of iron pillars along the curved upstage edge painted a grey-purple. It featured two entrances, one leading downstage and a large double door on the center upstage. The lighting created a very stimulating, imaginative space for the play. When the thin pillars were illuminated, the set took on the look of a birdcage. Hatano's extensively researched period costume designs, with their unique sense of shape, material and color, were beautiful and elegant.

Andromache *(Andromaque)*

Mirjam Grote Gansey (Netherlands)
Set & Costume Design

The performance of *Andromaque* presented a perfect synthesis of decor, costumes, light, sound and *mise-en-scène*, the result of the tight collaboration between director Peter te Nuyl and scenographer Mirjam Grote Gansey, who have formed a creative duo for many years.

Grote Gansey designed an irregular set, placing three asymmetrical screens in succession on stage, each one holding a transparent gauze printed with an image from 17th century tapestry of knights in battle. Passages in the centre of these screens simulated perspective and suggested spaces and time. She established the imbalance and also the timelessness of the theme even further in her costumes. Andromaque's outfit was, for example, rather asymmetric and eclectic in style: ancient Greek, 17th century, with hints from the 19th and 20th centuries.

Mirjam Grote Gansey received the gold medal for best set designer at PQ '91 for her oeuvre, the aforementioned design being a part of this exhibition.

The Merry Wives of Windsor

Wang Peisen (China)
Set Design

Designer Wang Peisen was inspired by the similarities between Shakespeare and traditional Chinese opera in terms of coherence and the uninterrupted flow of action. The set featured two symmetric rotating platforms. Gothic architecture was represented by iron-painting and paper-cutting—popular folk art in China—to highlight Chinese style.

Alice in Wonderland

Anthony Ward (UK)
Set & Costume Design

Alice in Wonderland was staged as one of the Lyric Hammersmith's famous Christmas productions. It provided an early platform for Anthony Ward to express the witty approach to design that can be seen in his later large-scale national and international work, including his work in opera and afterward musical theatre such as *Chitty Chitty Bang Bang* and *My Fair Lady*, as well as his work for the Royal Shakespeare Company, in particular *A Midsummer Night's Dream*. The inclusion of this piece in the UK's PQ'87 entry created wider recognition for Ward's work at an early stage of his career. The exuberance of these designs was no less than that of his later works, despite the low budget available at the Lyric.

drop dramatically following US stock market crash • World population reaches five billion • First "naked-eye" supernova since 1604 is observed • Margaret Thatcher elected UK prime minister for third time • Nazi war criminal Klaus Barbie found guilty of crimes against humanity • US Food and Drug Administration approves anti-AIDS drug AZT • First criminal convicted using DNA evidence in England

1987

• Work on channel tunnel joining UK and France begins • 1987 is shortened by 1 second to adjust to the Gregorian calendar • Disposable contact lenses became available for commercial distribution • Prozac makes its debut in the United States • The Simpsons seen on TV for the first time • Stock markets around the world drop dramatically following US stock market crash • World population reaches five billion • First "naked-eye" supernova since 1604 is observed • Margaret Thatcher elected UK prime minister for third time • Nazi war criminal Klaus Barbie found guilty of crimes against humanity • US Food and Drug Administration approves anti-AIDS drug AZT • First criminal convicted using DNA evidence in England • Work on channel tunnel joining UK and France begins • 1987 is shortened by 1 second to adjust to the Gregorian calendar • Disposable contact lenses became available for commercial distribution • Prozac makes its debut in the United States • The Simpsons seen on TV for the first time • Stock markets around the world drop dramatically following

The Good Woman of Setzuan
(Der gute Mensch von Sezuan)

Yan Long (China)
Set & Costume Design

When *The Good Woman of Setzuan*, written by a German, was staged in China, it did not appear either to be like German versions or a traditionally oriented Chinese version, but was an unfamiliar, alien, fresh, and thought-provoking production, beyond the imagination of many in the audience. At the time, it was unique.

The Fall of Singapore

Nigel Triffitt (Australia)
Set & Costume Design

Commissioned and produced for the 1987 Melbourne Festival, this production is a powerful representation of the work of Nigel Triffit—one of Australia's most significant theatre artists, who has had a distinguished career as a designer/director of visual theatre. The production subsequently toured to Brisbane and Sydney. *The Fall of Singapore* touched on experiences of Australian prisoners of war during World War II.

Odysseus

Josef Svoboda (Czechoslovakia/ Czech Republic)
Set & Costume Design

In the performance of *Odysseus*, Svoboda and his team's artistic and technical expertise crystallized to great effect on the stage of the Laterna Magika, working with that theatre's multimedia principles (a combination of projection, live stage action, and music). Svoboda even collaborated on the text of the performance based on Homer's epic, whose literary pictures inspired the creation of an impressive scenographic creation. Apart from the scenographer, the production's cameraman and creator of film sequences and the choreographer of the live action, which sometimes bordered on acrobatics, also left their mark. Even though this project has the characteristics of a piece by Svoboda, this expressive visual element can be considered a collective effort. The model of the set was part of the collection for which Svoboda received the Gold Medal for Scenography at PQ'87.

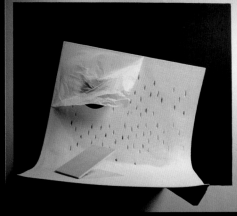

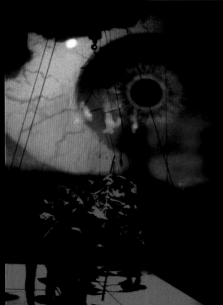

1987

Azuchi—Play With Music

Kappa Senoh (Japan)
Set Design

Kappa Senoh was born in Kobe, Japan, in 1930. As a boy, Senoh demonstrated a talent for drawing, and on leaving school a few years after the end of World War II, he worked as a graphic designer. When he was in his twenties, he became a stage designer. He has since been the set designer for numerous operas, theatre productions, and musicals and is recognized as one of Japan's leading designers, winning many awards for his work.

Love and Intrigue

Li Zhiliang (China)
Scenic Design

Not creating a realistic environment for the story to unfold gave this stage design and the production a space to develop. A cross made of aluminum plate set against a wall connected by plywood—two totally different materials and geometric images—together created the formal beauty of symbols and revealed the love tragedy.

The Cherry Orchard
(O jardim das cerejas)

José Manuel Castanheira (Portugal)
Set Design

One of the substantial ideas of this design was a redefinition of the classical scene, working with models taken from illusionist theatre and subverting them with unexpected openings, fragile boundaries, and above all a great deal of color. Red cherry wood enclosed an abstract saturated space, almost claustrophobic, with no direct link to a house interior, which was in stark contrast to the historical costumes. The rear wall of the set opened during the performance, initially as a crack and at the end completely, an empty abyss into which all the elements fall.

The text refers to several environments that are not part of the central action, a second level resolved in many productions through sound. This design used a second setting, seen through gateways coated with mirrors, which the audience was invited to perceive through an inverted image.

Like a huge closet, the house and its memories became a small stage within a stage, an empty space where the last character rested, a crystallization of the root-like textures seen in its wood panels.

During this time Yolanda Sonnabend made a considerable impact as both painter and scenic designer in close collaboration with Kenneth McMillan, among others. Part of a career that spans half a century, *Swan Lake* is one of the designs for which Sonnabend is best known. It exemplifies the ornate, painterly style that is characteristic of her work in ballet. The intention was to give the ballroom a glittering, jeweled, Fabergé quality which the costumes reflect. Sonnabend's expressive style has influenced emerging designers, particularly through her work as a teacher at the Slade School of Fine Art.

This version of *Swan Lake* continues to be re-staged by the Royal Ballet, and in 2007 it was the first of its productions to be shown as part of the BP Summer Big Screen events, broadcast live to audiences in Trafalgar Square and nine other locations across the UK.

Swan Lake *(Lebedínoye Ózero)*

Yolanda Sonnabend (South Africa/UK)
Set & Costume Design

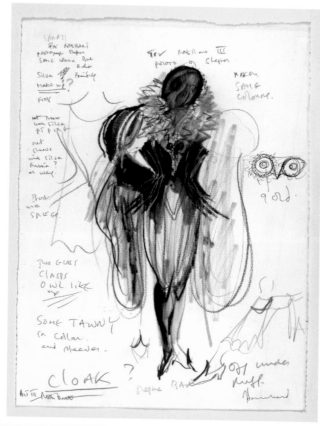

Waiting for Godot

Frank Haenig (Germany FRG)
Set & Costume Design

This was one of the first productions by
Frank Haenig at the state theatre in Dresden.

Together with director Wolfgang Engels he
looked for new ways to express the decadence
of the late GDR. This production was very
important for his national career, because it
was the first staging of a Beckett play in the
GDR in 35 years and was quite symbolic. He
and Engel did many productions together.

The production was especially important
for the Dresden theatre, because it received
much more attention than the theatre had
ever enjoyed. It became one of the first
productions to help initiate the enormous
social and political changes that brought
about the fall of the wall in November 1989.

Death and the King's Horseman

Eni Jones Umuko (Nigeria)
Set & Costume Design

For the designer, the director, and the Paul Robeson team, this was a groundbreaking production
project which tried successfully to transcend the demands of the University of Nigeria Arts
Theatre proscenium stage to accommodate Wole Soyinka's very demanding play whose scenes
shift very quickly from a country road, to and teeming market in the centre of the village, to the
colonial mansion to host a costume ball and then into a prison cell. The flexible design adopted
showed what was possible within the contstraints of a fixed stage to accommodate an African
world of spirits, ancestors gods and humans. For the team it was the culmination of many years
of experimentation.

Tristan and Isolde (Tristan und Isolde)

Annelies Corrodi (Switzerland)
Set & Costume Design

Annelies Corrodi is one of the world's leading projected scenography artists, the only Swiss working in the field. She specializes in opera, especially those of Richard Wagner.

It is very difficult to understand Annelies Corrodi's projection scenography only from pictures, because the scenography is a constantly changing 3D technique. To draw one of the main slides, which she does herself, takes about 30 to 35 hours. For one production about 80 to 120 slides, each measuring 18x18 cm, are used. Several projectors project a number of slides simultaneously to create an impressive atmosphere. Most of the time Corrodi uses a cyclorama to project on, which has positive effects on the acoustic, too. The projections can be adjusted in very small steps, so no pauses need to be made for scene changes.

Said Corrodi, "To work on stage projection means to design the space primarily with the use of light. By using the technical expedient of fading in and out the space is changing exactly in line with the music, i.e. as with the music, the time and variation factors assume enormous importance: Controlled developments and progression can be composed optically."

Corrodi's stage design for *Tristan and Isolde* was an expressive, painted lightcomposition for 12 Pani-projectors and a cyclorama. The scenery changed slowly, as if breathing, in exact relation to the musical score. The collaboration with director Lotfi Mansouri and lighting designer Michael Whitfield was highly inspiring and harmonic.

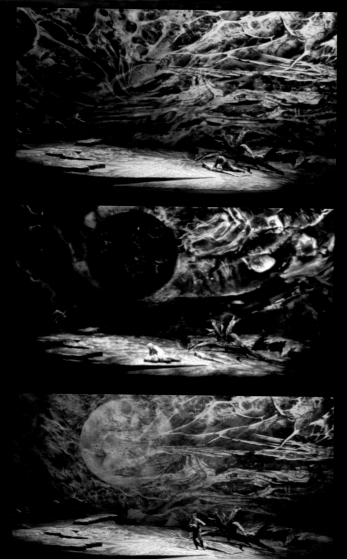

Nixon in China
Adrianne Lobel (USA)
Set Design

"Adrianne Lobel's set for the original [1987 Peter] Sellars production took its cue from Communist Chinese iconography. Reds, blues, and greens were bright and unmodulated, imparting the look and feel of old propananda literature from the Cultural Revolution. The arrival of the Nixon delegation in Act I, a coup du theatre worthy of *Aida*... featured an immense replica of Air Force One, the Presidential 747 from which Nixon, Pat and Kissinger descend to be greeted by a long line of identically clad Chinese officials." [Description by composer John Adams, earbox.com]

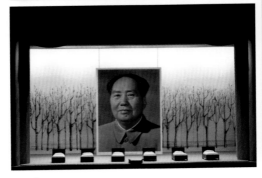

The Huguenots *(Les Huguenots)*

Gottfried Pilz (Austria/Germany)
Set & Costume Design

The Huguenots deals with the oppression of the
Protestant Church in France. In post-war Germany, the
opera had a clear association with the extermination of
the Jews by the Third Reich. This production in 1987
in West Berlin gave it a completely new meaning. The
designer compared the oppressive situation in the opera
with the Berlin Wall, which cut one city in two. His
set was mostly inspired by the song "Ein feste Burg ist
unser Gott" ("A Mighty Fortress is Our God") written
by Martin Luther and ironically quoted in the opera. To
create an sense of oppression and as a cynical contrast
to the song, Gottfried Pilz designed a set of closed
walls whose outer appearance was a reproduction of
deserted houses close to the Berlin Wall. This created an
atmosphere of menace and anger on stage such as could
be experienced in Berlin at that time. The final scene
played against a reproduction of part of the wall, with
the first line of the song written on it as graffiti.

The Hunger Artist

Robert Israel (USA)
Set & Costume Design

Robert Israel's theatre work reflects the influence of the intellectual, philosophical, and aesthetic environment around him at that time, distinguishing his designs as ones in which spatial images probe the tension between illusion and reality, rather than function as illustration or decor. Israel's work in Europe early in his career reinforced the aesthetic of the abstract, deconstructed metaphor, which he brought to the United States both as a designer and teacher of design.

Israel received the Obie Award in 1987 for his set and costume design for *The Hunger Artist*. The *New York Times* review describes the design: "With the aid of Paul Gallo's exquisitely ominous lighting and Robert Israel's striking set—an expansive graveyard of dark earth in the foreground, a pinched room out of Beckett in the rear—the director [Martha Clarke] does at times open a door on the murky psychological landscape where Kafka's anguished figures reside." [Frank Rich, *New York Times*, 27 February 1987]

City in the Water

Wang Ren (China)
Set & Costume Design

Wang adopted anti-logical and non-traditional scenery to carry the images of this absurdist play. Scenes were combined and constructed in a abstract space. Rather than concretely portraying the drama, it symbolized the philosophical and ideological implications of the drama *City in the Water*.

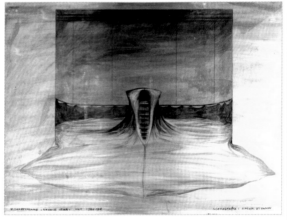

King Lear (Regele Lear)

Emilia Jivanov (Romania)
Set & Costume Design

On a dramatically illuminated background, in the middle of an almost bare stage, is the symbolic device of power, so difficult to gain and guard and so easy to lose.

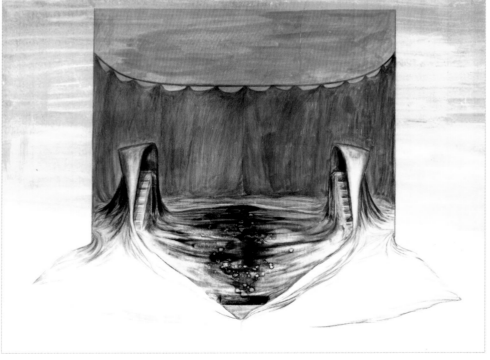

Alchemy of Sorrow (Алхимия на скръбта)

Marina Raytchinova (Bulgaria)
Costume Design

This was the first production Marina Raytchinova designed after graduating from the Academy of Arts, and it was staged by a group of young actors led by emerging avant-garde director Ivan Stanev. Many of the members of the group are now prominent theatre artists working in Sofia and abroad.

The script was put together during rehearsals. The designer was present at all rehearsals, and the costume design emerged and evolved during the rehearsal process, with the final sketches created as portraits of the characters. The design won the Union of Bulgarian Actors annual award for costume design in 1987.

The Magic Circle (*Noitaympyrä*)

**Måns Hedström
& Kimmo Viskari** (Finland)
Set & Costume Design

The Magic Circle is a stage adaptation of one
of author Pentti Haanpää's most popular
books that tells the story of a lumberjack and
the challenges of living in Finnish society.

Don Giovanni

George Tsypin (Kazakhstan/USA)
Set Design

Don Giovanni—reset in the violent, backstreets of New York's Spanish Harlem in the 1980s—was one of three Mozart operas produced at the Pepsico Summerfare and directed by Peter Sellars. The other two were *The Marriage of Figaro*, set in Trump Tower (1988), and *Cosi Fan Tutte*, set in an American diner (1986).

"...the action unfolds on George Tsypin's magnificent, brooding set of squalid urban buildings, apartments above a store, and an abandoned washeteria. Dunya Ramicova's costumes define an ethnic mix of characters who live on the fringe of society; the props are guns, knives, and needles." [Review by Richard Dyer, *Boston Globe*, 18 July 1987]

The Winter's Tale

Mary Moore (UK/Australia)
Set & Costume Design

This production is an example of the set and costume designs of Mary Moore. In her words, "*The Winter's Tale* is a play set in two worlds. This design contrasted a traditional old world of an imaginary mono-cultural Northern Europe—vertical, classical, and monochrome—with an an idealised imaginary new world of Australia—harmoniously multicultural, embraced by a rainbow, and bursting with colour."

The Dragon's Trilogy

Robert Lepage (Canada)
Design Collaboration

The original version *The Dragons' Trilogy* was first performed on 6 June 1987 at Hangar 9 of the Vieux-Port de Montréal as part of the Festival de théâtre des Amériques. In the beginning, there was nothing, or almost nothing: Six actors (including the director who had brought them together), two set designers, and a producer, all looking for the road to the Orient. A vacant lot turned into a parking space, where imagination and memory would have to start working. *The Dragons' Trilogy* gained Robert Lepage an international reputation, quickly followed by *Vinci* (1986), *Polygraph* (1987), and *Tectonic Plates* (1988).

Into the Woods

Tony Straiges (USA)
Set Design

The characters in Stephen Sondheim's musical, *Into the Woods*, "...travel into a dark, enchanted wilderness to discover who they are and how they might grow up and overcome the eternal, terrifying plight of being alone. ...The designer, Tony Straiges, transports us from a mock-proscenium set redolent of 19th-century picturebook illustration into a thick, asymetrical, Sendakesque woods whose Rorschach patterns, eerily lighted by Richard Nelson, keep shifting to reveal hidden spirits and demons." [Review by Frank Rich, *New York Times*, 6 November 1987]

Straiges was nominated for the 1988 Tony and Drama Desk Awards for his scenic design for *Into the Woods*.

Montedemo

João Brites (Portugal)
Set Design

This was an advance for João Brites in his quest for subversive and telluric aspects of folk traditions—this time in the open spaces of a woods. Based on a short story by Hélia Correia with the same title, *Montedemo*—a word that can be translated as "devil's mountain"—tells of a young woman who becomes pregnant during the festivities that take place in a small fishing village, linked to Carnival and the ancient rites of fertility. The discovery that the baby is black enrages the population, and she is accused of witchcraft.

Several wagons, various agricultural tools and other props were dispersed in the fields, and the spectators were invited to move around, each with a lantern to light the way, allowing for different paces and rhythms. The props were real wooden or iron everyday objects. Combined with costumes in rags, heavy makeup and masks, the production, a moving vindication of feminist values as much as a critical view of religious prejudice, created an enchanting atmosphere.

Sarafina!

Sarah Roberts (South Africa)
Set Design

Perhaps more than any other South African playwright, composer and director Mbongeni Ngema has made the ensemble the defining feature of his work. Here, a fictional class at Morris Isaacson High School is constructed around the figure of Sarafina, who herself represents the spirit of resistance leadership. In a complete break with conventional norms, *Sarafina!* was rehearsed, designed, and performed without the "script" being reduced to writing. Lighting cues and additional calls were made from a cue sheet rather than an entire prompt book. It was only on arrival at Lincoln Centre, New York that the absence of such a document was "remedied" with an individual appointed to generate a written document, so that the stage management team had an orthodox means of interfacing with the production.

Solo vocalists and dance leaders emerged from within the group without any particular significance (or status) being attached to their role. What appears to be a homogenous group, however, is consistently revealed as heterogeneous. The monochrome black, white and grey school uniforms worn by the Morris Isaacson pupils operate in direct antithesis to a neutral mask. They draw attention to the face and the distinctive features of each individual. The use of uniforms thus becomes a potent, if ironic, intervention.

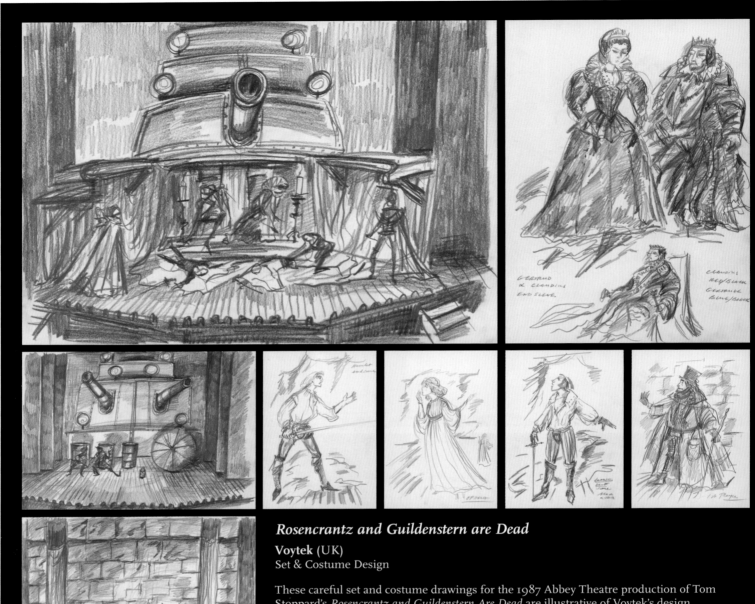

Rosencrantz and Guildenstern are Dead

Voytek (UK)
Set & Costume Design

These careful set and costume drawings for the 1987 Abbey Theatre production of Tom Stoppard's *Rosencrantz and Guildenstern Are Dead* are illustrative of Voytek's design aesthetic, and part of a great body of work that he produced around the UK and Ireland, where he worked as a designer for more than 30 years in theatre and musicals as well as film, a testament to his influence and importance.

He was given the 1983 Critics Circle Best Designer Award for *Great and Small*, the West End production of a play by Botho Strauss.

Triumph in the Midnight

Dai Yannian (China)
Set Design

Using non-realistic techniques, Dai designed a constant, neutral, and multi-meaning ladder-like structure on the stage. He abandoned a realistic description of the environment, and instead emphasized the expressiveness and generalization of the formal structure. He tried to fire the audience's imagination about the plot and setting by playing with the space-time elements and the development of the action in an effort to make the performance an uninterrupted stream of consciousness and to provide a free, broad, and symbolic space for the actors.

Cirque Réinventé

André Caron (Canada)
Set Design

Cirque du Soleil, a Quebec-based company producing a "dramatic mix of circus arts and street entertainment," has grown from a local troupe performing a single show for hundreds in 1984 to an international producer of some 20 productions seen by millions around the globe. Among the features that hallmark the work of Cirque du Soleil are the rich, unique, and imaginative set, costume, lighting, and sound designs.

"The entrance of the characters, through the cloud of red smoke, evoking a red curtain, was a strong emotional moment." —Arthur Hoffmester, chief editor of *De Piste* Magazine, in describing *Cirque Réinventé*.

The Indiade or India of Their Dreams
(*L'Indiade ou l'Inde de leurs rêves*)

Guy-Claude François (France)
Set Design

'The spatial metaphor is one that allows the message to be transmitted. I hate those sets and space which are made redundant when the message is there already. Design should be a support, a base for what is going to be told, played. I always forbid myself to make something 'beautiful.' What is right is beautiful." (Interview with Guy-Claude François, Construire pour le temps d'un regard, ... *Editions Fage*, 2009).

A true base, the naked space of the *Indiade* makes one think of Copeau's bare stage, an association acknowledged by Mnouchkine in her search for an ideal theatre (an impossible search, of course). The space depicts the immensity of pre-partition India. The marble of the palaces at the central crossroads and the brick oof the suburbs for the base and the outer zones make the metaphor of this land that structures its society into different castes.

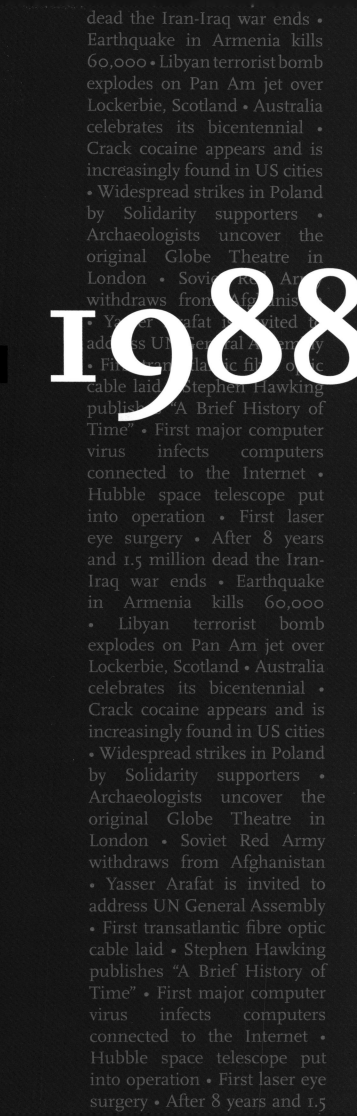

dead the Iran-Iraq war ends • Earthquake in Armenia kills 60,000 • Libyan terrorist bomb explodes on Pan Am jet over Lockerbie, Scotland • Australia celebrates its bicentennial • Crack cocaine appears and is increasingly found in US cities • Widespread strikes in Poland by Solidarity supporters • Archaeologists uncover the original Globe Theatre in London • Soviet Red Army withdraws from Afghanistan • Yasser Arafat is invited to address UN General Assembly • First transatlantic fibre optic cable laid • Stephen Hawking publishes "A Brief History of Time" • First major computer virus infects computers connected to the Internet • Hubble space telescope put into operation • First laser eye surgery • After 8 years and 1.5 million dead the Iran-Iraq war ends • Earthquake in Armenia kills 60,000 • Libyan terrorist bomb explodes on Pan Am jet over Lockerbie, Scotland • Australia celebrates its bicentennial • Crack cocaine appears and is increasingly found in US cities • Widespread strikes in Poland by Solidarity supporters • Archaeologists uncover the original Globe Theatre in London • Soviet Red Army withdraws from Afghanistan • Yasser Arafat is invited to address UN General Assembly • First transatlantic fibre optic cable laid • Stephen Hawking publishes "A Brief History of Time" • First major computer virus infects computers connected to the Internet • Hubble space telescope put into operation • First laser eye surgery • After 8 years and 1.5

1988

Tiger Amulet

Ma Weili (China)
Set Design

Scenic images of *Tiger Amulet* adopted variations of pre-Ch'in bronzeware pattern design as well as the color and textures of silk painting to create the atmosphere and environment. A heavy curtain, tailor-made according to Singapore theatre style, was also used. Instead of a neutral stage curtain, the curtains were painted with intensive patterns, broadening the space, creating a striking visual effect, and enhancing the play's momentum. Major attention was paid to help express the hero's "sacrifice for justice."

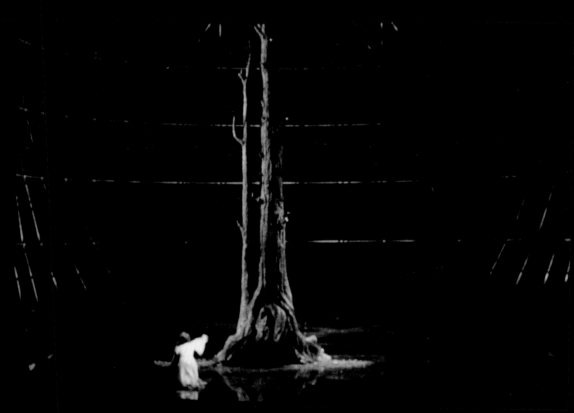

Tannhauser

Yukio Horio (Japan)
Set Design

Most of Yukio Horio's set designs for opera create symbolic and dynamic spaces for the directors and singers to work in. His drawing skill are very good, the results of his studies at the Musashino Art University. This composition of the space for the opera by Richard Wagner was exceptionally successful.

Germania Death in Berlin
(Germania Tod in Berlin)

Johannes Schütz (Germany FRG)
Set Design

The design and the production had a long-lasting effect on the Bochum theatre. It was performed for the first time in 1988, one year before the fall of the wall. East German playwright Heiner Mueller began writing the play in the 1950s, completing it in 1971. It deals with the history of the early GDR, from its foundation in 1949 through the upheavals in 1953. For citizens in West Germany, East German history was very remote, but this production provided them with a closer view. The production was very popular and was performed after the fall of the wall in November 1989. The interest of West Germans in East German life and history evidently rose. A set featuring Stalin and the hammer and sickle and a play about a country that no longer existed was a peculiar thing. In early 1989, this production was chosen by the Soviet Theatre Association to be shown in Moscow. The impression of images of Stalin coming from capitalist West Germany in an East German play must have been rather spectacular; the Russians apparently were very enthusiastic about it.

1000 Airplanes on the Roof:
A Science Fiction Music Drama

Jerome Sirlin (USA)
Set & Projection Design

The creators (Glass, Hwang, and Sirlin) consider this piece to have bee "co-authored," elevating the standards of collaboration and positioning the designer as the creative equal to the playwright and composer.

The photographic montage technique that Sirlin used to create projections for this production maximized the available technology— essentially photography, slides, and slide projection, achieving a fluidity and integral presence that moved this piece beyond the existing realm of multi-media production. By all accounts, the effect was stunning, creating a completely amorphous environment that

changed in an instant from one imaginal place to another, foreshadowing the visual complexity of digital imaging and projection used in today's theatrical designs.

Sirlin's remarkable "holographic" projection technique, in which he created complexly layered photographic images that were projected onto a sculptural set, was used as the primary scenic element and was technically and artistically well beyond anything most had seen. Sirlin is one of a handful of set designers who paved the way for theatre artists whom we now call projection designers.

The premiere took place in the Vienna Airport Hangar #3, and was site specific in that the single character in the piece, "M," is ostensibly abducted by extraterrestrials and transported from New York City to other realities. "M's" telling of the story explores the meaning of our existence in time and space, physically and mentally. Whether the experience is itself real or a disintegration of "M's" psychological state is an ambiguity that is created through the seamless and ever-changing landscapes of Sirlin's projections.

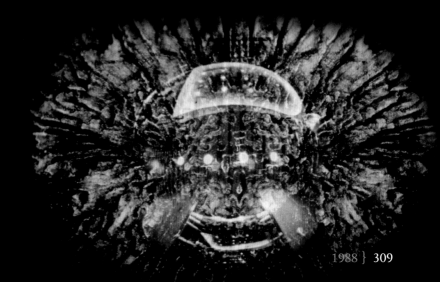

Romeo and Juliet

Marta Roszkopfová (Czechlslovakia/Czech Republic)
Set & Costume Design
The scenography for this performance was based on an
abstract stage design and an exaggerated decorativeness
in the costumes and accessories. The contrast of these
elements reflects not only contemporary scenographic
practice, but also shows the distinctive expressive voice
of the designer, who in her drawings presented the
characters in costume as if already in a dramatic situation.

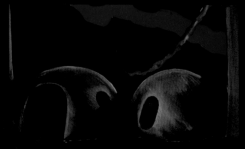

Too Clever By Half

Richard Hudson (Kenya/UK)
Set & Costume Design

Too Clever by Half, although directed by Richard Jones, was staged as part of Jonathan Millar's first season as artistic director of the Old Vic. Having never worked with Millar previously, Richard Hudson was employed to design all eight productions, firmly helping to establish his career. Referring to this period of work, Goodwin describes Hudson as "the new architect of gravitational riot" identifying unexpected angles and an absent ceiling as two methods employed by Hudson to manipulate space. It was carried out as part of an ongoing collaboration between Hudson and Jones. The design was part of a season which heralded a new period for the Old Vic under Jonathan Millar's directorship and contributed towards Hudson's emergence as a practitioner of international standing.

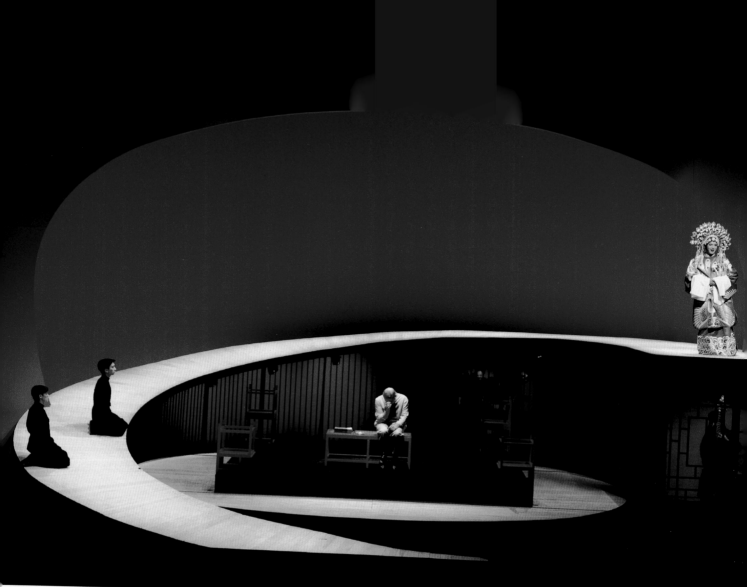

M. Butterfly

Eiko Ishioka (Japan)
Set & Costume Design

"Using Eiko Ishioka's towering, blood-red Oriental [abstract set], the director stirs together Mr. Hwang's dramatic modes and settings until one floats to a purely theatrical imaginative space suspended in time and place." [Review by Frank Rich, *New York Times*, 21 March 1988]

Nominated for Tony Award for the stage and costume design of the Broadway play *M. Butterfly*, Eiko Ishioka graduated from the Tokyo National University of Fine Arts and Music. Her work is included in the permanent collection of museums throughout the world, including the Museum of Modern Art in New York. In 1992 she was selected to be a member of the New York Art Directors Club Hall of Fame.

Francisco Maniago

Salvador Bernal (Philippines)
Set & Costume Design

"Bernal's most radical experimentation with the Little Theatre proscenium stage was his set for Tanghalang Pilipino's *Francisco Maniago*. Working on [director Felix] Padilla's suggestion of the hourglass as metaphor of history, Bernal created three huge sandboxes on different levels, which recalled the shapes of the ancient timepiece. The largest and lowest sandbox, filled with real gray sand, fanned out over the theatre apron and thrust out into the auditorium, covering about five rows of seats, which has to be compensated by tiered bleachers on the stage itself. The three sand boxes were surrounded on stage by rows of upright coconut trees from Laguna, which simultaneously alluded to the impermeable walls of the naos of Spain and evoked the tropical landscape of Pampanga. These openings, as well as the long ramps which cut into the house on either side of the sandbox-thrust, provided actors with entrances from anywhere on the stage and in the house in a full 360-degree circle. That thrust-stage-cum-bleachers effectively bridged the gap between audience and actors and allowed the historical play to 'spill over to the audience's lap.' Bernal's stage design for *Maniago* constituted a landmark in Philippine stage design. He was awarded the National Artist of Philippines on Theatre Design since 2010."

— *Salvador F. Bernal: Designing the Stage* by Nicanor G. Tiongson

The Dream of Akutagawa

Roh Matsushita (Japan)
Set Design

Roh Matsushita's paintings have been influenced by the social realism painters in the former Soviet Union. The resulting designs have had a powerful impact in Japanese theatre. His choice of colours is reflective of order of colours of power.

The Kingdom of Desire

Ching-Ru Lin (Taiwan)
Costume Design

Adapted from both *Macbeth* and the film *Throne of Blood*, *Kingdom of Desire* was a fusion of east and west. The whole scenography was conceived to evoke an historical past while also appealing to a contemporary audience's taste. There was much less reliance on traditional highly stylized makeup, and the costumes tended to be more realistic than was the custom. And in a marked departure from the norm, the normally flat lighting was replaced with a gloomy, starkly shadowed lighting that contributed to the ambience of each scene. The production was revived in 1990.

The Dybbuk *(Der Dybuk)*

Andrzej Wajda & Krystyna Zachwatowicz (Poland)
Production Design

In the dynamic between Andrzej Wajda and his designer Krystyna Zachwatowicz, the landscape of Szymon An-ski's *Dybbuk* was one of death, graves, and abandoned cemeteries. The principal set was the interior of a synagogue, with some basic furniture and a colorful stained glass with a Star of David in the background. Behind it laid one of the many Jewish cemeteries in Poland, a reminder of the nation that once lived here. Tulle mesh was stretched over the proscenium.

Using interesting concept drawnings by Wajda, Zachwatowicz created a magical mood drawn from Jewish beliefs, giving the people and settings a place among the living dead. The scene in the synagogue in Act I resembled an image in the books of Joseph Messer, and the preparation for the wedding in Act II was a quote from an iconographic oil painting by Maurice Gottlieb, "A Jewish Wedding."

In 1989, Zachwatowicz's designs for this production won an award at the 15th Opole Theatre Confrontations.

Electra (*Ηλέκτρα*)

Giorgos Ziakas (Greece)
Set & Costume Design

This design for *Electra* by Giogos Ziakas, presented at the 1989 Epidaurus Festival, proved to be a milestone, and had an extremely significant influence on other Greek theatre artists.

Nothing Sacred

Mary Kerr (Canada)
Set & Costume Design

The set was from the mind of Bazarov, who spoke of blowing things up and creating a new world. Mary Kerr realigned the squared opening of the proscenium with a deconstructed false proscenium that forced the pine floorboards to flow in an undulating, lava-like manner from upstage to downstage in forced perspective and over the edge of the stage into the auditorium. There were little flat levels built in — not obvious to audience but clear to actors — where furniture and other objects were placed. Doorways held by the asymmetrical forced perspective of the canvas walls, with the four doors in each wall decreasing in size from 16 feet downstage to 5 feet upstage.

The show began downstage in a graphic wooden forest with a proscenium curtain of birch trees. The trees were made of four types of unpainted layered wood. For interior scenes, the small back wall with an unframed door flew in to complete the box set. For exteriors it flew out to reveal the cyclorama beyond, while cutouts of pine trees from 3 feet to 16 feet flew in that were influenced by folk art and Bilibin's illustrations of Russian folk tales. The costumes were period outlines but simplified, and their colors related to emotional/character states.

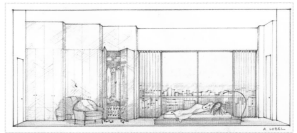

The Marriage of Figaro *(Le Nozze di Figaro)*

Adrianne Lobel (USA)
Set Design

In his 1988 production of *The Marriage Figaro* for the PepsiCo Summerfare, director Peter Sellars wanted to remind his audience that it's not just popular art that deals in provocative themes. He set this satire of an arrogant upper class and a scheming lower class on the 52nd floor of Manhattan's Trump Tower.

"...The action [was set] in a fantasy Trump Tower, which looks small-scaled and tacky in Adrianne Lobel's settings for the first two acts, but opens up in grand (if still properly vulgar) fashion in the third. The fourth act takes place on an outdoor terrace...and is as dark and muddled as it usually is." [Review by John Rockwell, *New York Times*, 15 July 1988]

The stage production was subsequently videotaped in Vienna for broadcast in various countries, including PBS Great Performances in the US.

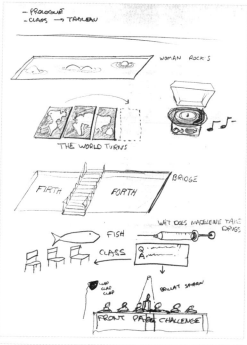

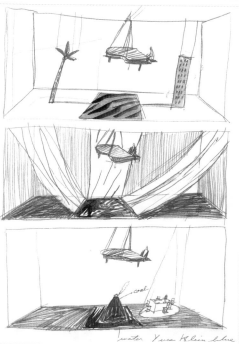

Tectonic Plates

Michael Levine (Canada)
Set, Costume & Lighting Design

This production marked the first collaboration between Michael Levine and Robert Lepage. It also was one of Lepage's first forays into the English Canadian theatre scene. Levine joined the production after its run in Quebec City. The upper sketch, by Lepage, is for the Quebec production, while the lower sketch, by Levine, is for Toronto. It subsequently toured Britain.

The du Maurier theatre stage was converted into a pool of water in which the action took place, while an orchestra was suspended overhead. The du Maurier had undergone extensive renovations from its previous life as an ice storage facility. This was one of the first shows produced after the renovations were complete, and it was an extraordinary original use of an alternative space.

Metropolis

Ralph Koltai (Germany/UK)
Set & Costume Design

One of Ralph Koltai's most renowned designs, it illustrates the importance of found objects to his work. In accordance with his oft-quoted aim, to "recognize the accident when it happens," the starting point for *Metropolis* occurred when he found an old car gearbox. While Koltai himself maintains that his design style does not lend itself to the West End, being not naturalistic enough, this musical proved his versatility and cemented his popularity. According to the show's book writer Dusty Hughes, when the company appeared on the set for the first time it was like a group of wild children let loose in Disneyland, climbing all over the moving lifts and through the honeycombed steel towers. The work also illustrates a design approach that emerges from an abstract concept to make a strong visual statement, while applying his trademark use of industrial engineering elements in the set design. Koltai has been frequently honored at PQ, with this design part of the British exhibit that won the Golden Triga at PQ'91.

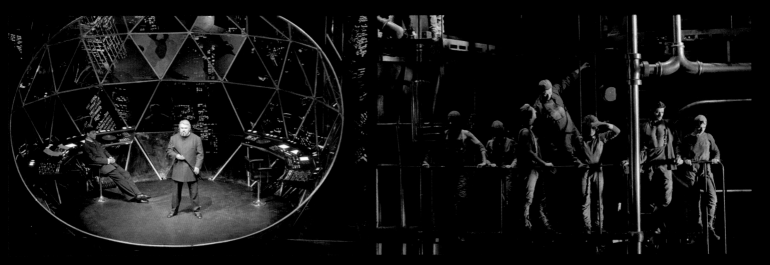

In the Land of Spirits

Mary Kerr (Canada)
Set & Costume Design

This production is considered the first "official" aboriginal ballet in Canada. It was a mix of the legend of Winona and the Great Spirit and the more contemporary theme of recovery from addiction. The design challenge was to create images that would bridge to a non-aboriginal audience and still be true in spirit to the first nation's audience.

The stage worlds moved from the shabby reserve, where the old stories were ridiculed by young people leaving for the city to the mysterious space where Winona was captured by the evil spirit, represented by a sensational wall of silk fabric swirled onto the full height of the stage, enwrapping Winona and swirling her off stage.

The stage had a huge birch bark wheel of life hanging against the cyc, with abstract clouds floating in space as well as ground rows of landscape. The stage was in constant motion. Four seasons of trees turned to leather teepees, representing the tribes of the four directions in painted leather costumes. The hero's journey to healing moved from the beginning of time. In the mysterious land of spirits Kerr referenced Eskimo art: fantastic non-human white masks with six legs and arms to bone masks with bamboo. A black and metallic silver thunderbird set piece with wings that opened to fill the entire stage of the opera and blazing lasers in his eyes came down and ended the battle in favorr of the young man who then realized the power of the Great Spirit was in all of us.

The great thunderbird on the huge cyc behind him was realized by positioning a 'winged' dancer upstage of the cyc doing the same dance. The huge dancing silhouette gave the impression that the young man was transformed into a human thunderbird with spiritual wings. It was a breathtaking ending.

The Lake Boy

Elena Lutsenko (USSR/Russia)
Set & Puppet Design

The Lake Boy, staged by Valery Volkhovsky and designed by Yelena Lutsenko, exemplified the so-called "third genre" (i.e. when a performance is created at the junction of dramatic and puppet theatres). It convincingly proved that there is nothing wrong with a puppet theatre trying to stage a large-scale and genuine tragedy. The production was enormously popular with audiences. In 1988, it received the Grand Prix and the Public Choice Award at the Puppet Theatre Festival in Moscow. That same year it took the Grand Prix at "Golden Dolphin" Puppet Theatre Festival in Varna. In 1989 it won the Grand Prix at the International Festival in Pecs, Hungary, and the Public Choice Prize at the Festival in Neuchatel, Switzerland. The production toured extensively throughout Europe, and few spectators left the theatre with dry eyes.

Hura Tau
Iriti Hoto (Tahiti)
Costume Design

Iriti Hoto, director of the Heikura Nui company, began his training in the troupe of Madeleine Moura, a leading figure in the reanimation of Tahitian dance culture. Moura campaigned to lift the taboos on traditional Tahitian dance that were preventing the maintenance of distinctive traditions and discouraging the development of new performance ideas. This prize-winning Hura Tau dance narrative owes its existence to individuals such as Moura and her commitment to the preservation of Tahitian dance forms.

This particular performance, which extends and modifies traditional ideas, won first prize for its integration of costumes into the dance narrative and for its musicianship and choreography. A young boy is symbolically filled with knowledge, and one of the dancers from the corps de ballet traces the movements of a tortoise, representative of the shadow of the gods and the strength and sovereignty of Tahiti.

Kafka's Trilogy (Trilogia Kafka)
Daniela Thomas (Brazil)
Set Design

Kafka's Trilogy involved three works by Kafka adapted for one show. The design is one of Daniela Thomas' most striking, and remains one of most important theatre designs of the second half of the 20th century. She received many awards for it, including the Moliere, the most important honor in Brazilian theatre.

The space featured a huge library, imprisoning the words of Kafka in a mausoleum of words. The design imagined a play set against a wall of thousands of old books, making is a "tomb of reason" for the absurd world of Kafka.

Thomas was part of the Brazilian delegation PQ'95 when the country received the Golden Triga. Among the designers in that same delegation were also JC Serroni and José de Anchieta. She had previously taken part in the PQ'7 when Brazil received an honorable mention.

Vast

Andrew Carter (Australia)
Set Design

In 1988 Graeme Murphy was commissioned by the Australian Bicentennial Authority to create *Vast*, the National Bicentennial Dance Event. Involving 70 dancers from four dance companies—Australian Dance Theatre, West Australian Ballet, the Queensland Ballet, and Sydney Dance Company—the production premiered at the Palais Theatre, Melbourne, on 4 March 1988 before touring nationally to Adelaide, Perth, Brisbane, and Sydney.

Tristan and Isolde

Hans Dieter Schaal (Germany)
Set Design

This production design was metaphorical, with a marked psychological dimension, rather decorative. The moon was a symbol for romance. Structures reminiscent of a stream suggested a more or less forced and aimless wandering. Finally, when the moon descends and destroys the stream, the wandering ends. Hans Dieter Schaal constructs very concrete-looking set architecture. In their interpretations, however, they are astonishingly non-concrete and can be viewed in many ways. He also renounces color for the set, reducing it to white. Structure and color come to life through light and shadow. The elements that can be identified are highly symbolic and can be understood universally. What was remarkable about this production was the "East-West" combination of the creative team, crossing what was then the "Iron Curtain." Direction, costume, and dramaturgy were from the "East," while the set and the opera house were "West."

Inferno and Paradise
(Inferno und Paradies)

Martin Rupprecht (Germany FGR)
Set Design

In this spectacular show on the Wannsee, a lake near Berlin, the design was the motor for the open-air performance. At that time, open-air shows of this dimension were not yet very common in Germany, and this show served as a model for many others to follow. This production marked an important step in the careers of the designer and director. Rupprecht had always been very diversified in his work, which ranged from opera and ballet to experimental theatre and other events. Director Winfried Bauernfeind had been working as an assistant director at the Deutsche Oper Berlin. This project was a new direction in his career. For both Rupprecht and Bauernfeind the large-scale production of *Inferno and Paradise* became a big reference in their careers.

Indessen wir den toten Sumpf dunk fuhren war einer ganz voll schlamm zu mir geraten und sprach / Wer bist du der zu früh gekommen, und ich zu Ihm: ich komme nicht zu bleiben. Doch wer bist du der sich so abschätig machte? Er gab zur Antwort: sicher wie...

Lulu
Gerardo Vera (Spain)
Set & Costume Design

An industrial set, with elevators going up and going down, contrasts with the elegant attire of the actors.

Celestina (La Celestina)
Carlos Cytrynowski (Spain)
Set & Costume Design

In the set's circular space, concentric circles made reference to the orchestra of the Greek theatre and provided the setting for this production of the seminal late medieval text. The sinuous form of the exterior circle allowed for the different comings and goings so important for the text. The illumination with warm colours evoked Castile in late summer.

The Three Musketeers

Tony Geddes (New Zealand)
Set Design

This production represents the innovative approach that Geddes used to transform The Court Theatre, and exemplifies the quality of works that he produced over this period. It resolved the problems of presenting a large-scale production in the shallow space of The Court Theatre, where there is no fly tower. *The Three Musketeers* has a significant amount of movement between locations, so Geddes' set resolved many of these issues with a large revolving center stage. The act of walking between the cities of Paris and London was evoked through the use of this revolve. The production was a big success for The Court Theatre. While the script appears to have little consequence to NZ culture or the antipodean context, this production of *The Three Musketeers* had some relevance. NZ was for a time a contested territory with France, and Akaroa (near Christchurch) was established in 1840 with the intent of claiming South Island for the French. Geddes' design for this production involved overt heraldic imagery and references to the "mappa mundi" of 18th- and 19th century colonial conquest. The large revolve became a compass on the map, and it extended over several levels of the stage, becoming a map of the heavens on its topmost plane. This gave the production some significance to the Christchurch audience, especially since it was produced only three years after the French bombing of Greenpeace's anti-nuclear protest vessel "The Rainbow Warrior" in Auckland Harbor.

Away

Joe Hayes (New Zealand)
Lighting Design

The Court Theatre has been Christchurch's premier theatre company and production house since 1971. Joe Hayes' body of work here demonstrates his ability to transform space and extend spatial horizons with lighting design. His designs rendered this very small venue in a number of diverse ways that kept the space in flux, expanding and contracting with each new production, so that the architectural limitations became blurred. This kept the audience's imagination alive for season after season, ensuring (in collaboration with set and direction) that audiences never entered the same space.

1989

Pro democracy protesters clash with Chinese security forces • Tokyo stock market crash ends long period of Japanese economic growth • Violence in South African black townships worsen • New South Africa prime minister de Klerk starts to dismantle apartheid • Free elections in Poland bring Solidarity to power • Protesters in Prague call for the resignation of communist government in the "Velvet Revolution" • Hundreds of demonstrators killed during Tiananmen Square protests • George Bush becomes president of the United States • Exxon Valdez spills 240,000 barrels of oil after running aground • Cold War between East and West ends and the Berlin Wall comes down • Civil War in Lebanon increases between Christian and Islamic fundamentalists • Nintendo begins selling the Game Boy • Pro democracy protesters clash with Chinese security forces • Tokyo stock market crash ends long period of Japanese economic growth • Violence in South African black townships worsen • New South Africa prime minister de Klerk starts to dismantle apartheid • Free elections in Poland bring Solidarity to power • Protesters in Prague call for the resignation of communist government in the "Velvet Revolution" • Hundreds of demonstrators killed during Tiananmen Square protests • George Bush becomes president of the United States • Exxon Valdez spills 240,000 barrels of oil after running aground • Cold War between East and West ends and the Berlin Wall comes down •

Uncle Vanya *(Unchiul Vania)*

Stefania Cenean (Romania)
Set & Costume Design

This impressionistic design worked as
pictorial draft, featuring the interior and
exterior of a house, where the few pieces
of furniture were surrounded by a typically
Russian background of green and white
birch wood.

Fly toward the New Century

Sun Tianwei (China)
Set & Lighting Design

The design concept for musical drama should start with the form and style of the
stage. The theme and content should be created via subjective imagination. Such an
idea and techniques were employed here to highlight a series of visual symbols and
make the most of them via exaggeration, romanticizing, and construction so as to
achieve a new form and style on stage, and consequently a unique art effect.

Moth

Zhou Benyi (China)
Set Design

Moth reflected the fate of the
heroine Er (literally, "Moth")
in Chinese culture, which
was like a moth flying toward
a flame.

The Hamlet Machine
(Die Hamletmaschine)
Gottfried Pilz (Austria/Germany)
Set & Costume Design

Heiner Mueller's *Hamletmachine* is an adaptation of Hamlet's story set in post-war Germany. Composer Wolfgang Rihm found that the play could very well be transformed into an opera, because it was not a "closed" play and had an interesting rhythm. Gottfried Pilz designed the stage as a kind of parable of the author's life. The first part shows the world in ruins: instead of buildings, ruined human beings were shown in a fateful tangle. The second part included a breathtaking scene where a barbed wire wall is moved threateningly on to the stage. Later, tourists are seen viewing this monstrosity out of pure curiosity. In the end, the opera shows a kind of utopia, imagining the world after a peaceful revolution. Symbolically, Pilz wanted to open the wall. At first, he hesitated, because he was superstitious and thought that it would be a bad omen, but finally he made the design, and six months later the wall came down. After 1990, the final scene was always shown with a completely opened wall, and the production continued to be very successful.

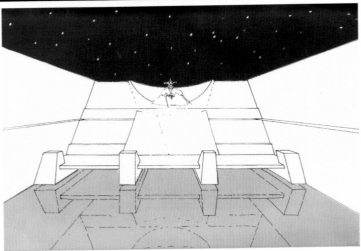
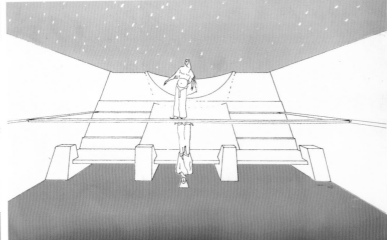

Scheherezade (Šeherezada)

Marko Japelj (Slovenia)
Set Design

This production was a major breakthrough for Marko Japelj as a designer as well as for Tomaž Pandur as a theatre director. The design promoted Japelj as one of the most influential younger set designers in the former Yugoslavia. The design enabled the choreographer to find an adequate dance space and allowed the director to fulfill his post-dramatic approach to textual and other components of the performance. Japelj's design was very important for the new identity of Mladinsko theatre's aesthetics in the 1980s. It was a strong accent of a new theatrical aesthetics. In a way it changed the idea of the Eastern European theatrical design.

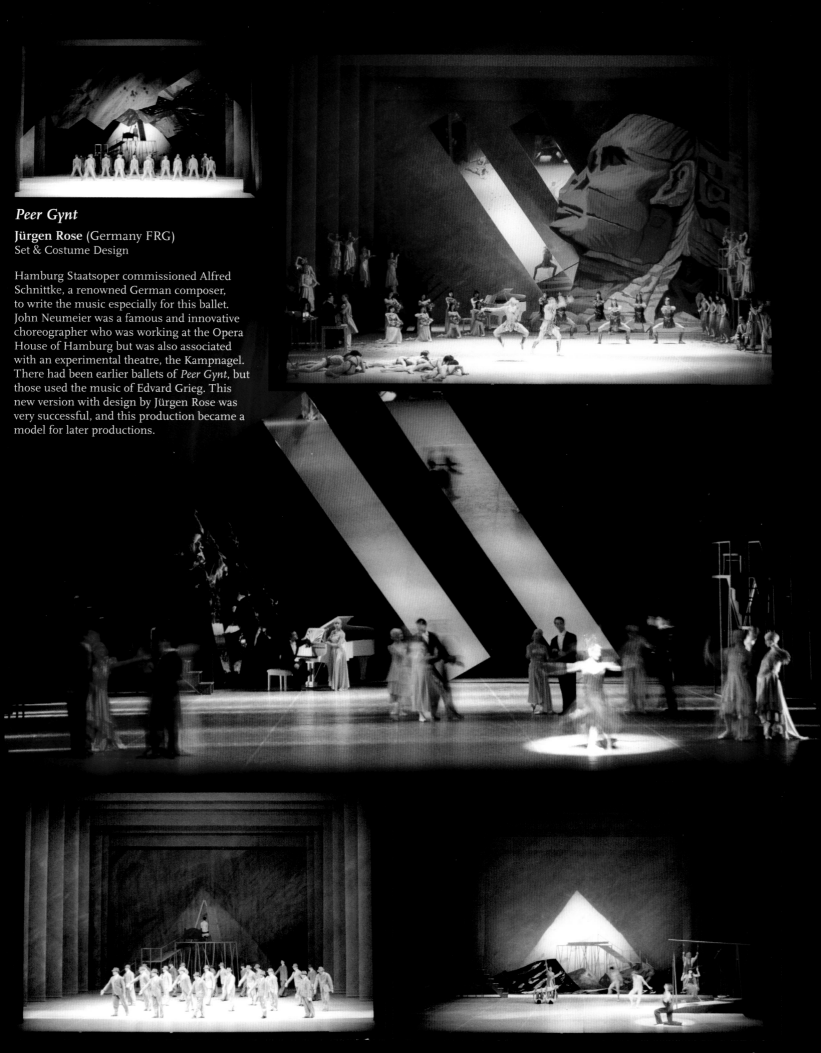

Peer Gynt

Jürgen Rose (Germany FRG)
Set & Costume Design

Hamburg Staatsoper commissioned Alfred
Schnittke, a renowned German composer,
to write the music especially for this ballet.
John Neumeier was a famous and innovative
choreographer who was working at the Opera
House of Hamburg but was also associated
with an experimental theatre, the Kampnagel.
There had been earlier ballets of *Peer Gynt*, but
those used the music of Edvard Grieg. This
new version with design by Jürgen Rose was
very successful, and this production became a
model for later productions.

The Jump Over the Shadow
(Der Sprung über den Schatten)
Gottfried Pilz (Austria/Germany)
Set & Costume Design

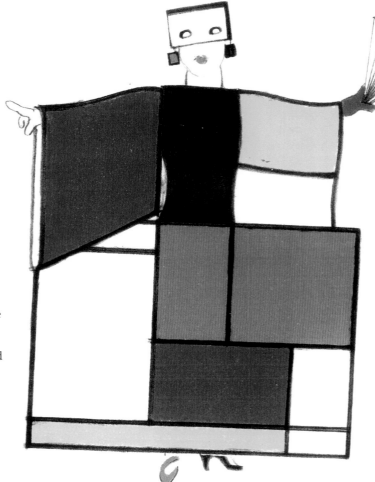

Between 1975 and 1998 under intendant Heiner Bruns and dramaturg Alexander Gruber, the Bielefeld Opera became internationally renowned as the "Bielefelder Opernwunder," producing a series of successful remountings and premiere performances, notably of forgotten or suppressed work of the 1920s. John Dew was the stage director, Gottfried Pilz the stage designer. This production was of an operetta by Ernst Krenek, who went into exile in the United States in 1938. It concerns a solution for a bourgeois society where everything finally remains as it is. Citizens try to "jump over the shadow" (i.e. do what had been oppressed before) by way of a telepathic healer. Behind the irony, there is a bitter and serious picture of prewar Europe. Pilz created a space that referenced modern music and experimented mainly with lighting. The space was abstract, inhabited by actors that were part of the set. A telephone also played an important role and was shown on stage. The production succeeded in conveying the ambiguous atmosphere of the 1920s, when society hovered between joy and depression. Pilz created a symbiosis of the art and music of that time, referring also to cubism and futurist design.

Yourcenar or Your Own Marguerite (Yourcenar o Cada quien su Marguerite)
Carlos Trejo (Mexico)
Set & Lighting Design

Yourcenar, o Cada Quien su Marguerite is a "sacred divertimento" based on French writer Marguerite Yourcenar's text *Qui n'a pas son Minotaure*, adapted and directed by Mexican theatre and performance artist Jesusa Rodríguez. Inspired by the Greek myth of Theseus, Ariadne, and the Minotaur, the play is a philosophical reflection on the desires, repressions, dreams, and sufferings of contemporary men and women. The triangle Ariadne-Theseus-Phaedra brings to the forefront dramatic conflicts rooted in a series of dualities: sensual/spiritual, constructive/destructive, idealist/pragmatic, male/female, to attack/to wait. The performance—full of poetic images, choreographic gestures, and mythic symbolism—renders the Minotaur a metaphor of these conflicts: each one of us confronts our own inner Minotaur.

The Enemies
(Los enemigos)

Tolita Figueroa (México)
Set & Costume Design

The Enemies was a polemic production on Mexican theatre. It was based on the play by Sergio Magaña (from 1970) and which implied another performance: the Mayan representation of "Rabinal Achí." But its esthetics and design were passed through the eyes of the European explorer who first wrote about the traditional Maya ceremony. It was also the reunion of a then young creative team (director and set designer) under the guidance of main design figure Alejandro Luna. Tolita Figueroa has since been a very successful costume designer, and has been honoured both in Mexico and abroad.

Quartet

Giorgos Patsas (Greece)
Set & Costume Design

Visual elements play a serious, important role for this theatre troupe. Caught in two rectangular rhombi, the protagonists bicker, exchange roles, and slowly die. The performance is based on the physicality of the two actors.

Lend Me a Tenor

William Ivey Long (USA)
Costume Design

"With its speedy gait, gleaming lighting (by Paul Gallo) and wildly luxurious Art Deco sets and costumes (by Tony Walton and by William Ivey Long), the play looks so much like a prime example of its genre..." [*New York Times*, Frank Rich, 3 March 1989]

"What helps the proceedings—not immeasurably, but measurably—is Jerry Zak's fleet-footed and sure-handed direction, and the smoothest, creamiest set by Tony Walton and (ditto) lighting by Paul Gallo, against which William Ivey Long's costumes are delirious rockets of color." [*New York Magazine*, John Simon, 13 March 1989]

Upon graduation from Yale in 1975, Long moved to New York City. A friend of his from Yale, Karen Schulz, who was the set designer for a Broadway revival of Nikolai Gogol's *The Inspector General*, suggested that Long be hired to do costume designs for the show. This marked Long's first Broadway production; he has since designed more than 50 Broadway shows.

Long won the 1989 Drama Desk Award for outstanding costume design and a Tony nomination for his costumes for *Lend Me a Tenor*. He has been nominated for 11 Tony Awards, winning five (for *Nine, Crazy for You, The Producers, Hairspray,* and *Grey Gardens*). He has also won the Drama Desk Award for outstanding costume design for *Hairspray, The Producers, Guys and Dolls, Lend Me a Tenor,* and *Nine*.

Much Ado About Nothing
(ΠολύΚακόγιατοΤίποτα)

Stefanos Athienitis (Cyprus)
Set & Costume Design

Stefanos Athienitis is a leading figure in Cypriot stage and costume design, and has made an enormous contribution to theatre, television, and cinema. The costume design shown here was significant for its use of modern materials, such as denim, on historical costumes, creating an interesting combination of the old and the new, applied with a large helping of humour.

From the Street (De la calle)

Gabriel Pascal (Mexico)
Set & Lighting Design

This powerful set design by Gabriel Pascal and the well-known images created by director Julio Castillo turned a drama about abandoned children who live in Mexico City's streets into a universal story. This production was honored by all critics associations and was so significant that the venue changed its name to Teatro Julio Castillo after his death a few years later.

From the Street was a very significant production in Mexican theatre. The creative teams and the esthetics developed at the University of Mexico theatres took over the main official venues in the country and reached wider audiences. At the same time, it opened the way to the reunion of Mexican directors and authors who had been separated by their ideals during the 1960s and 1970s. It led to an impressive list of stage productions by directors and designers who were finally able to connect with a national heritage and characters.

Grand Hotel

Santo Loquasto, Tony Walton & Jules Fisher (USA)
Set, Costume & Lighting Design

The 1989 Broadway musical *Grand Hotel* was adapted from the 1932 film that focused on events taking place over the course of a weekend in an elegant Berlin hotel.

"The musical ... [is] dedicated to creating the tumultuous atmosphere of the setting: an opulent way station at a distant crossroads of history in Berlin—that of 1928. Think of a three-dimensional collage...filled with the smoky light, faded gilt fixtures, dirty secrets, lost mementos and ghostly people of its time and place.

"Tony Walton's stunning set, in which an orchestra occupies the lofty second tier, is but a deep, dilapidated shell in which dreamy abstract imagery (strings of pearls floating inside transparent structural pillars) stands in for a literal hotel floor plan. Santo Loquasto's costumes and Jules Fisher's lighting—equally brilliant evocations of Expressionism—don't try to wow the audience with Technicolor eruptions but instead hold to a dark crimson-to-sepia palette that suggests the vanished luxury pictured on frayed antique postcards and the fever dreams of a world on the brink of Depression and war." [Review by Frank Rich, *New York Times*, 13 November 1989]

Loquasto and Fisher won the 1990 Tony and Drama Desk Awards for outstanding costume and lighting design for their work on the production.

Tevye Tevel

Daniil Lider (Ukraine)
Set Design

This production was Daniil Lider's last and probably most philosophic work for theatre, blending two fundamental elements of human existence: the microcosm of the protagonist and the macrocosm of the universe. The small private world was expressed in the clay milk-jug, neatly covered with a clean white cloth, which stood in the middle of the huge open space of the stage, the very center of this "earth" of human beings. Lit by vertical light from "heaven," it carried a very strong symbolic meaning. Stretching above it was the infinite cosmos of the Milky Way. The stars descended in an arc from stage left to stage right, continued by candles that became progressively smaller along the same axis, the smallest one barely smoldering. The same candles in the hands of the characters lit their earthly travels. The open space in this production was of paramount importance for Lider. As he noted, he needed the "colossal emptiness" to rise above daily routine.

Void *(Vacío)*

Jesusa Rodríguez (Mexico)
Set Design

This production was the creative summit of the Sombras Blancas group under the direction of Julio Castillo. Later on, the actresses involved would continue to work with Jesusa Rodriguez on important productions like *Don Giovanni* and *Yourcenar*.

Based on the life and writing of American poet Sylvia Plath, the production featured a collection of poetical and dramatic images. It opened the door to highly visual theatre in Mexico. It was honored locally, toured internationally, and was filmed by artist R. W. Fassbinder.

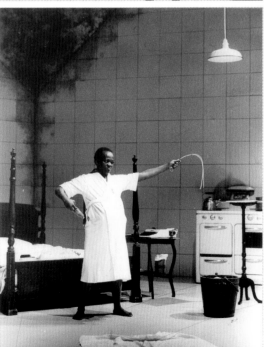

Open Weave

Mary Moore (UK/Australia)
Set & Costume Design

This production is an example of Mary Moore's work as a designer for contemporary dance. In her words: "*Open Weave* was a formalist experiment in creating a kinetic design out of a technology common to all proscenium theatres: the counterweight flying system. I created a second visible counterweight system with 16 chrome bars that were 'flown' to create patterns that enhanced the choreography and produced a performing space in perpetual motion."

Prayer for the Dead
(Pominalnaya Molitva)

Oleg Sheintsis (Russia)
Set Design

The stage of the Lenkom theatre was fenced off with pictures of the old Jewish quarter, a long-gone world. There the snow was falling gently on the lop-sided dome of the small synagogue and the stunted trees, where a white horse stood throughout the performance. A board was knocked off the fence to become a platform-table. The white figures of Tevye's daughters appeared in the resulting opening, a white bird soaring above them. The bride and the groom walked the platform, showered ritualistically by paper petals, and at that moment blue flowers bloomed miraculously on the branches of the trees. In the closing scene, objects from the broken lives of the expelled Jews were thrown onto the platform-table.

In 1992, *Prayer for the Dead* was awarded the State Prize of the Russian Federation. It is still playing at the Lenkom Theatre.

Our Country's Good

Tony Tripp (Australia)
Set & Costume Design

Tony Tripp was resident designer at the Melbourne Theatre Company for many years. During that time, he developed a particularly rich creative partnership with the artistic director, Roger Hodgman. The play is based on the Thomas Kenneally novel *The Playmaker*, the story of the first play produced in Australia, *The Recruiting Officer*, staged not long after the first fleet had arrived in Australia. The production was highly regarded and was an eloquent example of their collaborative work. It played on alternate nights in repertoire with a production of *The Recruiting Officer*, also directed by Hodgman and designed by Tripp.

KITE
The Recruiting Officer

Tripp 89

ROBERT SIDEWAY

The Recruiting Officer

CAPTAIN PHILLIP

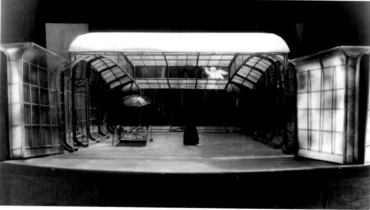

North Side Paradise (Paraíso Zona Norte)

JC Serroni (Brazil)
Set Design

During the 1980s, director Antunes Filho chose to work with a simple stage, always presenting his work in a black box, searching for theatricality in the actors, costumes, and stage props. In *Paraíso Zona Norte* by Nelson Rodrigues—considered Brazil's greatest playright—Antunes sought for an extremely expressive collaboration in the scenography. He began a partnership with designer J.C. Serroni, and together they created one of the most important moments of the Brazilian theatre in the last decade. The show ran for five years, opening in Sao Paulo and touring the major Brazilian cities and South America. With the collaboration of Max Keller, one of the most important lighting designers in the world, the space designed for *Paraíso Zona Norte* always a referenced Brazilian scenography.

The design for *Paraíso Zona Norte* emphasized the weight of the structures and the circumscription of the characters. A scrim trimmed by decorative elements that referenced an indistinct past revealed a static metallic grid with a longitudinal cut made of a neon column. It was an oppressive environment, forcing the actors move as if they were commanded, their wills annihilated.

The production won many honors, and the show's model was exhibited at PQ'91, which, due to a strike in Air France, wasn't set up in time for the jury evaluation.

Threepenny Opera

Mary Kerr (Canada)
Set & Costume Design

This is the third in a series of 12 natural-wood lathe set explorations. The design was a deliberate departure from the standard Berliner Ensemble approach to Brechtian design and created a brazen abstracted industrial image of a decaying city collapsing in on itself. The machine gun rhythm of Kurt Weill's score and Brecht's hammer-stroke lyrics find visual counterparts in the repeated patterning of tilting wood lathe walls and industrial materials spiraling and deconstructing inwards, with backlighting creating a parallel rhythm to the score. A disjointed broken circle intersected by an extreme spiraling rake gave a cubistic, multi-perspective impression of an enormous, exploding sculpture.

The Conductor in white face and a tux entered in a gondola from the flies and remained in view throughout, conducting the orchestra on the fourth level of the collapsing wall like Weill conducting from heaven. The literalized costume designs in black, white, and red suggested not only magazine illustration of the time and the stark contrasts of German Expressionism, but also the parade-ground graphics of the Third Reich. The stenciled texts on costumes and props, cross hatching lines of buttons, distorted white cabaret makeup, and the actors' stylized movement reinforced Brecht's and Weill's harsh critique of a corrupt bourgeois world.

Woyzeck

Achim Freyer (Germany)
Set and Costume Design

This production of *Woyzeck*, a social drama, was very different from other interpretations. Usually, directors have tried to fill the empty spaces of what in fact is only a fragment. Interpretations were put on to the play as a second layer. Freyer chose the opposite way. He conceived a seemingly simple stage, consisting of a big wooden plate from which the figures could easily fall. The simplicity and clarity of the set and the dramaturgy showed a new way of seeing this drama and were therefore influential on many other theatre artists. The production was invited to the "Theatertreffen Berlin," the annual theatre festival where the ten best productions of German language theatre are shown.

Achim Freyer won the Gold Medal for his lifetime achievement at the PQ'99.

Madame de Sade
(Sado Kōshaku Fujin)
Charles Koroly (Sweden/USA)
Set & Costume Design

Charles Koroly works in Sweden and internationally as a scenographer and costume designer in theatre, musicals, film and television. He trained at the Hornsey School of Art in London and at the University College of Film and Theatre in Stockholm. His designs hover between extremes and he has given the Swedish theatre strong spaces and splendid costumes, for example in *Madame de Sade* directed by Ingmar Bergman. Koroly maintains that a constant conversation is a condition for successful co-operation between the scenographer and the director. His role as a co-creator is really important and he thinks he has the same responsibility for the result as everyone else in the process.

Koroly was awarded the Theatre Prize of the Swedish newspaper *Expressen* in 1989.

Legend of Mt. Ararat
(Ağrıdağı Efsanesi)
Atıl Yalkut (Turkey)
Set & Costume Design

The Legend of Mount Ararat was adapted from the most popular novel by the world-renowned Turkish novelist Yashar Kemal and staged in the Municipal Theatre of Istanbul during the 1989-90 theatre season. The action took place on the heights of the mountain, and the *mise en scene* needed appropriate play-space for the large cast and chorus. On the other hand, the existence of a bigger group of players on the stage would provide a rich visual background with their colorful authentic costumes. So the decision of the creative team was to adopt a realistic approach in the costume design, with a highly stylistic and monochrome stage setting. Dramatic stage lighting would color the scene and fuse every element in the same magical atmosphere.

"The main principle of my design interpretation was to create a dynamic, minimalistic, and functional acting space, but one with charm. It was a one-set play, with linked flights of steps providing different acting spaces on different levels for different scenes. I was inspired by the look of mineral crystals under the microscope for the rough and icy look of the mountain rocks on the heights. The biggest problem of the realisation process was to find a suitable material for the surface of my construction. Finally I found some soft plastic mirror plates used mainly for house decoration, and after many tests with different solutions, I achieved the glimmering effect I was seeking. It worked perfectly under the limelights."
—Atıl Yalkut

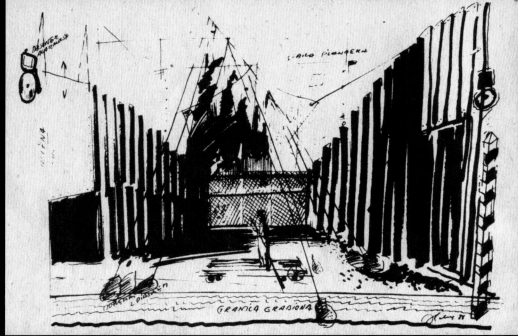

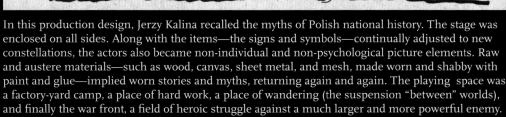

In this production design, Jerzy Kalina recalled the myths of Polish national history. The stage was enclosed on all sides. Along with the items—the signs and symbols—continually adjusted to new constellations, the actors also became non-individual and non-psychological picture elements. Raw and austere materials—such as wood, canvas, sheet metal, and mesh, made worn and shabby with paint and glue—implied worn stories and myths, returning again and again. The playing space was a factory-yard camp, a place of hard work, a place of wandering (the suspension "between" worlds), and finally the war front, a field of heroic struggle against a much larger and more powerful enemy.

Kalina created a place where the ceremony of recalling and replaying of the nation's history could take place. This was shown in the multiplicity of borrowings and interconnected references to literature, film, theatre, and historical iconography. Attributes of war were deliberately taken from different historical periods—from the Hussar wings; through the Uhlan uniforms, scythes, swords, and bayonets; to the modern "tank" symbolically constructed from a group of soldiers in helmets, clad in common great coat.

Pilgrims and Wanderers
(Pielgrzymi i tułacze)

Jerzy Kalina (Poland)
Set & Costume Design

Una Pooka

Monica Frawley (Ireland)
Set & Costume Design

Trained at the National College of Art and Design in Dublin and the Central School of Art and Design in London, Monica Frawley continues to be one of Ireland's most prolific set and costume designers, working freelance with all major Irish theatre companies and venues. Her work with some of the best writers and directors in the country has garnered many awards and nominations. Her set for *Una Pooka*, the 1989 premiere of Michael Harding's play, is an excellent example of Frawley's stylised and graphic designs, showing extreme forced perspective and a threatening tone, but not without humour.

The Flying Dutchman
(Der fliegende Holländer)

Stefanos Lazaridis (Ethiopia/UK)
Set & Costume Design

Writing Lazaridis' obituary in *The Independent*, the director David Pountney referred to *The Flying Dutchman* as the first of Lazaridis' three most striking productions, all created for the lake stage at Bregenz. Pountney stated that "the opportunity to work on this scale somehow triggered Stefan's most sensitive dramaturgical instincts, allied to his phenomenal aesthetic sense, and understanding of scale."

The other productions Lazaridis designed at Bregenz were *Nabucco* (1991) and *Fidelio* (1995).

reunite • Saddam Hussein orders Iraq invasion of neighbouring Kuwait • Lech Walesa becomes president of Poland • Earthquake in Iran kills 50,000 • Nelson Mandela is released from prison in South Africa after 28 years • A stampede of religious pilgrims in Mecca leaves 1,400 dead • Soviet Union leader Mikhail Gorbachev is awarded the Nobel Peace Prize • Channel Tunnel workers meet 40 metres beneath the English Channel seabed, establishing the first ground connection between the UK and the mainland of Europe • Namibia gains independence from South Africa • Boris Yeltsin becomes president of the Russian republic • Depletion of the ozone layer is discovered above the North Pole • East and West Germany reunite • Saddam Hussein orders Iraq invasion of neighbouring Kuwait • Lech Walesa becomes president of Poland • Earthquake in Iran kills 50,000 • Nelson Mandela is released from prison in South Africa after 28 years • A stampede of religious pilgrims in Mecca leaves 1,400 dead • Soviet Union leader Mikhail Gorbachev is awarded the Nobel Peace Prize • Channel Tunnel workers meet 40 metres beneath the English Channel seabed, establishing the first ground connection between the UK and the mainland of Europe • Namibia gains independence from South Africa • Boris Yeltsin becomes president of the Russian republic • Depletion of the ozone layer is discovered above the North Pole • East and West Germany reunite • Saddam

1990

Mephisto
Eli Sinai (Germany/Israel)
Set Design

Eli Sinai's design for *Mephisto* has been a major breakthrough for the Be'er Sheva Theatre, demonstrating that a highly atmospheric and flexible design can be creat on a small, cramped and ill-equipped stage.

M Butterfly
Justin Hill (Australia/Singapore)
Set Design

The Theatreworks Singapore company was given the rights for the show by the playwright after its London season, so this was a coup for the company. Unlike the London version, this design sought to evoke a sense of Chinese Imperial order. It was a most important production in Singapore, as it headlined the city's Arts Festival. Racial issues and overt stage nudity dominated the debate over the production. Permission to perform was granted only after tickets were fully sold out.

2nd Nature

Teresa Przybylski (Poland/Canada)
Set & Costume Design

"This production offered a tremendous challenge. It was very complex. The small stage of The Theatre Centre had to accommodate projections and videos, support the story with several levels metaphorically and specifically and at the same time to be functional and safe for the actors. Deanne Taylor was very involved in the whole process of the design. We decided to use an ellipse as a configuration for the set because this shape offers a friendly perspective and the lines that can be drawn out of the ellipsoid shape contributed to organisation of the space. Costumes for all the characters who impersonated parts of the body and its functions were really fun to design. They had to be very clear to support the abstract concept of the play." — Teresa Przybylski

The Flying Dutchman
(Der Fliegende Holländer)

Jürgen Rose (Germany FRG)
Set & Costume Design

Juergen Rose had collaborated with Dieter Dorn for many years in theatre, but they had also done opera productions together. Their new production of *The Flying Dutchman*—following a successful mounting by Harry Kupfer—was a great challenge, but they created a very successful production that was shown for seven years in Bayreuth. Their production placed the opera in a bourgeois world that resembled a doll's house, and they infused it with a bit of humor, giving a new and fresh view of the drama.

This opera by Richard Wagner allows contrary interpretations—from surrealist to psychological and pathological. Dorn and Rose revealed the drama of the sailor who cannot get back because he cursed God as a window into a world of bourgeois dreams and wishes. The stage was artificially reduced, also reducing the figures. The ship became like a nutshell, the house like a doll's house.

Critic Imre Fabian summarizes the production: "Dorn and Rose searched for—and found—their way. They did not rely on psychoanalytical abstraction or a lofty stage realism. Rose's conception of the scenery becomes most important here. The visual images have a fascinating theatricality, including film effects that help sharpen and focus the scenic interpretation."

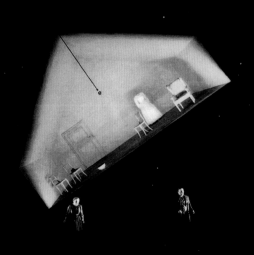

The Marriage of Figaro

Susan Benson (Canada)
Set & Costume Design

The unified design for *The Marriage of Figaro* by Susan Benson, with lighting by Michael J Whitfield, is evidence of a leading designer at the peak of her form. The four acts were gradually revealed by flying out one wall at a time, increasing the playing space as the scenes changed from the bedroom, to the Countess' chamber, the dining room, and eventually the graveyard. The fusion of scenic painting and costuming was exceptional, all united in a seamlessly appropriate lighting design. Originally performed at the Banff Centre for Fine Arts, the production design was rented to Pacific Opera Victoria and many other opera companies since.

Dance of the Devils (La Diablada)

Unknown (Bolívia)
Costume Design

Bolivia is a country with a rich cultural heritage, most importantly in music and dance. These form the basis of the "diabladas de oruro," named for Oruro, a mining city located about 150 km from La Paz.

The Diablada Orureña heritage comes from sacramental public ceremonies that date from the beginning of the Middle Ages in Spain, arriving in Bolivia at the end of the 18th century where they were integrated with local Indian rituals. It is not just music and dance put together, but includes a third component: very rich and theatrical costumes.

The performances use a script developed that represents the clash of good and evil. Elaborate masks and hats are strong ritualistic symbols in the parade. Its presentation through the streets of the city is very similar to the Brazilian carnival, but the theatrical and ritualistic aspects are stronger.

Wind in the Willows

Mark Thompson (UK)
Set & Costume Design

Designing animal costumes calls for imagination tempered with practicality. In Alan Bennett's *Wind in the Willows* at the National Theatre, all the characters, while recognizably animals, were also human types: Mark Thompson's witty costumes blended animal with human characteristics. There was no use of 3-D heads; the animals were defined by make-up and evocative costumes—the ferrets *en brosse*, the sideburns shaping the face, the studded braces, gloves and tail-hole, paws indicated by the gloves but with the fingers free—which, with the merest color change of nails, became paws and claws. The thin pencil moustaches for the stoats made them look like spivs, slick city types in country wear, with thin-brimmed bowler hats. There is a disturbing impression of creatures trying to hide their true selves.

In terms of set, this was the one of the first times that the Olivier stage and its drum revolve were really made to work, bringing up the riverbank creatures' houses from its lower level but also featuring various forms of transport moving above—Toad's car, a barge. It earned Mark Thompson an Olivier award and one from the Critics' Circle.

Platonov

Csaba Antal (Hungary)
Set & Costume Design

Csaba Antal's tinted drawings represent the spatial
concept for this 1990 production of Chekhov's *Platonov*
at the Katona József Theatre in Budapest, the most
renowned art theatre in the capital. A peculiarity of
the set was that it penetrated into the auditorium, yet
still managed to preserve the typically Chekhovian
atmosphere. Shortly after its premiere, the production
won the most prestigious award granted by the theatre
profession. It received the theatre critics' prize in two
categories: best performance and best direction. In the
same year it was also awarded the Quality Theatre Prize.

Dance of the Conquest *(Baile de la Conquista)*

Unknown (Guatemala)
Set & Costume Design

The *Baile de la Conquista* or *Dance of the Conquest* is a traditional folkloric dance
from Guatemala. The dance reenacts the invasion led by Spanish Conquistador
Don Pedro de Alvarado y Contreras and his confrontation with the K'iche' Maya
ruler Tecún Umán. Although the dance is more closely associated with Guatemalan
traditions, it has been performed in early colonial regions of Latin America at the
urging of Catholic friars and priests, as a method of converting various native
populations and African slaves to Christianity.

A scenographic spectacle that took place amongst the aboriginal people of
Guatemala, it had a ritualistic expression, including a synthesis of historical heritage
from the 16th-century Spanish conquerors. Today, these rituals remain with great
vigour and scenic strength. About eighty balls (performances) are presented still
in Guatemala. They do not have any commercial end and are presented during
festivities that are rooted in ritualistic traditions.

John Brown's Body

Pamela Howard (UK)
Set & Costume Design

This large-scale promenade performance represents the fruitful collaboration between Pamela Howard and John McGrath, cut short by his death in 2002. For Howard, working with McGrath was satisfying because it allowed her to work outside the hierarchical conventions of existing performance spaces. Her 2002 publication *What Is Scenography?* refers to the way that individuals contributed to the overall dramaturgy of this piece: "I saw how placing a well-chosen object could resonate with meaning and speak volumes. Each visual image in the play was tried out in many different ways, and assessed by the group of actors, technicians, assistant directors, and scenographers, all of whom had a voice."

Howard's definition and promotion of a scenographic approach to theatre making has influenced future generations through the publication mentioned above as well as her long career as a tutor and eventually course director at Central Saint Martin's College of Art and Design, where she established a scenography master's degree across three European centers. In 2008 she was awarded the OBE for Services to Drama.

Dancing at Lughnasa

Joe Vanek (Ireland)
Set & Costume Design

The design for *Dancing at Lughnasa* chose to move from the prescriptive to emphasizing the mood and sub-text in the script. This was a departure from traditional Irish drama, which had mostly been staged using realism and a staunch adherence to the playwright's visual concept.

The design was considered to be a major factor in the success of the premiere, and the production was much emulated in subsequent designs for the play and for many other "rural" Irish dramas.

It was seen internationally at the National Theatre in London and in the West End. It was subsequently produced on Broadway and in Australia with the original designs and toured in Ireland and the UK. It received two Tony nominations for set and costumes as well as Drama Desk and Critics Forum nominations. The play itself won awards in both London and New York.

This was the first collaboration between Peter Corrigan and Barrie Kosky, who went on to establish a highly successful collaborative partnership both in Australia and internationally, most recently with a production of *La Grande Macabre* at the Komische Oper in Berlin.

Belshazzar
Peter Corrigan (Australia)
Set & Costume Design

Peer Gynt
Huo Qidi (China)
Costume Design

The production not only focused on portraying the personality of each role, but also integrated all the characters into the plot development and the stage atmosphere. The characters' costumes reflected the local environmental and foreign culture.

The Magic Flute *(Die Zauberflöte)*
Yishiko Kunishima (Japan)
Set Design

Yishiko Kunishima's opera designs are constructed mostly of metal. For her sets she uses contemporary materials. Her work is especially popular in the southwestern Kansai region.

The Possessed (*The Devils*)
Eduard Kochergin (USSR/Russia)
Set Design

This production tried to avoid topical allusions, endeavoring instead to settle accounts not with the contemporary but with eternity, to somehow discern the crossing point of Good and Evil in the heart of mankind. Kochergin's set design was both philosophical and metaphorical, dividing the slanting stage into three acting zones with vertical pillars, along which moved wooden panels. The front panel, truncated at the bottom, functioned as a curtain whose sharp and crashing fall called up the image of the guillotine. The rear one served as a backdrop, a "blank sheet" for the actors. The movement of the panels and boards (like a swing) offered a wide range of spatial arrangements. The platforms, rising slantwise and toward one another, were "exposing" those standing on the brink. These narrow surfaces were like the sword of Fate falling on its victims. The performance consisted of three parts and played, with intermissions, from noon until 10 p.m. *The Possessed* premiered in Braunschweig, Germany, in November 1991, and later in St. Petersburg

The Fall of the House of Usher
Trina Parker & David Murray (Australia)
Set Design

"Trina Parker's awesome design strips back the Merlyn Theatre...creating a Gothic cavern. Only a thin band of furniture, 'profuse, comfortless, antique and tattered,' defines the bulwark the Ushers hold against the encroaching darkness. The furniture takes on its own significance, creating Poe's 'atmosphere of sorrow,' an unbearable nostalgia for a lost, corrupt beauty. It is moved around the naked stage as scene changes demand by two servants, whose formality creates a sense of somber ritual. What gives expressive life to the design is David Murray's spectacular lighting, which works as a definer of physical space and to evoke the emotional dimensions of the story..." [Review by Alison Croggon]

The Ghost Sonata
Xu Xiang (China)
Set Design

A rotten, corrupt, and metallic space, contrasted with a plain, clear, and expressive space, created a three-dimensional and flowing environment for the play.

Katsura Harudanji

Shiro Takeuchi (Japan)
Set Design

Shiro Takeuchi's set designs dexterously use the limited space of the theatre to the fullest. He is also a famous calligrapher and uses his skills to design the publicity materials for his productions. He is also an excellent mentor for theatre designers in the southwestern Kansai region.

Cao Zhi

Xu Haishan (China)
Set Design

The design adopted a combination of virtuality and reality, and used as its basic structure two huge dragon pillars and several groups of platforms that could be combined in diverse ways. In addition, shifting colors, lights, and sounds were employed to reveal the profound implication of the play.

My Name Is Edward Kelly

Kenneth Rowell (Australia)
Set & Costume Design

My Name Is Edward Kelly was commissioned by the Australian Ballet and formed part of a triple bill that premiered in Melbourne. It focused on the legendary Australian historical figure Ned Kelly. The music was composed by renowned Australian composer Peter Sculthorpe.

An Encounter

Sun-Hi Shin (Korea)
Set Design

Sun-Hi Shin: "Encounters of human beings are at once crisscrossing and colliding with each other. I think of such a struggle for encounters as a leap of a spider which spins its webs. When spinning its web in all directions, a spider leaps about in the air. After setting up an outer space with eight webs, it hops onto the center to weave dense longitudinal webs, sitting on webs it has already made.

"The perfect plan and intense leaps of the spider to build her web are well reflected by the leaps and passionate music in this work. Rubber bands are tied up and down to the bars, so that dancers can design their spatial movements."

The Resistable Rise of Arturo Ui
(ΗΆνοδοςκαιΗΠτώσητουΑρτούροοΟυί)

Andy Bargilly (Cyprus)
Set Design

Andy Bargilly is a leading stage designer who introduced the minimalist approach to stage design in Cyprus. This design is important to his career, not only because of its minimalism but for its innovative use of industrial-looking metal construction, something that appears again and again in varying forms in his later theatre work.

Ubu *(Ubu Roi, Татко Юбю)*

Marina Raytchinova (Bulgaria)
Set, Costume & Lighting Design

This was the first production of this famous play in Bulgaria after it had been banned during the Communist period, and it was performed more than 150 times in Sofia. The set design can be categorized as "action scenography," and consisted of three kinetic but useless machines made of waste materials—a metaphor for the chaos of the period immediately following the collapse of the Communist regime in Bulgaria. The first project in a long collaboration between designer Marina Raytchinova and composer Assen Avramov, it also marked one of the first productions by the Little City Theatre Off the Channel, still one of the most successful companies in Bulgaria today. Performed at the Pompidou Centre during the 1991 Paris Autumn Festival, it received very positive reviews in the French media.

Lady Macbeth of Mtsensk

David Borovsky (Russia)
Set Design

Invited to design the sets for Shostakovitch's opera for the Hamburg State Opera, Borovsky naturally recalled his experience of working on the piece in Kiev in 1965. The central visual idea of the heroine's life space enclosed within dark log walls was transferred from that old staging to Lyubimov's production. These walls rose to the very top of the stage, leaving only a narrow strip of the sky with church domes with crosses. However, this time Borovsky made the walls transformable: they functioned in different ways in different episodes, creating different arrangements of the space. But no matter what transformations were performed, whatever apertures appeared in the walls, the sense of the lockup in which the heroine was destined to live remained predominant.

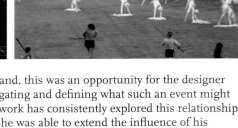

Commonwealth Games Auckland 1990 Opening Ceremony: Cultural Display

Joe Bleakley (New Zealand)
Event Design

With large-scale ceremonies a rarity in New Zealand, this was an opportunity for the designer and the collaborators to work together on investigating and defining what such an event might be in New Zealand and Pacific terms. Bleakley's work has consistently explored this relationship between the spectacle and the community. Here he was able to extend the influence of his designs to an international level: expressing what it is to be a New Zealander and providing a uniquely antipodean slant on the ritualistic elements of the opening ceremony. Issues of colonialism, biculturalism, and national identity became significant features of the ceremony.

Most significantly this design was the first of its kind to use storytelling and scenography in an opening ceremony. It had a profound influence on similar event designs that followed it. The 1992 Barcelona Summer Olympics consulted with members of the creative team for the design of its own opening.

Staged only two weeks before the 150th anniversary of the signing of the Treaty of Waitangi, this event became an important moment in reconciling New Zealand's colonial and indigenous backgrounds. The event started with a traditional Maori welcome (powhiri) and continued to review New Zealand history with a ceremonial pageant that featured the arrival of the Maori seafarers from the Pacific, and the images of Captain James Cook's ships arriving on the shores of the country. This integration of the diverse elements of New Zealand culture into the ceremony allowed athletes and citizens to participate in an expression of cultural diversity and dynamic biculturalism.

Medea

Apostolos Vettas (Greece)
Set & Costume Design

One of the most important projects undertaken for the Thessaloniki theatre and one of the most interesting produced at the Festival of Epidaurus, this production of *Medea* opened up new avenues for expression with its post-modern approach. The design gave a visual emphasis to the ancient tragedy through the use of additional elements from the Argonaut myth cycle.

The skeleton of the ship Argo was a major theatrical device, providing the exiled Medea with a makeshift refuge outside ancient Corinth. Once a reminder of what had originally been a shelter for their love affair, the ruined vessel became a setting for the unfolding tragedy, acted out mainly between Medea and Jason.

In the play's climax, the high prow of the ship was transformed into a dragon-shaped winged chariot of the sun, while in the bowels of the ship's wooden shell lay the tragic conclusion waiting for the now solitary Jason.

A Midsummer Night's Dream
(Sonho de uma Noite de Verão)

José de Anchieta (Brazil)
Set & Costume Design

This production of *Midsummer's Night Dream* may be been one of Brazil's greatest theatre productions of the last decades, and it was the summit of the many productions done by one of the most important Brazilian theatre groups, Ornitorrinco, directed by Caca Rosset. It was produced in New York City and it had its opening night at Central Park during the summer theater festival.

In Brazil, it ran for more than two years in Sao Paulo and Rio de Janeiro in addition to many other Brazilian capitals. José de Anchieta's design was part of the PQ'95 exhibition, where it received a Golden Triga.

De Anchieta, scenographer and costume designer for more than four decades, is today one of the most influential names in Brazilian scenography, and his work has been collected in a book, *Auleum*. He also works with television, commercials, and movies, and he is one of the country's finest scenography educators.

The Brigades of Beauty *(Brigade Lepote)*

Vlado G. Repnik (Slovenia)
Set & Costume Design

Vlado Repnik, together with theatre director Bojan Jablanovec and theatre architect Aljoša Kolenc, set the foundation for his later theatre research-oriented work in the project THEATRE [GLEDALIŠČE]. In 1988, THEATRE produced the performance piece, *Helios*, based on Bertolt Brecht's *Galileo Galilei*, created with the students from the Academy of Theatre, Radio, Film, and Television. Repnik's subsequent theatre productions are marked by continual conceptual shifts, while the projects move along the edges of the visual arts and theatre. In 1990, Repnik created the acclaimed Mladinsko Theatre performance, *Brigades of Beauty (Brigade lepote)*, which was also presented at the Evrokaz Festival.

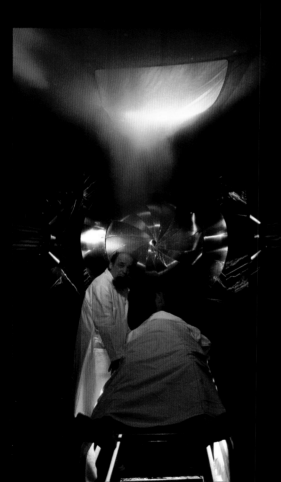

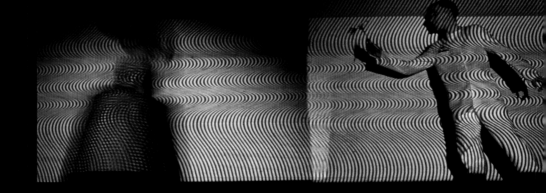

Phoenician Women
(Φοίνισσες)

Angelos Angeli (Cyprus)
Set Design

Angelos Angeli is an important stage and costume designer for Cypriot theatre, responsible for both set and costume in a large number of well-received productions. The design seen here was an important, innovative, and meaningful design of a ancient Greek drama

Odysseus and Son, or
on the World and Home Home
(Odisej & Sin Ili Svijet I Dom)

Dalibor Laginja (Croatia)
Set Design

Slovenian poet Veno Taufer's most famous play is Odysseus & Son or on the World and Home. The Zagreb Youth Theatre is known for presenting plays in a new or "youthful" style, rather than just plays for younger audiences. The repertoire is often radical or experimental. This production of Odysseus was at the start of a change in direction for the company to a more pluralistic one in which a much broader audience can find a home. This was an early work of Dalibor Laginja, who has designed hundreds of productions and received many awards.

La Boheme

Catherine Martin (Australia)
Set & Costume Design

This production marked an important step in the partnership of Catherine Martin and Baz Luhrmann, who have gone on to have one of the most successful collaborative partnerships in Australian theatre. It was an enormously successful production that ultimately made its way to an extended season at the Broadway Theatre in New York in 2002.

Coffee Foxes (*Raposas do Café*)
José Carlos Serroni (Brazil)
Set Design

Raposas do Café was produced by TAPA, one of the most important permanent companies in Brazil for the last three decades.

JC Serroni's scenography was made of big reversible bookshelves, functioning like a great chest filled with the characters and stage elements. It was a landmark production in that all materials used were recycled. All of the props and furniture were donated and restored, and no money was spent on materials, only restorative work. It played in a warehouse of coffee beans sacks, where 500 empty sacks made of natural fiber filled with rice straw were piled up

The show ran for three years, and the design received many awards, including the well-respected Moliére award sponsored by Air France. The model, project, sketches, and pictures were part of the Brazilian section of PQ'91.

A Month in the Country (*Mjesec Dana Na Selu*)
Dinka Jeričević (Yugoslavia/Croatia)
Set Design

This was a very early design in the career of Dinka Jeričević and was a collaboration with Georgij Paro late in his time at the helm of the Croatian National theatre. It is typical of her aesthetic of scenography, being both imaginative and functional.

{ PRODUCTION CREDITS }

[16]

The Rocky Horror Show
Brian Thomson (Australia) & **Sue Blane** (UK)
Set & Costume Design

Company: **The Royal Court Theatre**
Venue: **Theatre Upstairs, Royal Court**
Location: **London, UK**
Opening/First Night: **June 1973**
[also Roxy Theatre, Los Angeles, March 1974; New Arts Cinema, Sydney, April 1974; Regent Palace, Melbourne, October 1975]

Author: **Richard O'Brien**
Composer: **Richard O'Brien**
Scenic Designer: **Brian Thomson**
Costume Designer: **Sue Blane**
Lighting Designer: **Gerry Jenkinson** (London), **Chip Monk** (LA), **John Saltzer** (Sydney)
Director: **Jim Sharman**
Conductor: **Richard Hartley** (London), **Roy Ritchie** (Sydney)

Contributing Researcher: **Richard Roberts & Madeline Taylor**

Image Credits: **Sue Blane, John Haynes, Brian Thompson, & Victoria and Albert Museum, London**

[17]

Equus
John Napier (UK)
Set & Costume Design

Company: **Royal National Theatre**
Venue: **The Old Vic**
Location: **London, UK**
Opening/First Night: **17 July 1973**

Author: **Peter Shaffer**
Scenic Designer: **John Napier**
Costume Designer: **John Napier**
Lighting Designer: **Andy Phillips**
Director: **John Dexter**
Choreographer: **Claude Chagrin**
Composer: **Marc Wilkinson**

Contributing Researcher: **Kate Dorney**

Image Credit: **Victoria and Albert Museum, London**

[18]

The Money Tree
Julian Beck & William Shari (USA)
Set Design

Company: **The Living Theatre**

Venue: **Homestead**
Location: **Pittsburgh, Pennsylvania USA**
Opening/First Night: **1975**

Author: Collective Creation, written down by **Julian Beck, Judith Malina, Hanon Reznikov**
Scenic Designer: **Julian Beck & William Shari**
Costume Designer: **Julian Beck**
Director: **Julian Beck, Judith Malina; collective creation by the Company**

Contributing Researcher: **Thomas Walker & Eric Fielding**

Image Credit: **Judith Malina**

[18]

Samoan Fire Knife Dance (Siva Aailao)
Aggie Grey's Resort (Western Samoa)
Performance Design

Company: **Aggie Grey's**
Venue: **Aggie Grey's Resort**
Location: **Apia, Western Samoa**
Opening/First Night: **1975-1990**, continuous performances

Author: **Chief Letuli Olo Misilagi** & others
Choreographer: **Chief Letuli Olo Misilagi** & others
Contributors: **Tama Matua, Kinilau Tavita Lauifi**

Contributing Researcher: **Keren Chiaroni**

Image Credits: **Aggie Grey's Resort, Giovanni Rossi, Laura Wadsworth**

[19]

A Little Night Music
Boris Aronson (Russia/USA), **Florence Klotz** & **Tharon Musser** (USA)
Set Design

Venue: **Shubert Theatre**
Location: **New York, New York, USA**
Opening/First Night: **25 February 1973**

Composer: **Stephen Sondheim**
Lyrics: **Stephen Sondheim**
Author: **Hugh Wheeler**
Scenic Designer: **Boris Aronson**
Costume Designer: **Florence Klotz**
Lighting Designer: **Tharon Musser**
Director: **Harold Prince**
Choreographer: **Patricia Birch**

Contributing Researcher: **Eric Fielding**

Image Credit: **Martha Swope © The New York Public Library for the Performing Arts**

[20]

Split Enz Costumes
Noel Crombie (New Zealand)
Costume Design

Company: **Split Enz**
Venue: **Various**
Location: **World Tour**
Opening/First Night: **1975**

Composer: **Split Enz**
Costume Designer: **Noel Crombie**
Lighting Designer: **Raewyn Turner**

Contributing Researcher: **Sam Trubridge**

Image Credits: **Alan Wild, Noel Crombie**

[20]

Ivanov
Mart Kitaev (Latvia)
Set Design

Company: **Latvian Theatre for Young Spectators**
Location: **Riga, Latvia**
Opening/First Night: **1975**

Author: **Anton Chekhov**
Scenic Designer: **Mart Kitaev**
Director: **Adolf Shapiro**

Contributing Researcher: **Inna Mirzoyan**

Image Credit: **Mart Kitaev**

[21]

Romeo and Juliet
Sergei Barkhin (USSR/Russia)
Set Design

Company: **Boris Shchukin Theatre Institute**
Venue: **School Theatre**
Location: **Moscow, USSR/Russia**
Opening/First Night: **1975**

Author: **William Shakespeare**
Scenic Designer: **Sergei Barkhin**
Director: **Albert Burov**

Contributing Researcher: **Inna Mirzoyan**

Image Credit: **Sergei Barkhin**

[22]

Strider: The Story of a Horse (Kholstomer)
Eduard Kochergin (USSR/Russia)
Set Design

Venue: **Bolshoi Drama Theatre**
Location: **Leningrad (St.Petersburg), USSR/Russia**
Opening/First Night: **1975**

Author: **Leo Tolstoy** (original story)
Scenic Designer: **Eduard Kochergin**
Director: **Georgy Tovstonogov**

Contributing Researcher: **Inna Mirzoyan**

Image Credit: **Eduard Kochergin**

[24]

The Red Eagle (Al Nesr Al Ahmar)
Sakina Mohamed Ali (Egypt)
Set & Costume Design

Company: **The Artistic Theatre House**
Venue: **Egyptian National Theatre**
Location: **Cairo, Egypt**
Opening/First Night: **September, 1975**

Author: **Abdel Rahman Elsharkawy**
Scenic Designer: **Sakina Mohamed Ali**
Costume Designer: **Sakina Mohamed Ali**
Director: **Karam Metawaa**

Contributing Researcher: **Hazem Shebl**

Image Credit: **Sakina Mohamed Ali**

[24]

The Little Square (Il campiello)
Luciano Damiani (Italy)
Set & Costume Design

Company: **Strehler's Company**
Venue: **Piccolo Teatro di Milano**
Location: **Milano, Italy**
Opening/First Night: **May 1975**

Author: **Carlo Goldoni**
Scenic Designer: **Luciano Damiani**
Costume Designer: **Luciano Damiani**
Sound Designer: **Fiorenzo Carpi**
Director: **Giorgio Strehler**

Contributing Researcher: **Daniela Sacco**

Image Credits: **Luigi Ciminaghi/Piccolo Teatro di Milano & Teatro d›Europa**

[25]

A Chorus Line
Robin Wagner & Tharon Musser (USA)
Set & Lighting Design

Company: **New York Shakespeare Festival**
Venue: **Shubert Theatre**
Location: **New York City, New York, USA**
Opening/First Night: **25 July 1975**

Author: **James Kirkwood & Nicholas Dante**
Composer: **Marvin Hamlish**
Lyrics: **Edward Kleban**
Scenic Designer: **Robin Wagner**
Costume Designer: **Theoni V. Aldredge**
Lighting Designer: **Tharon Musser**
Sound Designer: **Abe Jacob**
Director: **Michael Bennett**
Choreographer: **Michael Bennett & Bob Avian**
Conductor/Musical Director: **Donald Pippin**
Producer: **Joseph Papp**

Contributing Researcher: **Delbert Unruh & Eric Fielding**

Image Credit: **Martha Swope © The New York Public Library for the Performing Arts**

[26]

Brand
Ilmars Blumbergs (Latvia)
Set, Costume & Lighting Design

Company: **Latvian Daile Theatre**
Venue: **Latvian Daile Theatre**
Location: **Riga, Latvia**
Opening/First Night: **25 September 1975**

Author: **Henrik Ibsen**
Scenic Designer: **Ilmars Blumbergs**
Costume Designer: **Ilmars Blumbergs**
Lighting Designer: **Ilmars Blumbergs**
Director: **Arnolds Linins**
Choreographer: **Modris Tenisons**

Contributing Researcher: **Edite Tisheizere**

Image Credits: **Yuri Ikonnikov, Juris Kalnins**

[27]

The Lady Bagdat (Bağdat Khatun)
Refik Eren (Turkey)
Set Design

Company: **Turkish State Theatres**
Venue: **Istanbul State Theatre, Venüs Stage**
Location: **Istanbul, Turkey**
Opening/First Night: **October 1975**

Author: **Güngör Dilmen**
Composer: **Sabahattin Kalender**
Scenic Designer: **Refik Eren**
Costume Designer: **Hale Eren**
Lighting Designer: **Nuri Özakyol**
Director: **Cüneyd Gökçer**

Contributing Researcher: **Evcimen Percin**

Image Credit: **Refik Eren**

[27]

Ivan the Terrible
Simon Vrisaladze (USSR/Russia)
Set Design

Company: **State Academic Bolshoi Theatre**
Location: **Moscow, USSR/Russia**
Opening/First Night: **1975**

Composer: **Sergei Prokofiev**
Scenic Designer: **Simon Vrisaladze**
Choreographer: **Yuri Grigorovich**

Contributing Researcher: **Inna Mirzoyan**

Image Credit: **Simon Vrisaladze**

[28]

Fragments from an Unfinished Novel
(*Útržky z nedokončeného románu*)
Jan Konečný (Czechoslovakia/Czech
Republic)
Set Design

Company: Hanácké Theatre, Prostějov
Venue: State Theatre Brno
Location: Brno, Czechoslovakia/Czech
Republic
Opening/First Night: 13 June 1975

Author: Arnošt Goldflam
Scenic Designer: Jan Konečný
Costume Designer: Katarína Kissoczyová
Director: Arnošt Goldflam

Contributing Researcher: Daniela Pařízková
& Marie Zdeňková

Image Credit: Jaroslav Prokop, Prague
Quadrennial Archive

[28]

Optimistic Tragedy (*Optimistinen tragedia*)
Måns Hedström (Finland)
Set & Costume Design

Company: KOM Theatre
Venue: KOM Theatre
Location: Helsinki, Finland
Opening/First Night: 22 January 1975

Author: Vsevolod Vishnevsky
Composer: Kaj Chydenius
Scenic Designer: Måns Hedström
Costume Designer: Måns Hedström
Lighting Designer: Reima Vähämäki
Director: Kaisa Korhonen
Conductor: Kaj Chydenius

Contributing Researcher: Pälvi Laine

Image Credit: Måns Hedström, Klaus
Hedström; The Theatre Museum Archive
(Finland)

[29]

American Anti-Bicentennial Pageant
Peter Schumann (Germany/USA)
Puppet Design

Company: Bread and Puppet Theater
Location: New York City, USA
Opening/First Night: 1975

Author: Peter Schumann
Puppet Designer: Peter Schumann
Director: Peter Schumann

Contributing Researcher: Eric Fielding

Image Credit: © Theodore Shank

[30]

Rake's Progress
David Hockney (UK)
Set & Costume Design

Company: Glyndebourne Festival Opera
Venue: Glyndebourne Festival Theatre
Location: Sussex, UK
Opening/First Night: June 1975

Composer: Igor Stravinsky
Libretto: W. H. Auden & Chester Kallman
Scenic Designer: David Hockney
Costume Designer: David Hockney
Lighting Designer: Robert Bryan
Conductor: Bernard Haitinik
Director: John Cox

Contributing Researcher: Madeline Taylor

Image Credit: © David Hockney,
Collection: David Hockney Foundation

[32]

Tent of the Underdogs
(*La Carpa de los Rasquachis*)
Luis Valdez (USA)
Set Design

Company: El Teatro Campesino
Location: San Juan Bautista, California,
USA
Opening/First Night: 1974

Author: Luis Valdez
Composer: Traditional Corrido (public
domain)
Scenic Designer: Luis Valdez & El Teatro
Campesino
Costume Designer: Luis Valdez & El Teatro
Campesino
Director: Luis Valdez
Choreographer: Luis Valdez

Contributing Researcher: Eric Fielding

Image Credit: El Teatro Campesino

[33]

By Feet and Hands (*De Pies y Manos*)
Guillhermo de la Torre (Argentina)
Set Design

Venue: Teatro Nacional Cervantes
Location: Buenos Aires, Argentina
Opening/First Night: 1984

Author: Roberto Cossa
Scenic Designer: Guillhermo de la Torre
Director: Omar Grasso

Contributing Researcher: JC Serroni

Image Credit: Guillhermo de la Torre

[33]

Baal
Raul Belem (Brazil)
Set & Costume Design

Venue: Palace of Arts
Location: Belo Horizonte, Brazil
Opening/First Night: June 1975

Author: Bertolt Brecht
Scenic Designer: Raul Belem
Costume Designer: Raul Belem
Lighting Designer: Paulo Laender
Director: Ronaldo Brandão

Contributing Researcher: JC Serroni

Image Credit: Paulo Lacerda

[34]

The Cherry Orchard
Valery Levental (USSR/Russia)
Set Design

Company: Taganka Theatre
Location: Moscow, USSR/Russia
Opening/First Night: 1975

Author: Anton Chekhov
Scenic Designer: Valery Levental
Director: Anatoly Efros

Contributing Researcher: Inna Mirzoyan

[35]

The Revenger's Tragedy
Kristian Fredrikson (New Zealand/
Australia)
Set & Costume Design

Company: Melbourne Theatre Company
Venue: St Martin's Theatre
Location: Melbourne, Australia
Opening/First Night: October 1975

Author: Cyril Tourneur
Composer: Helen Gifford
Scenic Designer: Kristian Fredrikson
Costume Designer: Kristian Fredrikson
Lighting Designer: Jamieson Lewis
Director: David Myles
Choreographer: Graeme Murphy

Contributing Researcher: Richard Roberts

Image Credit: Kristian Fredrikson

[36]

Till Eulenspiegel (*Thyl Ulenspegel*)
Evgeni Lysik (Ukraine)
Design

Company: Ukraine Ivan Franko Academic
Opera & Ballet Theatre
Location: Lviv, Ukraine
Opening/First Night: 1975

Composer: Evgeni Glebov
Scenic Designer: Evgeni Lysik
Choreographer: Mikhail Zaslavsky

Contributing Researcher: Inna Mirzoyan

Image Credit: Prague Quadrennial Archive

[36]

Gee Girls—The Liberation is Near
(*Jösses flickor – befrielsen är nära*)
Måns Hedström (Sweden)
Set & Costume Design

Venue: Stockholms Stadsteater
Location: Stockholm, Sweden
Opening/First Night: 29 November 1974

Author: Margareta Garpe & Suzanne Osten
Composer: Gunnar Edander
Scenic Designer: Måns Hedström
Costume Designer: Måns Hedström
Lighting Designer: Olle Öster
Director: Susanne Osten

Contributing Researcher: Ammy
Kjellsdotter

Image Credit: Måns Hedström

[36]

The Resistible Rise of Arturo Ui
(*Der aufhaltsame Aufstieg des Arturo Ui*)
Daniil Lider (Ukraine)
Set Design

Company: Khmelnitsk Music and Drama
Theatre
Location: Khmelnitsk, Ukraine
Opening/First Night: 1975

Author: Bertolt Brecht
Scenic Designer: Daniil Lider
Director: V. Bulatova

Contributing Researcher: Inna Mirzoyan

Image Credit: Daniil Lider

[37]

Clowns of Avignon (*Klauni z Avugnonu*)
Helena Anýžová (Czechoslovakia/Czech
Republic)
Costume Design

Venue: F. X. Šalda Theatre
Location: Liberec, Czechoslovakia/Czech
Republic
Opening/First Night: 13 June 1975

Author: Günter Weisenborn
Scenic Designer: Vratislav Habr
Costume Designer: Helena Anýžová
Director: Milan Vobruba

Contributing Researcher: Daniela Pařízková
& Marie Zdeňková

Image Credit: Helena Anýžová

[37]

The Miracle in Sargan (*Čudo u Šarganu*)
Petar Pašić (Serbia/Yugoslavia)
Set Design

Company: Theatre Atelje 212
Venue: Theatre Atelje 212
Location: Belgrade, Serbia/Yugoslavia
Opening/First Night: 24 October 1975

Author: Ljubomir Simović
Composer: Vojislav Kostić
Scenic Designer: Petar Pašić
Scenic Artist: Dušan Škorić
Costume Designer: Vladislav Lalicki
Lighting Designer: Petar Stojković
Sound Designer: Đuro Sanader
Director: Mira Trailović

Contributing Researcher: Radivoje
Dinulović

Image Credit: Museum of Theatrical Arts
of Serbia

[38]

Peter Grimes
Timothy O'Brien & Tazeena Firth (UK)
Set Design

Company: Royal Opera House
Venue: Covent Garden
Location: London, UK
Opening/First Night: May 1975

Composer: Benjamin Britten
Scenic Designer: Timothy O'Brien &
Tazeena Firth
Costume Designer: Timothy O'Brien &
Tazeena Firth
Lighting Designer: David Hersey
Director: Elijah Moshinsky
Choreographer: Eleanor Fazan
Conductor: Colin Davis

Contributing Researcher: Donatella Barbieri

Image Credits: Victoria and Albert
Museum, London & Timothy O'Brien

[40]

The Dead Class (*Umarła klasa*)
Tadeusz Kantor (Poland)
Set & Costume Design

Company: Teatr Cricot 2
Venue: Teatr Cricot 2
Location: Kraków, Poland
Opening/First Night: 15 November 1975

Author: Tadeusz Kantor
Scenic Designer: Tadeusz Kantor
Costume Designer: Tadeusz Kantor
Director: Tadeusz Kantor

Contributing Researcher: Agnieszka Kubaś

Image Credit: Tadeusz Kantor; © Maria
Kantor & Dorota Krakowska, Archive of The
Centre for the Documentation of the Art
of Tadeusz Kantor CRICOTEKA (Kraków);
Dalman & Smith, George Oliver

[41]

Heartbreak House
Michael Annals (UK)
Set & Costume Design

Company: **National Theatre Company**
Location: **Old Vic Theatre, London, UK**
Opening/First Night: **25 February 1975**

Author: **George Bernard Shaw**
Scenic Designer: **Michael Annals**
Costume Designer: **Michael Annals**
Lighting Designer: **Richard Pilbrow**
Sound Designer: **Sylvia Carter**
Director: **John Schlesinger**

Contributing Researcher: **Ian Herbert**

Image Credit: **Victoria and Albert Museum, London**

[42]

Macbeth *(Makbet)*
Vladimir Marenić (Croatia/Serbia)
Set Design

Company: **National Theatre**
Venue: **National Theatre**
Location: **Belgrade, Serbia/Yugoslavia**
Opening/First Night: **27 June 1975**

Author: **William Shakespeare**
Scenic Designer: **Vladimir Marenić**
Costume Designer: **Milena Jeftić Ničeva Kostić**
Director: **Arsenije Jovanović**

Contributing Researcher: **Radivoje Dinulović**

Image Credit: **Museum of Theatre Arts of Serbia**

[43]

The Corsair (Der Korsar)
Toni Businger (Switzerland)
Set & Costume Design

Company: **Bregenzer Festspiele**
Venue: **Bregenzer Festspiele Seebuhne**
Location: **Bregenz, Austria**
Opening/First Night: **2 August 1975**

Composer: **Adolphe Adam**
Libretto: **Jules Henri Vernoy de Saint-Georges** (based on the novel *The Corsair* by Lord Byron)
Scenic Designer: **Toni Businger**
Costume Designer: **Toni Businger**
Director: **Wazlaw Orlikowsky**
Choreographer: **Wazlaw Orlikowsky, Joseph Mazilier**
Conductor: **Niksa Bareza**

Contributing Researcher: **Sandra Gredig**

Image Credit: **Bregenzer Festspiele**

[43]

A Night in Venice (Eine Nacht in Venedig)
Toni Businger (Switzerland)
Set & Costume Design

Company: **Bregenzer Festspiele**
Venue: **Bregenzer Festspiele Seebühne**
Location: **Bregenz, Austria**
Opening/First Night: **17 July 1975**

Composer: **Johann Strauss II**
Author: **Camillo Walzel & Richard Genée**
Scenic Designer: **Toni Businger**
Costume Designer: **Toni Businger**
Director: **Wolfgang Weber**
Choreographer: **Wazlav Orlikov**
Conductor: **Heinz Wallberg**

Contributing Researcher: **Sandra Gredig**

Image Credit: **Bregenzer Festspiele**

[44]

Oedipus at Colonus
Dionysis Fotopoulos (Greece)
Set & Costume Design

Company: **National Theatre of Greece**
Venue: **Epidaurus Festival**
Location: **Epidaurus, Greece**
Opening/First Night: **1975**

Author: **Sophocles**
Scenic Designer: **Dionysis Fotopoulos**
Costume Designer: **Dionysis Fotopoulos**

Contributing Researcher: **Dio Kangelari**

Image Credit: **Dionysis Fotopoulos**

[44]

White Marriage (Białe małżeństwo)
Zofia de Ines (Poland)
Costume Design

Venue: **Teatr Współczesny**
Location: **Wrocław, Poland**
Opening/First Night: **11 August 1975**

Author: **Tadeusz Różewicz**
Composer: **Mirosław Jastrzębski**
Scenic Designer: **Piotr Wieczorek**
Costume Designer: **Zofia de Ines**
Director: **Kazimierz Braun**
Choreographer: **Waldemar Fogiel**

Contributing Researcher: **Agnieszka Kubas**

Image Credits: **Tadeusz Drankowski, Private Archive of Zofia de Ines**

[45]

Gilgamesh, What He Saw
Maija Pekkanen (Finland)
Costume Design

Company: **Helsinki City Theatre**
Venue: **Helsinki City Theatre**
Location: **Helsinki, Finland**
Opening/First Night: **23 January 1975**

Author: **Antti Einari Halonen and Jukka Kajava**
Composer: **Toni Edelmann**
Scenic Designer: **Markku Sirén**
Costume Designer: **Maija Pekkanen**
Director: **Antti Einari Halonen and Jukka Kajava**

Contributing Researcher: **Pälvi Laine**

Image Credit: **© Kari Hakli; The Theatre Museum Archive (Finland)**

[46]

The Cherry Orchard
(Wiszniewyj sad, Wiśniowy sad)
Jerzy Juk Kowarski (Poland)
Set & Costume Design

Venue: **Stary Teatr im. Heleny Modrzejewskiej**
Location: **Kraków, Poland**
Opening/First Night: **1 February 1975**

Author: **Anton Chekov**
Composer: **Zygmunt Konieczny**
Scenic Designer: **Jerzy Juk Kowarski**
Director: **Jerzy Jarocki**

Contributing Researcher: **Agnieszka Kubas**

Image Credit: **Wojciech Plewiński, Private archive of Jerzy Juk-Kowarski**

[47]

The Tempest (Der Sturm)
Eva-Maria Viebeg (Germany GDR)
Set & Costume Design

Company: **Deutsches Theater**
Venue: **Deutsches Theater**
Location: **Berlin, Germany GDR**
Opening/First Night: **12 December 1974**

Author: **William Shakespeare**
Scenic Designer: **Eva-Maria Viebeg**
Costume Designer: **Eva-Maria Viebeg**
Mask: **Wolfgang Utzt**
Director: **Friedo Solter**

Contributing Researcher: **Karin Winkelsesser**

Image Credits: **Akademie der Kuenste Berlin, Eva-Maria Viebeg Archive**

[47]

The Misanthrope (Le Misanthrope)
Igor Ivanov (USSR/Russia)
Set Design

Company: **State Academic Comedy Theatre**
Location: **Leningrad (St.Petersburg), USSR/Russia**
Opening/First Night: **1975**

Author: **Molière**
Scenic Designer: **Igor Ivanov**
Director: **Pyotr Fomenko**

Contributing Researcher: **Inna Mirzoyan**

Image Credit: **Prague Quadrennial Archive**

[48]

The Marriage
Valery Levental (USSR/Russia)
Set Design

Company: **Malaya Bronnaya Theatre**
Location: **Moscow, USSR/Russia**
Opening/First Night: **1975**

Author: **Nikolai Gogol**
Scenic Designer: **Valery Levental**
Director: **Anatoly Efros**

Contributing Researcher: **Inna Mirzoyan**

Image Credit: **Valery Levental**

[49]

The Devils of Loudun (Diabły z Loudun)
Andrzej Majewski (Poland)
Set & Costume Design

Company: **Teatr Wielki**
Venue: **Teatr Wielki**
Location: **Warsaw, Poland**
Opening/First Night: **8 June 1975**

Author/Creator: **Krzysztof Penderecki**
Scenic Designer: **Andrzej Majewski**
Costume Designer: **Andrzej Majewski**
Director: **Kazimierz Dejmek**

Contributing Researcher: **Agnieszka Kubaś**

Image Credit: **Andrzej Majewski, Archive of The Centre of Polish Scenography in Katowice; Edward Hartwig**

[52]

Firebird
Tetsuhiko Maeda (Japan)
Set Design

Company: **Maki Asami Ballet Company**
Venue: **Mel Park Hall**
Location: **Tokyo, Japan**
Opening/First Night: **July 1976**

Composer: **Igor Stravinsky**
Scenic Designer: **Tetsuhiko Maeda**
Choreographer: **Asami Maki**

Contributing Researcher: **Kazue Hatano**

Image Credit: **Tetsuhiko Maeda**

[52]

The Misadventures of The New Satan
(or The New Devil of Hellsbottom)
(Põrgupõhja Uus Vanapagan)
Georg Sander (Estonia)
Set Design

Design Company: **Theatre Vanemuine**
Location: **Tallinn, Estonia**
Opening/First Night: **25 January 1976**

Author: **Anton Hansen Tammsaare, O. Tooming**
Scenic Designer: **Georg Sander**
Director: **Jaan Tooming**

Contributing Researcher: **Nicole Leclercq/ Monika Larini**

Image Credits: **Raivo Velsker, Estonian Theatre and Music Museum**

[53]

Storm (Arashi)
Akaji Maro (Japan)
Set Design

Company: **Dairakudakan**
Venue: **Nihon Seinenkan Hall**
Location: **Tokyo, Japan**
Opening/First Night: **27 September 1976**

Author: **Dairakudakan**
Scenic Designer: **Akaji Maro**
Costume Designer: **Dairakudakan**
Lighting Designer: **Yoshiro Abe**
Sound Designer: **Kazuo Oaku**
Director: **Akaji Maro**
Choreographer: **Akaji Maro**

Contributing Researcher: **Kazue Hatano**

Image Credit: **Akaji Maro**

[54]

Book of Splendors (le Livre des Splendeurs)
Richard Foreman (USA)
Set, Costume & Lighting Design

Company: **Ontological-Hysteric Theater**
Venue: **Festival d'Autumn, Bouffes du Nord**
Location: **Paris, France**
Opening/First Night: **1976**

Author: **Richard Foreman**
Scenic Designer: **Richard Foreman**
Costume Designer: **Richard Foreman**
Lighting Designer: **Richard Foreman**
Director: **Richard Foreman**

Contributing Researcher: **Eric Fielding**

Image Credit: **© Theodore Shank**

[55]

Midsummer Night's Dream
Susan Benson (Canada)
Set & Costume Design

Company: **Stratford Festival**
Venue: **The Festival Stage**
Location: **Stratford, Ontario, Canada**
Opening/First Night: **18 August 1976**

Author: **William Shakespeare**
Composer: **Alan Laing**
Scenic Designer: **Susan Benson**
Costume Designer: **Susan Benson**
Lighting Designer: **Michael J. Whitfield**
Director: **Robin Phillips**

Contributing Researcher: **Susan Benson**

Image Credit: **Susan Benson**

389

[56]

The Good Woman of Setzuan
(*Der gute mench von Sezuan*)
Nina Schiøttz (Denmark)
Set & Costume Design

Venue: **Aalborg Teater**
Location: **Aalborg, Denmark**
Opening/First Night: **28 October 1976**

Author: **Bertolt Brecht**
Composer: **Paul Dessau**
Scenic Designer: **Nina Schiøttz**
Costume Designer: **Nina Schiøttz**
Director: **Asger Bonfils**
Conductor: **Bente Frendrup**

Contributing Researcher: **Camilla Bjørnvad**

Image Credit: **Nina Schiøttz**

---

[57]

The Little Square (*Il Campiello*)
Deirdre Clancy (UK)
Costume Design

Company: **National Theatre**
Venue: **Olivier Theatre**
Location: **London, UK**
Opening/First Night: **25 October 1976**

Author: **Carlo Goldoni**, English version by
Susanna Graham-Jones & Bill Bryden
Scenic Designer: **Hayden Griffin**
Costume Designer: **Deirdre Clancy**
Lighting Designer: **Rory Dempster**
Director: **Bill Bryden**
Composer: **Michael Nyman**
Choreographer: **Romayne Grigorova**

Contributing Researcher: **Ian Herbert**

Image Credit: **Victoria and Albert Museum, London**

---

[57]

The Shadows
Tatiana Selvinskaya (USSR/Russia)
Set & Costume Design

Company: **Kirov Drama Theatre**
Location: **Kirov, USSR/Russia**
Opening/First Night: **1976**

Author: **Mikhail Saltykov-Shchedrin**
Scenic Designer: **Tatiana Selvinskaya**
Costume Designer: **Tatiana Selvinskaya**
Director: **Felix Berman**

Contributing Researcher: **Inna Mirzoyan**

Image Credit: **Tatiana Selvinskaya**

---

[58]

Romeo & Juliet
Phillip Silver (Canada)
Set & Lighting Design

Company: **Citadel Theatre**
Venue: **Shoctor Theatre**
Location: **Edmonton, Alberta**
Opening/First Night: **13 November 1976**

Author: **William Shakespeare**
Composer: **David Lovett**
Scenic Designer: **Phillip Silver**
Costume Designer: **David Lovett**
Lighting Designer: **Phillip Silver**
Director: **John Neville**
Choreographer: **Ronald Holgerson**

Contributing Researcher: **Phillip Silver**

Image Credit: **Phillip Silver**

---

[58]

Jakov Bogomolov
Vladimir Serebrovsky (USSR/Russia)
Set Design

Company: **Drama Theatre**
Location: **Magdeburg, Germany DDR**
Opening/First Night: **1976**

Author: **Maxim Gorki**
Scenic Designer: **Vladimir Serebrovsky**
Director: **Vladimir Andreyev**

Contributing Researcher: **Inna Mirzoyan**

Image Credit: **Vladimir Serebrovsky**

---

[59]

Jesus Christ Superstar
Kaoru Kanamori (Japan)
Set & Costume Design

Company: **Shiki Theatre Company**
Venue: **Nissei Theatre**
Location: **Tokyo, Japan**
Opening/First Night: **April 1976**

Composer: **Andrew Lloyd Webber**
Author: **Tim Rice**
Scenic Designer: **Kaoru Kanamori**
Costume Designer: **Kaoru Kanamori**
Lighting Designer: **Yuji Sawada**
Director: **Keita Asari**
Choreographer: **Taku Yamada**

Contributing Researcher: **Kazue Hatano & Eric Fielding**

Image Credits: **Kaoru Kanamori, Eric Fielding**

---

[60]

Ivanov
David Borovsky (USSR/Russia)
Set & Costume Design

Company: **Moscow Art Theatre** (MXAT)
Location: **Moscow, USSR/Russia**
Opening/First Night: **1976**

Author: **Anton Chekhov**
Scenic Designer: **David Borovsky**
Costume Designer: **David Borovsky**
Director: **Oleg Yefremov**

Contributing Researcher: **Inna Mirzoyan**

Image Credit: **David Borovsky**

---

[61]

Pacific Overtures
Boris Aronson (Russia/USA)
Set Design

Venue: **Winter Garden Theatre**
Location: **New York City, New York, USA**
Opening/First Night: **11 January 1976**

Composer: **Stephen Sondhiem**
Lyrics: **Stephen Sondhiem**
Author: **John Weidman**
Scenic Designer: **Boris Aronson**
Costume Designer: **Florence Klotz**
Lighting Designer: **Tharon Musser**
Sound Designer: **Jack Mann**
Kabuki Consultant: **Haruki Fujimoto**
Director: **Harold Prince**
Choreographer: **Patricia Birch**
Musical Director/Conductor: **Paul Gemignani**

Contributing Researcher: **Delbert Unruh**

Image Credits: **Martha Swope, Boris Aronson**

---

[61]

Empty Days (*Los Dias Vacios*)
Osvaldo Reyno (Uruguay)
Set Design

Venue: **Comedia Nacional Theatre**
Location: **Montevideo, Uruguay**
Opening/First Night: **1976**

Author: **Robert W. Anderson**
Scenic Designer: **Osvaldo Reyno**
Costume Designer: **Drugstore y Adam**
Lighting Designer: **Carlos Torres**
Director: **Elena Zuasti**

Contributing Researcher: **JC Serroni**

Image Credit: **Osvaldo Reyno**

---

[62]

Leonce and Lena (*Leonce a Lena*)
Jaroslav Malina (Czechoslovakia/Czech Republic)
Set & Costume Design

Venue: **Z. Nejedlý State Theatre**
Location: **Prague, Czechoslovakia/Czech Republic**
Opening/First Night: **22 April 1976**

Author: **Georg Büchner**
Scenic Designer: **Jaroslav Malina**
Costume Designer: **Jaroslav Malina**
Director: **Ivan Rajmont**

Contributing Researcher: **Daniela Pařízková & Marie Zdeňková**

Image Credit: **Prague Quadrennial Archive**

---

[63]

At the Nice View (*Kod lepog izgleda*)
Dušan Ristić (Serbia)
Set Design

Company: **Theatre Atelje 212**
Venue: **Theatre Atelje 212**
Location: **Belgrade, Serbia**
Opening/First Night: **19 March 1976**

Author: **Eden von Horvat**
Composer: **Vojislav Kostić**
Scenic Designer: **Dušan Ristić**
Scenic Artist: **Miljan Kljaković**
Costume Designer: **Božana Jovanović**
Lighting Designer: **Petar Stojković**
Sound Designer: **Đuro Sanader**
Director: **Paolo Magelli**

Contributing Researcher: **Radivoje Dinulović**

Image Credit: **Museum of Theatrical Arts of Serbia**

---

[63]

Tales of Ensign Stål (*Fänrik Ståls sägner*)
Ralf Forsström (Finland)
Set Design

Venue: **The Swedish Theatre, Helsinki**
Location: **Helsinki, Finland**
Opening/First Night: **31 August 1976**

Author: **Johan Ludvig Runeberg**, edited by
Frej Lindqvist and Bengt Ahlfors
Composer: **Otto Donner**
Scenic Designer: **Ralf Forsström** (after
Albert Edelfelt)
Costume Designer: **Annika Piha**
Lighting Designer: **Torolf Söderqvist**
Sound Designer: **Kristian Strömberg**
Director: **Frej Lindqvist**
Choreographer: **Fred Negendanck**
Conductor: **Nacke Johansson**

Contributing Researcher: **Hanna Helavuori**

Photographer: **Peter Widén**

Image Credit: **Ralf Forsström**

---

[64]

Long Day's Journey into Night
(*Lungul drum al zilei catre noapte*)
Dan Jitianu (Romania)
Set Design

Venue: **Lucia Sturza Bulandra Theatre**
Location: **Bucharest, Romania**
Opening/First Night: **10 January 1976**

Author: **Eugene O'Neill**
Scenic Designer: **Dan Jitianu**
Costume Designer: **Doris Jurgea**
Director: **Liviu Ciulei**

Contributing Researcher: **Jean Cazaban**

Image Credit: **Dan Jitia**

---

[64]

The Wedding (*Casatoria*)
Paul Bortnovschi (Romania)
Set Design

Company: **National Theatre**
Location: **Bucharest, Romania**
Opening/First Night: **1976**

Author: **N. Gogol**
Scenic Designer: **Paul Bortnovschi**
Costume Designer: **Elena Patrascu-Veakis**
Director: **Sanda Manu**

Contributing Researcher: **Jean Cazaban**

Image Credit: **Paul Bortnovschi**

---

[65]

The Left-hander (*Levsha*)
Boris Messerer (USSR/Russia)
Set & Costume Design

Company: **Kirov State Academic Opera & Ballet Theatre**
Venue: **Mariinsky Theatre**
Location: **Leningrad (St.Petersburg), USSR/Russia**
Opening/First Night: **1976**

Author: adapted from **Nikolai Leskov**'s story
Levsha
Scenic Designer: **Boris Messerer**
Costume Designer: **Boris Messerer**
Choreographer: **Konstantin Sergeev**

Contributing Researcher: **Inna Mirzoyan**

Image Credit: **Prague Quadrennial Archive**

---

[66]

Cervantes
Józef Szajna (Poland)
Set Design

Company: **Teatr Studio**
Venue: **Teatr Studio**
Location: **Warsaw, Poland**
Opening/First Night: **30 December 1976**

Author: **Józef Szajna**
Scenic Designer: **Józef Szajna**
Director: **Józef Szajna**

Contributing Researcher: **Agnieszka Kubas**

Image Credit: **Stefan Okołowicz**

---

[67]

To Clothe the Naked (*Vestire gli ignudi*)
Maurizio Balò (Italy)
Set Design

Venue: **Teatro Santa Chiara**
Location: **Brescia, Italy**
Opening/First Night: **1976**

Author: **Luigi Pirandello**
Scenic Designer: **Maurizio Balò**
Costume Designer: **Maurizio Balò**
Director: **Massimo Castri**

Contributing Researcher: **Daniela Sacco**

Image Credit: **Maurizio Balò**

[70]

The Journey to Golgotha
(Olugendo lwe Gologoosa)
Leonard Ondur (Uganda)
Set & Lighting Design

Company: **African Artists Association**
Venue: **National Theatre**
Location: **Kampala, Uganda**
Opening/First Night: **20 March 1977**

Author: **Wycliff Kiyingi**
Scenic Designer: **Leonard Ondur**
Costume Designer: **Wycliff Kiyingi**
Lighting Designer: **Leonard Ondur**
Sound Designer: **Leonard Ondur**
Director: **Wycliff Kiyingi**

Contributing Researcher: **Sam Kasule**

Image Credit: **Samuel Kasule**

[70]

Hamlet
Ezio Toffolutti (Italy)
Set & Costume Design

Company: **Festival d' Avignon**
Venue: **Corte dei Papi**
Location: **Avignon, France**
Opening/First Night: **July 1977**

Author: **William Shakespeare**
Scenic Designer: **Ezio Toffolutti**
Costume Designer: **Ezio Toffolutti**
Director: **Benno Besson**

Contributing Researcher: **Daniela Sacco**

Image Credit: **Ezio Toffolutti, National Library for Martone**

[70]

The Last Car (*O Ultimo Carro*)
Germano Blum (Brazil)
Set Design

Company: **Grupo Opiniao**
Venue: **Pavilhoao da Bienal**
Location: **São Paulo, Brazil**
Opening/First Night: **October 1977**

Author: **João das Neves**
Scenic Designer: **Germano Blum**
Lighting Designer: **João das Neves**
Sound Designer: **Antonio Camaleão**
Director: **João das Neves**

Contributing Researcher: **JC Serroni**

Image Credit: **Ruth Amorim Toledo**

[71]

Dead Souls
Valery Levental (USSR/Russia)
Set Design

Company: **State Academic Bolshoi Theatre**
Location: **Moscow, USSR/Russia**
Opening/First Night: **1977**

Composer: **Rodion Shchedrin**
Scenic Designer: **Valery Levental**
Director: **Boris Pokrovsky**

Contributing Researcher: **Inna Mirzoyan**

Image Credit: **Valery Levental**

[72]

Mother Courage
Metin Deniz (Turkey)
Set Design

Company: **Istanbul Municipal Theatre**
Venue: **Taksim Experimental Stage**
Location: **Istanbul, Turkey**
Opening/First Night: **October 1977**

Author: **Bertolt Brecht**
Scenic Designer: **Metin Deniz**
Director: **Beklan Algan**

Contributing Researcher: **Evcimen Percin**

Image Credit: **Metin Deniz**

[72]

Vienna Waltzes
Rouben Ter-Arutunian (Georgia/USA)
Set Design

Company: **New York City Ballet**
Venue: **New York State Theater, Lincoln Center**
Location: **New York, New York, USA**
Opening/First Night: **23 June 1977**

Composer: **Johann Strauss, Jr., Franz Lehár & Richard Strauss**
Scenic Designer: **Rouben Ter-Arutunian**
Costume Designer: **Karinska**
Lighting Designer: **Ronald Bates**
Choreographer: **George Balanchine**
Conductor: **Robert Irving**

Contributing Researcher: **Barbara Cohen-Stratyner & Eric Fielding**

Image Credit: **Martha Swope © The New York Public Library for the Performing Arts**

[73]

Untitled
Pilobolus Collective (USA)
Choreographic Design

Company: **Pilobolus Dance Theatre**
Venue: **Nikolais-Louis Theatre Lab**
Location: **New York, New York**
Opening/First Night: **1977**

Author: **Moses Pendleton, Robby Barnett, Jonathan Wolken & Michael Tracy**
Composer: **Robert Dennis**
Costume Designer: **Pilobolus Collective**
Lighting Designer: **Neil Peter Jampolis**
Choreographer: **Pilobolus Collective**

Contributing Researcher: **Jan Chambers**

Image Credit: **Tim Matson**

[74]

Macbeth
Hugh Colman (Australia)
Set & Costume Design

Company: **State Theatre Company of South Australia**
Venue: **The Playhouse, Adelaide Festival Centre**
Location: **Adelaide, Australia**
Opening/First Night: **1977**

Author: **William Shakespeare**
Scenic Designer: **Hugh Colman**
Costume Designer: **Hugh Colman**
Lighting Designer: **Nigel Levings**
Director: **Colin George**
Choreographer: **Michael Fuller**

Contributing Researcher: **Richard Roberts**

Image Credit: **Hugh Colman**

[75]

Danton's Death (*Dantonin kuolema*)
Juha Lukala (Finland)
Set Design

Company: **Turku City Theatre**
Venue: **Turku City Theatre**
Location: **Turku, Finland**
Opening/First Night: **4 February 1977**

Author: **Georg Büchner**
Composer: **Heikki Aaltoila**
Scenic Designer: **Juha Lukala**
Costume Designer: **Liisi Tandefelt**
Lighting Designer: **Osmo Salo and Timo Grönroos**
Director: **Ralf Långbacka**

Contributing Researcher: **Hanna Helavuori & Pälvi Laine**

Image Credit: **Juha Lukala**

[75]

The Tempest
Luciano Damiani (Italy)
Set Design

Company: **Strehler's Company**
Venue: **Piccolo Teatro di Milano**
Location: **Milano, Italy**
Opening/First Night: **July 1977**

Author: **William Shakespeare**
Scenic Designer: **Luciano Damiani**
Costume Designer: **Luciano Damiani**
Sound Designer: **Fiorenzo Carpi**
Director: **Giorgio Strehler**

Contributing Researcher: **Daniela Sacco**

Image Credits: **Luigi Ciminaghi/Piccolo Teatro di Milano/Teatro d'Europa**

[76]

Danton's Death
(*A Morte de Danton, Dantons Tod*)
Luis Carlos Mendes Ripper (Brazil)
Set Design

Venue: **Gallery of the Subway**
Location: **Rio de Janeiro, Brazil**
Opening/First Night: **1977**

Author: **Georg Büchner**
Scenic Designer: **Luis Carlos Mendes Ripper**

Contributing Researcher: **JC Serroni**

Image Credit: **Luis Carlos Mendes Ripper**

[76]

The Tower of Babel
(*Torre de Babel, La tour de Babel*)
Luis Carlos Mendes Ripper (Brazil)
Set Design

Location: **São Paulo, Brazil**
Opening/First Night: **1977**

Author: **Fernando Arrabal**
Scenic Designer: **Luis Carlos Mendes Ripper**
Costume Designer: **Luis Carlos Mendes Ripper**

Contributing Researcher: **JC Serroni**

Image Credit: **Luis Carlos Mendes Ripper**

[77]

The Cherry Orchard
Santo Loquasto (UK)
Set & Costume Design

Company: **New York Shakespeare Festival**
Venue: **Beaumont Theatre, Lincoln Center**
Location: **New York, New York, USA**
Opening/First Night: **17 February 1977**

Author: **Anton Chekhov**
Scenic Designer: **Santo Loquasto**
Costume Designer: **Santo Loquasto**
Lighting Designer: **Jennifer Tipton**
Director: **Andrei Serban**

Contributing Researcher: **Eric Fielding**

Image Credits: **Santo Loquasto, Randy Rupert**

[78]

Rumstick Road
Jim Clayburgh & Elizabeth LeCompte (USA)
Production Design

Company: **The Wooster Group**
Venue: **The Performing Garage**
Location: **New York, New York, USA**
Opening/First Night: **25 March 1977**

Author/Composer: **Spalding Gray & Elizabeth LeCompte**, in collaboration with Libby Howes, Bruce Porter, and Ron Vawter
Design: **Jim Clayburgh & Elizabeth LeCompte**
Director: **Elizabeth LeCompte**

Contributing Researcher: **Eric Fielding & Clay Hapaz**

Image Credits: **© Clem Fiori, © Elizabeth LeCompte, © Ken Kobland**

[79]

Michelangelo Buonarroti
Miodrag Tabački (Yugoslavia/Serbia)
Set & Costume Design

Company: **Drama Ensemble, Split Summer Festival**
Venue: **Croatian National Theatre**
Location: **Split, Yugoslavia/Croatia**
Opening/First Night: **30 July 1977**

Author: **Miroslav Krleža**
Scenic Designer: **Miodrag Tabački**
Costume Designer: **Miodrag Tabački**
Director: **Ljubiša Ristić**
Choreographer: **Nada Kokotović**

Contributing Researcher: **Lada Cale Feldman & Visnja Rogosic**

Image Credit: **Ljubomir Garbin, Croatian National Theatre Archive, Split**

[80]

The Merchant of Venice
Ichiro Takada (Japan)
Set Design

Company: **Haiyuza (Actors) Theatre Company**
Venue: **Toyoko Theatre**
Location: **Tokyo, Japan**
Opening/First Night: **January 1982**

Author: **William Shakespeare**
Composer: **Shinichiro Ikebe**
Scenic Designer: **Ichiro Takada**
Lighting Designer: **Sumio Yoshii**
Director: **Toshikiyo Masumi**

Contributing Researcher: **Kazue Hatano**

Image Credit: **Ichiro Takada**

[80]

He Who Gets Slapped
(Ten, který dostává políčky)
Fára Libor (Czechoslovakia/Czech Republic)
Set Design

Company: **Činoherní Club Prague**
Venue: **State Theatre Studio**
Location: **Prague, Czechoslovakia/Czech Republic**
Opening/First Night: **37 September 1977**

Author: **Leonid Andrejev**
Scenic Designer: **Libor Fára**
Costume Designer: **Jarmila Konecčná**
Director: **Miroslav Macháček**

Contributing Researcher: **Daniela Pařízková & Marie Zdeňková**

Image Credit: **Prague Quadrennial Archive**

[81]

The Trojan Women (Troades)
Yannis Tsarouchis (Greece)
Set & Costume Design

Company: **Yannis Tsarouchis Company**
Location: **Athens, Greece**
Opening/First Night: **Summer 1977**

Author: **Euripides**
Scenic Designer: **Yannis Tsarouchis**
Costume Designer: **Yannis Tsarouchis**
Director: **Yannis Tsarouchis**

Contributing Researcher: **Dio Kangelari**

Image Credit: **Yannis Tsarouchis**

[82]

Variations (Warjacje)
Jerzy Grzegorzewski (Poland)
Set Design

Company: **Teatr Dramatyczny**
Location: **Warsaw, Poland**
Opening/First Night: **30 December 1977**

Author: **Jerzy Grzegorzewski**
Composer: **Stanisław Radwan**
Scenic Designer: **Jerzy Grzegorzewski**
Director: **Jerzy Grzegorzewski**

Contributing Researcher: **Agnieszka Kubaś**

Image Credit: **Marek Holzman (ZPAF), Private archive of Ewa Bułhak**

[83]

Les Canadiens
Astrid Janson (Canada)
Set & Costume Design

Company: **Toronto Workshop Productions (TWP)**
Venue: **Toronto Workshop Productions**
Location: **Toronto, Canada**
Opening/First Night: **20 October 1977**

Author: **Rick Salutin**
Composer: **Pierre Lenoir**
Scenic Designer: **Astrid Janson**
Costume Designer: **Astrid Janson**
Lighting Designer: **Simon Reeve**
Sound Designer: **Victor Svenningson**
Director: **George Luscombe**

Contributing researcher: **Mary Kerr**

Image Credits: **Toronto Reference Library, Prague Quadrennial Archive**

[83]

The Tent Project
(Tältprojektet: vi äro tusenden...)
Sören Brunes (Sweden)
Set Design

Company: **Nationalföreningen för arbetarrörelsen i Sverige/Tältprojektet ideell förening**
Venue: **Heden**
Location: **Gothenburg, Sweden**
Opening/First Night: **1 May 1977**

Author: **Berit Persson, Ninne Olsson, Håkan Wennberg, Peter Wahlquist**
Composer: **Christer Boustedt, Ulf Dageby, Bertil Goldberg**
Scenic Designer: **Sören Brunes**
Costume Designer: **Aja Ericsson, Ann-Margret Fyregård**
Mask Designer: **Eva-Lena Jönsson, Stefan Wårdsäter**
Lighting Designer: **Lars Jacob Jakobsson, Figge Holmberg**
Sound Designer: **Peter Sikström, Kristina Firman, Tarzan Wågstam**
Director: **Björn Granath, Henric Holmberg, Med Reventberg**

Contributing Researcher: **Ammy Kjellsdotter**

Image Credits: **Sören Brunes**

[84]

Volpone or the Fox
Drago Turina (Yugoslavia/Croatia)
Set Design

Company: **Summer Festival of Split**
Venue: **Town Square in Trogir**
Location: **Trogir, Yugoslavia/Croatia**
Opening/First Night: **Summer 1977**

Author: **Ben Johnson**
Scenic Designer: **Drago Turina**
Director: **Bozidar Violić**

Contributing Researcher: **Ivana Bakal**

Image Credit: **Drago Turnia**

[84]

Julius Caesar
Ichiro Takada (Japan)
Set Design

Company: **Haiyuza (Actors) Theatre Company**
Venue: **Toyoko Theatre**
Location: **Tokyo, Japan**
Opening/First Night: **January 1977**

Author: **William Shakespeare**
Composer: **Shinichiro Ikebe**
Scenic Designer: **Ichiro Takada**
Lighting Designer: **Mitsuo Ushimaru**
Director: **Toshikiyo Masumi**

Contributing Researcher: **Kazue Hatano**

Image Credit: **Ichiro Takada**

[85]

Shadows (Сенки)
Georgi Ivanov (Bulgaria)
Set & Lighting Design

Company: **National Theatre "Ivan Vazov"**
Location: **Sofia, Bulgaria**
Opening/First Night: **1977**

Author: **W. Shchedrin**
Scenic Designer: **Georgi Ivanov**
Lighting Designer: **Georgi Ivanov**
Director: **Krastyo Mirski**

Contributing Researcher: **Marina Raytchinova**

Image Credit: **Georgi Ivanov**

[85]

Oresteia
Niels Hamel (Netherlands)
Design

Company: **De Appel**
Location: **Amsterdam, Netherlands**
Opening/First Night: **16 December 1977**

Author: **Aeschylus**
Scenic Designer: **Niels Hamel**
Costume Designer: **Niels Hamel**
Director: **Eric Vos**

Contributing Researcher: **Joke van Pelt**

Photographer: **Pan Sok** (Netherlands)

Image Credit: **Pan Sok**

[88]

Angel
Ming Cho Lee (China/USA)
Set Design

Venue: **Minskoff Theatre**
Location: **New York City, New York, USA**
Opening/First Night: **4 May 1978**

Composer: **Gary Geld**
Book & Lyrics: **Peter Udell** & **Ketti Frings**, based on the novel, *Look Homeward Angel*, by Thomas Wolfe
Scenic Designer: **Ming Cho Lee**
Costume Designer: **Pearl Somner**
Lighting Designer: **John Gleason**
Director: **Philip Rose**
Choreographer: **Robert Tucker**

Contributing Researcher: **Eric Fielding**

Image Credit: **Collection of the McNay Art Museum, Gift of Robert L. B. Tobin**

[88]

Faust - a Fantasy (Faust en fantasi)
Claus Rostrup (Denmark)
Set & Costume Design

Venue: **Gladsaxe Teater**
Location: **Copenhagen, Denmark**
Opening/First Night: **10 October 1978**

Author/Creator: **Goethe, Kaspar Rostrup**
Composer: **Fuzzy**
Scenic Designer: **Claus Rostrup**
Costume Designer: **Claus Rostrup**
Lighting Designer: **Benny Rünitz**
Director: **Kaspar Rostrup**
Choreographer: **Per Møller-Nielsen**
Conductor: **Poul Erik Christensen**

Contributing Researcher: **Camilla Bjørnvad**

Image Credit: **Klaus Lindewald, Royal Library Archive**

[89]

Shijima: The Darkness Calms Down in Space
Ushio Amagatsu (Japan)
Production Design

Company: **Sankai Juku**
Venue: **Théâtre de la Ville**
Location: **Paris, France**
Opening/First Night: **April 1988**

Composer: **Ushio Amagatsu**
Scenic Designer: **Ushio Amagatsu**
Costume Designer: **Ushio Amagatsu**
Lighting Designer: **Ushio Amagatsu**
Director: **Ushio Amagatsu**
Choreographer: **Ushio Amagatsu**

Contributing Researcher: **Kazue Hatano**

Image Credit: **Ushio Amagatsu**

[90]

On The Twentieth Century
Robin Wagner (USA)
Set Design

Venue: **St. James Theatre**
Location: **New York, New York, USA**
Opening/First Night: **19 February 1978**

Composer: **Cy Coleman**
Book & Lyrics: **Betty Comden & Adolph Green**
Scenic Designer: **Robin Wagner**
Costume Designer: **Florence Klotz**
Lighting Designer: **Ken Billington**
Director: **Harold Prince**
Choreographer: **Larry Fuller**

Contributing Researcher: **Eric Fielding**

Image Credits: **Martha Swope © The New York Public Library for the Performing Arts; Collection of the McNay Art Museum, Gift of Robert L. B. Tobin**

[91]

Zoot Suit
Roberto Morales & Thomas A. Walsh (USA)
Set Design

Company: **Center Theatre Group**
Venue: **Mark Taper Forum**
Location: **Los Angeles, California, USA**
Opening/First Night: **17 August 1978**

Author: **Luis Valdez**
Composer: **Daniel Valdez & Lalo Guerrero**
Scenic Designer: **Roberto Morales & Thomas A. Walsh**
Costume Designer: **Peter J. Hall**
Lighting Designer: **Dawn Chiang**
Sound Designer: **Abe Jacob**
Director: **Luis Valdez**
Choreographer: **Patricia Birch**

Contributing Researcher: **Alma Martinez & Eric Fielding**

Image Credit: **Center Theatre Group**

[91]

Project Round Tower (Projekt Rundetårn)
Kirsten Dehlholm & Per Flink Basse (Denmark)
Set & Costume Design

Venue: **Billedstofteater i Rundetårn**
Location: **Copenhagen, Denmark**
Opening/First Night: **1978**

Scenic Designer: **Kirsten Dehlholm**
Costume Designer: **Per Flink Basse**

Contributing Researcher: **Camilla Bjørnvad**

Image Credit: **Kirsten Dehlholm**

[92]

Antichrist (Антихрист)
Neyko Neykov (Bulgaria)
Set, Costume & Lighting Design

Company: **Plovdiv Drama Theatre**
Venue: **Plovdiv Drama Theatre**
Location: **Plovdiv, Bulgaria**
Opening/First Night: **1978**

Author: **Emiliyan Stanev**
Scenic Designer: **Neyko Neykov**
Costume Designer: **Neyko Neykov**
Lighting Designer: **Neyko Neykov**
Sound Designer: **Kiril Grozdanov**
Director: **Ivan Dobchev**

Contributing Researcher: **Marina Raytchinova**

Image Credit: **Drama Theatre Plovdiv**

[94]
Betrayal
John Bury (UK)
Set Designs

Company: **National Theatre**
Venue: **Lyttelton**
Location: **London, UK**
Opening/First Night: **18 November 1978**

Author: **Harold Pinter**
Scenic Designer: **John Bury**
Costume Designer: **John Bury**
Lighting Designer: **John Bury**
Director: **Peter Hall**

Contributing Researcher: **Ian Herbert**

Image Credits: **Douglas H Jeffery, Victoria and Albert Museum, London; National Theatre Archive**

[95]
The Insect Play (*Ze života hmyzu*)
Jan Vančura (Czechoslovakia/Czech Republic)
Set & Costume Design

Venue: **F. X. Šalda Theatre**
Location: **Liberec, Czechoslovakia/Czech Republic**
Opening/First Night: **10 June 1978**

Author: **Karel & Josef Čapové**
Scenic Designer: **Jan Vančura**
Costume Designer: **Jan Vančura**
Director: **Karel Kříž**

Contributing Researcher: **Daniela Pařízková**

Image Credit: **Prague Quadrennial Archive**

[96]
Kabuki Macbeth
Shozo Sato (Japan/USA)
Set & Costume Design

Company: **University of Illinois Department of Drama**
Venue: **Festival Theater, Krannert Center for the Performing Arts**
Location: **Urbana, Illinois, USA**
Opening/First Night: **1978**

Author: **Shozo Sato**, after William Shakespeare
Scenic Designer: **Shozo Sato**
Costume Designer: **Shozo Sato**
Lighting Designer: **Ray Caton**
Sound Designer: **Michael Cerri**
Director: **Shozo Sato**
Choreographer: **Shozo Sato**
Text editor: **Tom Heenan**

Contributing Researcher: **Jan Chambers**

Image Credit: **Shozo Sato**

[98]
Cracow Crib (*Szopka krakowska*)
Adam Kilian (Poland)
Set, Costume & Puppet Design

Company: **Teatr Lalek Pleciuga**
Venue: **Teatr Lalek Pleciuga**
Location: **Szczecin, Poland**
Opening/First Night: **19 November 1978**

Author: **Tadeusz & Stanisław Estreicher**
Composer: **Jerzy Dobrzański**
Scenic Designer: **Adam Kilian**
Costume Designer: **Adam Kilian**
Puppet Designer: **Adam Kilian**
Director: **Bohdan Radkowski**
Choreographer: **Zygmunt Zdanowicz**

Contributing Researcher: **Anna Ochman**

Image Credit: **Jacek Pawłowski, Archive of The Puppets Theatre 'Pleciuga' in Szczecin (Poland); Adam Kilian**

[99]
Woyzeck
Cristina Reis (Portugal)
Set Design

Company: **The Cornucopia Theatre**
Venue: **Teatro do Bairro Alto**
Location: **Lisbon, Portugal**
Opening/First Night: **18 July 1978**

Author: **Georg Büchner**
Composer: **Paulo Brandão**
Scenic Designer: **Cristina Reis**
Costume Designer: **Cristina Reis**
Lighting Designer: **Jorge Silva Melo, Luís Miguel Cintra, Abílio Henriques**
Director: **Jorge Silva Melo, Luís Miguel Cintra**

Contributing Researcher: **Paulo Eduardo Carvalho & Maria Helena Serôdio**

Image Credits: **Cristina Reis, Paulo Cintra Gomes**

[99]
Spartacus
Boris Messerer (USSR/Russia)
Set Design

Company: **Spendiarov Opera and Ballet Theatre**
Location: **Yerevan, USSR/Armenia**
Opening/First Night: **1978**

Composer: **Aram Khachaturian**
Scenic Designer: **Boris Messerer**
Choreographer: **Vilen Galstian**

Contributing Researcher: **Inna Mirzoyan**

Image Credit: **Prague Quadrennial Archive**

[100]
The End of the World (*El Fin del Mundo*)
El Teatro Campesino (USA)
Scenic Design

Company: **El Teatro Campesino**
Location: **San Juan Bautista, California, USA**
Opening/First Night: **1978**

Author: **Luis Valdez**
Composer: **Luis Valdez**
Scenic Designer: **El Teatro Campesino**
Costume Designer: **El Teatro Campesino**
Lighting Designer: **El Teatro Campesino**
Sound Designer: **El Teatro Campesino**
Director: **Luis Valdez**
Choreographer: **Luis Valdez**

Contributing Researcher: **Alma Martinez & Eric Fielding**

Image Credit: **El Teatro Campesino**

[100]
Oedipus
Maurizio Balò (Italy)
Set & Costume Design

Venue: **Piazza del Foro**
Location: **Brescia, Italy**
Opening/First Night: **1978**

Author: **L. A. Seneca**
Scenic Designer: **Maurizio Balò**
Costume Designer: **Maurizio Balò**
Director: **Massimo Castri**

Contributing Researcher: **Daniela Sacco**

[101]
Oedipus Rex
Cameron Porteous (Canada)
Set & Costume Design

Company: **Vancouver Playhouse**
Venue: **Vancouver Playhouse Theatre**
Location: **Vancouver, Canada**
Opening/First Night: **7 January 1978**

Author: **Sophocles**
Composer: **Michael Richards**
Scenic Designer: **Cameron Porteous**
Costume Designer: **Cameron Porteous**
Lighting Designer: **Jeffrey Dallas**
Director: **Yurk Bogodawitz** (Bogajewicz)

Contributing Researcher: **Peter McKinnon**

Image Credit: **Eric Fielding**

[104]
The Second Handshake
Zhang Lian (China)
Set & Costume Design

Company: **The G.F.K.W. Art Troupe**
Venue: **The 5th Unit Theatre of The Second Machinery Department**
Location: **China**
Opening/First Night: **October 1979**

Author: **The G.F.K.W. Art Troupe**
Scenic Designer: **Zhang Lian**
Costume Designer: **Zhang Lian**
Lighting Designer: **Qi Yinghou**
Director: **Lou Kai**

Contributing Researcher: **Xu Xiang**

Image Credit: **Zhang Lian**

[105]
The Bourgeois Gentleman (*Úrhatnám polgár*)
Nelly Vágó (Hungary)
Costume Design

Company: **National Theatre**
Venue: **National Theatre**
Location: **Budapest, Hungary**
Opening/First Night: **1979**

Author: **Molière**
Composer: **Jean-Baptiste de Lully**
Scenic Designer: **Gyula Pauer**
Costume Designer: **Nelly Vágó**
Director: **Gábor Székely**
Choreographer: **Sándor Ivánka**

Contributing Researcher: **Eva Nemeth**

Image Credit: **Benkő Imre, MTI Photo Archive (Magyar Távirati Iroda - Hungarian News Agency)**

[106]
Chikamatsu Lovers' Suicide Story
Setsu Asakura (Japan)
Set Design

Company: **Toho Company**
Venue: **Imperial Theatre** (Teikoku gekijou)
Location: **Tokyo, Japan**
Opening/First Night: **February 1979**

Author: **Matsuyo Akimoto**
Composer: **Ryudou Uzaki**
Scenic Designer: **Setsu Asakura**
Costume Designer: **Jusaburou Tsujimura**
Lighting Designer: **Sumio Yoshii**
Sound Designer: **Akira Honma**
Director: **Yukio Ninagawa**

Contributing Researcher: **Kazue Hatano**

Image Credit: **Setsu Asakura**

[107]
Richard III
Mirian Shveldidze (USSR/Georgia)
Set Design

Company: **Shota Rustaveli Academic Drama Theatre**
Location: **Tblisi, USSR/Georgia**
Opening/First Night: **1979**

Author: **William Shakespeare**
Scenic Designer: **Mirian Shveldidze**
Director: **Robert Sturua**

Contributing Researcher: **Inna Mirzoyan**

Image Credit: **Mirian Shveldidze**

[107]
The Tempest (*Furtuna*)
Liviu Ciulei (Romania)
Set Design

Venue: **Lucia Sturza Bulandra Theatre**
Location: **Bucharest, Romania**
Opening/First Night: **1979**

Author: **William Shakespeare**
Composer: **Theodor Grigoriu**
Scenic Designer: **Liviu Ciulei**
Costume Designer: **Doina Levintza**
Director: **Liviu Ciulei**
Choreographer: **Adina Cezar & Sergiu Anghel**

Contributing Researcher: **Jean Cazaban**

Image Credit: **Liviu Ciulei**

[108]
The Seagull
Sergei Barkhin (Russia)
Set Design

Company: **Lithuanian State Youth Theatre**
Location: **Vilnius, Lithuania**
Opening/First Night: **1979**

Author: **Anton Chekhov**
Scenic Designer: **Sergei Barkhin**
Director: **Dalia Tamulyavichyute**

Contributing Researcher: **Inna Mirzoyan**

Image Credit: **Sergei Barkhin**

[108]
Macunaíma
Naum Alves de Souza (Brazil)
Costume Design

Company: **Macunaima Group**
Venue: **Anchieta Theater**
Location: **São Paulo, Brazil**
Opening/First Night: **1979**

Author: **Mario de Andrade**
Scenic Designer: **Naum Alves de Souza**
Costume Designer: **Naum Alves de Souza**
Lighting Designer: **Sandro Apolônio**
Director: **Antunes Filho**

Contributing Researcher: **JC Serroni**

Image Credits: **Paulo Henrique, Carvalho, Derly Barroso**

[109]

Bouquet (Kytice)
Jana Zbořilová (Czechoslovakia/
Czech Republic)
Set & Costume Design

Company: **Theatre on a String**
Venue: **State Theatre Brno**
Location: **Brno, Czecholslovakia/
Czech Republic**
Opening/First Night: **22 December 1979**

Author: **Rudolf Těsnohlídek, Miloš Štědroň**
Scenic Designer: **Jana Zbořilová**
Costume Designer: **Jana Zbořilová**
Director: **Zdeněk Pospíšil**

Contributing Researcher: **Daniela Pařízková
& Marie Zdeňková**

Image Credit: **Prague Quadrennial Archive**

[110]

*The Passion and Death of Our Lord Jesus
Christ (Passio et mors Domini Nostri Iesu
Christi secundum, Pasja)*
Andrzej Majewski (Poland)
Set Design

Company: **Teatr Wielki**
Venue: **Teatr Wielki**
Location: **Warsaw, Poland**
Opening/First Night: **14 January 1979**

Composer: **Krzysztof Penderecki**
Scenic Designer: **Andrzej Majewski**
Director: **Andrzej Majewski**
Conductor: **Jacek Kasprzyk**

Contributing Researcher: **Agnieszka Kubaś**

Image Credit: **Andrzej Majewski, Archive
of The Centre of Polish Scenography in
Katowice; Leon Myszkowski**

[111]

Ten Characters of Date
Kumaji Kugimachi (Japan)
Set Design

Company: **Ichikawa Ennosuke Kabuki**
Venue: **Kabukiza Theatre**
Location: **Tokyo, Japan**
Opening/First Night: **July 1979**

Author: **Tsuruya Nanboku**, adapted by
Shouji Nakagawa
Scenic Designer: **Kumaji Kugimachi**
Lighting Designer: **Kiyotsune Soma**
Director: **Kanjurou Fujima**
Choreographer: **Kanjurou Fujima**

Contributing Researcher: **Kazue Hatano**

Image Credit: **Kumaji Kugimachi**

[111]

Chalk (Giz)
Alvaro Apocalypse (Brazil)
Puppet Design

Company: **Group Giramundo**
Location: **Belo Horizonte, Brazil**
Opening/First Night: **1979**

Author: **Alvaro Apocalypse**
Puppet Designer: **Alvaro Apocalypse**
Director: **Alvaro Apocalypse**

Contributing Researcher: **JC Serroni**

Image Credit: **Enzo Giaquinto**

[112]

*Sweeney Todd, The Demon Barber
of Fleet Street*
Eugene Lee & Franne Lee (USA)
Set & Costume Design

Venue: **Uris Theatre**
Location: **New York, New York, USA**
Opening/First Night: **1 March 1979**

Composer: **Stephen Sondheim**
Lyrics: **Stephen Sondheim**
Author: **Hugh Wheeler**
Scenic Designer: **Eugene Lee**
Costume Designer: **Franne Lee**
Lighting Designer: **Ken Billington**
Sound Designer: **Jack Mann**
Director: **Harold Prince**
Choreographer: **Larry Fuller**

Contributing Researcher: **Eric Fielding**

Image Credit: **Martha Swope © The New
York Public Library for the Performing Arts**

[113]

Three Sisters
Vladimir Serebrovsky (Russia)
Set Design

Company: **Drama Theatre**
Location: **Magdeburg, Germany DDR**
Opening/First Night: **1979**

Author: **Anton Chekhov**
Scenic Designer: **Vladimir Serebrovsky**
Director: **Vladimir Andreyev**

Contributing Researcher: **Inna Mirzoyan**

Image Credit: **Vladimir Serebrovsky**

[114]

The Duelist (Rváč)
Otakar Schindler (Czechoslovakia/
Czech Republic)
Set & Costume Design

Company: **E. F. Burian Theatre**
Location: **Prague, Czechoslovakia/
Czech Republic**
Opening/First Night: **14 November 1979**

Author: **Ivan Sergeyevič Turgeněv**
(Translation by Antonín Máša)
Scenic Designer: **Otakar Schindler**
Costume Designer: **Otakar Schindler**
Director: **Jan Kačer**

Contributing Researcher: **Daniela Pařízková
& Marie Zdeňková**

Image Credit: **Prague Quadrennial Archive**

[114]

Beautiful Vida (Lepa Vida)
Meta Hočevar (Slovenia)
Set & Costume Design

Company: **SLG Celje**
Location: **Celje, Slovenia**
Opening/First Night: **28 September 1979**

Author: **Ivan Cankar**
Scenic Designer: **Meta Hočevar**
Costume Designer: **Meta Hočevar**
Director: **Mile Korun**
Dramaturg: **Igor Lampret**
Music: **Darijan Božič**

Contributing Researcher: **Nicole Leclercq**

Image Credit: **Meta Hočevar**

[115]

Hamlet
Hugh Colman (Australia)
Set & Costume Design

Company: **State Theatre Company of South
Australia**
Venue: **The Playhouse, Adelaide Festival
Centre**
Location: **Adelaide, Australia**
Opening/First Night: **1979**

Author: **William Shakespeare**
Scenic Designer: **Hugh Colman**
Costume Designer: **Hugh Colman**
Lighting Designer: **Nigel Levings**
Director: **Colin George**
Choreographer: **Michael Fuller**

Contributing Researcher: **Richard Roberts**

Image Credit: **Hugh Colman**

[115]

Vassa Zheleznova
Igor Popov (USSR/Russia)
Set Design

Company: **Stanislavsky Drama Theatre**
Location: **Moscow, USSR/Russia**
Opening/First Night: **1979**

Author: **Maxim Gorki**
Scenic Designer: **Igor Popov**
Director: **Anatoly Vasiliev**

Contributing Researcher: **Inna Mirzoyan**

Image Credit: **Igor Popov**

[116]

The Third Pole (A treia teapa)
Vittorio Holtier (Romania)
Set & Costume Design

Venue: **Municipal Theatre**
Location: **Ploiesti, Romania**
Opening/First Night: **1979**

Author: **Marin Sorescu**
Scenic Designer: **Vittorio Holtier**
Costume Designer: **Vittorio Holtier**
Director: **Letitia Popa**

Contributing Researcher: **Jean Cazaban**

Image Credit: **Vittorio Holtier**

[116]

Richard III
Tatiana Selvinskaya (USSR/Russia)
Set & Costume Design

Company: **Primorsk (Seaside) Drama
Theatre**
Location: **Vladivostok, USSR/Russia**
Opening/First Night: **1979**

Author: **William Shakespeare**
Scenic Designer: **Tatiana Selvinskaya**
Costume Designer: **Tatiana Selvinskaya**
Director: **Efim Tabachnikov**

Contributing Researcher: **Inna Mirzoyan**

Image Credit: **Tatiana Selvinskaya**

[117]

*Sinking of the Titanic
(Der Untergang der Titanic)*
Martin Rupprecht (Germany FGR)
Set & Costume Design

Company: **Deutsche Oper Berlin**
Venue: **Deutsche Oper**
Location: **Berlin, Germany FRG**
Opening/First Night: **6 September 1979**

Author: **Wilhelm Dieter Siebert**
Scenic Designer: **Martin Rupprecht**
Costume Designer: **Martin Rupprecht**
Director: **Winfried Bauernfeind**
Conductor: **Caspar Richter**

Contributing Researcher: **Karin
Winkelsesser**

Image Credit: © **Martin Rupprecht**

[118]

Idomeneo
John Truscott (Australia)
Set & Costume Design

Company: **Victorian State Opera**
Venue: **Princess Theatre**
Location: **Melbourne, Australia**
Opening/First Night: **1979**

Composer: **Wolfgang Amadeus Mozart**
Scenic Designer: **John Truscott**
Costume Designer: **John Truscott**
Director: **Robin Lovejoy**

Contributing Researcher: **Richard Roberts**

[119]

Amadeus
John Bury (UK)
Set, Costume & Lighting Design

Company: **National Theatre**
Venue: **Olivier Theatre** (followed by West
End and Broadway transfers)
Location: **London, UK**
Opening/First Night: **26 October 1979**

Author: **Peter Shaffer**
Scenic Designer: **John Bury**
Costume Designer: **John Bury**
Lighting Designer: **John Bury**
Director: **Peter Hall**

Contributing Researcher: **Donatella Barbieri
& Ian Herbert**

Image Credits: **Douglas H Jeffery, Victoria
and Albert Museum, London;** © **Nobby
Clark/Arenapal**

[122]

The Suppliants (Ικέτιδες)
Giorgos Ziakas (Greece)
Set & Costume Design

Company: **Cyprus Theatre Organisation**
Venue: **Epidaurus Festival**
Location: **Nicosia, Cyprus**
Opening/First Night: **30 July 1980**

Author: **Aeschylus**
Scenic Designer: **Giorgos Ziakas**
Costume Designer: **Giorgos Ziakas**
Director: **Nikos Charalambous**

Contributing Researcher: **Dio Kangelari**

Image Credit: **Giorgos Ziakas, Andreas
Coutas**

[122]

Montserrat
Mao Jingang (China)
Set & Costume Design

Company: **The Youth Art Theatre**
Venue: **The Youth Art Theatre**
Location: **China**
Opening/First Night: **1980**

Author: **E. Roblus**
Scenic Designer: **Mao Jingang**
Costume Designer: **Mao Jingang**
Lighting Designer: **Guo Rongchen**
Director: **Cen Rong**

Contributing Researcher: **Xu Xiang**

Image Credit: **Mao Jingang**

[123]

The Elephant Man
Kaoru Kanamori (Japan)
Set Design

Company: **Shiki Theatre Company**
Venue: **Nissei Theatre**
Location: **Tokyo, Japan**
Opening/First Night: **September 1980**

Author: **Bernard Pomerance**
Scenic Designer: **Kaoru Kanamori**
Costume Designer: **Hiroshi Tomi**
Lighting Designer: **Yuji Sawada**
Director: **Keita Asari**

Contributing Researcher: **Kazue Hatano &
Eric Fielding**

Image Credits: **Kaoru Kanamori, Eric
Fielding**

[124]

Parintins Street Festival
(*Festa Popular de Parintins*)
Group Caprichoso (Brazil)
Set Design

Company: **Group Caprichoso**
Location: **Manaus, Amazonas, Brazil**
Opening/First Night: **1980**

Scenic Designer: **Collective Creation**
Costume Designer: **Collective Creation**

Contributing Researcher: **JC Serroni**

Image Credit: **Andreas Valentin**

[125]

Genroku Minato Uta
Setsu Asakura (Japan)
Set Design

Company: **Toho Company**
Venue: **Imperial Theatre** (Teikoku gekijou)
Location: **Tokyo, Japan**
Opening/First Night: **September 1980**

Author: **Matsuyo Akimoto**
Scenic Designer: **Setsu Asakura**
Lighting Designer: **Sumio Yoshii**
Sound Designer: **Akira Honma**
Director: **Yukio Ninagawa**

Contributing Researcher: **Kazue Hatano**

Image Credit: **Setsu Asakura**

[125]

Waiting for Godot (*Asteptand pe Godot*)
Paul Bortnovski (Romania)
Set Design

Venue: **National Theatre**
Location: **Bucharest, Romania**
Opening/First Night: **1980**

Author: **Samuel Beckett**
Scenic Designer: **Paul Bortnovski**
Costume Designer: **Constantin Russu**
Director: **Grigore Gonta**

Contributing Researcher: **Jean Cazaban**

Image Credit: **Paul Bortnovski**

[126]

Cruel Games
Oleg Sheintsis (USSR/Russia)
Set Design

Company: **Lenkom Theatre**
Location: **Moscow, USSR/Russia**
Opening/First Night: **1980**

Author: **Aleksey Arbuzov**
Scenic Designer: **Oleg Sheintsis**
Director: **Mark Zakharov**

Contributing Researcher: **Inna Morzoyan**

Image Credit: **Oleg Sheintsis**

[126]

The Hundredth Bride
Wang Linyou (China)
Set Design

Company: **The Central Opera Theatre**
Venue: **The Tianqiao Playhouse**
Opening/First Night: **1980**

Author: **Li Shusheng, Wang Shiguang, Xu
Xueda, Hu Xianting**
Composer: **Wang Shiguang**
Scenic Designer: **Wang Linyou**
Costume Designer: **Situ Ping**
Lighting Designer: **Liu Rui**
Director: **Liu Lianchi**

Contributing Researcher: **Xu Xiang**

Image Credit: **Wang Linyou**

[127]

The Sunny South
Ian Robinson (Australia)
Set Design

Company: **Sydney Theatre Company**
Venue: **Drama Theatre, Sydney Opera
House**
Location: **Sydney, Australia**
Opening/First Night: **January 1980**

Author: **George Darrell**
Scenic Designer: **Ian Robinson**
Costume Designer: **Vicky Feitscher**
Director: **Richard Wherrett**

Contributing Researcher: **Richard Roberts**

Image Credit: **Peter Holderness**

[127]

The Haggadah: A Passover Cantata
Julie Taymor (USA)
Set & Costume Design

Company: **New York Shakespeare Festival**
Venue: **The Public Theater**
Location: **New York City, New York, USA**
Opening/First Night: **1980**

Author: **Elizabeth Swados**
Composer: **Elizabeth Swados**
Scenic Designer: **Julie Taymor**
Costume Designer: **Julie Taymor**
Puppet and Mask Designer: **Julie Taymor**
Lighting Designer: **Arden Fingerhut**
Director: **Elizabeth Swados**

Contributing Researcher: **Eric Fielding**

Image Credit: **Martha Swope © The New
York Public Library for the Performing Arts**

[128]

Danton's Death (*Dantons Tod*)
Jürgen Rose (Germany FRG)
Set Design

Company: **Kammerspiele München**
Venue: **Kammerspiele München**
Location: **Munich, Germany**
Opening/First Night: **1980**

Author: **Georg Buechner**
Scenic Designer: **Jürgen Rose**
Costume Designer: **Jürgen Rose**
Lighting Designer: **Max Keller**
Director: **Dieter Dorn**

Contributing Researcher: **Karin
Winkelsesser**

Image Credit: **Jürgen Rose**

[130]

Satyagraha
Robert Israel (USA)
Set & Costume Design

Company: **National Opera of the
Netherlands, Utrechts Symfonie Orkest**
Venue: **Stadsschouwburg**
Location: **Rotterdam, Netherlands**
Opening/First Night: **5 September 1980**

Composer: **Phillip Glass**
Librettist: **Constance De Jong**, based on the
Hindu scripture, the Bhagavad Gita
Scenic Designer: **Robert Israel**
Costume Designer: **Robert Israel**
Lighting Designer: **Richard Riddell**
Director: **David Pountney** (Netherlands),
Hans Nieuwenhuis (New York)

Contributing Researcher: **Jan Chambers**

Image Credit: **Richard Riddell**

[131]

Sideshow Alley
Ian Robinson (Australia)
Set Design

Venue: **Paris Theatre**
Location: **Sydney, Australia**
Opening/First Night: **October 1980**

Author: **Robyn Archer**
Composer: **Robyn Archer**
Scenic Designer: **Ian Robinson**
Costume Designer: **Ron Williams**
Lighting Designer: **Peter Holderness**
Director: **Rodney Fisher**
Choreographer: **Keith Bain**

Contributing Researcher: **Richard Roberts**

Image Credit: **Peter Holderness**

[131]

Tear Heart (*Rasga Coração*)
Marcos Flaksman (Brazil)
Set & Costume Design

Venue: **Sergio Cardoso Theater**
Location: **Sao Paulo, Brazil**
Opening/First Night: **October 1980**

Author: **Oduvaldo Viana Filho**
Composer: **John Neschling & Segio Scolo**
Scenic Designer: **Marcos Flaksman**
Costume Designer: **Marcos Flaksman**
Lighting Designer: **Jorginho de Carvalho**
Director: **Jose Renato**
Choreographer: **Lucia Aratanha & Helena
Moreira**

Contributing Researcher: **JC Serroni**

Image Credit: **Nani Góis**

[132]

Lola
Hysen Devolli (Albania)
Set Design

Venue: **The National Theatre of Opera and
Ballet**
Location: **Tirana, Albania**
Opening/First Night: **12 October 1980**

Composer: **Sergei Nikiforovich Vasilenko**
Scenic Designer: **Hysen Devolli**
Costume Designer: **Hysen Devolli**
Choreographer: **Agron Aliaj**

Contributing Researcher: **Ilir Martini**

Photo: **Ilir Martini**

Image Credit: **Hysen Devolli**

[132]

The Cunning Little Vixen
(*Příhody Lišky Bystroušky*)
Maria Björnson (UK/France)
Costume Design

Company: **Scottish Opera**
Location: **Glasgow, Scotland**
Opening/First Night: **1980**

Composer: **Leoš Janáček**
Scenic Designer: **Maria Björnson**
Costume Designer: **Maria Björnson**
Lighting Designer: **Nick Chelton**
Director: **David Pountney**

Contributing Researcher: **Ian Herbert &
Donatella Barbieri**

Image Credit: **Victoria and Albert Museum,
London; Prague Quadrennial Archive**

[133]

Wielopole, Wielopole
Tadeusz Kantor (Poland)
Set & Costume Design

Company: **Teatr Cricot 2**
Venue: **Teatr Cricot 2**
Location: **Kraków, Poland**
Opening/First Night: **23 June 1980**

Author: **Tadeusz Kantor**
Scenic Designer: **Tadeusz Kantor**
Costume Designer: **Tadeusz Kantor**
Director: **Tadeusz Kantor**

Contributing Researcher: **Agnieszka Kubaś**

Image Credit: **Tadeusz Kantor, © Maria
Kantor & Dorota Krakowska, Archive of The
Centre for the Documentation of the Art of
Tadeusz Kantor CRICOTEKA in Kraków;
Leszek Dziedzic**

[134]

Don Juan is Coming Back from War
(Don Žuan se vraća iz rata)
Dušan Ristić (Croatia/Serbia)
Set Design

Company: **Yugoslav Drama Theatre**
Venue: **Yugoslav Drama Theatre**
Location: **Belgrade, Yugoslavia/Serbia**
Opening/First Night: **4 September 1980**

Author: **Eden von Horvat** (Ödön von Horváth)
Composer: **Zoran Simjanović**
Scenic Designer: **Dušan Ristić**
Costume Designer: **Božana Jovanović**
Director: **Paolo Magelli**

Contributing Researcher: **Radivoje Dinulović**
Author's sketch: **Museum of Theatre Arts of Serbia**
Photographs: **Yugoslav Drama Theatre**

Image Credit: **Museum of Theatrical Arts of Serbia**

---

[134]

Caligula
Paul Bortnovski (Romania)
Set Design

Venue: **National Theatre**
Location: **Bucharest, Romania**
Opening/First Night: **1980**

Author: **Albert Camus**
Scenic Designer: **Paul Bortnovski**
Costume Designer: **Doina Levintza**
Director: **Horea Popescu**

Contributing Researcher: **Jean Cazaban**

---

[135]

Maestro and Margaret
(Maestrul si Margareta)
Lia Mantoc (Romania)
Costume Design

Venue: **Teatrul Mic**
Location: **Bucharest, Romania**
Opening/First Night: **1980**

Author: **Mihaela Tonitza & Catalina Buzoian**, adapted from novel by Mihail Bulgakov
Composer: **Mircea Florian**
Scenic Designer: **Andrei Both**
Costume Designer: **Lia Mantoc**
Director: **Catalina Buzoianu**
Choreographer: **Miriam Raducanu**

Contributing Researcher: **Jean Cazaban**

Image Credit: **Lia Mantoc, Bucharest**

---

[138]

Juno and Avos (*Yunona i Avos*)
Oleg Sheintsis & Valentina Komolova (USSR/Russia)
Set & Costume Design

Company: **Lenkom Theatre**
Location: **Moscow, USSR/Russia**
Opening/First Night: **1981**

Author: **Andrei Voznesensky**
Composer: **Aleksey Rybnikov**
Scenic Designer: **Oleg Sheintsis**
Costume Designer: **Valentina Komolova**
Lighting Designer: **Peter Pchelyntsev**
Director: **Mark Zakharov**

Contributing Researcher: **Inna Mirzoyan**

Image Credit: **Valentina Komolova**

---

[140]

The True Story of Ah Q
Xue Dianjie (China)
Set & Costume Design

Company: **The Central Experimental Drama Theatre**
Venue: **The Cultural Palace of Nationalities of Beijing**
Location: **Beijing, China**
Opening/First Night: **August 1981**

Author: **Lu Xun**, adapted by Chen Baichen
Scenic Designer: **Xue Dianjie**
Costume Designer: **Xue Dianjie**
Lighting Designer: **Zhang Wenchang**
Director: **Yu Cun, Wen Xingyu**

Contributing Researcher: **Xu Xiang**

Image Credit: **Xue Dianjie**

---

[140]

The Seven against Thebes (*Επτά επί Θήβας*)
Giorgos Ziakas (Greece)
Set & Costume Design

Company: **National Theatre of Greece**
Venue: **Epidaurus Festival**
Location: **Athens, Greece**
Opening/First Night: **18 July 1981**

Author: **Aeschylus**
Scenic Designer: **Giorgos Ziakas**
Costume Designer: **Giorgos Ziakas**
Sound Designer: **Michalis Christodoulidis** (music)
Director: **Nikos Charalambous**

Contributing Researcher: **Dio Kangelari**

Image Credit: **Giorgos Ziakas**

---

[141]

The Alphabet Story (*Хождение по буквам*)
Silva Bachvarova (Bulgaria)
Set, Costume & Puppet Design

Company: **State Puppet theatre**
Location: **Plovdiv, Bulgaria**
Opening/First Night: **1981**

Author: **Valeri Petrov**
Composer: **Traditional Bulgarian Church Chants**
Scenic Designer: **Silva Bachvarova**
Costume Designer: **Silva Bachvarova**
Sound Designer: **Alexandra Kaloyanova**
Director: **Slavcho Malenov**

Contributing Researcher: **Marina Raytchinova**

Image Credit: **Silva Bachvarova**

---

[142]

One String of Koto
Yasuhiro Ishii (Japan)
Set Design

Company: **Toho Company**
Venue: **Imperial Theatre** (Teikoku Gekijou)
Location: **Tokyo, Japan**
Opening/First Night: **March 1981**

Author: **Tomiko Miyao**, adapted By Ikuko Ouyabu
Composer: **Shinichiro Ikebe**
Scenic Designer: **Yasuhiro Ishii**
Lighting Designer: **Mitsugu Asanuma**
Sound Designer: **Akira Honma**
Director: **Toshikiyo Masumi**
Choreographer: **Otojiro Hanayagi**

Contributing Researcher: **Kazue Hatano**

Image Credit: **Yasuhiro Ishii**

---

[142]

Woza Albert
Mbongeni Ngema, Percy Mtwa & Barney Simon (South Africa)
Set Design

Company: **Earth Players**
Location: **South Africa**
Opening/First Night: **1981**

Author: based on idea by **Mbongeni Ngema & Percy Mtwa**
Designer: **Mbongeni Ngema, Percy Mtwa & Barney Simon**
Director: **Barney Simon**

Contributing Researcher: **Sarah Roberts**

Image Credit: **Ruphin Coudyzer FPPSA**

---

[143]

Songs for Faidra (*Lauluja Faidralle*)
Juha Lukala (Finland)
Set Design

Company: **Turku City Theatre**
Venue: **Turku City Theatre**
Location: **Turku, Finland**
Opening/First Night: **29 October 1971**

Author: **Per Olov Enquist**
Composer: **Matti Puurtinen**
Scenic Designer: **Juha Lukala**
Costume Designer: **Merja Levo**
Lighting Designer: **Osmo Salo & Timo Grönroos**
Sound Effects Designer: **Tapio Nylander**
Director: **Jotaarkka Pennanen**
Hairdressing and makeup: **Merja Kuntsi**

Contributing Researcher: **Hanna Helavuori/ Pälvi Laine**

Image Credit: **Juha Lukala**

---

[143]

Orphan of Zhao Family
Zhao Yingmian (China)
Set Design

Company: **The National Academy of Chinese Theatre Arts**
Venue: **The National Academy of Chinese Theatre Arts**
Location: **China**
Opening/First Night: **July 1981**

Author: **Ji Junxiang**, adapted by Wang Yan
Scenic Designer: **Zhao Yingmian**
Costume Designer: traditional Beijing Opera costume
Lighting Designer: **Li Dianhua**
Director: **Lu Xingcai**

Contributing Researcher: **Xu Xiang**

Image Credit: **Zhao Yingmian**

---

[144]

Cats
John Napier (UK)
Set & Costume Design

Company: **Really Useful Theatre Co.**
Venue: **New London**
Location: **London, UK**
Opening/First Night: **1981**

Composer: **Andrew Lloyd Webber**
Lyrics: **T S Eliot**
Scenic Designer: **John Napier**
Costume Designer: **John Napier**
Lighting Designer: **David Hersey**
Sound Designer: **Martin Levan**
Director: **Trevor Nunn**
Choreographer: **Gillian Lynne**

Contributing Researcher: **Ian Herbert**

Image Credit: **John Napier**

---

[146]

Madame Butterfly
Kappa Senoh (Japan)
Set Design

Company: **Fujiwara Opera Company**
Venue: **Shinjuku Bunka Hall**
Location: **Tokyo, Japan**
Opening/First Night: **July 1981**

Composer: **Giuseppe Puccini**
Author: **Ruigi Irikka**
Scenic Designer: **Kappa Senoh**
Lighting Designer: **Michio Akimoto**
Director: **Hideo Kanze**

Contributing Researcher: **Kazue Hatano**

Image Credit: **Kappa Senoh**

---

[146]

Translations
Eileen Diss (UK)
Set Design

Venue: **Hampstead Theatre**
Location: **London, UK**
Opening/First Night: **1981**

Author: **Brian Friel**
Scenic Designer: **Eileen Diss**
Costume Designer: **Lindy Hemming**
Lighting Designer: **Gerry Jenkinson, Ronnie Cox**
Director: **Donald McWhinnie**

Contributing Researcher: **Ian Herbert**

Image Credit: **Victoria and Albert Museum, London; John Haynes**

---

[147]

Yerma
Giorgos Patsas (Greece)
Set & Costume Design

Company: **National Theatre of Northern Greece**
Location: **Thessaloniki, Greece**
Opening/First Night: **1981**

Author: **Federico Garcia Lorca**
Translator: **Alexis Solomos**
Scenic Designer: **Giorgos Patsas**
Costume Designer: **Giorgos Patsas**
Director: **Theodoros Terzopoulos**

Contributing Researcher: **Dio Kangelari**

Image Credit: **Chryssa Kyriakidou**

---

[148]

Scaffolding (*Echafaudages*)
Pat Van Hemelrijck (Belgium)
Set Design

Company: **Radeis**
Venue: **Shaffy Theatre** (Zuilenzaal)
Location: **Amsterdam, The Netherlands**
Opening/First Night: **26 September 1981**

Author: **Radeis**
Composer: **Union**
Scenic Designer: **Pat Van Hemelrijck**
Lighting Designer: **Reinier Tweebeke**
Director: **Pat Van Hemelrijck**

Contributing Researcher: **Rose Werckx**

Image Credit: **Michiel Hendrickx**

[149]

Pirosmani, Pirosmani...
Adomas Yatsovskis (Lithuania)
Set Design

Company: **Lithuanian State Youth Theatre**
Location: **Vilnius, Lithuania**
Opening/First Night: **1981**

Author: **Vadim Korostyliov**
Scenic Designer: **Adomas Yatsovskis**
Director: **Eimuntas Nekrosius**

Contributing Researcher: **Inna Morzoyan**

Image Credit: **Adomas Yatsovskis**

[150]

Dreamgirls
Robin Wagner & Tharon Musser (USA)
Set & Lighting Design

Venue: **Imperial Theatre**
Location: **New York, New York, USA**
Opening/First Night: **20 December 1981**

Composer: **Henry Krieger**
Book & Lyrics: **Tom Eyen**
Scenic Designer: **Robin Wagner**
Costume Designer: **Theoni V. Aldredge**
Lighting Designer: **Tharon Musser**
Sound Designer: **Otts Munderloh**
Director: **Michael Bennett**
Choreographer: **Michael Bennett & Michael Peters**
Conductor/Musical Supervisor: **Harold Wheeler**

Contributing Researcher: **Eric Fielding**

Image Credit: **Martha Swope © The New York Public Library for the Performing Arts**

[151]

Bluebeard (Kékszakáll)
Judit Schäffer (Hungary)
Costume Design

Company: **Hungarian State Opera House**
Venue: **Erkel Ferenc Theatre**
Location: **Budapest, Hungary**
Opening/First Night: **November 1981**

Composer: **Jacques Offenbach**
Libretto: **Henri Meilhac, Ludovic Halévy**
Scenic Designer: **Péter Makai**
Costume Designer: **Judit Schäffer**
Director: **András Békés**
Choreographer: **László Pethő**
Conductor: **Ferenc Nagy**

Contributing Researcher: **Eva Nemeth**

Image Credit: **Scenography Collection, Hungarian Theatre Museum and Institute**

[152]

The Man From Mukinupin
Anna French (Australia)
Set & Costume Design

Company: **Melbourne Theatre Company**
Venue: **Russell Street Theatre**
Location: **Melbourne, Australia**
Opening/First Night: **1981**

Author: **Dorothy Hewett**
Scenic Designer: **Anna French**
Costume Designer: **Anna French**
Lighting Designer: **Jamieson Lewis**
Director: **Judith Alexander**

Contributing Researcher: **Richard Roberts**

Image Credit: **Anna French**

[152]

Goldilocks (Zlatovláska)
Petr Matásek (Czechoslovakia/Czech Republic)
Set & Puppet Design

Company: **DRAK Theatre**
Location: **Hradec Králové, Czechoslovakia/ Czech Republic**
Opening/First Night: **17 October 1981**

Author: **Josef Kainar**
Scenic Designer: **Petr Matásek**
Puppet Designer: **Petr Matásek**
Director: **Josef Krofta**

Contributing Researcher: **Daniela Pařízková & Marie Zdeňková**

Image Credit: **Prague Quadrennial Archive**

[153]

Antigone
Isabel Echarri & Diego Echeverry (Spain)
Set & Costume Design

Location: **France**
Opening/First Night: **1981**

Author: **Sophocles**
Scenic Designer: **Isabel Echarri & Diego Echeverry**
Costume Designer: **Isabel Echarri & Diego Echeverry**

Contributing Researcher: **Eric Fielding**

Image Credit: **Prague Quadrennial Archive; Eric Fielding**

[153]

On foot (Pieszo)
Jerzy Juk Kowarski (Poland)
Set Design

Company: **Teatr Dramatyczny**
Venue: **Teatr Dramatyczny**
Location: **Warsaw, Poland**
Opening/First Night: **22 May 1981**

Author: **Sławomir Mrożek**
Composer: **Stanisław Radwan**
Scenic Designer: **Jerzy Juk Kowarski**
Director: **Jerzy Jarocki**

Contributing Researcher: **Agnieszka Kubaś**

Image Credit: **Marek Holzman (ZPAF)**

[154]

Nahod Simeon
Vladislav Lalicki (Yugoslavia/Serbia)
Set & Costume Design

Company: **Yugoslav Drama Theatre**
Venue: **Yugoslav Drama Theatre**
Location: **Belgrade, Yugoslavia/Serbia**
Opening/First Night: **5 February 1981**

Author: **Jovan Sterija Popović**
Composer: **Veljko Marić**
Scenic Designer: **Vladislav Lalicki**
Costume Designer: **Vladislav Lalicki**
Director: **Dejan Mijač**

Contributing Researcher: **Radivoje Dinulović**

Photo Credits: **Museum of Theatrical Arts of Serbia**

[154]

On the Razzle
Carl Toms (UK)
Set & Costume Design

Company: **National Theatre**
Venue: **Lyttelton Stage**
Location: **London, UK**
Opening/First Night: **22 September 1981**

Author: **Tom Stoppard**, adapted from Johan Nestroy (*Einen dux will er sich machen*)
Scenic Designer: **Carl Toms**
Costume Designer: **Carl Toms**
Lighting Designer: **Robert Bryan (Razzle)**
Director: **Peter Wood**

Contributing Researcher: **Ian Herbert**

Image Credits: **Douglas H Jeffery, Victoria and Albert Museum, London**

[155]

Danton's Death (Dantons Tod)
Volker Pfüller (Germany FRG)
Set & Costume Design

Company: **Alexander Lang**
Venue: **Deutsches Theater**
Location: **Berlin, Germany (GDR)**
Opening/First Night: **24 April 1981**

Author: **Georg Buechner**
Scenic Designer: **Volker Pfüller**
Costume Designer: **Volker Pfüller**
Director: **Alexander Lang**

Contributing Researcher: **Karin Winkelsesser**

Image Credit: **Volker Pfüller**

[158]

Antigone
Sally Jacobs (UK)
Set & Costume Design

Company: **New York Shakespeare Festival**
Venue: **The Public Theatre**, Martinson Hall
Location: **New York, New York, USA**
Opening/First Night: **1982**

Author: **Sophocles**, translation by John Chioles
Scenic Designer: **Sally Jacobs**
Costume Designer: **Sally Jacobs**
Lighting Designer: **Beverly Emmons**
Director: **Joseph Chaikin**

Contributing Researcher: **Barbara Cohen-Stratyner & Eric Fielding**

Image Credit: **Martha Swope © The New York Public Library for the Performing Arts**

[158]

White Weapons (Armas blancas)
Alejandro Luna (México)
Set, Costume & Lighting Design

Venue: **Sótano del Teatro Carlos Lazo**
Location: **Mexico City, Mexico**
Opening/First Night: **January 1982**

Author: **Víctor Hugo**
Translator: **Rascón Banda**
Scenic Designer: **Alejandro Luna**
Costume Designer: **Alejandro Luna**
Lighting Designer: **Alejandro Luna**
Director: **Julio Castillo**

Contributing Researcher: **Rodolfo Obregon Rodriguez**

Image Credits: **Fondo Julio Castillo, Archivo Alejandro Luna, INBA-CITRU, Biblioteca de las Artes-CENART, Mexico**

[159]

Rigoletto
Patrick Robertson (UK)
Set Design

Company: **English National Opera**
Venue: **Coliseum**
Location: **London, UK**
Opening/First Night: **1982**

Composer: **Giuseppe Verdi**
Scenic Designer: **Patrick Robertson**
Costume Designer: **Rosemary Vercoe**
Lighting Designer: **Robert Bryan**
Director: **Jonathan Miller**

Contributing Researcher: **Ian Herbert**

Image Credit: **Victoria and Albert Museum, London**

[160]

Nine
William Ivey Long (USA)
Costume Design

Venue: **46th Street Theatre**
Location: **New York, New York, USA**
Opening/First Night: **9 May 1982**

Composer: **Maury Yeston**
Lyrics: **Maury Yeston**
Author: **Arthur Kopit**
Scenic Designer: **Lawrence Miller**
Costume Designer: **William Ivey Long**
Lighting Designer: **Marcia Madeira**
Director: **Tommy Tune**
Choreographer: **Thommie Walsh**

Contributing Researcher: **Eric Fielding**

Image Credits: **Martha Swope © The New York Public Library for the Performing Arts; William Ivey Long**

[162]

New Genji Story
Hachiro Nakajima (Japan)
Set Design

Company: **Shochiku Company**
Venue: **Kabukiza Theatre**
Location: **Tokyo, Japan**
Opening/First Night: **June 1982**

Author: **Seiko Tanabe**, adapted by Naruo Dobashi
Scenic Designer: **Hachiro Nakajima**
Costume Designer: **Shochiku Costume Company**
Lighting Designer: **Kiyotsune Soma**
Director: **Naruo Dobashi**

Contributing Researcher: **Kazue Hatano**

Image Credit: **Hachiro Nakajima**

[163]

Susan Benson (UK/Canada)
The Mikado
Set & Costume Design

Company: **Stratford Festival**
Venue: **Festival Theatre**
Location: **Stratford, Canada**
Opening/First Night: **7 June 1982**

Author: **William S. Gilbert**
Composer: **Sir Arthur Sullivan**
Scenic Designer: **Susan Benson**
Costume Designer: **Susan Benson**
Lighting Designer: **Michael J. Whitfield**
Director: **Brian Macdonald**
Choreographer: **Brian Macdonald**

Contributing Researcher: **Peter McKinnon**

Image Credits: **Stratford Festival Archive, Peter McKinnon, Susan Benson**

[164]
Hecuba (*Hekuba*)
Zlatko Kauzlarić Atač (Croatia)
Set Design

Company: **Theatre Workshop Pozdravi**
Location: **Dubrovnik Days of a Young Theater**
City: **Dubrovnik, Croatia**
Opening/First Night: **7 August 1982**

Author: **Marin Držić**
Composer: **Davor Rocco**
Scenic Designer: **Zlatko Kauzlarić Atač**
Costume Designer: **Goranka Politeo**
Director: **Ivica Boban**
Fight Choreographer: **Ilija Smoljenović**

Contributing Researcher: **Lada Cale Feldman & Visnja Rogosic**

Image Credit: **Division for History of the Croatian Theater, Croatian Academy of Sciences and Arts**

[164]
The Thirteenth Chairman
(*Тринадесетият председател*)
Vassil Rokomanov (Bulgaria)
Set & Costume Design

Company: **State Drama Theatre**
Location: **Kardzali, Bulgaria**
Opening/First Night: **1982**

Author: **Azat Abdulin**
Scenic Designer: **Vassil Rokomanov**
Costume Designer: **Vassil Rokomanov**
Director: **Kamen Kostov**

Contributing Researcher: **Marina Raytchinova**

Image Credit: **Vassil Rokomanov**

[165]
Rush Hour (*Час Пик*)
Georgi Ivanov (Bulgaria)
Set & Lighting Design

Company: **Drama Theatre Pazardjik**
Location: **Pazardjik, Bulgaria**
Opening/First Night: **1982**

Author: **E. Stavinski**
Scenic Designer: **Georgi Ivanov**
Lighting Designer: **Georgi Ivanov**
Director: **N. Lyutzkanov**

Contributing Researcher: **Marina Raytchinova**

Image Credit: **Georgi Ivanov**

[166]
Kings and Queens (*Könige und Königinnen*)
Johannes Schütz (Germany FRG)
Set Design

Company: **Reinhild Hoffmann Company**
Venue: **Concordia Theatre**
Location: **Bremen, Germany**
Opening/First Night: **1982**

Author: **Reinhild Hoffmann**
Composer: **Peter Raaben**
Scenic Designer: **Johannes Schütz**
Costume Designer: **Claudia Flütsch**
Choreographer: **Reinhild Hoffmann**

Contributing Researcher: **Karin Winkelsesser**

Image Credit: **Johannes Schütz**

[167]
Amadeus
Kazue Hatano (Japan)
Set & Costume Design

Company: **Shochiku Company**
Venue: **Sunshine Theatre**
Location: **Tokyo, Japan**
Opening/First Night: **June 1982**

Author: **Peter Shaffer**
Scenic Designer: **Kazue Hatano**
Costume Designer: **Kazue Hatano**
Lighting Designer: **Kiyotsune Soma**
Sound Designer: **Ryoji Tsuji**
Director: **Giles Block**

Contributing Researcher: **Kazue Hatano**

Image Credit: **Kazue Hatano**

[167]
Sink the Ruined Capital
Kappa Senoh (Japan)
Set Design

Company: **Seibu Parco Company**
Venue: **Parco Part 3**
Location: **Tokyo, Japan**
Opening/First Night: **1982**

Author: **Makoto Sato**
Scenic Designer: **Kappa Senoh**
Lighting Designer: **Sumio Yoshii**
Director: **Makoto Sato**

Contributing Researcher: **Kazue Hatano**

Image Credit: **Kappa Senoh**

[168]
Giselle
Marie-Louise Ekman (Sweden)
Set & Costume Design

Company: **Cullberg Ballet**
Venue: **Royal Dramatic Theatre**
Location: **Stockholm, Sweden**
Opening/First Night: **6 July1982**

Composer: **Adolphe Adam**
Author: **Jules Perrot, Jean Corrali**
Scenic Designer: **Marie-Louise Ekman**
Costume Designer: **Marie-Louise Ekman**
Choreographer: **Mats Ek**

Contributing Researcher: **Ammy Kjellsdotter**

Image Credit: © **Lesley Leslie-Spinks**

[169]
Blood Wedding (*Bodas de sangre*)
Byong-boc Lee (Korea)
Set & Costume Design

Venue: **Munye Theater**
Location: **Seoul, Korea**
Opening/First Night: **1982**

Author: **Frederico Garcia Lorca**
Scenic Designer: **Byong-boc Lee**
Costume Designer: **Byong-boc Lee**

Contributing Researcher: **Kazue Hatano**

Image Credit: **Byong-Boc Lee**

[170]
A Man is a Man (*Mann ist Mann*)
Shigeo Okajima (Japan)
Set Design

Company: **Tokyo Ensemble**
Venue: **Brecht Raum Theatre**
Location: **Tokyo, Japan**
Opening/First Night: **1982**

Author: **Bertolt Brecht**
Composer: **Hikaru Hayashi**
Scenic Designer: **Shigeo Okajima**
Costume Designer: **Shigeo Kawamori**
Lighting Designer: **Sadahiko Tachiki**
Director: **Tsunetoshi Hirowatari**

Contributing Researcher: **Kazue Hatano**

Image Credit: **Teruto Kurahara**

[170]
Afonso Henriques
João Brites (Portugal)
Set Design

Company: **Teatro O Bando**
Venue: **Sala O Bando**
Location: **Lisbon, Portugal**
Opening/First Night: **November 1982**

Author: **Collective dramaturgy based on historical records**
Scenic Designer: **João Brites**
Director: **João Brites**

Contributing Researcher: **Maria Helena Serôdio**

Photography: **Archive of Teatro O Bando**

Image Credit: **João Brites**

[171]
The Mission (*Der Auftrag*)
Erich Wonder (Austria/Germany)
Set Design

Company: **Theatre Bochum**
Venue: **Schauspiel Bochum**
Location: **Bochum, Germany**
Opening/First Night: **13 February 1982**

Author: **Heiner Mueller**
Scenic Designer: **Erich Wonder**
Costume Designer: **Nina Ritter**
Director: **Heiner Mueller**

Contributing Researcher: **Karin Winkelsesser**

Image Credit: **Erich Wonder**

[172]
Too True to Be Good
Jim Plaxton (Canada)
Set & Costume Design

Company: **Shaw Festival**
Venue: **Courthouse Theatre**
Location: **Niagara-on-the-Lake, Canada**
Opening/First Night: **2 July 1982**

Author: **George Bernard Shaw**
Scenic Designer: **Jim Plaxton**
Costume Designer: **Jim Plaxton**
Lighting Designer: **Jeffrey Dallas**
Director: **Paul Bettis**

Contributing Researcher: **Peter McKinnon**

Image Credits: **Jim Plaxton, Eric Fielding**

[173]
Twelfth Night
Agim Zajmi (Albania)
Set Design

Venue: **The National Theatre**
Location: **Tirana, Albania**
Opening/First Night: **17 September 1982**

Author: **William Shakespeare**
Scenic Designer: **Agim Zajmi**
Costume Designer: **Agim Zajmi**
Director: **Pirro Mani**

Contributing Researcher: **Ilir Martini**

Image Credit: **Agim Zajmi**

[173]
The Dove and the Poppy (*Kyyhky ja unikko*)
Tiina Makkonen (Finland)
Set, Costume & Poster Design

Company: **Vaasa City Theatre**
Venue: **Vaasa City Theatre**
Location: **Vaasa, Finland**
Opening/First Night: **9 August 1982**

Author: **Timo K. Mukka**, dramatized by Väinö Vainio
Composer: **Matti Inkinen**
Scenic Designer: **Tiina Makkonen**
Costume Designer: **Tiina Makkonen**
Lighting Designer: **Tarmo Salminen**
Sound Designer: (effects: Kimmo Sillantie)
Director: **Juha Malmivaara**
Poster: **Tiina Makkonen**

Contributing Researcher: **Pälvi Laine**

Image Credit: **Tiina Makkonen, The Theatre Museum Archive (Finland)**

[174]
Le Grand Macabre
Timothy O'Brien (UK)
Set & Costume Design

Company: **English National Opera**
Venue: **Coliseum**
Location: **London, England**
Opening/First Night: **1982**

Composer: **György Ligeti**
Scenic Designer: **Timothy O'Brien**
Costume Designer: **Timothy O'Brien**
Lighting Designer: **Nick Chelton**
Director: **Elijah Moshinsky**

Contributing Researcher: **Kate Dorney**

Image Credit: **Timothy O'Brien**

[174]
Love and Pigeons
Olga Tvardovskaya & Vladimir Makushenko (USSR/Russia)
Set Design

Company: **Sovremennik Theatre**
Location: **Moscow, USSR/Russia**
Opening/First Night: **1982**

Author: **Vladimir Gurkin**
Scenic Designer: **Olga Tvardovskaya & Vladimir Makushenko**
Director: **Valery Fokin**

Contributing Researcher: **Inna Mirzoyan**

Image Credits: **Olga Tvardovskaya, Vladimir Makushenko**

[175]

The Magic Flute (*Die Zauberflöte*)
Achim Freyer (Germany)
Set & Costume Design

Company: **National Opera Hamburg**
Venue: **Hamburgische Staatsoper**
Location: **Berlin, Germany FRG**
Opening/First Night: **20 May 1982**

Composer: **Wolfgang Amadeus Mozart**
Libretto: **Emanuel Schikaneder**
Scenic Designer: **Achim Freyer**
Costume Designer: **Achim Freyer**
Director: **Achim Freyer**
Conductor: **Christoph von Dohnany**

Contributing Researcher: **Karin Winkelsesser**

Image Credits: **Monika Rittershaus; Akademie der Kuenste Berlin, Achim Freyer Archive**

[176]

Way Upstream
Alan Tagg (UK)
Set & Costume Design

Company: **Royal National Theatre**
Venue: **Lyttelton Theatre**
Location: **London, UK**
Opening/First Night: **4 October 1982**

Author: **Alan Ayckbourn**
Scenic Designer: **Alan Tagg**
Costume Designer: **Alan Tagg**
Lighting Designer: **Willian Bundy**
Director: **Alan Ayckbourn**

Contributing Researcher: **Ian Herbert**

Image Credits: **Douglas H Jeffery, Victoria and Albert Museum, London; © Nobby Clark/Arenapal**

[177]

The Hobbit (*Hobit*)
Geroslav Zarić (Yugoslavia/Serbia)
Set Design

Company: **Theatre Boško Buha**
Venue: **Theatre Boško Buha**
Location: **Belgrade, Yugoslavia/Serbia**
Opening/First Night: **11 November 1982**

Author: **J. R. R. Tolkien**, adapted by Dobrivoje Ilić
Composer: **Dušan Mitrović**
Scenic Designer: **Geroslav Zarić**
Costume Designer: **Božana Jovanović**
Director: **Paolo Magelli**
Choreographer: **Ferid Karajica**

Contributing Researcher: **Radivoje Dinulović**

Image Credits: **Museum of Theatrical Arts of Serbia**

[177]

The Tempest
Nadine Baylis (UK)
Set & Costume Design

Company: **Rambert Dance Company**
Location: **UK**
Opening/First Night: **1979**

Creator: **Glen Tetley**
Scenic Designer: **Nadine Baylis**
Costume Designer: **Nadine Baylis**
Lighting Designer: **John B Read**
Choreographer: **Glen Tetley**

Contributing Researcher: **Ian Herbert**

Image Credit: **Victoria and Albert Museum, London**

[178]

Hamlet
Gilles Aillaud (Germany)
Set Design

Company: **Schaubuehne Berlin**
Venue: **Schaubuehne Berlin**
Location: **Berlin, Germany FRG**
Opening/First Night: **11 December 1982**

Author: **William Shakespeare**
Scenic Designer: **Gilles Aillaud**
Costume Designer: **Moidele Bickel & Andrea Schmitt-Futterer**
Lighting Designer: **Wolfgang Göbbel**
Director: **Klaus Michael Grüber**

Contributing Researcher: **Karin Winkelsesser**

Image Credit: **Ruth Walz**

[179]

The Golubnjaca (*Golubnjača*)
Radovan Marušić (Bosnia & Herzegovina)
Set Design

Company: **Serbian National Theatre**
Venue: **Serbian National Theatre**
Location: **Novi Sad, Yugoslavia/Serbia**
Opening/First Night: **10 October 1982**

Author: **Jovan Radulović**
Composer: **Mladen & Predrag Vranešević**
Scenic Designer: **Radovan Marušić**
Costume Designer: **Jasna Petrović**
Director: **Dejan Mijač**

Contributing Researcher: **Radivoje Dinulović**

Photo Credits: **Museum of Theatrical Arts of Serbia**

Image Credit: **Radovan Marušić**

[180]

The Screens (*Les Paravents, Parawany*)
Jerzy Grzegorzewski (Poland)
Set & Costume Design

Company: **Teatr Studio**
Venue: **Teatr Studio**
Location: **Warsaw, Poland**
Opening/First Night: **19 December 1982**

Author: **Jean Genet**
Composer: **Stanisław Radwan**
Scenic Designer: **Jerzy Grzegorzewski**
Costume Designer: **Jerzy Grzegorzewski**
Director: **Jerzy Grzegorzewski**

Contributing Researcher: **Theatre Institute in Poland (Instytut Teatralny im. Raszewskiego)**

Image Credits: **Zygmunt Rytka/Zbigniew Raszewski Theatre Institute Archive**

[180]

Guys and Dolls
John Gunter (UK) & **Sue Blane** (UK)
Set & Costume Design

Company: **National Theatre**
Venue: **Olivier Stage**
Location: **London, UK**
Opening/First Night: **23 March 1982**

Author: **Frank Loesser**, from Damon Runyon
Composer: **Frank Loesser**
Book: **Jo Swerling & Abe Burrows**
Scenic Designer: **John Gunter**
Costume Designer: **Sue Blane**
Lighting Designer: **David Hersey**
Director: **Richard Eyre**
Choreographer: **David Toguri**
Musical director: **Tony Britten**

Contributing Researcher: **Donatella Barbieri, Ian Herbert & Liz Wright**

Image Credit: **Victoria and Albert Museum, London**

[181]

It is theatre as was to be expected and foreseeable. (Het is theater zoals te verwachten en te voorzien was.)
Jan Fabre (Belgium)
Set Design

Venue: **Klapstuk**
Opening/First Night: **1982**

Author: **Jan Fabre**
Scenic Designer: **Jan Fabre**

Contributing Researcher: **Rose Werckx**

Image Credits: **Bob Van Dantzig, Patrick T Sellito**

[184]

The Sun Festival
Joe Bleakley (New Zealand)
Event Design

Venue: **Oriental Bay**
Location: **Wellington, New Zealand**
Opening/First Night: **17 December 1983**

Author: **Jean Betts & Joe Bleakley**
Composer: **Jenny McLeod**
Scenic Designer: **Joe Bleakley**
Costume Designer: **Pam Vakidis & public**
Director: **Joe Bleakley**
Water Projections & Inventions: **Russell Collins**

Contributing Researcher: **Sam Trubridge**

Image Credit: **Mike Langford, Muller, Joe Bleakley, David Hamilton**

[185]

Cats (*Macskák*)
Béla Götz (Hungary)
Set Design

Company: **Madách Theatre**
Venue: **Madách Theatre**
Location: **Budapest, Hungary**
Opening/First Night: **March 1983**

Composer: **Andrew Lloyd Webber**
Lyrics: **T. S. Eliot, Trevor Nunn**
Book: **Andrew Lloyd Webber, Trevor Nunn, Gillian Lynne**
Scenic Designer: **Béla Götz**
Costume Designer: **Nelly Vágó**
Director: **Tamás Szirtes**
Choreographer: **László Seregi**

Contributing Researcher: **Eva Nemeth**

Image Credits: : **Götz Béla, Scenography Collection, Hungarian Theatre Museum and Institute; Ilovszky Béla, MTI Photo Archive (Magyar Távirati Iroda - Hungarian News Agency)**

[186]

A Bicycle
Sun-Hi Shin (Korea)
Set & Costume Design

Company: **Dongrang Drama Repertory Company**
Venue: **Munye Theatre**
Location: **Seoul, Korea**
Opening/First Night: **3 March 1983**

Author: **Tae-Seok On**
Scenic Designer: **Sun-Hi Shin**
Costume Designer: **Sun-Hi Shin**
Lighting Designer: **Duk-Hyung Yoo**
Director: **Woo-Ok Kim**

Contributing Researcher: **Kazue Hatano**

Image Credit: **Sun-Hi Shin**

[187]

K2
Ming Cho Lee (China/USA)
Set Design

Venue: **Arena Stage / Brooks Atkinson Theatre**
Location: **Washington, DC / New York City, USA**
Opening/First Night: **1983**

Author: **Patrick Meyers**
Scenic Designer: **Ming Cho Lee**
Costume Designer: **Noel Borden**
Lighting Designer: **Allen Lee Hughes**
Sound Designer: **David Schnirman**
Director: **Terry Schrieber**

Contributing Researcher: **Eric Fielding**

Image Credit: **Martha Swope © The New York Public Library for the Performing Arts**

[187]

Caesar and Cleopatra
Cameron Porteous (Canada)
Set & Costume Design

Company: **Shaw Festival**
Venue: **Festival Theatre**
Location: **Niagara-on-the-Lake, Canada**
Opening/First Night: **25 May 1983**

Author: **George Bernard Shaw**
Scenic Designer: **Cameron Porteous**
Costume Designer: **Cameron Porteous**
Lighting Designer: **Jeffrey Dallas**
Director: **Christopher Newton**

Contributing Researcher: **Peter McKinnon**

Image Credits: **Dean Palmer, Guelph Archives**

[188]

Don Giovanni/Donna Giovanni
Carmen Parra (Mexico)
& Tolita Figueroa (Mexico)
Set Design

Company: Divas, A.C.
Venue: Teatro Cervantes
Location: Guanajuato, Mexico
Opening/First Night: October 1983

Composer: W. A. Mozart
Librettist: L. Daponte
Scenic Designer: Carmen Parra & Tolita Figueroa
Costume Designer: Angela Dodson
Lighting Designer: Jesusa Rodríguez & E. Medina
Director: Jesutherland (Jesusa Rodríguez)
Composer: Alicia Urreta

Contributing Researcher: Rodolfo Obregon Rodriguez

Image Credit: INBA-CITRU, Biblioteca de las Artes-CENART, Mexico

---

[188]

The Spring and Autumn of the Taiping Heavenly Kingdom
Xing Dalun (China)
Set Design

Company: The Central Academy of Drama
Venue: The Experimental Theatre of The Central Academy of Drama
Location: China
Opening/First Night: 1983

Author: Yang Hansheng
Composer: Jiang Hongsheng, Chen Zidu
Scenic Designer: Xing Dalun
Costume Designer: Zhong Linxuan
Lighting Designer: Guo Qiang
Director: He Zhian, Jin Nanqian
Martial Arts Choreographer: Song Lifen

Contributing Researcher: Xu Xiang

Image Credit: Xiang Dalun

---

[189]

The Midsummer Marriage
Robin Don (UK)
Set & Costume Design

Company: San Francisco Opera
Location: San Francisco, USA
Opening/First Night: 1983

Composer: Michael Tippett
Scenic Designer: Robin Don
Costume Designer: Robin Don
Lighting Designer: Thomas Munn
Director: John Copley

Contributing Researcher: Ian Herbert

Image Credit: Ron Scherl, Robin Don

---

[189]

Mary Stuart
Shigeki Kawamori (Japan)
Costume Design

Company: Haiyuza (Actors') Theatre Company
Venue: Haiyuza Theatre
Location: Tokyo, Japan
Opening/First Night: May 1983

Author: Alexandre Dumas
Scenic Designer: Machi Abe
Costume Designer: Shigeki Kawamori
Lighting Designer: Toshihiko Shimizu
Director: Koreya Senda

Contributing Researcher: Kazue Hatano

Image Credit: Shigeki Kawamori

---

[190]

Wozzeck
Annelies Corrodi (Switzerland)
Set, Costume & Projection Design

Company: Opéra de Nice
Venue: Opéra de Nice
Location: Nice, France
Opening/First Night: May 2, 1984

Composer: Alban Berg
Author: Alban Berg (based on Georg Büchner's play *Woyzeck*)
Scenic Designer: Annelies Corrodi
Costume Designer: Annelies Corrodi
Projection Designer: Annelies Corrodi
Director: Pierre Médecin
Conductor: Berislav Klobucar
Photographer: Verena Moser

Contributing Researcher: Franziska K. Trefzer & Sandra Gredig

Image Credits: Verena Moser, Annelies Corrodi

---

[192]

OD on Paradise
Jim Plaxton (Canada)
Set & Lighting Design

Company: Theatre Passe Muraille
Venue: Theatre Passe Muraille
Location: Toronto, Canada
Opening/First Night: 15 January 1983

Author: Patrick Brymer & Linda Griffiths
Scenic Designer: Jim Plaxton
Costume Designer: Jim Plaxton
Lighting Designer: Jim Plaxton
Director: Clarke Rogers

Contributing Researcher: Cameron Porteous

Image Credits: Guelph Archive, Jim Plaxton

---

[192]

Peer Gynt
Liu Yuansheng (China)
Set Design

Company: The Central Academy of Drama
Venue: The Experimental Theatre of the Central Academy of Drama
Location: China
Opening/First Night: May 1983

Author: Henrik Ibsen
Scenic Designer: Liu Yuansheng
Costume Designer: Huo Qidi
Lighting Designer: Mu Baisuo
Director: Xu Xiaozhong

Contributing Researcher: Xu Xiang

Image Credit: Liu Yuansheng

---

[193]

Rusalka
Stefanos Lazaridis (Greece/UK)
Set & Costume Design

Company: English National Opera
Venue: Coliseum
Location: London, UK
Opening/First Night: 1983

Composer: Antonin Dvorak
Scenic Designer: Stefanos Lazaridis
Costume Designer: Stefanos Lazaridis
Lighting Designer: Nick Chelton
Director: David Pountney

Contributing Researcher: Ian Herbert

Image Credits: Prague Quadrennial Archive, Victoria and Albert Museum, London, Douglas H. Jeffery

---

[194]

Body
Tetsuhiko Maeda (Japan)
Set Design

Company: Midori Ishii, Katsuko Orita Dance Institute
Venue: Mel Park Hall
Location: Tokyo, Japan
Opening/First Night: March 1983

Scenic Designer: Tetsuhiko Maeda
Lighting Designer: Yuji Sawada
Director: Midori Ishii
Choreographer: Midori Ishii

Contributing Researcher: Kazue Hatano

Image Credit: Tetsuhiko Maeda

---

[194]

Do Not Deny The Love
(Не се отричай от любовта)
Vassil Rokomanov (Bulgaria)
Set & Costume Design

Company: State Drama Theatre
Location: Kardzali, Bulgaria
Opening/First Night: 1983

Author: Lyudmila Petrushevska
Scenic Designer: Vassil Rokomanov
Costume Designer: Vassil Rokomanov
Director: Alexander Galperin

Contributing Researcher: Marina Raytchinova

Image Credit: Vassil Rokomanov

---

[195]

On the Life of the Marionettes
(De la vida de las marionetas)
Alejandro Luna (Mexico)
Set, Costume & Lighting Design

Venue: Foro Sor Juana Inés de la Cruz
Location: Mexico City, Mexico
Opening/First Night: March 1983

Author: Ingmar Bergman
Scenic Designer: Alejandro Luna
Costume Designer: Alejandro Luna
Lighting Designer: Alejandro Luna
Director: Ludwik Margules
Choreographer: Nora Manneck

Contributing Researcher: Rodolfo Obregon Rodriguez

Image Credit: INBA-CITRU, Biblioteca de las Artes-CENART, Mexico

---

[195]

The Ring of the Nibelung
(Der Ring des Nibelungen)
Lars Juhl (Denmark)
Set & Costume Design

Company: Den Jyske Opera
Venue: Musikhuset
Location: Aarhus, Denmark
Opening/First Night: 27 August 1983
(*Valkyrie* 1983; *Rheingold*, 1984; *Siegfried*, 1985; *Gotterdammerung*, 1986; and entire Ring Cycle, 1987)

Composer: Richard Wagner
Scenic Designer: Lars Juhl
Costume Designer: Lars Juhl
Lighting Designer: Benny Rünitz
Director: Klaus Hoffmeyer
Conductor: Francesco Cristofoli

Contributing Researcher: Camilla Bjørnvad

Image Credit: Poul Ib Hendriksen

---

[196]

The Descent of the Middleclass
(Amurgul burghez)
Emilia Jivanov (Romania)
Set Design

Venue: National Theatre, Hungarian Department
Location: Targu Mures, Romania
Opening/First Night: 1983

Author: Romulus Guga
Scenic Designer: Emilia Jivanov
Costume Designer: Emilia Jivanov
Director: Dan Alecsandrescu

Contributing Researcher: Jean Cazaban

Image Credit: Emilia Jivanov

---

[197]

The Soldiers (Les Soldats, Die Soldaten)
Ralph Koltai (Germany/UK)
Set Design

Company: Opéra de Lyon
Venue: Opéra de Lyon
Location: Lyon, France
Opening/First Night: 1983

Composer: Bernd Alois Zimmermann
Scenic Designer: Ralph Koltai
Costume Designer: Annena Stubbs
Lighting Designer: Nick Chelton
Director: Ken Russell

Contributing Researcher: Ian Herbert

Image Credit: Ralph Koltai; Collection of the McNay Art Museum, Gift of the Tobin Endowment

---

[198]

Oedipus
Tony Geddes, Pamela Maling & Joe Hayes (New Zealand)
Set, Costume, & Lighting Design

Company: The Court Theatre
Venue: The Court Theatre
Location: Christchurch, New Zealand
Opening/First Night: 1983

Author: Sophocles
Composer: Dorothy Buchanan
Scenic Designer: Tony Geddes
Costume Designer: Pamela Maling
Lighting Designer: Joe Hayes
Director: Elric Hooper

Contributing Researcher: Sam Trubridge

Image Credit: Elric Hooper

---

[198]

Raymonda
Nicholas Georgiadis (Greece/UK]
Set & Costume Design

Company: Paris Opera Ballet
Venue: Garnier Theatre
Location: Paris, France
Opening/First Night: 1983

Choreographer: Rudolf Nureyev
Composer: Alexander Glazunov
Scenic Designer: Nicholas Georgiadis
Costume Designer: Nicholas Georgiadis

Contributing Researcher: Madeline Taylor

Image Credit: Victoria and Albert Museum, London

[199]

Lulu
David Borovsky (Russia)
Costume Design

Company: Teatro Regio di Torino
Location: Turin, Italy
Opening/First Night: 1983

Composer: Alban Berg
Scenic Designer: David Borovsky
Costume Designer: David Borovsky
Director: Yuri Lyubimov
Conductor: Zoltan Peshko

Contributing Researcher: Inna Morzoyan

Image Credit: David Borovsky

[202]

Solide Salad
Michel Lemieux (Canada)
Creative Director

Company: Lemieux Pilon 4D art
Venue: Spectrum
Location: Montreal, Canada
Opening/First Night: 20 September 1984

Author: Michel Lemieux, Alain Fournier &
Simon Pressey
Composer: Michel Lemieux
Scenic Designer: Robert Bobby Breton
Costume Designer: Louise Vincent & Denis
Lavoie
Lighting Designer: Alain Lortie
Multi-images opening number created by:
Paul St-Jean
Sound Designer: Simon Pressey & Alain
Thibault
Director: Michel Lemieux
Collaboration to the direction by: René
Richard Cyr, Sylvie Panet

Contributing Researcher: Peter McKinnon

Image Credit: R Marquis

[203}

Venice Preserv'd
Alison Chitty (UK)
Set & Costume Design

Company: Royal National Theatre
Venue: Lyttleton Theatre
Location: London, UK
Opening/First Night: 12 April 1984

Author: Thomas Otway
Composer: Dominic Muldowney
Scenic Designer: Alison Chitty
Costume Designer: Alison Chitty
Lighting Designer: Stephen Wentworth
Director: Peter Gill

Contributing Researcher: Madeline Taylor

Image Credit: Alison Chitty; Douglas
H Jeffery, Victoria and Albert Museum,
London

[204]

Sunday in the Park with George
Tony Straiges, Patricia Zipprodt
& Ann Hould-Ward (USA)
Set & Costume Design

Venue: Booth Theatre
Location: New York, New York, USA
Opening/First Night: 2 May 1984

Composer: Stephen Sondheim
Lyrics: Stephen Sondheim
Author: James Lapine
Scenic Designer: Tony Straiges
Costume Designer: Patricia Zipprodt & Ann
Hould-Ward
Lighting Designer: Richard Nelson
Sound Designer: Tom Morse
Director: James Lapine
Choreographer: Randolyn Zinn
Conductor/Musical Director: Paul
Gemignani

Contributing Researcher: Jody L. Blake, Eric
Fielding & Jade Bettin

Image Credits: Photo by Martha Swope
© The New York Public Library for the
Performing Arts; Tony Straiges; Collection
of the McNay Art Museum, Gift of Robert
L. B. Tobin

[206]

The Mission
(A missão: Recordações de uma revolução)
Cristina Reis (Portugal)
Set Design

Company: The Cornucopia Theatre
Venue: Teatro do Bairro Alto
Location: Lisbon, Portugal
Opening/First Night: 16 February 1984

Author: Heiner Müller
Scenic Designer: Cristina Reis
Costume Designer: Cristina Reis
Lighting Designer: Luís Miguel Cintra,
Cristina Reis
Director: Luís Miguel Cintra, Cristina Reis
Translation: Anabela Mendes

Contributing Researcher: Maria Helena
Serôdio

Image Credits: Cristina Reis, Paulo Cintra
Gomes

[206]

Bumboat!
Kalyani Kausikan (Singapore)
Lighting Design

Venue: World Trade Centre Auditorium
Location: Singapore, Singapore
Opening/First Night: 1984

Author: Dick Lee
Composer: Dick Lee
Scenic Designer: Justin Hill
Lighting Designer: Kalyani Kausikan
Director: Tzi Mah

Contributing Researcher: Justin Hill

Image Credit: Justin Hill

[207]

The Snow Queen (Снежната Кралица)
Asen Stoychev (Bulgaria)
Set, Costume & Lighting Design

Company: "Salza I Smyah" Theatre
Location: Sofia, Bulgaria
Opening/First Night: 1984

Author: Evgeni Shvartz
Scenic Designer: Asen Stoychev
Costume Designer: Asen Stoychev
Lighting Designer: Asen Stoychev
Director: Dimitar Stoyanov

Contributing Researcher: Marina
Raytchinova

Image Credit: Asen Stoychev

[207]

Puck (Пук)
Silva Bachvarova (Bulgaria)
Set, Costume & Puppet Design

Company: State Puppet theatre
Location: Plovdiv, Bulgaria
Opening/First Night: 1984

Author: Valeri Petrov
Composer: Yury Stupel
Scenic Designer: Silva Bachvarova
Costume Designer: Silva Bachvarova
Sound Designer: Nelly Lazarova
Director: Peter Pashov

Contributing Researcher: Marina
Raytchinova

Image Credit: Silva Bachvarova

[208]

Rapunzel in Suburbia
Kim Carpenter (Australia)
Set & Costume Design

Company: Marionette Theatre of Australia
Location: Sydney, Australia
Opening/First Night: 1984

Author: Kim Carpenter (based on the book
of poems by Dorothy Hewett)
Composer: Richard Vella
Scenic Designer: Kim Carpenter
Costume Designer: Kim Carpenter
Lighting Designer: John Rayment
Director: Kim Carpenter

Contributing Researcher: Richard Roberts

Image Credit: Kim Carpenter

[209]

The Vampires
Adrianne Lobel (USA)
Set Design

Venue: Astor Place Theater
Location: New York, New York, USA
Opening/First Night: 11 April 1984

Author: Harry Kondoleon
Scenic Designer: Adrianne Lobel
Costume Designer: Rita Ryack
Lighting Designer: William Armstrong
Sound Designer: Paul Garrity
Director: Harry Kondoleon

Contributing Researcher: Eric Fielding

Image Credit: Adrianne Lobel

[209]

The Archaeology of Sleep
Julian Beck (USA)
Set Design

Company: The Living Theatre
Venue: Joyce Theater
Location: New York City, USA
Opening/First Night: January 1984

Author: Julian Beck
Scenic Designer: Julian Beck
Costume Designer: Julian Beck
Lighting Designer: Julian Beck
Director: Judith Malina

Contributing Researcher: Thomas Walker &
Eric Fielding

Image Credit: Thomas Walker

[210]

Birds (Όρνιθες)
Apostolos Vettas (Greece)
Set & Costume Design

Company: Diadromi Theatre & Unlimited
Group, Sydney
Location: Thessaloniki, Greece
Opening/First Night: Summer 1984

Author: Aristophanes
Composer: Kostas Vomvolos
Scenic Designer: Apostolos Vettas
Costume Designer: Apostolos Vettas
Director: Despina Pantazi
Choreographer: Ronaldo Cameron

Contributing Researcher: Dio Kangelari

Image Credit: Apostolos Vettas

[210]

The Flight (Menekülés)
László Székely (Hungary)
Set Design

Company: Katona József Theatre
Venue: Katona József Theatre
Location: Budapest, Hungary
Opening/First Night: 1984

Author: Mihail Bulgakov
Scenic Designer: László Székely
Costume Designer: Nelly Vágó
Director: Gábor Székely

Contributing Researcher: Eva Nemeth

Image Credit: Benkő Imre, MTI Photo
Archive (Magyar Távirati Iroda - Hungarian
News Agency)

[211]

Masquerade (Maskarada)
Drago Turina (Yugoslavia/Croatia)
Set Design

Venue: Croatian National Theatre
Location: Osijek , Yugoslavia/Croatia
Opening/First Night: 26 April 1984

Author: Mikhail Lermontov
Scenic Designer: Drago Turina
Costume Designer: Ingrid Begovic
Director: Josko Juvančić

Contributing Researcher: Ivana Bakal

Image Credit: Drago Turnia

[212]

The Big Magic (*La grande magia*)
Ezio Frigerio (Italy)
Set Design

Company: **Strehler's company**
Venue: **Piccolo Teatro di Milano**
Location: **Milan, Italy**
Opening/First Night: **May 1984**

Author: **Eduardo de Filippo**
Scenic Designer: **Ezio Frigerio**
Costume Designer: **Luisa Spinatelli**
Sound Designer: **Fiorenzo Carpi**
Director: **Giorgio Strehler**

Contributing Researcher: **Daniela Sacco**

Image Credit: **Luigi Ciminaghi/Piccolo Teatro di Milano/Teatro d'Europa**

---

[212]

Folichon
Acar Başkut (Turkey)
Set Design

Company: **Istanbul State Opera and Ballet**
Venue: **Atatürk Cultural Center**
Location: **Istanbul, Turkey**
Opening/First Night: **October 1984**

Author: **Ekrem Reşit Rey**
Composer: **Cemal Reşit Rey**
Scenic Designer: **Acar Başkut**
Director: **Tod Bolender**

Contributing Researcher: **Evcimen Percin**

Image Credit: **Acar Başkut**

---

[213]

Blue Snake
Jerrard Smith (Canada)
Set & Costume Design

Company: **The National Ballet of Canada**
Venue: **The O'Keefe Centre**
Location: **Toronto, Canada**
Opening/First Night: **1984**

Author: **Robert Desrosiers**
Composer: **John Lang & Ahmed Hassan**
Scenic Designer: **Jerrard Smith**
Costume Designer: **Jerrard Smith**
Lighting Designer: **Robert Thomson**
Choreographer: **Robert Desrosiers**

Contributing Researcher: **Jerrard Smith**

Image Credits: **Jerrard Smith; Owais Lightwala, Courtesy of Metro Toronto Library; National Ballet of Canada Archives**

---

[214]

Revelation and Fall
Michael Pearce (Australia)
Set & Costume Design

Company: **Australian Dance Theatre**
Venue: **Festival Theatre**
Location: **Adelaide, Australia**
Opening/First Night: **March 1984**

Composer: **Peter Maxwell Davies**
Scenic Designer: **Michael Pearce**
Costume Designer: **Michael Pearce**
Lighting Designer: **William Akers**
Choreographer: **Glen Tetley**
Conductor: **Stuart Challender**

Contributing Researcher: **Richard Roberts**

Image Credit: **Michael Pearce**

---

[215]

The Mask
Kuan-Yen Nieh (Taiwan)
Set & Lighting Design

Company: **An-Lin Theatre**
Venue: **National Dr. Sun Yat-sen Memorial Hall**
Location: **Taipei, Taiwan**
Opening/First Night: **1984**

Author: **Lee-Chen Lin**
Scenic Designer: **Kuan-Yen Nieh**
Costume Designer: **Jung-Lin Huo**
Lighting Designer: **Kuan-Yen Nieh**
Director: **Ming Zhuo**

Contributing Researcher: **Kazue Hatano**

Image Credit: **Kuan-Yen Nieh**

---

[215]

Sacra Conversazione
Peter McKinnon (Canada)
Lighting Design

Company: **Banff Centre for the Arts**
Venue: **Eric Harvie Theatre**
Location: **Banff, Canada**
Opening/First Night: **26 July 1984**

Author: **David Earle**
Composer: **W.A. Mozart**
Costume Designer: **Julia Tribe**
Lighting Designer: **Peter McKinnon**
Choreographer: **David Earle**

Contributing Researcher: **Peter McKinnon**

Image Credit: **Banff Centre, Ed Ellis**

---

[216]

the CIVIL warS: a tree is best measured when it is down (The Knee Plays)
Robert Wilson (USA)
Set, Costume & Lighting Design

Venue: **Walker Art Center**
Location: **Minneapolis, Minnesota, USA**
Opening/First Night: **April 1984**

Author: **Robert Wilson**
Composer: **David Byrne**
Scenic & Costume Designer: **Robert Wilson David Byrne, & Jun Matsuno**
Lighting Designer: **Robert Wilson & Julie Archer**
Director: **Robert Wilson**
Choreographer: **Suzushi Hanayagi**

Contributing Researcher: **Eric Fielding**

Image Credits: **Geoffrey Clements, Herman Baus, Kees de Graaff, Silas Jackson, JoAnn Verburg, Richard Feldman, Robert Wilson, The Watermill Center**

---

[218]

Good
Kazue Hatano (Japan)
Set & Costume Design

Company: **Shochiku Company**
Venue: **Sunshine Theatre**
Location: **Tokyo, Japan**
Opening/First Night: **May 1984**

Author: **C. P. Taylor**
Composer: **George Fenton**
Scenic Designer: **Kazue Hatano**
Costume Designer: **Kazue Hatano**
Lighting Designer: **Kiyotsune Soma**
Sound Designer: **Ryouji Tsuji**
Director: **Howard Davies**
Choreographer: **Saburo Nakagawa**

Contributing Researcher: **Kazue Hatano**

Image Credit: **Kazue Hatano**

---

[218]

Waiting for Godot
Axel Manthey (Germany)
Set & Costume Design

Company: **Schauspiel Köln**
Venue: **Schauspiel Köln**
Location: **Cologne, Germany**
Opening/First Night: **17 November 1984**

Author: **Samuel Beckett**
Scenic Designer: **Axel Manthey**
Costume Designer: **Axel Manthey**
Director: **Juergen Gosch**

Contributing Researcher: **Dr. Renae Raetz**

Image Credits: **Clärchen+Hermann Baus, Akadmie der Kuenste Berlin, Axel-Manthey Archive**

---

[219]

The King Goes Forth to France
(*Kuningas lähtee Ranskaan*)
Ralf Forsström (Finland)
Set & Costume Design

Company: **Savonlinna Opera Festival**
Venue: **Savonlinna Opera Festival, Olavinlinna Castle**
Location: **Savonlinna, Finland**
Opening/First Night: **7 July 1984**

Libretto: **Paavo Haavikko**
Composer: **Aulis Sallinen**
Scenic Designer: **Ralf Forsström**
Costume Designer: **Ralf Forsström**
Lighting Designer: **Jukka Kuuranne**
Sound Designer: **Kari Tiitinen**
Makeup: **Helena Lindgren**
Director: **Kalle Holmberg**
Choreographer: **Pauli Pöllänen & Jens-Ole Walentinsson**
Conductor: **Okko Kamu**

Contributing Researcher: **Hanna Helavuori & Pälvi Laine**

Image Credit: **Matti Kolho, Savonlinna Opera Festival**

---

[220]

The Niebelung (*Nibelungen*)
Jochen Finke (Germany GDR)
Set Design

Company: **National Theatre Dresden**
Venue: **Schauspielhaus Dresden**
Location: **Dresden, Germany GDR**
Opening/First Night: **27 March 1984**

Author: **Friedrich Hebbel**
Scenic Designer: **Jochen Finke**
Costume Designer: **Jutta Harnisch**
Lighting Designer: **Dieter Frank**
Director: **Wolfgang Engel**

Contributing Researcher: **Karin Winkelsesser**

Image Credit: **Jochen Finke**

---

[220]

A Midsummer Night's Dream
(*San Ivanjske Noći*)
Drago Turina (Yugoslavia/Croatia)
Set Design

Venue: **Gavella Drama Theatre**
Location: **Zagreb, Yugoslavia/Croatia**
Opening/First Night: **11 October 1984**

Author: **William Shakespeare**
Scenic Designer: **Drago Turina**
Costume Designer: **Jasna Novak**
Director: **Dino Radivojević**

Contributing Researcher: **Ivana Bakal**

Image Credit: **Drago Turina**

---

[221]

A Loud Solitude (*Hlučná samota*)
Jan Dušek (Czechoslovakia/Czech Republic)
Set & Costume Design

Venue: **Theatre on the Balustrade**
Location: **Prague, Czechoslovakia/Czech Republic**
Opening/First Night: **7 March 1984**

Author: **Bohumil Hrabal, Evald Schorm**
Scenic Designer: **Jan Dušek**
Costume Designer: **Jan Dušek**
Director: **Evald Schorm**

Contributing Researcher: **Daniela Pařízková & Marie Zdeňková**

Image Credit: **Prague Quadrennial Archive**

---

[222]

The Ring of the Nibelung
(*Ring des Nibelungen*)
Peter Sykora (Poland/Germany)
Set & Costume Design

Company: **Deutsche Oper Berlin**
Venue: **Deutsche Oper Berlin**
Location: **Berlin, FDR**
Opening/First Night: **September 1984**

Composer: **Richard Wagner**
Scenic Designer: **Peter Sykora**
Costume Designer: **Peter Sykora**
Director: **Goetz Friedrich**
Conductor: **Jesus Lopez Cobos**

Contributing Researcher: **Karin Winkelsesser**

Image Credit: **Peter Sykora**

---

[224]

Oedipus
Axel Manthey (Germany)
Set & Costume Design

Company: **Schauspiel Köln**
Venue: **Schauspiel Köln**
Location: **Cologne, Germany**
Opening/First Night: **13 March 1984**

Author: **Sophocles**
Scenic Designer: **Axel Manthey**
Costume Designer: **Axel Manthey**
Director: **Jürgen Gosch**

Contributing Researcher: **Karin Winkelsesser**

Image Credit: **Axel Manthey**

---

[225]

Nippon no Yoake
Akaji Maro (Japan)
Set Design

Company: **Dairakudakan**
Venue: **Nihon Toshi Center Hall**
Location: **Tokyo, Japan**
Opening/First Night: **30 April 1984**

Author: **Dairakudakan**
Scenic Designer: **Akaji Maro**
Costume Designer: **Dairakudakan**
Lighting Designer: **Yoshiro Abe**
Sound Designer: **Kazuo Oaku**
Director: **Akaji Maro**
Choreographer: **Akaji Maro**

Contributing Researcher: **Kazue Hatano**

Image Credit: **Akaji Maro**

[226]

Henry V
Bob Crowley (Ireland/UK)
Set & Costume Design

Company: **Royal Shakespeare Company**
Venue: **Royal Shakespeare Theatre**
Location: **Stratford-upon-Avon, UK**
Opening/First Night: **22 March 1984**

Author: **William Shakespeare**
Scenic Designer: **Bob Crowley**
Costume Designer: **Bob Crowley**
Lighting Designer: **Robert Bryan**
Director: **Adrian Noble**

Contributing Researcher: **Madeline Taylor**

Image Credits: **Douglas H Jeffery, Victoria and Albert Museum, London; Bob Crowley**

---

[226]

In The Summer House (In het Tuinhuis)
Paul Gallis (Netherlands)
Set & Costume Design

Company: **Zuidelijk Toneet Globe**
Location: **Netherlands**
Opening/First Night: **1984**

Author: **Jane Bowles**
Scenic Designer: **Paul Gallis**
Costume Designer: **Paul Gallis**
Director: **Gerardian Rijnders**

Contributing Researcher: **Joke van Pelt**

Image Credit: **Gerrit Buys**

---

[227]

Turandot
Andrzej Majewski (Poland)
Set & Costume Design

Company: **Teatr Wielki**
Venue: **Teatr Wielki**
Location: **Warsaw, Poland**
Opening/First Night: **15 December 1984**

Composer: **Giacomo Puccini**
Scenic Designer: **Andrzej Majewski**
Costume Designer: **Andrzej Majewski**
Director: **Marek Grzesiński, Andrzej Majewski**
Choreographer: **Marek Wesołowski**

Contributing Researcher: **Agnieszka Kubaś**

Image Credits: **Juliusz Multarzyński, Archive of The Centre of Polish Scenography in Katowice (Poland)**

---

[228]

Three Sisters (Drei Schwestern, Tri sestry)
Karl-Ernst Hermann (Germany)
Set Design

Company: **Schaubuehne Berlin**
Venue: **Schaubuehne Berlin**
Location: **Berlin, Germany FRG**
Opening/First Night: **2 February 1984**

Author: **Anton Chekhov**
Scenic Designer: **Karl-Ernst Herrmann**
Costume Designer: **Moidele Bickel**
Lighting Designer: **Wolfgang Göbbel & Konrad Lindenberg**
Director: **Peter Stein**

Contributing Researcher: **Karin Winkelsesser**

Image Credit: **Ruth Walz**

---

[230]

Animal Farm
Jennifer Carey (UK)
Set, Mask & Costume Design

Company: **National Theatre**
Venue: **Cottesloe Theatre**
Location: **London, UK**
Opening/First Night: **1984**

Author: **Peter Hall**, adapted from George Orwell
Composer: **Richard Peaslee**
Lyrics: **Adrian Mitchell**
Scenic Designer: **Jennifer Carey**
Costume Designer: **Jennifer Carey**
Mask Designer: **Jennifer Carey**
Lighting Designer: **John Bury**
Director: **Peter Hall**

Contributing Researcher: **Donatella Barbieri**

Image Credit: **Douglas H Jeffery, Victoria and Albert Museum, London**

---

[230]

Rough Crossing
Carl Toms (UK)
Set & Costume Design

Company: **National Theatre**
Venue: **Lyttelton Stage**
Location: **London, UK**
Opening/First Night: **1984**

Author: **Tom Stoppard**, adapted from *Play at the Castle* by Ference Molnar
Scenic Designer: **Carl Toms**
Costume Designer: **Carl Toms**
Lighting Designer: **David Hersey**
Director: **Peter Wood**

Contributing Researcher: **Ian Herbert**

Image Credit: **Douglas H Jeffery, Victoria and Albert Museum, London**

---

[231]

The Cherry Orchard
Joe Hayes (New Zealand)
Lighting Design

Company: **The Court Theatre**
Venue: **The Court Theatre**
Location: **Christchurch, New Zealand**
Opening/First Night: **1984**

Author: **Anton Chekhov**
Scenic Designer: **Tony Geddes**
Lighting Designer: **Joe Hayes**
Director: **Elric Hooper**

Contributing Researcher: **Sam Trubridge**

Image Credit: **Elric Hooper**

---

[231]

Crime and Punishment (Priestuplenije i nakazanije, Zbrodnia i kara)
Krystyna Zachwatowicz (Poland)
Set & Costume Design

Company: **Stary Teatr im. Modrzejewskiej**
Venue: **Stary Teatr im. Modrzejewskiej**
Location: **Kraków, Poland**
Opening/First Night: **5 October 1984**

Author: **Fiodor Dostoyevsky**
Scenic Designer: **Krystyna Zachwatowicz**
Costume Designer: **Krystyna Zachwatowicz**
Director: **Andrzej Wajda**

Contributing Researcher: **Agnieszka Kubaś**

Image Credit: **Stanisław Markowski**

---

[234]

The Mahabharata
Jean-Guy Lecat (France)
Set Design

Company: **Centre International de Recherche Théâtrale**
Venue: **Avignon Festival/Théâtre des Bouffes du Nord**
Location: **Avignon/Paris, France**
Opening/First Night: **1985**

Author: **Jean-Claude Carriere & Peter Brook**
Scenic Designer: **Jean-Guy Lecat**
Costume Designer: **Chloe Obolensky**
Director: **Peter Brook**

Contributing Researcher: **Eric Fielding**

Image Credit: **Jean-Guy Lecat**

---

[236]

Three Venetian Twins (Trei gemeni venetieni)
Stefania Cenean (Romania)
Set & Costume Design

Venue: **National Theatre**
Location: **Craiova, Romania**
Opening/First Night: **1985**

Author: **A.C. Collalto Mattiuzzi**
Scenic Designer: **Stefania Cenean**
Costume Designer: **Stefania Cenean**
Director: **Mihai Manolescu**

Contributing Researcher: **Jean Cazaban**

Image Credit: **Stefania Cenean**

---

[236]

Julius Caesar
Lennart Mörk (Sweden)
Set & Costume Design

Company: **Royal Dramatic Theatre**
Venue: **Royal Dramatic Theatre, Stora scenen**
Location: **Stockholm, Sweden**
Opening/First Night: **24 January 1985**

Author: **William Shakespeare**
Composer: **William Runnström**, after *La Valse* by Ravel
Scenic Designer: **Lennart Mörk**
Costume Designer: **Lennart Mörk**
Lighting Designer: **Klas Möller**
Director: **Staffan Roos**
Choreographer: **Donya Feuer**

Contributing Researcher: **Ammy Kjellsdotter**
Photographer: **Bengt Wanselius**

Image Credit: **Lennart Mörk**

---

[237]

The Rake's Progress
Alejandro Luna & **Lucile Donay** (México)
Set, Costume & Lighting Design

Company: **Compañía Nacional de Ópera**
Venue: **Teatro del Palacio de Bellas Artes**
Location: **Mexico City, Mexico**
Opening/First Night: **1985**

Composer: **Igor Stravinsky**
Librettist: **W. H. Auden**
Scenic Designer: **Alejandro Luna**
Costume Designer: **Lucile Donay**
Lighting Designer: **Alejandro Luna**
Director: **Ludwik Margules**

Contributing Researcher: **Rodolfo Obregon Rodriguez**

Image Credits: **INBA-CITRU, Biblioteca de las Artes-CENART, Mexico; Fondo Ludwik Margules**

---

[238]

Tartuffe
Måns Hedström, Riitta Riihonen & Kimmo Viskari (Finland)
Set and Costume Design

Company: **Helsinki City Theatre**
Venue: **Helsinki City Theatre**
Location: **Helsinki, Finland**
Opening/First Night: **4 December 1985**

Author: **Molière**
Scenic Designer: **Måns Hedström, Riitta Riihonen & Kimmo Viskari**
Costume Designer: **Måns Hedström, Riitta Riihonen & Kimmo Viskari**
Lighting Designer: **Juhani Leppänen & Kimmo Lehtonen**
Director: **Kalle Holmberg**

Contributing Researcher: **Hanna Helavuori**

Image Credit: © **Tapio Vanhatalo, The Theatre Museum Archive (Finland)**

---

[239]

Cerceau
Igor Popov (USSR/Russia)
Set Design

Company: **Taganka Theatre**
Location: **Moscow, USSR/Russia**
Opening/First Night: **1985**

Author: **Viktor Slavkin**
Scenic Designer: **Igor Popov**
Director: **Anatoly Vasiliev**

Contributing Researcher: **Inna Mirzoyan**

Image Credit: **Igor Popov**

---

[240]

The Ring Cycle (Der Ring des Nibelungen)
Robert Israel (USA)
Set & Costume Design

Company: **Seattle Opera**
Venue: **Seattle Opera House**
Location: **Seattle, Washington, USA**
Opening/First Night: **1985**

Composer: **Richard Wagner**
Scenic Designer: **Robert Israel**
Costume Designer: **Robert Israel**
Director: **Francois Rochaix**
Conductors: **Armin Jordan & Manuel Rosenthal**

Contributing Researcher: **Jan Chambers**

Image Credit: © **Ron Scherl**

---

[242]

Lima Barreto
José Dias (Brazil)
Set Design

Venue: **Theater Culture Center Brazil Bank**
Location: **Rio de Janeiro, Brazil**
Opening/First Night: **March 1985**

Author: **Luis Alberto de Abreu**
Composer: **Tato Taborda**
Scenic Designer: **José Dias**
Lighting Designer: **Aurelio de Simone**
Director: **Aderbal Freire Filho**

Contributing Researcher: **JC Serroni**

Image Credit: **José Dias**

[242]

The Kalevala
Reija Hirvikoski (Finland)
Set & Costume Design

Company: **Helsinki City Theatre**
Venue: **Helsinki City Theatre**
Location: **Helsinki, Finland**
Opening/First Night: **14 May 1985**

Author: **Jorma Uotinen**
Composer: **Matti Bergström**
Scenic Designer: **Reija Hirvikoski**
Costume Designer: **Jorma Uotinen and Reija Hirvikoski**
Lighting Designer: **Claude Naville**
Director: **Jorma Uotinen**
Choreographer: **Jorma Uotinen**

Contributing Researcher: **Pälvi Laine**

Image Credit: **The Theatre Museum Archive (Finland)**

---

[243]

Lohengrin
Kenneth Rowell (Australia)
Set & Costume Design

Company: **Victorian State Opera**
Venue: **State Theatre, Victorian Arts Centre**
Location: **Melbourne, Australia**
Opening/First Night: **1985**

Composer: **Richard Wagner**
Scenic Designer: **Kenneth Rowell**
Costume Designer: **Kenneth Rowell**
Lighting Designer: **Nick Schlieper**
Director: **August Everding**

Contributing Researcher: **Richard Roberts**

Image Credit: **Kenneth Rowell**

---

[244]

Grotesque (*Groteska*)
Petr Lébl (Czechoslovakia/Czech Republic)
Set & Costume Design

Company: **Doprapo**
Location: **Prague, Czechoslovakia/Czech Republic**
Opening/First Night: **20 March 1985**

Author: **Kurt Vonnegut**, adapted by Petr Lébl
Scenic Designer: **Petr Lébl**
Costume Designer: **Petr Lébl**
Director: **Petr Lébl**

Contributing Researcher: **Daniela Pařízková & Marie Zdeňková**

Image Credit: **Prague Quadrennial Archive**

---

[244]

Les Miserables
John Napier (UK)
Set Design

Company: **Royal Shakespeare Company**
Venue: **Barbican**
Location: **London, UK**
Opening/First Night: **8 October 1985**

Composer: **Alain Boublil, Claude-Michel Schönberg**
Lyrics: **Herbert Kretzmer**
Scenic Designer: **John Napier**
Costume Designer: **Andreane Neofitou**
Lighting Designer: **David Hersey**
Director: **Trevor Nunn, John Caird**

Contributing Researcher: **Ian Herbert**

Image Credits: © **Chris Davies**

---

[245]

Asinamali
Mannie Manim (South Africa)
Lighting Design

Location: **South Africa**
Opening/First Night: **1985**

Author: **Mbongeni Ngema**
Lighting Designer: **Mannie Manim**
Director: **Mbongeni Ngema**

Contributing Researcher: **Sarah Roberts**

Image Credits: **Ruphin Coudyzer FPPSA**

---

[245]

The Cherry Orchard
Raymond Boyce (Great Britain/New Zealand)
Set Design

Company: **Downstage Theatre**
Venue: **The Hannah Playhouse**
Location: **Wellington, New Zealand**
Opening/First Night: **25 October 1985**

Author: **Anton Chekhov**
Scenic Designer: **Raymond Boyce**
Costume Designer: **Raymond Boyce**
Lighting Designer: **Stephen Blackburn**
Director: **Colin McColl**

Contributing Researcher: **Sam Trubridge**

Image Credit: **Phillip Merry, Glen Morris, Alexander Turnbull Library**

---

[246]

Everybody Wants to Live
(*Kulam Rutzim Lich'yot*)
Ruth Dar (Israel)
Set & Costume Design

Company: **Cameri Theatre**
Venue: **Cameri Theatre**
Location: **Tel Aviv, Israel**
Opening/First Night: **1985**

Author: **Hanoch Levin**
Scenic Designer: **Ruth Dar**
Costume Designer: **Ruth Dar**
Director: **Hanoch Levin**

Contributing Researcher: **Ben Tzion Munitz**

Image Credit: **Ruth Dar**

---

[246]

Matthew Honest (*Matěj Poctivý*)
Miroslav Melena (Czechoslovakia/Czech Republic)
Set & Costume Design

Venue: **Studio Y, Jiří Wolker Theatre**
Location: **Prague, Czechoslovakia/Czech Republic**
Opening/First Night: **23 May 1985**

Author: **Arnošt Dvořák, Ladislav Klíma**
Scenic Designer: **Miroslav Melena**
Costume Designer: **Miroslav Melena**
Director: **Jan Schmid**

Contributing Researcher: **Daniela Pařízková & Marie Zdeňková**

Image Credit: **Prague Quadrennial Archive**

---

[247]

Electra (*Électre*)
Yannis Kokkos (Greece/France)
Set & Costume Design

Name of Company: **Théâtre National de Chaillot**
Location: **Paris, France**
Opening/First Night: **1985**

Author : **Sophocles**
Scenic Designer: **Yannis Kokkos**
Costume Designer: **Yannis Kokkos**
Director: **Antoine Vitez**

Contributing Researcher: **Eric Fielding**

Image Credit: **Eric Fielding**

---

[248]

Les Liaisons Dangereuses
Bob Crowley (UK)
Set & Costume Design

Company: **Royal Shakespeare Company**
Venue: **The Other Place**
Location: **Stratford-on-Avon, England**
Opening/First Night: **24 September 1985**

Author: **Christopher Hampton**; from the novel by Choderlos de Laclos
Scenic Designer: **Bob Crowley**
Costume Designer: **Bob Crowley**
Lighting Designer: **Chris Parry**
Director: **Howard Davies**

Contributing Researcher: **Eric Fielding**

Image Credit: **Martha Swope** © **The New York Public Library for the Performing Arts; Prague Quadrennial Archive**

---

[249]

The Mysteries
William Dudley (UK)
Set & Costume Design

Company: **National Theatre**
Venue: **Cottesloe Stage**
Location: **London, UK**
Opening/First Night: **1985**

Author: **Unknown**
Adaptor: **Tony Harrison**
Scenic Designer: **William Dudley**
Costume Designer: **William Dudley**
Lighting Designer: **William Dudley & Laurence Clayton**
Director: **Bill Bryden**

Contributing Researcher: **Ian Herbert**

Image Credit: © **Nobby Clark/Arenapal; Douglas H Jeffery, Victoria and Albert Museum, London**

---

[250]

Princess of the Stars
Jerrard Smith (Canada)
Set & Costume Design

Company: **Banff Centre for the Arts**
Venue: **Two Jack Lake**
Location: **Banff, Canada**
Opening/First Night: **summer 1985**

Author: **Murray Schaeffer**
Composer: **Murray Schaeffer**
Scenic Designer: **Jerrard Smith**
Costume Designer: **Jerrard Smith**
Musical Director/Conductor: **Murray Schaeffer**

Contributing Researcher: **Peter McKinnon**

Image Credit: **Jerrard Smith**

---

[251]

The Cherry Orchard (*Livada de visini*)
Romulus Fenes (Romania)
Set & Costume Design

Venue: **National Theatre**
Location: **Targu Mures, Romania**
Opening/First Night: **1985**

Author: **Anton Chekhov**
Scenic Designer: **Romulus Fenes**
Costume Designer: **Romulus Fenes**
Director: **Harag György**

Contributing Researcher: **Jean Cazaban**

Image Credit: **Jean Cazaban, Bucharest**

---

[252]

Confiteor (*Konfiteor*)
Miodrag Tabački (Yugoslavia/Serbia)
Set Design

Company: **National Theatre**
Venue: **National Theatre**
Location: **Belgrade, Yugoslavia/Serbia**
Opening/First Night: **1 March 1985**

Author: **Slobodan Šnajder**
Composer: **Gregor F. Strniša**
Scenic Designer: **Miodrag Tabački**
Costume Designer: **Doris Kristić**
Lighting Designer: **Dušan Kotorčević**
Director: **Janez Pipan**
Choreographer: **Damir Zlatar-Frey**

Contributing Researcher: **Radivoje Dinulović**

Image Credit: **Museum of Theatrical Arts of Serbia**

---

[253]

Xerxes
David Fielding (UK)
Set & Costume Design

Company: **English National Opera**
Venue: **Coliseum**
Location: **London, UK**
Opening/First Night: **1985**

Composer: **Georg Frederick Handel**
Scenic Designer: **David Fielding**
Costume Designer: **David Fielding**
Lighting Designer: **Paul Pyant**
Director: **Nicholas Hytner**

Contributing Researcher: **Ian Herbert**

Image Credit: **Victoria and Albert Museum, London;** © **Catherine Ashmore**

---

[254]

Tsar Maximilian (*Cara Maksymilian*)
Rajmund Strzelecki (Poland)
Puppet Design

Company: **Teatr Lalek "Arlekin"**
Venue: **Teatr Lalek "Arlekin"**
Location: **Łódź, Poland**
Opening/First Night: **10 November 1985**

Author: **Aleksiej Remizow**
Puppet Designer: **Rajmund Strzelecki**
Scenic Designer: **Zenobiusz Strzelecki**
Director: **Stanisław Ochmański**

Contributing Researcher: **Agnieszka Kubaś**

Image Credit: **Rajmund Strzelecki, ???**

[255]

The Mother (Matka)
Jan Banucha (Poland)
Set & Costume Design

Company: **Teatr Współczesny**
Venue: **Teatr Współczesny**
Location: **Szczecin, Poland**
Opening/First Night: **14 June 1985**

Author: **Stanisław Ignacy Witkiewicz**
Composer: **Andrzej Głowiński**
Scenic Designer: **Jan Banucha**
Costume Designer: **Jan Banucha**
Director: **Ryszard Major**
Choreographer: **Henryk Walentynowicz**

Contributing Researcher: **Agnieszka Kubaś**

Photographer: **Jacek Fijałkowski**

Image Credit: **Jacek Fijałkowski, Archive of The Centre of Polish Scenography in Katowice (Poland), Jan Banucha**

[258]

Titus Andronicus
Hu Miaosheng (China)
Set Design

Company: **Shanghai Theatre Academy**
Venue: **The Experimental Theatre of Shanghai Theatre Academy**
Location: **Shanghai, China**
Opening/First Night: **1986**

Author: **William Shakespeare**
Scenic Designer: **Hu Miaosheng**
Costume Designer: **Chen Hongguang**
Lighting Designer: **Jin Changlie**
Director: **Xu Quping**

Contributing Researcher: **Xu Xiang**

Image Credit: **Hu Miaosheng**

[258]

Mr Puntila and His Man Matti
(Herr Puntila und sein Knecht Matti)
Nicos Kouroushis (Cyprus)
Set Design

Company: **Cyprus Theatre Organisation (National)**
Venue: **Nicosia Municipal Theatre**
Location: **Nicosia, Cyprus**
Opening/First Night: **April 1986**

Author: **Bertolt Brecht**
Composer: **Paul Dessau**
Scenic Designer: **Nicos Kouroushis**
Costume Designer: **Nicos Kouroushis**
Lighting Designer: **Grigoris Papageorgiou**
Director: **Volker Geissler**
Sculpture of bull: **Leonidas Spanos**

Contributing Researcher: **Nicole Leclercq. Andy Bargilly**

Image Credit: **Nicos Kouroushis**

[259]

Čaruga (Galócza)
László Székely (Hungary)
Set Design

Company: **Katona József Theatre**
Venue: **Katona József Theatre**
Location: **Budapest, Hungary**
Opening/First Night: **March 1986**

Author: **Ivan Kušan**
Composer: **János Másik**
Scenic Designer: **László Székely**
Costume Designer: **Márta Pilinyi**
Director: **Miklós Benedek**

Contributing Researcher: **Eva Nemeth**

Image Credit: **Scenography Collection, Hungarian Theatre Museum and Institute**

[260]

Phantom of the Opera
Maria Bjonson (France/UK)
Set & Costume Design

Company: **Really Useful Theatre Co.**
Venue: **Her Majesty's Theatre**
Location: **London, UK**
Opening/First Night: **9 October 1986**

Composer: **Andrew Lloyd Webber**
Lyrics: **Charles Hart**
Book: **Richard Stilgoe & Andrew Lloyd Webber**, from Gaston Leroux novel
Scenic Designer: **Maria Björnson**
Costume Designer: **Maria Björnson**
Lighting Designer: **Andrew Bridge**
Sound Designer: **Martin Levan**
Director: **Harold Prince**

Contributing Researcher: **Donatella Barbieri & Ian Herbert**

Image Credits: **Redcase Limited/Maria Bjornson Archive; Victoria and Albert Museum, London; © Clive Barda/Arenapal**

[262]

Shakespeare the Sadist (Film und Frau)
Tihomir Milovac (Yugoslavia/Croatia)
Set Design

Company: **CEKADE/Coccolemocco**
Venue: **Mali lapidarij**
Location: **Zagreb, Yugoslavia/Croatia**
Opening/First Night: **26 July 1986**

Author: **Wolfgang Bauer**
Composer: **Damir Prica, Mario Berišin, Ivan Vinski**
Scenic Designer: **Tihomir Milovac**
Costume Designer: **Nina Silobrčić**
Film: **Tomislav Gotovac**
Director: **Branko Brezovec**

Image Credit: **Tihomir Milovac**

[262]

Event in the City of Goga
(Dogodek v mestu gogi)
Meta Hočevar (Slovenia)
Set & Costume Design

Company: **Slovene National Theatre**
Location: **Ljubljana, Slovenia**
Opening/First Night: **26 December 1986**

Author: **Slavko Grum**
Scenic Designer: **Meta Hočevar**
Costume Designer: **Meta Hočevar**
Director: **Meta Hočevar**
Dramaturg: **Dominik Smole**
Composer: **Aldo Kumar**

Contributing Researcher: **Nicole Leclercq**

Image Credit: **Meta Hočevar**

[263]

The Werewolf (Libahunt)
Aime Unt (Estonia)
Set Design

Design Company: **Rakvere Theatre**
Location: **Rakvere, Estonia**
Opening/First Night: **20 April 1986**

Author: **August Kitzberg**
Scenic Designer: **Aime Unt**
Director: **Mikk Mikiver**

Contributing Researcher: **Nicole Leclercq/ Monika Larini**

Image Credit: **Estonian Theatre and Music Museum**

[263]

Have You Seen Zandile?
Sarah Roberts (South Africa)
Set Design

Location: **South Africa**
Opening/First Night: **1986**

Author: **Gcina Mhlope**
Scenic Designer: **Sarah Roberts**
Director: **Maralin van Reenen**

Contributing Researcher: **Sarah Roberts**

Image Credit: **Ruphin Coudyzer FPPSA**

[264]

The Threepenny Opera
(Die Dreigroschenoper, Opera za trzy grosze)
Barbara Hanicka (Poland)
Set & Costume Design

Company: **Teatr Studio**
Venue: **Teatr Studio**
Location: **Warsaw, Poland**
Opening/First Night: **9 February 1986**

Author: **Bertolt Brecht**
Composer: **Kurt Weill**
Scenic Designer: **Barbara Hanicka**
Costume Designer: **Barbara Hanicka**
Director: **Jerzy Grzegorzewski**

Contributing Researcher: **Agnieszka Kubaś**

Image Credit: **Wojciech Plewiński, Polish Theatre Institute Archive/Private archive of Barbara Hanicka**

[266]

Grimmoire de Grimm
Metin Deniz (Turkey)
Set & Costume Design

Company: **Théâtre à Venir**
Location: **Paris, France**
Opening/First Night: **October 1986**

Author: **Richard Soudee**
Scenic Designer: **Metin Deniz**
Costume Designer: **Metin Deniz**
Director: **Işıl Kasapoğlu**

Contributing Researcher: **Evcimen Percin**

Image Credit: **Metin Deniz**

[267]

Uncle Vanya
Nadezhda Gultiajeva (Lithuania)
Set Design

Company: **Lithuanian State Youth Theatre**
Location: **Vilnius, Lithuania**
Opening/First Night: **1986**

Author: **Anton Chekhov**
Scenic Designer: **Nadezhda Gultiajeva**
Director: **Eimuntas Nekrosius**

Contributing Researcher: **Inna Morzoyan**

Image Credit: **Nadeshda Gultiajeva**

[268]

Robert Lewis Stephenson's
The Strange Case of Dr. Jekyll & Mr. Hyde
Ladislav Vychodil (Sslovakia)
Set Design

Company: **San Diego Repertory Theatre**
Venue: **San Diego Repertory Theatre Lyceum Stage**
Location: **San Diego, California, USA**
Opening/First Night: **1986**

Author: **D. W. Jacobs**
Scenic Designer: **Ladislav Vychodil**
Costume Designer: **Mary Gibson**
Lighting Designer: **Don Childs**
Composer/Sound Designer: **Burnham Joiner & Linda Vickerman**
Director: **D. W. Jacobs**
Fight Choreographer: **Christopher Villa**

Contributing Researcher: **Eric Fielding**

Image Credits: **D. W. Jacobs, Ladislav Vychodil**

[270]

The Tempest
Vadim Fomitšev (Estonia)
Set Design

Design Company: **Estonian Drama Theatre**
Location: **Tallinn, Estonia**
Opening/First Night: **12 November 1986**

Author: **William Shakespeare**
Scenic Designer: **Vadim Fomitšev**
Director: **Evald Hearmaküla**

Contributing Researcher: **Nicole Leclercq/ Monika Larini**

Image Credit: **Estonian Theatre and Music Museum**

[270]

You Strike the Woman, You Strike the Rock
(WaThint'Abafazi, wathint'umbokotho)
Sarah Roberts (South Africa)
Set Design

Company: **Market Theatre**
Location: **South Africa**
Opening/First Night: **1986**

Scenic Designer: **Sarah Roberts**
Director: **Phyllis Klotz**

Contributing Researcher: **Sarah Roberts**

Image Credit: **Ruphin Coudyzer FPPSA**

[271]

The Merchant of Venice
Judit Schäffer (Hungary)
Costume Design

Company: **National Theatre**
Venue: **National Theatre**
Location: **Budapest, Hungary**
Opening/First Night: **March 1986**

Author: **William Shakespeare**
Scenic Designer: **Árpád Csányi**
Costume Designer: **Judit Schäffer**
Director: **Ferenc Sík**

Contributing Researcher: **Eva Nemeth**

Image Credit: **Tóth István Csaba, MTI Photo Archive (Magyar Távirati Iroda - Hungarian News Agency)**

[272]

The Mask of Orpheus
Jocelyn Herbert (UK)
Set & Costume Design

Company: **English National Opera**
Venue: **Coliseum**
Location: **London, UK**

Opening/First Night: **1986**

Composer: **Harrison Birtwistle**
Scenic Designer: **Jocelyn Herbert**
Costume Designer: **Jocelyn Herbert**
Lighting Designer: **Andy Phillips**
Director: **David Freeman**

Contributing Researcher: **Ian Herbert & Liz Wright**

Image Credits: **Catherine Ashmore; Jocelyn Herbert; Douglas H Jeffery, Victoria and Albert Museum, London**

---

[274]

Isis
Sakina Mohamed Ali (Egypt)
Set & Costume Design

Venue: **Egyptian National Theatre**
Location: **City, Egypt**
Opening/First Night: **Day/Month/1986**

Author: **Tawfiq el-Hakim**
Scenic Designer: **Sakina Mohamed Ali**
Costume Designer: **Sakina Mohamed Ali**
Director: **Karam Metawea**

Contributing Researcher: **Hazem Shebl**

Image Credit: **Sakina Mohamed Ali**

---

[275]

A Doll's House
Kazue Hatano (Japan)
Set & Costume Design

Company: **Mingei Theatre Company**
Venue: **Sunshine Theatre**
Location: **Tokyo, Japan**
Opening/First Night: **September 1986**

Author: **Henrik Ibsen**
Scenic Designer: **Kazue Hatano**
Costume Designer: **Kazue Hatano**
Lighting Designer: **Kazuhisa Hakariya**
Sound Designer: **Taikei Yamamoto**
Director: **Jun Uchiyama**

Contributing Researcher: **Kazue Hatano**

Image Credit: **Kazue Hatano**

---

[275]

Andromache (Andromaque)
Mirjam Grote Gansey (Netherlands)
Set & Costume Design

Company: **Haagse Comedie**
Location: **Netherlands**
Opening/First Night: **1986**

Author: **Jean Racine**
Scenic Designer: **Mirjam Grote Gansey**
Costume Designer: **Mirjam Grote Gansey**
Lighting Designer: **Jeroen Visser**
Director: **Peter te Nuyl**

Contributing Researcher: **Joke van Pelt**

Image Credit: **Mirjam Grote Gansey; Pan Sok, Netherlands**

---

[276]

The Merry Wives of Windsor
Wang Peisen (China)
Set Design

Company: **The Central Experimental Drama Theatre**
Venue: **The Cultural Palace of Nationalities of Beijing**
Location: **Beijing, China**
Opening/First Night: **March 1986**

Author: **William Shakespeare**
Scenic Designer: **Wang Peisen**
Costume Designer: **Yan Long**
Lighting Designer: **Zhang Wenchang**
Director: **Yang Zongzheng**

Contributing Researcher: **Xu Xiang**

Image Credit: **Wang Peisen**

---

[276]

Alice in Wonderland
Anthony Ward (UK)
Set & Costume Design

Venue: **Lyric Hammersmith**
Location: **London, UK**
Opening/First Night: **18 December 1986**

Author: **Lewis Carroll**, adapted by John Wells
Composer: **Carl Davis**
Scenic Designer: **Anthony Ward**
Costume Designer: **Anthony Ward**
Lighting Designer: **Richard Caswell**
Director: **Ian Forrest**

Contributing Researcher: **Ian Herbert**

Image Credit: **Douglas H Jeffery, Victoria and Albert Museum, London; Anthony Ward**

---

[277]

Alcestis
Robert Wilson (USA)
Set, Costume & Lighting Design

Company: **American Repertory Theater**
Venue: **Loeb Drama Center**
Location: **Cambridge, Massachusetts, USA**
Opening/First Night: **March 1986**

Author: **Robert Wilson**, adapted from Euripides' play as translated by Dudley Fitts & Robert Fitzgerald
Composer: **Laurie Anderson**
Scenic Designer: **Tom Kamm & Robert Wilson**
Costume Designer: **John Conklin & Robert Wilson**
Lighting Designer: **Jennifer Tipton & Robert Wilson**
Director: **Robert Wilson**

Contributing Researcher: **Eric Fielding**

Image Credit: **Collection of the McNay Art Museum, Gift of Robert L. B. Tobin**

---

[278]

Sophiatown
William Kentridge & Sarah Roberts (South Africa)
Set & Costume Design

Company: **Junction Avenue Theatre Company**
Venue: **Market Theatre**

Location: **City, South Africa**
Opening/First Night: **1986**

Scenic Designer: **William Kentridge & Sarah Roberts**
Costume Designer: **Sarah Roberts**
Director: **Malcolm Purkey**

Contributing Researcher: **Sarah Roberts**

Image Credit: **Ruphin Coudyzer FPPSA**

---

[278]

Piebald Dog Running Along the Seashore
Gennady Sotnikov (USSR/Russia)
Set Design

Company: **Yakutsk Drama Theatre**
Location: **Yakutsk, USSR/Russia**
Opening/First Night: **1986**

Author: adapted from story by **Chingiz Aitmatov**
Scenic Designer: **Gennady Sotnikov**
Director: **Andrei Borisov**

Contributing Researcher: **Inna Mirzoyan**

Image Credit: **Gennady Sotnikov**

---

[279]

The Cherry Orchard (El Jardín de los cerezos)
Gerardo Vera (Spain)
Set & Costume Design

Company: **Centro Dramático Nacional**
Venue: **Teatro María Guerrero de Madrid**
Location: **Madrid, Spain**
Opening/First Night: **11 April 1986**

Author: **Anton Chekhov**
Composer: **Mariano Díaz**
Scenic Designer: **Gerardo Vera**
Costume Designer: **Gerardo Vera**
Lighting Designer: **José Luis Rodríguez**
Director: **José Carlos Plaza & William Layton**

Contributing Researcher: **Angel Martinez Roger**

Image Credit: **Chicho Ros Ribas**

---

[279]

The Public (El Público)
Fabia Puigserver (Spain)
Set & Costume Design

Company: **Centro Dramático Nacional (CDN)**
Venue: **Teatro María Guerrero de Madrid**
Location: **Madrid, Spain**
Opening/First Night: **16 January 1987**
[Piccolo Teatro Studio de Milán, 12 December 1986]

Author: **Federico García Lorca**
Composer: **Josep María Arrizabalaga**
Scenic Designer: **Fabia Puigserver**
Costume Designer: **Fabia Puigserver**
Director: **Lluís Pasqual**
Choreographer: **Cesc gelabert & Lydia Azzopardi**

Contributing Researcher: **Angel Martinez Roger**

Image Credit: **Bielva, "Centro de Documentación Teatral" del INAEM del Gobierno de España**

---

[282]

The Good Woman of Setzuan
(*Der gute Mensch von Sezuan*)
Yan Long (China)
Set & Costume Design

Company: **The Third Theatre of Sichuan Opera of Cheng Du**
Venue: **The Theatre of Beijing People's Art**
Location: **Beijing, China**
Opening/First Night: **July 1987**

Author: **Bertolt Brecht**, adapted by Liu Shaocong & Wu Xiaofei
Composer: **He Guojing**
Scenic Designer: **Yan Long**
Costume Designer: **Yan Long**
Lighting Designer: **Zhang Ange**
Director: **Li Liuyi**

Contributing Researcher: **Xu Xiang**

Image Credit: **Yan Long**

---

[282]

The Fall of Singapore
Nigel Triffitt (Australia)
Set & Costume Design

Company: **Melbourne Festival**
Venue: **Melbourne Town Hall**
Location: **Melbourne, Australia**
Opening/First Night: **September 1987**

Author: **Nigel Triffitt**
Scenic Designer: **Nigel Triffitt**
Costume Designer: **Nigel Triffitt**
Lighting Designer: **Phillip Lethlean**
Puppetry: **Peter Wilson**
Director: **Nigel Triffitt**

Contributing Researcher: **Richard Roberts**

Image Credit: **Nigel Triffitt**

---

[283]

Odysseus
Josef Svoboda (Czechoslovakia/ Czech Republic)
Set & Lighting Design

Company: **Laterna Magika**
Venue: **National Theatre**
Location: **Prague, Czechoslovakia/ Czech Republic**
Opening/First Night: **10 September 1987**

Author: **Evald Schorm, Jaroslav Kučera, Jindřich Smetana, Michael Kocáb**
Composer: **Michael Kocáb**
Scenic Designer: **Josef Svoboda**
Costume Designer: **Šárka Hejnová**
Lighting Designer: **Josef Svoboda**
Film designer: **Jindřich Smetana**
Cinematographer: **Jaroslav Kučera**
Director: **Evald Schorm, Jaroslav Kučera**
Choreographer: **Ondrej Šoth**

Contributing Researcher: **Daniela Parizkova & Marie Zdenkova**

Image Credit: **Prague Quadrennial Archive**

---

[284]

Azuchi—Play With Music
Kappa Senoh (Japan)
Set Design

Company: **Ginza Season Company**
Venue: **Ginza Season Theatre**
Location: **Tokyo, Japan**
Opening/First Night: **October 1987**

Author: **Shinichi Ichikawa**
Composer: **Yuzuru Hisaishi**
Scenic Designer: **Kappa Senoh**
Lighting Designer: **Tamotsu Harada**
Director: **Choku Kato**
Choreographer: **Yoshijiro Hanayagi**

Contributing Researcher: **Kazue Hatano**

Image Credit: **Kappa Senoh**

[285]

Love and Intrigue
Li Zhiliang (China)
Scenic Design

Company: People's Liberation Army Art
Academy
Venue: Hai Dian Theatre
Location: China
Opening/First Night: June 1987

Author: Friedrich Schiller
Scenic Designer: Li Zhiliang
Costume Designer: Xu Gefei
Lighting Designer: Duan Zhongxin
Director: Feng Jitang

Contributing Researcher: Xu Xiang

Image Credit: Li Zhiliang

---

[285]

The Cherry Orchard (*O jardim das cerejas*)
José Manuel Castanheira (Portugal)
Set Design

Company: Novo Grupo
Venue: Teatro Aberto
Location: Lisbon, Portugal
Opening/First Night: January 1987

Author: Anton Chekhov
Composer: Eduardo Paes Mamede
Scenic Designer: José Manuel Castanheira
Costume Designer: Lídia Lemos
Puppets: José Carlos Barros
Lighting Designer: Paulo Barreira
Director: João Lourenço
Dramaturg: Vera San Payo de Lemos

Contributing Researcher: Paulo Eduardo
Carvalho & Maria Helena Serôdio

Image Credit: José Manuel Castanheira

---

[286]

Swan Lake (*Lebedínoye Özero*)
Yolanda Sonnabend (South Africa/UK)
Set & Costume Design

Company: The Royal Ballet
Venue: Royal Opera House, Covent Garden
Location: London, UK
Opening/First Night: 1987

Choreographer: Marius Petipa, Lev Ivanov
Composer: P I Tchaïkovsky
Scenic Designer: Yolanda Sonnabend
Costume Designer: Yolanda Sonnabend
Lighting Designer: John B Read
Director: Anthony Dowell

Contributing Researcher: Ian Herbert &
Liz Wright

Image Credits: Leslie Spatt; Douglas H
Jeffery, Victoria and Albert Museum,
London

---

[288]

Waiting for Godot
Frank Haenig (Germany FRG)
Set & Costume Design

Company: Staatsschauspiel Dresden
Location: Dresden, GDR
Opening/First Night: 5 May 1987

Author: Samuel Beckett
Scenic Designer: Frank Haenig
Costume Designer: Frank Haenig
Director: Wolfgang Engel

Contributing Researcher: Karin
Winkelsesser

Image Credit: Hans-Ludwig Boehme

---

[288]

Death and the King's Horseman
Eni Jones Umuko (Nigeria)
Set & Costume Design

Company: Paul Robeson Players
Venue: Arts Theatre, University of Nigeria
Location: Nsukka, Nigeria
Opening/First Night: 1 February 1987

Author: Wole Soyinka
Scenic Designer: Eni Jones Umuko & Chris
Nwachukwu
Costume Designer: Eni Jones Umuko &
Kola Ogunjobi
Sound Designer: Chris Femi Faseun
Director: Eni Jones Umuko
Choreographer: Esiaba Irobi & Eni Jones
Umuko

Contributing Researcher: Osita Okagbue

Image Credit: Ngozi Awa

---

[289]

Tristan and Isolde (*Tristan und Isolde*)
Annelies Corrodi (Switzerland)
Set & Costume Design

Company: Canadian Opera Company
Venue: O'Keefe Centre
Location: Toronto, Canada
Opening/First Night: 23 September 1987

Composer: Richard Wagner
Scenic Designer: Annelies Corrodi
Costume Designer: Annelies Corrodi
Lighting Designer: Michael J Whitfield
Director: Lotfi Mansouri
Music Director/Conductor: Berislav
Klobucar
Chorus Master: Donald Palumbo

Contributing Researcher: Franziska K.
Trefzer & Sandra Gredig

Image Credits: Verena Moser, Annelies
Corrodi

---

[290]

Nixon in China
Adrianne Lobel (USA)
Set Design

Company: Houston Grand Opera
Location: Houston, Texas, USA
Opening/First Night: 22 October 1987
(New production, Metropolitan Opera, 2011)

Composer: John Adams
Libretto: Alice Goodman
Scenic Designer: Adrianne Lobel
Costume Designer: Dunya Ramicova
Lighting Designer: James F. Ingalls
Director: Peter Sellars
Choreographer: Mark Morris

Contributing Researcher: Eric Fielding

Image Credit: The Metropolitan Opera

---

[292]

The Huguenots (*Les Huguenots*)
Gottfried Pilz (Austria/Germany)
Set & Costume Design

Company: Deutsche Oper Berlin
Venue: Deutsche Oper Berlin
Location: Berlin, Germany
Opening/First Night: 9 May 1987

Author: Eugène Scribe
Composer: Giaccomo Meyerbeer
Scenic Designer: Gottfried Pilz
Costume Designer: Gottfried Pilz
Lighting Designer: Hans-Albrecht Neelsen
Sound Designer: Rolf Rietshausen
Director: John Dew
Conductor: Jesus Lopez Cobos
Choir director: Marcus Creed

Contributing Researcher: Karin
Winkelsesser

Image Credit: Gottfried Pilz

---

[293]

The Hunger Artist
Robert Israel (USA)
Set & Costume Design

Company: Music Theater Group & Kennedy
Center
Venue: St. Clements 46th St
Location: New York, New York, USA
Opening/First Night: 1987

Author: Martha Clarke
Composer: Richard Peaslee
Scenic Designer: Robert Israel
Costume Designer: Robert Israel
Lighting Designer: Paul Gallo
Illusions: Ben Robinson
Director: Martha Clarke
Choreographer: Martha Clarke

Contributing Researcher: Jan Chambers

Image Credit: © Carol Rosegg

---

[294]

City in the Water
Wang Ren (China)
Set & Costume Design

Company: The Central Academy of Drama
Venue: The Middle Theatre of the Central
Academy of Drama
Location: China
Opening/First Night: November 1987

Author: Kobo Abe
Scenic Designer: Wang Ren
Costume Designer: Wang Ren
Lighting Designer: Mu Baisuo
Director: Ishizawa Shūji

Contributing Researcher: Xu Xiang

Image Credit: Lv Hong

---

[294]

King Lear (*Regele Lear*)
Emilia Jivanov (Romania)
Set & Costume Design

Venue: National Theatre
Location: Timisoara, Romania
Opening/First Night: 1987

Author: William Shakespeare
Scenic Designer: Emilia Jivanov
Costume Designer: Emilia Jivanov
Director: Ioan Ieremia

Contributing Researcher: Jean Cazaban

Image Credit: Emilia Jivanov

---

[295]

Alchemy of Sorrow (Алхимия на скръбта)
Marina Raytchinova (Bulgaria)
Costume Design

Company: Lovetch Drama Theatre
Venue: Drama Theatre—Lovetch
Location: Lovetch, Bulgaria
Opening/First Night: May 1987

Author: A.P. Chehov, J. Ionesco, Ingmar
Bergman, Ludvig Vitgenstein
Scenic Designer: Marina Raytchinova
Costume Designer: Marina Raytchinova
Lighting Designer: Marina Raytchinova

Contributing Researcher: Marina
Raytchinova

Image Credit: Marina Raytchinova

---

[296]

The Magic Circle (*Noitaympyrä*)
Måns Hedström & Kimmo Viskari
(Finland)
Set & Costume Design

Company: Helsinki City Theatre
Venue: Helsinki City Theatre
Location: Helsinki, Finland
Opening/First Night: 6 November 1987

Author: Ritva Holmberg, after Pentti
Haanpää's novels and short stories
Composer: Jukka Linkola
Scenic Designer: Måns Hedström & Kimmo
Viskari
Costume Designer: Måns Hedström &
Kimmo Viskari
Lighting Designer: Juhani Leppänen &
Kimmo Lehtonen
Sound Designer: Kalle Holmberg
Director: Kalle Holmberg

Contributing Researcher: Pälvi Laine

Image Credit: Måns Hedström, The Theatre
Museum Archive (Finland)

---

[297]

Don Giovanni
George Tsypin (Kazakhstan/USA)
Set Design

Venue: Pepsico Summerfare
Location: Purchase, New York, USA
Opening/First Night: 1987

Composer: W A Mozart
Scenic Designer: George Tsypin
Costume Designer: Dunya Ramicova
Lighting Designer: James F. Ingalls
Director: Peter Sellars

Contributing Researcher: Eric Fielding

Image Credits: George Tsypin; Collection
of the McNay Art Museum, Gift of Robert
L. B. Tobin

---

[298]

The Winter's Tale
Mary Moore (UK/Australia)
Set & Costume Design

Company: State Theatre Company of South
Australia
Venue: Playhouse, Adelaide Festival Centre
Location: Adelaide, Australia
Opening/First Night: July 1987

Author: William Shakespeare
Composer: Moya Henderson
Scenic Designer: Mary Moore
Costume Designer: Mary Moore
Lighting Designer: John Comeadow
Director: Gale Edwards & John Gaden

Contributing Researcher: Richard Roberts

Image Credit: Mary Moore

[299]

The Dragon's Trilogy
Robert Lepage (Canada)
Design Collaboration

Company: **Ex Machina**
Location: **Montreal, Quebec, Canada**
Opening/First Night: **6 June 1987**

Author: **Robert Lepage**
Composer: **Robert Caux**
Scenic Designer: **Jean François Couture, Gilles Dubé**
Costume Designer: **Marie-Chantale Vaillancourt**
Lighting Designer: **Louis-Marie Lavoie, Lucie Bazzo**
Director: **Robert Lepage**
Text: **Marie Brassard, Jean Casault, Lorraine Côté, Marie Gignac, Robert Lepage, Marie Michaud**

Contributing Researcher: **Peter McKinnon**

Image Credits: **Claudel Huot, Érick Labbé**

[299]

Into the Woods
Tony Straiges (USA)
Set Design

Venue: **Martin Beck Theatre**
Location: **New York, New York, USA**
Opening/First Night: **5 November 1987**

Composer: **Stephen Sondheim**
Lyrics: **Stephen Sondheim**
Author: **James Lapine**
Scenic Designer: **Tony Straiges**
Costume Designer: **Ann Hould-Ward**
Lighting Designer: **Richard Nelson**
Sound Designer: **Alan Stieb & James Brousseau**
Director: **James Lapine**

Contributing Researcher: **Eric Fielding**

Image Credit: **Hey Tait Fraser**

[300]

Montedemo
João Brites (Portugal)
Set Design

Company: **Teatro O Bando**
Venue: **Woods at Tondela**, gardens of the Calouste Gilbenkian Foundation
Location: **Lisbon, Portugal**
Opening/First Night: **July 1987** (also Berlin 1988)

Author: **Hélia Correia**
Composer: **Luís Pedro Faro**
Scenic Designer: **João Brites**
Costume Designer: **Jasmim**
Director: **João Brites**
Choreographer: **Paula Massano**

Contributing Researcher: **Maria Helena Serôdio & Paulo Eduardo Carvalho**

Image Credit: **João Brites; Archive of Teatro O Bando, Jorge Barros**

[301]

Sarafina!
Sarah Roberts (South Africa)
Set Design

Location: **South Africa**
Opening/First Night: **1987**

Author: **Mbongeni Ngema**
Composer: **Mbongeni Ngema**
Scenic Designer: **Sarah Roberts**
Lighting Designer: **Mannie Manim**
Sound Designer: **Marc Malherbe**
Director: **Mbongeni Ngema**

Contributing Researcher: **Sarah Roberts**

Image Credit: **Ruphin Coudyzer FPPSA**

[302]

Rosencrantz and Guildenstern are Dead
Voytek (UK)
Set & Costume Design

Company: **Abbey Theatre Company**
Venue: **Abbey Theatre**
Location: **Dublin, UK**
Opening/First Night: **6 April 1987**

Author: **Tom Stoppard**
Scenic Designer: **Voytek**
Costume Designer: **Voytek**
Lighting Designer: **Tony Wakefield**
Director: **Brian de Salvo**

Contributing Researcher: **Ian Herbert**

Image Credit: **Victoria and Albert Museum, London**

[302]

Triumph in the Midnight
Dai Yannian (China)
Set Design

Company: **Air Force Political Department's Theatre**
Venue: **The Theatre of Air Force Political Department**
Location: **China**
Opening/First Night: **March 1987**

Author: **Han Jingting**
Scenic Designer: **Dai Yannian**
Costume Designer: **Xue Xiangsheng**
Lighting Designer: **Liu Qingchang**
Director: **Wang Gui**

Contributing Researcher: **Xu Xiang**

Image Credit: **Wang Ren**

[303]

Cirque Réinventé
André Caron (Canada)
Set Design

Company: **Cirque du Soleil**
Venue: **Under the Big Top**
Location: **Montreal, Canada**
Opening/First Night: **1987**

Author: **Guy Caron & Franco Dragone**
Composer: **René Dupéré**
Scenic Designer: **André Caron**
Costume Designer: **Michel Crête**
Lighting Designer: **Luc Lafortune**
Director: **Franco Dragone**
Choreographer: **Debra Brown**
Musical Director/Conductor: **Benoît Jutras**

Contributing Researcher: **Sylvia François**

Image Credit: **Cirque du Soleil**

[303]

The Indiade or India of Their Dreams
(*L'Indiade ou l'Inde de leurs rêves*)
Guy-Claude François (France)
Set Design

Company: **Théâtre du Soleil**
Venue: **Cartoucherie de Vincennes**
Location: **Paris, France**
Opening/First Night: **30 September 1987**

Author: **Hélène Cixous**
Composer: **Jean-Jacques Lemêtre**
Scenic Designer: **Guy-Claude François**
Costume Designer: **Jean-Claude Barriera & Nathalie Thomas**
Lighting Designer: **Jean-Noël Cordier**
Choreographer: **Maitreyi** (Bhârata-nâtyam)
Director: **Ariane Mnouchkine**

Contributing Researcher: **Marcel Freydefont**

Image Credit: **Theatre du Soleil**

[306]

Tiger Amulet
Ma Weili (China)
Set Design

Company: **The Central Academy of Drama**
Venue: **The Experimental Theatre of the Central Academy of Drama**
Location: **China**
Opening/First Night: **1988**

Author: **Guo Moruo**
Composer: **Wang Liping**
Scenic Designer: **Ma Weili**
Costume Designer: **Li Jun, Huang Shuli & Jiang Ruirong**
Lighting Designer: **Jiang Yuejin, Wu Chunli, Liu Fuxiang, Zhang Zhenming & Shao Jingtao**
Director: **He Bingzhu & Guan Yin**
Choreographer: **Zhang Daying & Song Lifen**

Contributing Researcher: **Xu Xiang**

Image Credit: **Ma Weili**

[306]

Tannhauser
Yukio Horio (Japan)
Set Design

Company: **NikiKai Opera**
Venue: **Tokyo Bunka Kaikan Hall**
Location: **Tokyo, Japan**
Opening/First Night: **February 1988**

Composer: **Richard Wagner**
Author: **Ludwig Tieck**
Scenic Designer: **Yukio Horio**
Lighting Designer: **Sumio Yoshii**
Director: **Keiichi Nishizawa**

Contributing Researcher: **Kazue Hatano**

Image Credit: **Ukio Horio**

[307]

Germania Death in Berlin
(*Germania Tod in Berlin*)
Johannes Schütz (Germany FRG)
Set Design

Venue: **Schauspielhaus Bochum**
Location: **Bochum, Germany**
Opening/First Night: **10 August 1988**

Author: **Heiner Müller**
Scenic Designer: **Johannes Schuetz**
Director: **Frank-Patrick Steckel**

Contributing Researcher: **Karin Winkelsesser**

Image Credit: **Johannes Schütz**

[308]

1000 Airplanes on the Roof:
A Science Fiction Music Drama
Jerome Sirlin (USA)
Set & Projection Design

Venue: **Vienna International Airport Hangar #3** (World Premiere) / **The American Music Theatre Festival** (USA Premiere)
Location: **Vienna, Austria / Philadelphia, USA**
Opening/First Night: **15 July 1988** (Vienna) / **September 1988** (Philadelphia)

Author: **David Henry Hwang**
Composer: **Philip Glass**
Scenic Designer: **Jerome Sirlin**
Lighting Designer: **Robert Wierzel**
Projection Design: **Jerome Sirlin**
Sound Designer: **Kurt Munkacsi**
Director: **Philip Glass**
Music Direction: **Martin Goldray**

Contributing Researcher: **Jan Chambers**

Image Credit: **Jerome Sirlin**

[310]

Romeo and Juliet
Marta Roszkopfová (Czechoslovakia/ Czech Republic)
Set & Costume Design

Company: **Theatre of P. Bezruč**
Venue: **State Theatre Ostrava**
Location: **Ostrava, Czechlslovakia/Czech Republic**
Opening/First Night: **9 April 1988**

Author: **William Shakespeare**
Scenic Designer: **Marta Roszkopfová**
Costume Designer: **Marta Roszkopfová**

Contributing Researcher: **Daniela Pařízková & Marie Zdeňková**

Image Credit: **Prague Quadrennial Archive**

[311]

Too Clever By Half
Richard Hudson (UK)
Set & Costume Design

Company: **Old Vic Company**
Venue: **The Old Vic**
Location: **London, UK**
Opening/First Night: **June 1988**

Author: **Alexander Ostrovsky**, from the Russian play, *Diary of a Scoundrel*, translated by Rodney Ackland
Scenic Designer: **Richard Hudson**
Costume Designer: **Richard Hudson**
Lighting Designer: **Davy Cunningham**
Director: **Richard Jones**

Contributing Researcher: **Ian Herbert**

Image Credit: **Richard Hudson**

[312]

M. Butterfly
Eiko Ishioka (Japan)
Set & Costume Design

Venue: **Eugene O'Neill Theatre**
Location: **New York, New York, USA**
Opening/First Night: **20 March 1988**

Author: **David Henry Hwang**
Scenic Designer: **Eiko Ishioka**
Costume Designer: **Eiko Ishioka**
Lighting Designer: **Andy Phillips**
Sound Designer: **Peter J. Fitzgerald**
Director: **John Dexter**

Contributing Researcher: **Eric Fielding, Tracy Roberts**

Image Credit: **Eiko Ishioka, Kuni Shinohara, Haruo Takino**

[314]

Hecuba (Εκάβη / Ekavi)
Stavros Antonopoulos (Cyprus)
Costume Design

Company: **Cyprus Theatre Organisation** (State Theatre)
Venue: **Makarios III Amphitheatre**
Location: **Nicosia, Cyprus**
Opening/First Night: **July 1988**

Author: **Euripides**
Composer: **Michalis Christodoulides**
Scenic Designer: **Stavros Antonopoulos**
Costume Designer: **Stavros Antonopoulos**
Masks: **Stavros Antonopoulos, Varnavas Kyriazis**
Lighting Designer: **Grigoris Papageorgiou**
Director: **Nicos Haralambous**

Contributing Researcher: **Andy Bargilly**

Image Credits: **Evis Ioannides, Stavros Antonopoulos**

[315]

The Number One Restaurant in China
(Tian Xia Di Yi Lou)
Huang Qingze (China)
Set Design

Company: **Beijing People's Art Theatre**
Venue: **The Capital Theater**
Location: **Beijing, China**
Opening/First Night: **June 1988**

Author: **He Jiping**
Scenic Designer: **Huang Qingze**
Costume Designer: **Yan Xiumin**
Lighting Designer: **Fang Kunlin**
Director: **Xia Chun & Gu Wei**

Contributing Researcher: **Xu Xiang**

Image Credit: **Huang Quingze**

[315]

Exercise #1 (Exercício Nº 1)
Fernando Mello da Costa (Brazil)
Set Design

Venue: **Banco Brasil Culture Center**
Location: **São Paulo, Brazil**
Opening/First Night: **1988**

Scenic Designer: **Fernando Mello da Costa**
Director: **Bia Lessa**

Contributing Researcher: **JC Serroni**

Image Credit: **Fernando Mello da Costa**

[316]

Xica da Silva
JC Serroni (Brazil)
Set & Costume Design

Company: **Group Macunaima Theatre—CPT SESC**
Venue: **SESC Anchieta Theater**
Location: **São Paulo, Brazil**
Opening/First Night: **1988**

Author: **Luis Alberto de Abreu**
Scenic Designer: **JC Serroni**
Costume Designer: **JC Serroni**
Lighting Designer: **Davi de Brito**
Sound Designer: **Macunaima Group, Bartho di Haro & Raul Teixeira**
Director: **Antunes Filho**

Contributing Researcher: **JC Serroni**

Image Credits: **JC Serroni, Emidio Luigi, Paulo Henrique de Carvalho**

[318]

Francisco Maniago
Salvador Bernal (Philippines)
Set & Costume Design

Venue: **CCP Tanghalang Aurello Tolentino**
Location: **Manila, Philippines**
Opening/First Night: **5 February 1988**

Author: **Paul Dumol**
Scenic Designer: **Salvador Bernal**
Costume Designer: **Salvador Bernal**
Director: **Nonon Padilla**

Contributing Researcher: **Kazue Hatano**

Image Credit: **Salvador Bernal**

[318]

The Dream of Akutagawa
Roh Matsushita (Japan)
Set Design

Company: **Khabarovsk Drama Theatre**
Location: **Khabarovsk, USSR**
Opening/First Night: **May 1988**

Author: **Tachiana Zalevskaya**
Scenic Designer: **Roh Matsushita**
Director: **Yuli Beligyin**

Contributing Researcher: **Kazue Hatano**

Image Credit: **Roh Matsushita**

[319]

The Kingdom of Desire
Ching-Ru Lin (Taiwan)
Costume Design

Company: **The Contemporary Legend Theatre**
Venue: **National Theatre**
Location: **Taipei, Taiwan**
Opening/First Night: **1988**

Author: **Huei-Ming Li**
Scenic Designer: **Kuen-Yen Deng**
Costume Designer: **Ching-Ru Lin**
Lighting Designer: **Ken-Hua Lin**
Director: **Hsing-Kuo Wu**

Contributing Researcher: **Kazue Hatano**

Image Credit: **Contemporary Legend Theatre**

[320]

The Dybbuk (Der Dybuk)
Andrzej Wajda & Krystyna Zachwatowicz (Poland)
Production Design

Company: **Stary Teatr im. Modrzejewskiej**
Venue: **Stary Teatr im. Modrzejewskiej**
Location: **Kraków, Poland**
Opening/First Night: **12 March 1988**

Author: **Szymon An-ski**
Composer: **Zygmunt Konieczny**
Scenic Designer: **Krystyna Zachwatowicz**
Costume Designer: **Krystyna Zachwatowicz**
Director: **Andrzej Wajda**
Choreographer: **Janusz Józefowicz**

Contributing Researcher: **Agnieszka Kubas**

Image Credit: **Stanisław Markowski; Archive of The Manggha Centre of Japanese Art and Technology in Kraków (Poland)**

[321]

Electra (Ηλέκτρα)
Giorgos Ziakas (Greece)
Set & Costume Design

Company: **Municipal & Regional Theatre of Larissa**
Venue: **Thessalian Theatre**
Location: **Larissa, Greece**
Opening/First Night: **1988**

Author: **Euripides**
Scenic Designer: **Giorgos Ziakas**
Costume Designer: **Giorgos Ziakas**
Director: **Costas Tsianos**

Contributing Researcher: **Dio Kangelari**

Image Credit: **Giorgos Ziakas**

[322]

Nothing Sacred
Mary Kerr (Canada)
Set & Costume Design

Company: **CentreStage**
Venue: **Bluma Appel Theatre**
Location: **Toronto, Canada**
Opening/First Night: **1988**

Author: **George F. Walker**
Scenic Designer: **Mary Kerr**
Costume Designer: **Mary Kerr**
Lighting Designer: **Lynne Hyde**
Director: **Bill Glassco**

Contributing Researcher: **Peter MᶜKinnon**

Image Credit: **Mary Kerr, Metro Toronto Reference Library**

[324]

The Marriage of Figaro (Le Nozze di Figaro)
Adrianne Lobel (USA)
Set Design

Venue: **PepsiCo Summerfare**
Location: **Purchase, New York, USA**
Opening/First Night: **1988**

Composer: **W A Mozart**
Scenic Designer: **Adrianne Lobel**
Costume Designer: **Dunya Ramicova**
Lighting Designer: **James F. Ingalls**
Director: **Peter Sellars**

Contributing Researcher: **Eric Fielding**

Image Credit: **Adrianne Lobel; Collection of the McNay Art Museum, Museum purchase with funds from the McNay Theatre Group**

[325]

Tectonic Plates
Michael Levine (Canada)
Set, Costume & Lighting Design

Company: **Harbourfront Centre**
Venue: **duMaurier Theatre**
Location: **Toronto, Canada**
Opening/First Night: **3 June 1988**

Author: **Robert Lepage, Marie Gignac, Richard Fréchette, Sylvie Gagnon**
Scenic Designer: **Michael Levine & Robert Lepage**
Costume Designer: **Michael Levine**
Lighting Designer: **Michael Levine**
Director: **Robert Lepage & Sylvie Gagnon**

Contributing Researcher: **Mary Kerr**

Image Credit: **Michael Levine, Ex Machina**

[326]

Metropolis
Ralph Koltai (Germany/UK)
Set & Costume Design

Venue: **Piccadilly Theatre**
Location: **London, UK**
Opening/First Night: **8 March 1988**

Author: **Joe Brooks & Dusty Hughes**, based on Fritz Lang's film
Composer: **Joe Brooks**
Scenic Designer: **Ralph Koltai**
Costume Designer: **Ralph Koltai**
Lighting Designer: **David Hersey**
Director: **Jerome Savary**

Contributing Researcher: **Liz Wright**

Image Credit: **Douglas H Jeffery, Victoria and Albert Museum, London**

[328]

In the Land of Spirits
Mary Kerr (Canada)
Set & Costume Design

Venue: **National Arts Centre**
Location: **Ottawa**
Opening/First Night: **16 November 1988**

Composer: **John Kim Bell**
Scenic Designer: **Mary Kerr**
Costume Designer: **Mary Kerr**
Director: **John Kim Bell**

Contributing Researcher: **Michael Greyeyes**

Image Credit: **Mary Kerr**

[328]

The Lake Boy
Elena Lutsenko (USSR/Russia)
Set & Puppet Design

Company: **Voronezh State Puppet Theatre Shuut** (Bafon)
Location: **Voronezh, USSR/Russia**
Opening/First Night: **1988**

Author: adapted from **Pavel Vezhinov**'s story
Scenic Designer: **Elena Lutsenko**
Puppet Designer: **Elena Lutsenko**
Director: **Valery Volkhovsky**

Contributing Researcher: **Inna Mirzoyan**

Image Credit: **Elena Lutsenko**

[329]

Hura Tau
Iriti Hoto (Tahiti)
Costume Design

Company: **Heikura Nui**
Venue: **Tarahoi Square**
Location: **Papeete, Tahiti**
Opening/First Night: **29 June 1988**

Author: **Heikura Nui Dance Troupe**
Costume Designer: **Iriti Hoto**
Director: **Iriti Hoto**

Contributing Researcher: **Keren Chiaroni**

Image Credits: **Marie Odile Boisard, Gilles Delemazure**

[329]

Kafka's Trilogy (Trilogia Kafka)
Daniela Thomas (Brazil)
Set Design

Venue: **Teatro Ruth Escobar**
Location: **Rio de Janeiro, Brazil**
Opening/First Night: **1988**

Author: **Franz Kafka**
Scenic Designer: **Daniela Thomas**
Costume Designer: **Daniela Thomas**
Lighting Designer: **Gerald Thomas and Wagner Pinto**
Director: **Gerald Thomas**

Contributing Researcher: **JC Serroni**

Image Credit: **Ary Brandi**

[330]

Vast
Andrew Carter (Australia)
Set Design

Company: **Sydney Dance Company/
Australian Dance Theatre/West Australian
Ballet/Queensland Ballet**
Venue: **Palais Theatre**
Location: **Melbourne, Australia**
Opening/First Night: **March 1988**

Choreographer: **Graeme Murphy**
Composer: **Barry Conyngham**
Scenic Designer: **Andrew Carter**
Costume Designer: **Jennifer Irwin**
Lighting Designer: **Kenneth Rayner**
Conductor: **John Hopkins**

Contributing Researcher: **Richard Roberts**

Image Credit: **Andrew Carter**

[331]

Tristan and Isolde
Hans Dieter Schaal (Germany)
Set Design

Company: **Hans Dieter Schaal**
Venue: **Hamburgische Staatsoper**
Location: **Hamburg, Germany**
Opening/First Night: **March 1988**

Author/Creator: **Hamburgische Staatsoper**
Composer: **Richard Wagner**
Scenic Designer: **Hans Dieter Schaal**
Costume Designer: **Marie-Luise Strandt**
Director: **Ruth Berghaus**
Conductor: **Zoltan Pesko**

Contributing Researcher: **Karin
Winkelsesser**

Image Credits: **Maria Steinefldt, Hans-
Dieter Schaal**

[332]

Inferno and Paradise (*Inferno und Paradies*)
Martin Rupprecht (Germany FGR)
Set Design

Venue: **Deutsche Oper**
Location: **Berlin, Germany FRG**
Opening/First Night: **22 July 1988**

Author: **After Dante's Divina Commedia**
Scenic Designer: **Martin Rupprecht**
Director: **Winfried Bauernfeind**
Conductor: **Caspar Richter**

Contributing Researcher: **Karin
Winkelsesser**

Image Credit: © **Martin Rupprecht**

[334]

Lulu
Gerardo Vera (Spain)
Set & Costume Design

Venue: **Teatro dela Zarzuela de Madrid**
Location: **Madrid, Spain**
Opening/First Night: **19 March 1988**

Composer: **Alban Berg**
Scenic Designer: **Gerardo Vera**
Costume Designer: **Gerardo Vera**
Director: **Arturo Tamayo, Jose Carlos Plaza**

Contributing Researcher: **Angel Martinez
Roger**

Image Credit: **Gerardo Vera**

[334]

Celestina (*La Celestina*)
Carlos Cytrynowski (Spain)
Set & Costume Design

Venue: **Teatro dela Comedia de Madrid**
Location: **Madrid, Spain**
Opening/First Night: **18 April 1988**

Author: **Fernando de Rojas**, adaptation by
Gonzalo Torrente Ballester
Scenic Designer: **Carlos Cytrynowski**
Costume Designer: **Carlos Cytrynowski**
Director: **Adolfo Marsillach**

Contributing Researcher: **Angel Martinez
Roger**

Image Credit: **Chicho Ros Ribas**

[335]

The Three Musketeers
Tony Geddes (New Zealand)
Set Design

Company: **The Court Theatre**
Venue: **The Court Theatre**
Location: **Christchurch, New Zealand**
Opening/First Night: **1988**

Author: **Simon Philips** (based on the novel
by Alexander Dumas)
Scenic Designer: **Tony Geddes**
Costume Designer: **Pamela Maling**
Director: **Elric Hooper**

Contributing Researcher: **Sam Trubridge**

Image Credits: **Tony Geddes, Elric Hooper**

[335]

Away
Joe Hayes (New Zealand)
Lighting Design

Company: **The Court Theatre**
Venue: **The Court Theatre**
Location: **Christchurch, New Zealand**
Opening/First Night: **1988**

Author: **Michael Gow**
Scenic Designer: **David Thornley**
Lighting Designer: **Joe Hayes**
Director: **Elric Hooper**

Contributing Researcher: **Sam Trubridge**

Image Credit: **Elric Hooper**

[338]

Moth
Zhou Benyi (China)
Set Design

Company: **Ha Erbin's Drama Theatre**
Venue: **The Theatre of Ha Erbin's Drama
Theatre**
Location: **China**
Opening/First Night: **July 1989**

Author: **Che Lianbin**
Scenic Designer: **Zhou Benyi**
Lighting Designer: **Jin Changlie**
Director: **Xiao Zhicheng**

Contributing Researcher: **Xu Xiang**

Image Credit: **Zhou Benyi**

[338]

Uncle Vanya (*Unchiul Vania*)
Stefania Cenean (Romania)
Set & Costume Design

Venue: **National Theatre of Craiova**
Location: **Craiova, Romania**
Opening/First Night: **1989**

Author: **Anton Chekhov**
Scenic Designer: **Stefania Cenean**
Costume Designer: **Stefania Cenean**
Director: **Mircea Cornisteanu**

Contributing Researcher: **Jean Cazaban**

Image Credit: **Stefania Cenean**

[338]

Fly toward the New Century
Sun Tianwei (China)
Set & Lighting Design

Company: **The League of Air Force Mission
of Political Literature's Theatre**
Venue: **Sky Theatre**
Location: **China**
Opening/First Night: **October 1989**

Author: **Chen Hong**
Composer: **Yang Ming**
Scenic Designer: **Sun Tianwei**
Costume Designer: **Hui Jing**
Lighting Designer: **Sun Tianwei**
Director: **Yang Yuelin**
Choreographer: **Yang Yuelin**

Contributing Researcher: **Xu Xiang**

Image Credit: **Sun Tianwei**

[339]

The Hamlet Machine (*Die Hamletmaschine*)
Gottfried Pilz (Austria/Germany)
Set & Costume Design

Company: **Hamburgische Staatsoper**
Venue: **Hamburgische Staatsoper**
Location: **Hamburg, Germany**
Opening/First Night: **2 April 1989**

Author: **Heiner Mueller**
Composer: **Wolfgang Rihm**
Scenic Designer: **Gottfried Pilz**
Costume Designer: **Gottfried Pilz**
Lighting Designer: **Gerhard Kretschmer&
Jürgen Zoch**
Sound Designer: **Wolfgang Köhnsen**
Director: **John Dew**
Conductor: **Lothar Zagrosek**
Choir director: **Nicola Panzer**

Contributing Researcher: **Karin
Winkelsesser**

Image Credit: **Gottfried Pilz**

[340]

Scheherezade (*Šeherezada*)
Marko Japelj (Slovenia)
Set Design

Company: **Slovensko Mladinsko Gledališče**
Location: **Ljubljana, Slovenia**
Opening/First Night: **9 February 1989**

Author: **Ivo Svetina**
Composer: **Ljupčo Konstantinov**
Scenic Designer: **Marko Japelj**
Costume Designer: **Svetlana Visintin, Leo
Kulaš**
Lighting Designer: **Igor Berginc**
Director: **Tomaž Pandur**
Choreographer: **Maja Milenović Workman**

Contributing Researcher: **Nicole Leclercq**

Image Credit: **Marko Japelj**

[341]

Peer Gynt
Jürgen Rose (Germany FRG)
Set & Costume Design

Venue: **Hamburgische Staatsoper**
Location: **Hamburg, Germany**
Opening/First Night: **22 January 1989**

Author: based on **Henrik Ibsen**
Composer: **Alfred Schnittke**
Scenic Designer: **Jürgen Rose**
Costume Designer: **Jürgen Rose**
Choreographer: **John Neumeier**
Conductor: **Eric Klas**

Contributing Researcher: **Karin
Winkelsesser**

Image Credit: **Jürgen Rose**

[342]

The Jump Over the Shadow
(*Der Sprung über den Schatten*)
Gottfried Pilz (Austria/Germany)
Set & Costume Design

Company: **Stadttheater Bielefeld**
Venue: **Stadttheater Bielefeld**
Location: **Berlin, Germany**
Opening/First Night: **Spring 1989**

Author: **Ernst Krenek**
Scenic Designer: **Gottfried Pilz**
Costume Designer: **Gottfried Pilz**
Director: **John Dew**
Choreographer: **Calvin Jackson**
Conductor: **David de Villiers**

Contributing Researcher: **Karin
Winkelsesser**

Image Credit: **Gottfried Pilz**

[342]

Yourcenar or Your Own Marguerite
(*Yourcenar o Cada quien su Marguerite*)
Carlos Trejo (Mexico)
Set & Lighting Design

Company: **Dirección de Teatro y Danza
(UNAM) y Divas A. C.**
Venue: **Foro Sor Juana Inés de la Cruz**
Location: **Mexico City, Mexico**
Opening/First Night: **12 July 1989**

Author: **Marguerite Yourcenar**
Scenic Designer: **Carlos Trejo**
Costume Designer: **Carlos Roces**
Lighting Designer: **Carlos Trejo**
Director: **Jesusa Rodríguez**

Contributing Researcher: **Rodolfo Obregon
Rodriguez**

Image Credit: **INBA-CITRU, Biblioteca de
las Artes-CENART, Mexico**

[343]

The Enemies (*Los enemigos*)
Tolita Figueroa (México)
Set, costume Design

Company: **Compañía Nacional de Teatro
(INBA)**
Venue: **Julio Castillo**
Location: **México City, México**
Opening/First Night: **October 1989**

Author: **Sergio Magaña**
Composer: **Federico Ibarra**
Scenic Designer: **Tolita Figueroa**
Costume Designer: **Tolita Figueroa**
Lighting Designer: **Alejandro Luna**
Sound Designer: **Xavier Villalpando**
Director: **Lorena Maza**
Choreographer: **Lidya Romero**

Contributing Researcher: **Rodolfo Obregon
Rodriguez**

Image Credit: **INBA-CITRU, Biblioteca de
las Artes-CENART, Mexico**

[344]
Quartet
Giorgos Patsas (Greece)
Set & Costume Design

Company: **ATTIS Theatre**
Location: **Athens, Greece**
Opening/First Night: **1989**

Author: **Heiner Müller**
Translator: **Heleni Varopoulou**
Scenic Designer: **Giorgos Patsas**
Costume Designer: **Giorgos Patsas**
Director: **Theodoros Terzopoulos**

Contributing Researcher: **Dio Kangelari**
Photographer: **Chryssa Kyriakidou, Archive of Giorgos Patsas**

Image Credit: **Giorgos Patsas**

[345]
Lend Me a Tenor
William Ivey Long (USA)
Costume Design

Venue: **Royale Theatre**
Location: **New York, New York, USA**
Opening/First Night: **2 March 1989**

Author: **Ken Ludwig**
Scenic Designer: **Tony Walton**
Costume Designer: **William Ivey Long**
Lighting Designer: **Paul Gallo**
Sound Designer: **Aural Fixation**
Director: **Jerry Zaks**

Contributing Researcher: **Eric Fielding**

Image Credit: **William Ivey Long, Martha Swope**

[346]
From the Street (*De la calle*)
Gabriel Pascal (Mexico)
Set & Lighting Design

Company: **Compañía Nacional de Teatro (INBA)**
Venue: **Teatro del Bosque**
Location: **Mexico City, Mexico**
Opening/First Night: **1989**

Author: **Jesús González Dávila Delgado, Rafael Matías Fabián**
Scenic Designer: **Gabriel Pascal**
Costume Designer: **Ángela Dodson**
Lighting Designer: **Gabriel Pascal**
Director: **Julio Castillo**
Assistant Director: **Philippe Amand**
Composers: **Salvador Matías Fabián, Arturo Cornejo Vargas, Juan Manuel Solís**

Contributing Researcher: **Rodolfo Obregon Rodriguez**

Image Credit: **INBA-CITRU, Biblioteca de las Artes-CENART, Mexico**

[346]
Much Ado About Nothing
(*ΠολύΚακόγιατοΤίποτα*)
Stefanos Athienitis (Cyprus)
Set & Costume Design

Company: **Cyprus Theatre Organisation (State)**
Venue: **Nicosia Municipal Theatre**
Location: **Nicosia, Cyprus**
Opening/First Night: **December 1989**

Author: **William Shakespeare**
Composer: **Lenia Serghi**
Scenic Designer: **Stefanos Athienitis**
Costume Designer: **Stefanos Athienitis**
Lighting Designer: **Grigoris Papageorgiou**
Director: **Nicos Haralambous**

Contributing Researcher: **Andy Bargilly**

Image Credits: **Costas Farmakas**

[347]
Grand Hotel
Santo Loquasto, Tony Walton & Jules Fisher (USA)
Set, Costume & Lighting Design

Venue: **Martin Beck Theatre**
Location: **New York City, USA**
Opening/First Night: **12 November 1989**

Composer: **Robert Wright & George Forrest**
Lyrics: **Robert Wright & George Forrest**
Author: **Luther Davis**
Scenic Designer: **Tony Walton**
Costume Designer: **Santo Loquasto**
Lighting Designer: **Jules Fisher**
Sound Designer: **Otts Munderlog**
Director: **Tommy Tune**
Choreographer: **Tommy Tune**

Contributing Researcher: **Eric Fielding**

Image Credits: **Martha Swope © The New York Public Library for the Performing Arts; Santo Loquasto**

[348]
Tevye Tevel
Daniil Lider (Ukraine)
Set Design

Company: **Ivan Franko Drama Theatre**
Location: **Kiev, Ukraine**
Opening/First Night: **1989**

Author: adapted from **Sholom Aleichem**'s Tevye the Milkman
Scenic Designer: **Daniil Lider**
Director: **Sergei Danchenko**

Contributing Researcher: **Inna Mirzoyan**

Image Credit: **Daniil Lider**

[349]
Void (*Vacío*)
Jesusa Rodríguez (Mexico)
Set Design

Company: **Grupo Sombras Blancas**
Venue: **Foro Sor Juana Inés de la Cruz**
Location [City]: **Mexico City, Mexico**
Opening/First Night: **February 1980**

Author: Based on the life and writing of Sylvia Plath
Scenic Designer: **Jesusa Rodríguez**
Costume Designer: **Jesusa Rodríguez**
Sound Designer: **Francis Laboriel**
Director: **Julio Castillo**
Contributing Researcher: **Rodolfo Obregon Rodriguez**

Image Credit: **INBA-CITRU, Biblioteca de las Artes-CENART, Mexico**

[350]
Open Weave
Mary Moore (UK/Australia)
Set & Costume Design

Company: **Australian Dance Theatre**
Venue: **Noarlunga College Theatre**
Location: **Adelaide, Australia**
Opening/First Night: **March 1989**

Composer: **Robert Lloyd**
Scenic Designer: **Mary Moore**
Costume Designer: **Mary Moore**
Lighting Designer: **Keith Tucker**
Choreographer: **Nanette Hassell**

Contributing Researcher: **Richard Roberts**

Image Credit: **Mary Moore**

[351]
Prayer for the Dead (*Pominalnaya Molitva*)
Oleg Sheintsis (Russia)
Set Design

Company: **Lenkom Theatre**
Location: **Moscow, Russia**
Opening/First Night: **1989**

Author: **Grigori Gorin**, adapted from Sholom Aleichem works
Scenic Designer: **Oleg Sheintsis**
Director: **Mark Zakharov**

Contributing Researcher: **Inna Mirzoyan**

Image Credit: **Oleg Sheintsis**

[352]
Our Country's Good
Tony Tripp (Australia)
Set & Costume Design

Company: **Melbourne Theatre Company**
Venue: **Playhouse, Victorian Arts Centre**
Location: **Melbourne, Australia**
Opening/First Night: **June 1989**

Author: **Timberlake Wertenbaker**
Scenic Designer: **Tony Tripp**
Costume Designer: **Tony Tripp**
Lighting Designer: **Jamieson Lewis**
Sound Designer: **Kerry Saxby**
Director: **Roger Hodgman**

Contributing Researcher: **Richard Roberts**

Image Credit: **Tony Tripp**

[353]
North Side Paradise (*Paraíso Zona Norte*)
JC Serroni (Brazil)
Set Design

Company: **CPT, Theater Research Center**
Venue: **SESC Anchieta Theater**
Location: **São Paulo, Brazil**
Opening/First Night: **April 1989**

Author: **Nelson Rodrigues**
Scenic Designer: **JC Serroni**
Costume Designer: **JC Serroni**
Lighting Designer: **Max Keller**
Director: **Antunes Filho**

Contributing Researcher: **JC Serroni**

Image Credit: **JC Serroni**

[354]
Threepenny Opera
Mary Kerr (Canada)
Set & Costume Design

Company: **Canadian Stage Company**
Venue: **Bluma Appel Theatre, St Lawrence Centre**
Location: **Toronto, Canada**
Opening/First Night: **1989**

Author: **Bertolt Brecht**
Composer: **Kurt Weill**
Scenic Designer: **Mary Kerr**
Costume Designer: **Mary Kerr**
Director: **Kelly Robinson**

Contributing Researcher: **Peter McKinnon**

Image Credits: **Mary Kerr; Courtesy of Metro Toronto Library**

[355]
Woyzeck
Achim Freyer (Germany)
Set and Costume Design

Company: **Burgtheater Vienna**
Venue: **Burgtheater Wien**
Location: **Vienna, Austria**
Opening/First Night: **22 April 1989**

Author: **Georg Büchner**
Scenic Designer: **Achim Freyer**
Costume Designer: **Achim Freyer**
Director: **Achim Freyer**

Contributing Researcher: **Karin Winkelsesser**

Image Credit: **Monika Rittershaus; Akademie der Kuenste Berlin, Achim Freyer Archive**

[356]
Madame de Sade (*Sado Kōshaku Fujin*)
Charles Koroly (Sweden/USA)
Set & Costume Design

Company: **Royal Dramatic Theatre**
Venue: **Royal Dramatic Theatre, Small stage**
Location: **Stockholm, Sweden**
Opening/First Night: **8 April 1989**

Author: **Yukio Mishima**, translated by Gunilla Lindberg-Wada & Per Erik Wahlund
Composer: **Ingrid Yoda**
Scenic Designer: **Charles Koroly**
Costume Designer: **Charles Koroly**
Lighting Designer: **Sven-Erik Jacobbson**
Sound Designer: **Jan-Erik Piper, Björn Lönnroos**
Choreographer: **Donya Feuer**
Conductor: **Kjell-Inge Stevensson**
Dramaturgy: **Ulla Åberg**
Director: **Ingmar Bergman**

Contributing Researcher: **Ammy Kjellsdotter**

Image Credits: **Bengt Wanselius, www.wanselius.com**

[356]
Legend of Mt. Ararat (*Ağrıdağı Efsanesi*)
Atıl Yalkut (Turkey)
Set & Costume Design

Company: **Istanbul Municipal Theatre**
Venue: **Taksim Stage**
Location: **Istanbul, Turkey**
Opening/First Night: **October 1989**

Author: **Yaşar Kemal**, adapted by Ali Taygun
Scenic Designer: **Atıl Yalkut**
Director: **Ali Taygun**

Contributing Researcher: **Evcimen Percin**

Image Credit: **Atýl Yalkut**

[357]
Pilgrims and Wanderers (*Pielgrzymi i tułacze*)
Jerzy Kalina (Poland)
Set & Costume Design

Company: **Teatr Studio**
Venue: **Teatr Studio**
Location: **Warsaw, Poland**
Opening/First Night: **7 April 1989**

Author: **Jerzy Kalina**
Composer: **Jan A.P. Kaczmarek**
Scenic Designer: **Jerzy Kalina**
Scenic Design Associate: **Kasper Kokczyński**
Costume Designer: **Jerzy Kalina**
Director: **Jerzy Kalina**

Contributing Researcher: **Agnieszka Kubaś**

Image Credit: **Jerzy Kalina; Zygmunt Rytka, Archive of The Zbigniew Raszewski Theatre Institute in Warszawa**

[358]
Una Pooka
Monica Frawley (Ireland)
Set & Costume Design

Company: **Abbey Theatre/Amharclann na Mainistreach**
Venue: **Peacock Theatre**
Location: **Dublin, Ireland**
Opening/First Night: **April 1989**

Author: **Michael Harding**
Scenic Designer: **Monica Frawley**
Costume Designer: **Monica Frawley**
Lighting Designer: **Tony Wakefield**
Sound Designer: **Dave Nolan**
Director: **Patrick Mason**

Contributing Researcher: **Jane Daly**
Photographs: **Abbey Theatre**

Image Credit: **Fergus Bourke, © Abbey Theatre; Monica Frawley**

[359]
The Flying Dutchman
(*Der fliegende Holländer*)
Stefanos Lazaridis (Ethiopia/UK)
Set & Costume Design

Company: **Bregenz Festival**
Venue: **Lake Stage**
Location: **Bregenz, Austria**
Opening/First Night: **1989**

Composer: **Richard Wagner**
Scenic Designer: **Stefanos Lazaridis**
Costume Designer: **Stefanos Lazaridis**
Director: **David Pountney**

Contributing Researcher: **Liz Wright**

Image Credit: **Bregenzer Festspiele**

[362]
Mephisto
Eli Sinai (Germany/Israel)
Set Design

Company: **Be'er Sheva Municipal Theatre**
Venue: **Be'er Sheva Municipal Theatre**
Location: **Be'er Sheva, Israel**
Opening/First Night: **1990**

Author: **Hillel Mittlelpunkt**, based on a novel by K. Mann
Scenic Designer: **Eli Sinai**
Costume Designer: **Eli Sinai**
Director: **Micha Levinson**

Contributing Researcher: **Ben Tzion Munitz**

Image Credit: **Eli Sinai**

[362]
M Butterfly
Justin Hill (Australia/Singapore)
Set Design

Company: **Theatreworks Singapore Ltd**
Venue: **Victoria Theatre**
Location: **Singapore, Singapore**
Opening/First Night: **29 May 1990**

Author: **David Henry Huang**
Scenic Designer: **Justin Hill**
Lighting Design: **Kalyani Kausikan & Lim Yu Beng**
Sound Design: **Ooi Yu-Lin & Loong Seng Onn**
Costume Design: **Lee Weng Kai**
Choreography: **Goh Siew Geok & Goh Lay Kuan**
Directors: **Krishen Jit & Christine Lim**

Contributing Researcher: **Justin Hill**

Image Credit: **Justin Hill**

[363]
2nd Nature
Teresa Przybylski (Poland/Canada)
Set & Costume Design

Venue: **The Theatre Centre**
Location: **Canada**
Opening/First Night: **1990**

Author: **Deanne Taylor**
Composer: **Brent Snyder**
Scenic Designer: **Teresa Przybylski**
Costume Designer: **Teresa Przybylski**
Lighting Designer: **Jim Plaxton**
Sound Designer: **Terry Crack**
Choreographer: **Susan McKenzie**

Contributing Researcher: **Peter McKinnon**

Image Credit: **Metro Toronto Library, Owais Lightwala**

[364]
The Flying Dutchman
(*Der Fliegende Holländer*)
Jürgen Rose (Germany FRG)
Set & Costume Design

Company: **Bayreuther Festspiele**
Venue: **Bayreuther Festspiele**
Location: **Bayreuth, Germany**
Opening/First Night: **25 July 1990**

Author/Creator: **William Shakespeare**
Scenic Designer: **Jürgen Rose**
Costume Designer: **Jürgen Rose**
Lighting Designer: **Manfred Voss**
Director: **Dieter Dorn**

Contributing Researcher: **Karin Winkelsesser**

Image Credit: **Jürgen Rose**

[366]
The Marriage of Figaro
Susan Benson (Canada)
Set & Costume Design

Venue: **The Banff Festival of the Arts**
Location: **Banff, Alberta, Canada**
Opening/First Night: **1990**

Composer: **W. A. Mozart**
Scenic Designer: **Susan Benson**
Costume Designer: **Susan Benson**
Lighting Designer: **Michael J. Whitfield**
Director: **Colin Graham**

Contributing Researcher: **Peter McKinnon**

Image Credit: **Banff Centre**

[367]
Dance of the Devils (*La Diablada*)
Unknown (Bolívia)
Costume Design

Venue: **Street Performance**
Location: **Oruro, Bolívia**
Opening/First Night: **1990**

Contributing Researcher: **JC Serroni**

Image Credit: **J. E. Calvo**

[367]
Wind in the Willows
Mark Thompson (UK)
Set & Costume Design

Company: **Royal National Theatre**
Venue: **Olivier Stage**
Location: **London, UK**
Opening/First Night: **1 December 1990**

Author: **Alan Bennett**
Composer: **Jeremy Sams**
Scenic Designer: **Mark Thompson**
Costume Designer: **Mark Thompson**
Lighting Designer: **Paul Pyant**
Director of movement: **Jane Gibson**
Director: **Nicholas Hytner**

Contributing Researcher: **Kate Dorney**

Image Credit: **Mark Thompson; Victoria and Albert Museum, London**

[368]
Platonov
Csaba Antal (Hungary)
Set & Costume Design

Company: **Katona József Theatre**
Venue: **Bouffes du Nord Theatre**
Location: **Paris, France**
Opening/First Night: **May 1990**

Author: **Anton Chekhov**
Scenic Designer: **Csaba Antal**
Costume Designer: **Nelly Vágó**
Director: **Tamás Ascher**

Contributing Researcher: **Eva Nemeth**

Image Credit: **Scenography Collection, Hungarian Theatre Museum and Institute**

[368]
Dance of the Conquest (*Baile de la Conquista*)
Collective Creation (Guatemala)
Set & Costume Design

Location: **Guatemala City, Guatemala**
Opening/First Night: **1990**

Author: **Traditional Folkloric Dance**
Scenic Designer: **Collective Creation**
Costume Designer: **Collective Creation**

Contributing Researcher: **JC Serroni**

Image Credit: **Paco Coronado**

[369]
John Brown's Body
Pamela Howard (UK)
Set & Costume Design

Company: **7.84 Theatre**
Venue: **Tramway**
Location: **Glasgow, Scotland, UK**
Opening/First Night: **1990**

Scenic Designer: **Pamela Howard**
Costume Designer: **Pamela Howard**
Director: **John McGrath**

Contributing Researcher: **Madeline Taylor**

Image Credit: **Pamela Howard**

[370]
Dancing at Lughnasa
TheTheJoe Vanek (Ireland)
Set & Costume Design

Company: **The Abbey Theatre**
Venue: **The Abbey Theatre**
Location: **Dublin, Ireland**
Opening/First Night: **24 April 1990**

Author: **Brian Friel**
Scenic Designer: **Joe Vanek**
Costume Designer: **Joe Vanek**
Lighting Designer: **Trevor Dawson**
Sound Designer: **Dave Nolan**
Director: **Patrick Mason**
Choreographer: **Terry John Bates**

Contributing Researcher: **Joe Vanek**

Image Credit: **Joe Vanek**

[372]
Peer Gynt
Huo Qidi (China)
Costume Design

Company: **Hong Kong Repertory Theatre**
Venue: **Hong Kong City Hall**
Location: **Hong Kong**
Opening/First Night: **November 1990**

Author: **Henrik Ibsen**
Composer: **Glenlyon**
Scenic Designer: **Liu Yuansheng**
Costume Designer: **Huo Qidi**
Lighting Designer: **Liang Ritian**
Director: **Xu Xiaozhong**
Choreographer: **Luo Yongfen**

Contributing Researcher: **Xu Xiang**

Image Credit: **Huo Qidi**

[372]
Belshazzar
Peter Corrigan (Australia)
Set & Costume Design

Company: **Treason of Images**
Location: **Melbourne, Australia**
Opening/First Night: **1990**

Composer: **George Frideric Handel**
Scenic Designer: **Peter Corrigan**
Costume Designer: **Peter Corrigan**
Director: **Barrie Kosky**
Conductor: **Warwick Stengards**

Contributing Researcher: **Richard Roberts**

Image Credit: **Peter Corrigan**

[373]
The Magic Flute (*Die Zauberflöte*)
Yishiko Kunishima (Japan)
Set Design

Company: **Kansai Opera Company**
Venue: **Archaic Hall**
Location: **Osaka, Japan**
Opening/First Night: **May 1990**

Composer: **W. A. Mozart**
Author: **C. M. Wieland**
Scenic Designer: **Yishiko Kunishima**
Lighting Designer: **Tsuneo Yanagihara**
Director: **Fumitaka Shibuya**

Contributing Researcher: **Kazue Hatano**

Image Credit: **Yishiko Kunishima**

[374]

The Possessed (The Devils)
Eduard Kochergin (USSR/Russia)
Set Design

Company: **Maly Drama Theatre**
Venue: **Theatre de L'Europe**
Location: **St. Petersburg, USSR/Russia**
Opening/First Night: **1990**

Author: **Lev Dodin**, adapted from Fyodor Dostoyevsky novel
Scenic Designer: **Eduard Kochergin**
Director: **Lev Dodin**

Contributing Researcher: **Inna Mirzoyan**

Image Credit: **Eduard Kochergin**

---

[375]

The Fall of the House of Usher
Trina Parker & David Murray (Australia)
Set Design

Company: **Chambermade Opera**
Venue: **Merlyn Theatre, Malthouse**
Location: **Melbourne, Australia**
Opening/First Night: **August 1990**

Composer: **Phillip Glass**
Author: **Edgar Allen Poe** (original story)
Scenic Designer: **Trina Parker**
Costume Designer: **Wiggy Brennan**
Lighting Designer: **David Murray**
Director: **Douglas Horton**
Conductor: **Brian Stacey**

Contributing Researcher: **Richard Roberts**

Image Credit: **Ponch Hawkes**

---

[375]

The Ghost Sonata
Xu Xiang (China)
Set Design

Company: **The Central Academy of Drama**
Venue: **The Experimental Theatre of the Central Academy of Drama**
Location: **China**
Opening/First Night: **1990**

Author: **August Strindberg**
Composer: **Wang Shi**
Scenic Designer: **Xu Xiang**
Costume Designer: **Wang Hong & Zhao Yue**
Lighting Designer: **Mu Baisuo**
Director: **Zhang Fuchen**
Choreographer: **Tian Zhenkun & Zhang Jingdi**
Conductor: **Wang Shi**

Contributing Researcher: **Xu Xiang**

Image Credit: **Xu Xiang**

---

[376]

Katsura Harudanji
Shiro Takeuchi (Japan)
Set Design

Company: **Fujita Makoto Production**
Venue: **Umeda Koma Theatre**
Location: **Osaka, Japan**
Opening/First Night: **February 1990**

Author: **Yukinobu Hasegawa**, adapted by Kikuo Umebayashi
Scenic Designer: **Shiro Takeuchi**
Lighting Designer: **Hideyuki Torii**
Director: **Hachiro Nakahata**

Contributing Researcher: **Kazue Hatano**

Image Credit: **Shiro Takeuchi**

---

[376]

Cao Zhi
Xu Haishan (China)
Set Design

Company: **Shanghai Theatre Academy**
Venue: **The Experimental Theatre of Shanghai Theatre Academy**
Location: **Shanghai, China**
Opening/First Night: **December 1990**

Author: **Zhou Shushan**
Scenic Designer: **Xu Haishan**
Costume Designer: **Yuan Xiaohong**
Lighting Designer: **Zhu Guangwu**
Director: **An Zhenji**

Contributing Researcher: **Xu Xiang**

Image Credit: **Xu Haishan**

---

[377]

My Name Is Edward Kelly
Kenneth Rowell (Australia)
Set & Costume Design

Company: **The Australian Ballet**
Venue: **State Theatre, Victorian Arts Centre**
Location: **Melbourne, Australia**
Opening/First Night: **June 1990**

Composer: **Peter Sculthorpe**
Scenic Designer: **Kenneth Rowell**
Costume Designer: **Kenneth Rowell**
Lighting Designer: **William Akers**
Choreographer: **Timothy Gordon**
Conductor: **Noel Smith/Ormsby Wilkins**

Contributing Researcher: **Richard Roberts**

Image Credit: **Kenneth Rowell**

---

[378]

An Encounter
Sun-Hi Shin (Korea)
Set Design

Company: **Ahn Ae-Soon Dance Company**
Venue: **Munye Theatre**
Location: **Seoul, Korea**
Opening/First Night: **3 November 1990**

Composer: **Ji-Wook Kim**
Scenic Designer: **Sun-Hi Shin**
Choreographer: **Ae-Soon Ahn**

Contributing Researcher: **Kazue Hatano**

Image Credit: **Sun-Hi Shin**

---

[378]

The Resistable Rise of Arturo Ui
(ΗΑνοδοςχαιΗΠτώσητουΑρτούροΟυί)
Andy Bargilly (Cyprus)
Set Design

Company: **Cyprus Theatre Organisation (State)**
Venue: **Municipal Theatre**
Location: **Nicosia, Cyprus**
Opening/First Night: **October 1990**

Author: **Bertolt Brecht**
Scenic Designer: **Andy Bargilly**
Costume Designer: **Glyn Hughes**
Lighting Designer: **Grigoris Papageorgiou**
Director: **Heinz Uwe Haus**

Contributing Researcher: **Stavros Antonopoulos & Andy Bargilly**

Image Credit: **Andy Bargilly**

---

[379]

Ubu (*Ubu Roi, Татко Юбю*)
Marina Raytchinova (Bulgaria)
Set, Costume & Lighting Design

Company: **Little City Theatre Off the Channel**
Venue: **Little City Theatre Off the Channel**
Location: **Sofia, Bulgaria**
Opening/First Night: **5 December 1990**

Author: **Alfred Jarry**
Composer: **Assen Avramov**
Scenic Designer: **Marina Raytchinova**
Costume Designer: **Marina Raytchinova**
Lighting Designer: **Marina Raytchinova**
Sound Designer: **Assen Avaramov**
Director: **Borislav Chakrinov**

Contributing Researcher: **Marina Raytchinova**

Image Credit: **Marina Raytchinova**

---

[379]

Lady Macbeth of Mtsensk
David Borovsky (Russia)
Set Design

Company: **Hamburg State Opera**
Location: **Hamburg, Germany**
Opening/First Night: **1990**

Composer: **Dmitri Shostakovitch**
Scenic Designer: **David Borovsky**
Director: **Yuri Lyubimov**
Conductor: **Maxim Shostakovitch**

Contributing Researcher: **Inna Mirzoyan**

Image Credit: **David Borovsky**

---

[380]

Commonwealth Games Auckland 1990
Opening Ceremony: Cultural Display
Joe Bleakley (New Zealand)
Event Design

Venue: **Mount Smart Stadium**
Location: **Auckland, New Zealand**
Opening/First Night: **24 January 1990**

Author: **Charlie Strachan, Joe Bleakley, Mary-Jane O'Reilly**, et al
Composer: **Wayne Laird**
Scenic Designer: **Joe Bleakley**
Costume Designer: **Barbara Darragh**
Choreographer: **Mary-Jane O'Reilly**
Producer: **Logan Brewer**
Maori Artistic Coordinator: **Pita Sharples**

Contributing Researcher: **Sam Trubridge**

Image Credit: **Jeff Worsnop**

---

[381]

Medea
Apostolos Vettas (Greece)
Set & Costume Design

Company: **National Theatre of Northern Greece**
Location: **Thessaloniki, Greece**
Opening/First Night: **14 July 1990**

Author: **Euripides**
Translator: **Giorgos Heimonas**
Scenic Designer: **Apostolos Vettas**
Costume Designer: **Apostolos Vettas**
Music: **Stamatis Kraounakis & Aigli Hava-Vayia**
Director: **Andreas Voutsinas**

Contributing Researcher: **Dio Kangelari**

Image Credit: **Stavros Antonopoulos, Archive of Apostolos Vettas**

---

[382]

A Midsummer Night's Dream
(Sonho de uma Noite de Verão)
José de Anchieta (Brazil)
Set & Costume Design

Company: **Ornitorrinco**
Venue: **Central Park**
Location: **New York, New York, USA**
Opening/First Night: **1990**

Author: **William Shakespeare**
Scenic Designer: **José de Anchieta**
Costume Designer: **José de Anchieta**
Lighting Designer: **Abel Copanski, Clovis Cardoso & Peter Kaczorowski**
Director: **Caca Rosset**

Contributing Researcher: **JC Serroni**

Image Credit: **Jose de Anchieta**

---

[383]

The Brigades of Beauty (*Brigade Lepote*)
Vlado G. Repnik (Slovenia)
Set & Costume Design

Company: **Gledalisce Helios/Theatre Helios**
Name of Venue: **Cankarjev Dom**
Location: **Ljubljana, Slovenia**
Opening/First Night: **24 February 1990**

Scenic Designer: **Vlado G. Repnik**
Costume Designer: **Lela B. Njatin & Felix Casio**
Lighting Designer: **Igor Berginc**
Director: **Vlado G. Repnik**
Composer: **Darko Majsek, Ivan Jug, Vanja Pegan**

Image Credit: **Vlado Repnik, Marko Modic**

---

[384]

Phoenician Women (*Φοίνισσες*)
Angelos Angeli (Cyprus)
Set Design

Company: **Cyprus Theatre Organisation (State)**
Venue: **Makarios III Amphitheatre**
Location: **Nicosia, Cyprus**
Opening/First Night: **June 1990**

Author: **Euripides**
Composer: **Giorgos Kouroupos**
Scenic Designer: **Angelos Angeli**
Costume Designer: **Angelos Angeli**
Lighting Designer: **Grigoris Papageorgiou**
Director: **Nicos Haralambous**
Masks: **Kika Harris**

Contributing Researcher: **Andy Bargilly**

Image Credit: **Evis Ionannides**

---

[384]

Odyssey or World and Home
(Odisej & Sin Ili Svijet I Dom)
Dalibor Laginja (Croatia)
Set Design

Company: **Zagreb Youth Theatre**
Location: **Hale Istra, Croatia**
Opening/First Night: **9 November 1990**

Author: **Veno Taufer**
Scenic Designer: **Dalibor Laginja**
Costume Designer: **Barbara Stupica**
Director: **Vito Taufer**
Choreographer: **Matjaž Farič**

Contributing Researcher: **Ivana Bakal**

Image Credit: **Dalibor Laginja**

[385]

La Boheme
Catherine Martin (Australia)
Set & Costume Design

Company: **The Australian Opera**
Venue: **Opera Theatre, Sydney Opera House**
Location: **Sydney, Australia**
Opening/First Night: **1990**

Composer: **Giacomo Puccini**
Scenic Designer: **Catherine Martin**
Costume Designer: **Catherine Martin**
Lighting Designer: **Nigel Levings**
Director: **Baz Luhrmann**

Contributing Researcher: **Richard Roberts**

Image Credit: **Opera Australia**

[386]

Coffee Foxes (*Raposas do Café*)
José Carlos Serroni (Brazil)
Set Design

Company: **TAPA**
Location: **São Paulo, Brazil**
Opening/First Night: **September 1990**

Author: **Antonio Bivar & Celso Luiz Paulini**
Composer: **Gustavo Kurlat**
Scenic Designer: **JC Serroni**
Costume Designer: **Lola Tolentino**
Lighting Designer: **Wagner Freire**
Director: Eduardo **Tolentino de Araujo**

Contributing Researcher: **JC Serroni**

Image Credit: **JC Serroni**

[386]

A Month in the Country (*Mjesec Dana Na Selu*)
Dinka Jeričević (Yugoslavia/Croatia)
Set Design

Venue: **Croatian National Theatre**
Location: **Zagreb, Yugoslavia/Croatia**
Opening/First Night: **28 May 1990**

Author: **Ivan Sergeyević Turgenev**
Scenic Designer: **Dinka Jeričević**
Costume Designer: **Zlatko Bourek**
Director: **Georgij Paro**
Choreographer: **Juraj Mofčan**

Contributing Researcher: **Ivana Bakal**

Image Credit: **Dinka Jeričević**

{ INDEX }

DESIGNERS

AUTHORS/ COMPOSERS

{ ACKNOWLEDGEMENTS }

A PROJECT OF

OISTAT Publications and Communications Commission

ENDORSED BY

FIRT | International Federation for Theatre Research

SIBMAS | International Association of Libraries and Museums of the Performing Arts

IATC | International Association of Theatre Critics

TLA | Theatre Library Association

ITI | International Theatre Institute

FINANCIALLY SUPPORTED BY

Social Sciences and Humanities Research Council of Canada

International Organisation of Scenographers, Theatre Architects and Technicians

Brigham Young University

York University

York University Faculty of Fine Arts

SPECIAL THANKS TO

the archivists and librarians of the world
for helping to preserve this important documentation

 Social Sciences and Humanities Research Council of Canada

{ ACKNOWLEDGEMENTS }

Archiv der Akademie der Künste
BERLIN, GERMANY

Abbey Theatre
DUBLIN, IRELAND

Brigham Young University
PROVO, UTAH, USA

Bund der Szenografen
BERLIN, GERMANY

Canadian Theatre Museum
TORONTO, ONTARIO, CANADA

The Gate Theatre
DUBLIN, IRELAND

Hungarian OISTAT Centre
BUDAPEST, HUNGARY

Hungarian Theatre Museum and Institute
BUDAPEST, HUNGARY

Zbigniew Raszewski Theatre Institute
WARSAW, POLAND

Irish Theatre Institute
DUBLIN, IRELAND

INBA–CITRU, Biblioteca de las Artes–CENART
MEXICO CITY, DF, MEXICO

ITI Germany
BERLIN, GERMANY

JATDT–Japan Association of Theatre Designers and Technicians
TOKYO, JAPAN

Massey University
CHRISTCHURCH, NEW ZEALAND

McNay Museum
SAN ANTONIO, TEXAS, USA

New York Public Library for the Performing Arts
NEW YORK CITY, USA

PaCPA–Pacific Creators for the Performing Arts
TOKYO, JAPAN

Prague Quadrennial Archive at the Arts & Theatre Institute
PRAGUE, CZECH REPUBLIC

Proscena Združenie
BRATISLAVA, SLOVAKIA

Russian National OISTAT Centre
MOSCOW, RUSSIA

Russian Theatre Union
MOSCOW, RUSSIA

Social Sciences and Humanities Research Council
OTTAWA, ONTARIO, CANADA

Slovak Theatre Institute
BRATISLAVA, SLOVAKIA

Stratford Festival Archives
STRATFORD, ONTARIO, CANADA

Svensk Teaterunion – ITI Swedish Centre
STOCKHOLM, SWEDEN

Theatre Institute in Poland
WARSAW, POLAND

Theater Instituut Nederland (TIN)
AMSTERDAN, NETHERLANDS

Theatre Info Finland
HELSINKI, FINLAND

Theatre Museum Finland
HELSINKI, FINLAND

Toronto Reference Library
TORONTO, ONTARIO, CANADA

ULUPUH
ZAGREB, CROATIA

University of Guelph Archives
GUELPH, ONTARIO, CANADA

University of Zagreb
ZAGREB, CROATIA

Victoria & Albert Museum
LONDON, ENGLAND

York University, Faculty of Fine Arts, Department of Theatre
TORONTO, ONTARIO, CANADA

WORLD SCENOGRAPHY 1975-1990
{ PROJECT STAFF }

EDITORS: Peter McKinnon & Eric Fielding

DESIGNER: Randal Boutilier at 12thirteen

TEXT EDITOR: Cecelia Fielding

RESEARCH ASSISTANTS: Owais Lightwala, Amelia Taverner, Laura Shordone,
Amelia Kerrigan, Sanaz Taghizadegan, Laura Andrew, Carter Thompson

---

AFRICA & MIDDLE EAST
ASSOCIATE EDITOR: Osita Okagbue

ASIA
ASSOCIATE EDITOR: Kazue Hatano

EUROPE
ASSOCIATE EDITOR: Ian Herbert
ASSISTANT EDITORS: Nicole Leclercq, Peter McKinnon

OCEANIA
ASSOCIATE EDITOR: Dorita Hannah

NORTH AMERICA
ASSOCIATE EDITOR: Eric Fielding

SOUTH AMERICA
ASSOCIATE EDITOR: J.C. Serroni
ASSISTANT EDITOR: Ana Paula Aquino

AFRICA (NORTH)
CONTRIBUTING RESEARCHER:
Victor Ukaegbu

AFRICA (EAST AND CENTRAL)
REGIONAL EDITOR: Sam Kasule

AFRICA (SOUTH)
CONTRIBUTING RESEARCHER:
Sarah Roberts
IMAGES: Ruphin Coudyzer

AFRICA (WEST)
REGIONAL EDITOR:
Duro Oni (Francophone),
Ossei Agyeman (Anglophone)
CONTRIBUTING RESEARCHER:
Cornelius Onyekaba

ALBANIA
CONTRIBUTING RESEARCHER:
Ilir Martini

ARGENTINA
COUNTRY EDITOR:
Richard A. Santana Pereira

AUSTRALIA
COUNTRY EDITOR: Richard Roberts

BELGIUM
CONTRIBUTING RESEARCHERS:
Jerome Maeckelbergh, Rose Werckx

BOLIVIA
COUNTRY EDITOR:
Richard A. Santana Pereira

BRAZIL
COUNTRY EDITORS:
Carmelinda Guimarães, José Dias,
Laura Reis, Sebastião Milaré,
Alberto Guzik
CONTRUBUTING RESEARCHERS:
Viviane Ramos, Márcia Pires,
Hugo Cabral
TRANSLATION TO ENGLISH:
Ana Paula Aquino

BULGARIA
CONTRIBUTING RESEARCHER:
Marina Raytchinova

CANADA
COUNTRY EDITOR: Peter McKinnon
CONTRIBUTING RESEARCHERS:
Susan Benson, Mary Kerr,
Cameron Porteous, Don Shipley

CHILE
COUNTRY EDITOR: Edith del Campo
CONTRIBUTING RESEARCHERS:
Richard A. Santana Pereira

CHINA
COUNTRY EDITOR: Xu Xiang
CONTRIBUTING RESEARCHERS:
Sun Daqing, Lu Ping
ASSISTANCE: Ma Wanqiu

COLOMBIA
COUNTRY EDITOR: Otavio Arbelaiz

CROATIA
CONTRIBUTING RESEARCHERS:
Ivana Bakal (ULUPUH),
Višnja Rogošić (University of Zagreb),
Lada Čale Feldman (University of Zagreb)

CYPRUS
CONTRIBUTING RESEARCHER:
Andy Bargilly

CZECH REPUBLIC
CONTRIBUTING RESEARCHERS:
Daniela Pařízková, Marie Zdeňková
ASSISTANCE:
Denisa Šťastná, Ondřej Svoboda,
Prague Quadrennial Archive at the Arts
and Theatre Institute Prague

DENMARK
CONTRIBUTING RESEARCHER:
Camilla Bjørnvad

EGYPT
CONTRIBUTING RESEARCHER: Hazem Shebl

ESTONIA
CONTRIBUTING RESEARCHER:
Monika Larini
IMAGES: Kirsten Simmo

FINLAND
CONTRIBUTING RESEARCHERS:
Hanna Helavuori (Theatre Info Finland),
Pälvi Laine (Theatre Museum Finland)

FRANCE
COUNTRY EDITORS:
Jean Chollet, Marcel Freydefont